Making War on Bodies

Series Editors: Victoria M. Basham and Sarah Bulmer

The Critical Military Studies series welcomes original thinking on the ways in which military power works within different societies and geopolitical arenas.

Militaries are central to the production and dissemination of force globally but the enduring legacies of military intervention are increasingly apparent at the societal and personal bodily levels as well, demonstrating that violence and war-making function on multiple scales. At the same time, the notion that violence is an appropriate response to wider social and political problems transcends militaries: from private security, to seemingly 'non-military' settings such as fitness training and schooling, the legitimisation and normalisation of authoritarianism and military power occurs in various sites. This series seeks original, high-quality manuscripts and edited volumes that engage with such questions of how militaries, militarism and militarisation assemble and disassemble worlds touched and shaped by violence in these multiple ways. It will showcase innovative and interdisciplinary work that engages critically with the operation and effects of military power and provokes original questions for researchers and students alike.

Titles in the *Advances in Critical Military Studies* series include:

Published:
Resisting Militarism: Direct Action and the Politics of Subversion
Chris Rossdale
Making War on Bodies: Militarisation, Aesthetics and Embodiment in International Politics
Catherine Baker

Forthcoming:
The Military-Peace Complex: Gender and Materiality in Afghanistan
Hannah Partis-Jennings
Inhabiting No-Man's-Land: Army Wives, Gender and Militarisation
Alexandra Hyde
Disordered Violence: Gendered Neo-Orientalism and Terrorism
Caron Gentry

Making War on Bodies

Militarisation, Aesthetics and Embodiment in International Politics

EDITED BY CATHERINE BAKER

EDINBURGH
University Press

Edinburgh University Press is one of the leading university presses in the UK. We publish academic books and journals in our selected subject areas across the humanities and social sciences, combining cutting-edge scholarship with high editorial and production values to produce academic works of lasting importance. For more information visit our website: edinburghuniversitypress.com

Edinburgh University Press Ltd
The Tun – Holyrood Road, 12(2f) Jackson's Entry, Edinburgh EH8 8PJ

First published in hardback by Edinburgh University Press 2020

Typeset in 10.5/13 ITC Giovanni Std by
IDSUK (DataConnection) Ltd

A CIP record for this book is available from the British Library

ISBN 978 1 4744 4618 1 (hardback)
ISBN 978 1 4744 4619 8 (paperback)
ISBN 978 1 4744 4620 4 (webready PDF)
ISBN 978 1 4744 4621 1 (epub)

CONTENTS

FIGURES

NOTES ON CONTRIBUTORS

Catherine Baker is Senior Lecturer in 20th Century History at the University of Hull. She specialises in the transnational cultural politics of militarism and nationalism, the everyday micropolitics of peacekeeping, and feminist and queer approaches to international politics, with an emphasis on how the affective geopolitics of war and nationhood play out in popular culture and everyday life. Her books include *Sounds of the Borderland: Popular Music, War and Nationalism in Croatia since 1991* (Ashgate, 2010), *Interpreting the Peace: Peace Operations, Conflict and Language in Bosnia-Herzegovina* (Palgrave Macmillan, 2013, with Michael Kelly) and *Race and the Yugoslav Region: Postsocialist, Post-Conflict, Postcolonial?* (Manchester University Press, 2018). Her articles have appeared in *European Journal of International Relations*, *International Feminist Journal of Politics* and elsewhere.

Federica Caso was awarded her doctorate from the University of Queensland in 2019, for a thesis titled 'Liberal Militarisation: Visualising the Military Body as a Form of Governance'. Her research explores everyday manifestations of militarism in liberal societies and the process of liberal militarisation. She is interested in the visual and aesthetic politics of subjugation and resistance. She is the co-editor of *Popular Culture and World Politics: Theories, Methods, Pedagogies* (E-IR, 2015), and her work has featured in the journal *Critical Military Studies*.

Dan Evans is a former academic, now a support worker and activist. He continues to research militarism and is currently working on a project about the role of schools within local military cultures. He also writes about Wales and socialist theory for popular platforms such as *Jacobin*, *Open Democracy*, *Planet* and *New Socialist*.

Sorana Jude is a Teaching Fellow in the School of Geography, Politics and Sociology at Newcastle University. Her research builds on the intersection of feminist international relations, communications and media studies, and critical military and security studies, and has a particular focus on the Israel Defense Forces. Her doctoral thesis, entitled 'Israel's Military: Emotions, Violence, and the Limits of Dissent', was completed at the International Politics Department of Aberystwyth University, and was awarded the Best Dissertation Award by the European International Studies Association in 2019.

Jennifer G. Mathers is a Senior Lecturer in the Department of International Politics at Aberystwyth University. She researches and teaches about Russian politics, Russia's foreign and security policy and gender and conflict. Her recent publications include 'Medals and American Heroic Military Masculinity after 9/11' in *Heroism and Global Politics*, which she co-edited with Veronica Kitchen (Routledge, 2019), and 'Even the Toys Are Demanding Free Elections: Humour and the Politics of Creative Protest in Russia' in *Cultural Forms of Protest in Russia*, edited by Birgit Beumers, Alexander Etkind, Olga Gurova and Sanna Turoma (Routledge, 2018). She is currently working on a book examining the contemporary crisis in Ukraine from the perspective of feminist security studies.

Daniel Møller Ølgaard is a doctoral candidate at the Department of Political Science, Lund University. His work is broadly concerned with the role of technology and emotions in global politics and war, and his doctoral research project examines how digital and social media manage and govern the mediated experience of distant suffering through algorithmic structures and interface design.

Henri Myrttinen is a researcher with the Berlin-based Mauerpark Institute. He has worked for numerous mom-governmental organisations (NGOs) and research institutions on gender, peace and security, focusing mostly on Southeast Asia, Central Asia and the Middle East (particularly Lebanon), as well as Central and Eastern Europe. He holds a PhD in Conflict Resolution and Peace Studies, having written his thesis on masculinities and urban violence in Timor-Leste. He has especially worked on critically engaging masculinities, integrating lesbian, gay, bisexual, trans, intersex and queer (LGBTIQ) perspectives into peace and security work as well as the gender dimension of small arms and light weapons, armed conflict and formal and informal security sector actors.

Amy Abugo Ongiri is Associate Professor and the Jill Beck Director of Film Studies at Lawrence University. Her book, *Spectacular Blackness: The Cultural Politics of the Black Power Movement and the Search for a Black Aesthetic* (University of Virginia Press, 2009), explores the cultural politics of the Black Power movement, particularly the Black Arts movement's search to define a 'Black Aesthetic'. Her academic work has been published in *College Literature, Journal of African American History, Camera Obscura, Postmodern Culture, Black Filmmaker*, the *Los Angeles Review of Books* and *Nka: The Journal of Contemporary African Art*. In addition to academic publications, she has also published creative non-fiction in *Black Girl Dangerous, Mutha Magazine, Glitterwolf, Black Lesbian Love Lab* and the *Rad Families* anthology.

Jane Tynan is Lecturer in Cultural and Historical Studies at Central Saint Martins, University of the Arts London. Her research concerns visual and material aspects of war and conflict, with a focus on militarised bodies. Publications include *British Army Uniform and the First World War: Men in Khaki* (Palgrave, 2013) and *Uniform: Clothing and Discipline in the Modern World* (co-edited with Lisa Godson, Bloomsbury, 2019). She is series editor for Palgrave Studies in Fashion and the Body.

ACKNOWLEDGEMENTS

This volume sprang to life with the encouragement of Victoria Basham, Sarah Bulmer and Jen Daly, and was nurtured by conversations with many colleagues who helped to guide its branches into its current shape, including Linda Åhäll, Katarina Birkedal, Amanda Chisholm, Jesse Crane-Seeber, Matt Davies, Maria-Adriana Deiana, Lola Frost, Holly Furneaux, Harriet Gray, Kyle Grayson, Marsha Henry, Alex Hyde, Kevin McSorley, Cynthia Miller-Idriss, Laura Mills, Jelena Obradović-Wochnik, Kandida Purnell, Melanie Richter-Montpetit, Nick Robinson, Joanna Tidy, Julia Welland, Annick T. R. Wibben, Lucie Whitmore, Katharine A. M. Wright and Marysia Zalewski. Particular thanks go to Synne Dyvik and participants in the 'Militarisation, Aesthetics and Embodiment' panels we co-organised at the International Studies Association annual convention in Baltimore in 2017, a parallel endeavour to this volume which nevertheless helped point the way towards explaining its intellectual and political scope. As editor, Catherine is especially grateful to Amanda Capern, Richard Gorski, Michael Gratzke, Simon Green, Chris Harris and Jenny Macleod for their support as I worked on the volume at Hull; to the series editors and anonymous reviewers, plus Jen Daly, Joannah Duncan, Sarah Foyle and David Lonergan at Edinburgh University Press, and Barbara Eastman for copy-editing; and to a very patient cat.

Making War on Bodies: Militarisation, Aesthetics and Embodiment in International Politics

Catherine Baker

War is a phenomenon made on bodies. Not only is war's purpose the destruction of bodies, as the phrase 'making war on bodies' would generally suggest; the ideologies, discourses and practices of war as a social institution are themselves revealed to be 'written on the body', as Synne Dyvik argues, by asking critical questions about how war and the military shape the ways that bodies move and appear.[1] The tools for advancing these questions come from an interdisciplinary, eclectic box: from feminist and postcolonial consciousness of how war and colonial violence permeate society; from historians tracing how social and cultural experiences of war have changed over time; from geographers exploring how the military transforms space and landscape; from sociologists, philosophers and critics theorising the body; from scholars of international politics putting experience and the senses back into how their notoriously bloodless discipline thinks about war. Together, they have made bodies a defining theme in current critical research on war and the military. They have also employed many fresh, insightful methods that make explicit the aesthetics of experiencing and representing war. Yet, even though war is so inherently made by, with or against bodies, it is still rare to see the turn towards aesthetics and the turn towards the body articulated explicitly together as part of understanding the process that Cynthia Enloe has inspired many to call 'militarisation' – that is, how ideas about the military and who should (not) belong to it are made normal, natural, attractive and unquestioned.

A few months into editing this volume, my desktop even produced its own unexpected resonance between militarisation, aesthetics and embodiment when I realised I had accidentally named the folder containing the volume's files (abbreviated *MAE*) after the Hollywood star

Mae West – whose own connection with militarised aesthetics of the body became one of World War II's many linguistic curiosities when Royal Air Force (RAF) airmen nicknamed their life-jacket after her because its inflated shape seemed to give wearers a bouncing bust.[2] West harnessed the persona of transatlantic Forces sweetheart to her risqué star image, writing seductively to the 'Boys of the RAF' in 1942:

> Yeah, it's kind of a nice thought to be flying all over with brave men, even if I'm only there by proxy in the form of a life-saving jacket . . . I always thought that the best way to hold a man was in your arms – but I guess when you're in the air a plane is safer. You've got to keep everything under control.'[3]

Just as Enloe turned a 'feminist curiosity' on international politics to the image of West's contemporary Carmen Miranda, revealing the sexualised and racialised imaginations behind US colonialism in Latin America and the international fruit trade,[4] approaching West's anecdote the same way might reveal a framework of gender relations in which it seems the world's most natural thing for aircrew to be men, for airmen to be brave, and for brave airmen to be attractive to a sex symbol like West. It might reveal the sexualisation of the US–British alliance in Allied media, and Hollywood's symbiotic relationship with the military then and now. It might even reveal some articulations between militarisation, aesthetics and embodiment of its own – such as the humour of military slang offsetting the other embodied emotions of high-risk missions, the sensations of activating the jacket after being shot down over the sea, or even the figure the RAF liked airmen to cut when modelling it in photographs. And certainly these are not the only articulations it could contain. By showing how the entanglement of aesthetics and embodiment produces the intimate politics of militarisation, this volume reveals militarisation as a process that is simultaneously personal and global, binding some bodies into identification with military projects and circumscribing others as in need of protection, compassion, pacification or death.

To study militarisation, aesthetics and embodiment is thus to study the combinations of how things are sensed and how bodies experience them, across contexts related to the military and its place in wider society. The affective logic of militarisation, as Linda Åhäll argues, operates through and between bodies, interacting with intimate desires and fantasies about the body and delimiting which bodies are even able to be militarised and which are marked as targets of martial violence.[5] That logic can be critiqued and contested, often using aesthetic methods which aim to engage the senses in alternative ways yet may not necessarily always escape the ideological orders they purport to resist.[6] Such tension between complicity and resistance stems from the way in which militarisation itself involves a continuum between what is inside and outside the military, with norms, values, practices and people moving in both directions across the imagined and material boundaries of military and civilian life. Even people living an ordinary civilian life with no direct connection to the military are still, as Christine Sylvester writes, living out embodied 'physical and emotional connections' to war and the military.[7] These connections exemplify both the aesthetics of how bodies sense, feel and perceive, and the aesthetics of how bodies appear.

Researching militarisation through the aesthetics of sensation, feeling and perception immediately raises the difficulties of writing, visualising and sounding embodied experiences of war to people who have not shared them. Literature and film scholars have long dealt with these matters, but they are newer material for some other disciplines that study the military and war, which have brought additional field-based and participatory methods to bear on them: key work on British mass-market military memoirs, which have shaped thousands of readers' common-sense knowledge about the physicality of service in Iraq and Afghanistan, has been done by two geographers, Rachel Woodward and K. Neil Jenkings.[8] Studying such material runs up against what historian Yuval Harari termed the notion of 'flesh-witnessing', the belief 'that war is something that must be experienced through and with the flesh', as veterans', war poets' and military memoirists' claim to authority.[9] The epistemological question Dyvik poses, on behalf of readers who like herself have never been to war, is how she can 'know' about wartime experiences when she '"wasn't over there"'.[10] Dyvik suggests the answer requires an 'engagement with *our own* embodiment as scholars of militarization, war and violence', and a reflexive appreciation of the acts of imagination and identification involved in reading these texts – which this volume too aims to display.[11] Researchers who write auto-ethnographically about their own embodied experiences in militarised settings, meanwhile, both use their body as sensory instruments of aesthetic experience, then engage the reader through writing (and/or other communicative methods) as an aesthetic device. The geographers Matthew Rech and Alison Williams, for instance, observe that the military airshows where they research are 'key location[s] where civilians are tied into broader currents of militarism, either directly through military recruitment, or more subtly through a range of embodied and aesthetic experiences' – including themselves.[12]

Alongside the aesthetics of how bodies perceive are the aesthetics of how bodies *are* perceived, or how bodies appear. Militaries' official and unofficial embodied practices, and even civilian appropriations of military style, combine to shape perceptions of militarised bodies as desirable and to create gendered, class-based, racialised and ethnicised ideals that bodies must meet to be so desired. This occurs both at the macro level of which categories of bodies can or must enter the military in which capacities, and the micro level of issues such as struggles over uniform design;[13] the phenomenon is historical as well as contemporary, as studies of uniform and fashion in World War I or even eighteenth-century Britain testify.[14] What Victoria Basham calls 'the process of becoming and remaining recognisable as a soldier' has been and is both aesthetic and embodied, in the past and present.[15] These processes are racialised and gendered in historically contingent ways, within militaries conscious that representations of their troops symbolise the military and the nation (or in certain cases the city-state, the kingdom or the empire) as collective bodies.[16] The 'embodied performativity' of particular military masculinities and femininities is shaped by armed forces for particular operations (such as counterinsurgency) but made material by troops' everyday bodily practices and experiences: producing embodiment thus means 'writing on' bodies by inscribing ideologies on them, in the phrase Dyvik adopts from Michel de Certeau.[17] However, the embodied aesthetic politics of militarisation do not just operate within military institutions; they are also produced in the civilian world.

Media and popular-cultural representations of contemporary, historical and imaginary militarised bodies (and, relationally, the bodies they exist to protect or destroy) are themselves sites of militarisation, engaging (sections of) the public in the pleasures of consuming them, and creating affective public investments in militarism and military intervention. In these processes, certain militarised bodies are frequently rendered 'hypervisible', and other bodies' existence rendered invisible – including personnel and veterans who have not lived up to the idealised qualifications for hypervisibility, and, especially, civilians and enemy combatants whom the military has injured and killed.[18] Masculinities, and femininities, must often be renegotiated when societies come to terms with the embodied realities of returning soldiers and those close to them after conflicts where many soldiers have been disabled, such as World War I or the wars in Iraq and Afghanistan.[19] Aesthetics are also what invest the horrific spectacle of the trophy body with its horror.[20] Indeed, this last practice exposes a continuum between militarisation and colonial violence that, as Alison Howell urges, the lens of critical race studies makes it imperative to recognise:[21] the history of the trophy body in the West runs both through the white supremacist spectacle of lynching,[22] and through the '[d]emonstrations of violence' under military orders through which European empires enforced colonial power.[23]

While manifestations of militarisation take many historically, politically and socially contingent forms, all interact with individuals' senses as embodied beings, and many evoke an aesthetics of embodiment themselves. Those exposing or resisting militarisation have also frequently done so by inventing and spreading alternative ways of imagining and inhabiting the body. These processes are always relational and intersubjective: Sara Ahmed famously describes the politics of emotion as occurring when 'emotions circulate between bodies',[24] and the disability theorist Tobin Siebers defines aesthetics as 'the way that some bodies make other bodies feel', through what they have created or just how they appear.[25] Both the pleasure and the pain of war, Dyvik writes, operate *through* and also *between* bodies.[26] Indeed, processes of militarisation have always depended on engaging the senses, charging embodied experiences with emotion, and fuelling desires and fantasies about the body: connecting militarisation, aesthetics and embodiment may seem theoretically fresh, but evidence of how they *are* connected is potentially as old as militaries themselves.

'Militarisation' as a concept still, however, makes assumptions about the normal relationship between the state, the public and violence which may not be transhistorically or even globally applicable. Does 'militarisation' only make sense regarding states and standing armies, or can it also offer insights into other forms of organised violence in the service of power? Though Enloe's own outlook on militarisation is avowedly global, in practice the literature on militarisation as a concept centres states positioning themselves in the Global North/West within an international order that continues to be racially stratified, despite the global dimensions and colonial legacies of militarisation revealed through research like Swati Parashar's on the 'postcolonial anxiety' of the Indian state's intimate relationship with militarism.[27] The militarised masculinities literature reaches somewhat wider, increasingly spotlighting masculinities which lie on social and global peripheries at once.[28] Contexts such as conscription and veterans in post-Soviet Russia, armed groups in Sierra Leone and South Sudan, Indonesian jihadism, or sexualised violence committed by Congolese government forces present important correctives to generalisations made from the Global North/West.[29] Widening the geographical scope of militarisation research is essential both to see militarisation itself as transnationally shaped and also to question whether it is equally relevant everywhere – a challenge this volume sets itself in articulating how the affective interplay of aesthetics and embodiment informs what we know as militarisation today.

What is Militarisation?

'Militarisation' as a scholarly term may have been popularised by Enloe's work in feminist international relations (IR), but other disciplines have long researched it even under different names: the historian Joanna Bourke, author of several books on war, masculinities and violence since the mid-1990s, notably adopted militarisation as a concept in her 2014 investigation of 'the extent to which the military and war-play invade our lives'.[30] Cultural historians' insights into 'popular memory' of war, showing for instance how television comedy has dominated how the public think about World War II Britain's Home Guard, say just as much about militarisation as they do memory.[31] Historians have likewise exposed the messy permeability of the separation between front line and home front, particularly but not only during and after the World Wars, and some like Graham Dawson place militarism and imperialism into a continuum that studies of present-day militarisation and coloniality could learn much from.[32] Among geographers, meanwhile, a critical turn in human geography in the 1990s/2000s inspired first the subfield of military geography, then the confrontation of geography's own complicity in the War on Terror and past exercises of military power.[33] Anthropologists reacting in real time to the outbreak of war and coercive atmospheres of nationalism in their home societies, most famously (for Anglophones) in the post-9/11 USA but also in 1990s Croatia and elsewhere, have offered rich ethnographic evidence of how war suffuses the everyday.[34]

The field of critical military studies (CMS) to which this volume contributes emerged as an endeavour to question 'the nature of military power and its effects' in which all these disciplines and more have joined.[35] In this endeavour, thinking about 'militarisation' helps scholars and activists recognise where assumptions about the military's role in society, and the gender order the military relies on, permeate everyday life.[36] This gender order is, as Marsha Henry argues, simultaneously racialised: even though the unexamined whiteness of much critical and feminist military research has overlooked the global politics of race, race *and* gender together constitute societies' patterns of thinking about which bodies belong inside or outside the military and what their roles should be in peace and war.[37]

These patterns manifest both within and around military institutions, especially in their hidden gendered and racialised divisions of labour, and equally in militarised artefacts', ideas', narratives' and aesthetics' reverberations into everyday civilian life. 'Militarisation', as Enloe framed it in a still-influential definition, stands for much more than what proportion of a national budget goes towards defence or how involved military officers are in national governments, as political science would once have had it:[38]

> Militarization is a step-by-step process by which a person or a thing gradually comes to be controlled by the military *or* comes to depend for its well-being on militaristic ideas. The more militarization transforms an individual or a society, the more that individual or society comes to imagine military needs and militaristic presumptions to be not only valuable but also normal. . . . To chart the spread of militarization, then, requires a host of skills: the ability to read budgets and interpret bureaucratic euphemisms, of course, but also the ability to understand the dynamics of memory, marriage, hero-worship, cinematic imagery, and the economies of commercial sex.[39]

Another common definition, particularly influential in geography, comes from Caroline Lutz's anthropological fieldwork around Fort Bragg.[40] Lutz too defined militarisation multi-dimensionally, but with less focus on gender, in writing about the USA soon after 9/11:

> [Militarization is] an intensification of the labor and resources allocated to military purposes, including the shaping of other institutions in synchrony with military goals. Militarization is simultaneously a discursive process, involving a shift in general societal beliefs and values in ways necessary to legitimate the use of force, the organization of large standing armies and their leaders, and the higher taxes or tribute used to pay for them. Militarization is intimately connected not only to the obvious increase in the size of armies and resurgence of militant nationalisms and militant fundamentalisms but also to the less visible deformation of human potentials into the hierarchies of race, class, gender, and sexuality, and to the shaping of national histories in ways that glorify and legitimate military action.[41]

Scholars investigating 'everyday geographies of militarization' in sites closely tied to the military followed Lutz in making contingencies of space and place increasingly important to militarisation research.[42]

Indeed, the pace of critical research into militarisation seemed to gather across disciplines in the late 2000s and 2010s. This was due to a political urgency of contesting militarisation at home that many

Western scholars described feeling during the War on Terror or even the World War I centenaries;[43] to developments in international security expanding perceptions of what might count as 'military', such as the growth of private military security companies (PMSCs) and the militarisation of border enforcement;[44] and to conceptual advances in social and political theory creating new possibilities for theorising militarisation, including the two advances this book draws together – a new emphasis on the aesthetic side of politics and new theorisations of embodiment and the body. These conceptual lenses, which IR scholars have termed the so-called 'aesthetic' and 'embodied' turns, focus attention on contingency, social practice and the everyday.

Such 'messiness' indeed suffuses current understandings of militarisation.[45] Marsha Henry and Katherine Natanel, for instance, describe it 'as a process which is constantly in flux as well as continually negotiated, reiterated and resisted' inside and outside the military – and, importantly, an '*unfinished*' one, certainly not predestined to succeed.[46] Laura Shepherd calls it a process 'that creates a positive public disposition towards the military and towards militaristic ideas', structuring and depoliticising how society understands violence and the use of force, associating masculinity with military power, and naturalising 'assumptions about how to engage with those people who are not part of that society' in border security and foreign deployments.[47] Rech, Jenkings, Williams and Woodward, like many authors, explain militarisation in relation to militarism: if militarism is 'an ideology which promotes the unproblematic acceptance of militaries' and the use of military power, militarisation comprises 'the processes and practices' letting militarism be (re)produced.[48] If militarisation is a process, these authors imply, its dynamics can be changed.

Feminist approaches have been particularly fruitful for linking militarisation into the aesthetic and embodied turns in social and political theory. Victoria Basham, for instance, notes militarism informs both national and individual identities, linking 'people's bodies and everyday experiences' with spaces, objects and discourses that have been invested with geopolitical significance.[49] Linda Åhäll returns to Enloe's metaphor of a militarising manoeuvre as a 'dance' not a struggle, albeit a dance 'among unequal partners', in rethinking practices of militarisation as 'part of sense-making in the everyday'.[50] Beyond understandings of militarisation as simply what is 'militarised as in *military-looking*', Åhäll conceives of militarisation as broader 'social and cultural preparation for the idea of war, which relies on a gendered logic and takes place in the mediatised everyday'.[51] The metaphor of dance, or bodies in collective and intersubjective motion, emphasises 'how bodies move us through non-verbal communication', and grounds this in 'a feminist questioning about how bodies matter politically' – a line of questioning where embodiment and aesthetics must be combined.[52]

What are Aesthetics?

Aesthetics, or the creative and representational practices with which artists and other creators engage the senses and emotions to convey human imagination and experience, are already at the heart of disciplines including art history, literature, film studies and a branch of philosophy. These explore the 'ways of seeing', and doing and making, that shape how the creators, spectators and users of images, texts and other artefacts perceive meaning and emotion.[53] Representations of war and the military, and the bodies involved in them, have long been among their subject matter. In IR, conversely, it is still comparatively novel to deal with how such representations achieve aesthetic effects.

In defining IR's then-nascent 'aesthetic turn' in 2001, Roland Bleiker contrasted his discipline's conventional 'mimetic' approaches against 'aesthetic' ones: while 'mimetic' approaches presume analysts are neutral observers addressing other neutral observers, representing political reality with the certainty of scientific measurement, aesthetic approaches recognise that research itself is a representation of politics, and that those representations too are 'incomplete'.[54] This insight inspired more and more studies of aesthetic artefacts, plus creative methodologies for conducting and communicating research.[55] Bleiker's praise for Enloe's Carmen Miranda discussion as an early foundational example of the 'aesthetic turn' suggests that this turn, and parallels in other disciplines, might be particularly productive for researching militarisation.[56]

Links between aesthetics and 'the political' are often made via the philosopher Jacques Rancière, whose idea of 'aesthetic regimes' (structures of ideas, moulded by power relations, 'that modulate what is seen and said') has particularly influenced critical security studies.[57] Rancière's idea of 'the sensible', or what is able to be sensed and felt, is often applied to media and visual cultures to explain how ideas (about the military, security regimes and other phenomena) become naturalised into consensus, and how 'politics' manifest as challenges to common sense through challenging what *can* be sensed.[58] Rancière's opposite to consensus is 'dissensus', 'a conflict of sensory worlds': political art seeks to create this, and political resistance perhaps requires it.[59] Rancière holds no monopoly on imagining these opposites: the postcolonial feminist scholars Anna

Agathangelou and L. H. M. Ling, for instance, described the 'poisies' in which 'worlds emerge from constant interplays . . . between selves and others', enactable through fiction and poetry.[60] Aesthetics in international politics are therefore about more than art, visual artefacts or 'how things look' (just as Åhall argues militarisation is about much more than 'military-looking' things[61]) – they are about the whole range of human senses and perceptions, and the (inter)subjectivity of representation itself.[62] Nevertheless, it often takes analysing particular '[a]esthetic sources' to illustrate this deeper point.[63]

More specific modes of human perception have also produced 'turns' in the study of international politics. These include a swell of interest in the aesthetics of how narrative produces feeling, opening space 'to engage with personal, lived, embodied experiences' of international politics which has obvious convergences with the study of militarisation, especially through military memoir, ethnography and autoethnography.[64] 'Visuality' (or meaning produced in still and moving images through the sense of sight) is likewise framed as a distinct aesthetic experience for making sense of international politics, within a literature fuelled by the international repercussions of certain iconic images like the destruction of the Twin Towers, the Abu Ghraib torture photographs, the Danish 'Muhammad cartoons' or Islamist execution videos, as well as the growing political importance digital media has afforded images' production, sharing and manipulation.[65] Many of these aesthetic artefacts and practices represent war and the military.[66]

What current critical military studies research adds to historians' and arts scholars' investigations of public and personal aesthetic representations of war, such as the contributions to the history of emotions based on World War I soldiers' letters and cultural production,[67] is a theoretical framework directly linking aesthetics and militarisation: through exploring how militaries use or suppress images and aesthetic practices to influence public opinion; through investigating the new aesthetic regimes of digital and interactive technology, which place viewers in ostensibly direct contact with soldiers' ways of seeing (potentially making their identification with soldiers more immediate); through studying entanglements of the military and militarism with popular culture and the entertainment media. The uptake of creative methodologies in military research has also opened new possibilities for exposing, and resisting, militarisation, such as Torika Bolatagici using photographic and video art to reflect on Fijian soldiers' and military contractors' 'lived and embodied experience' of 'express[ing] Fijian values through the body' outside Fiji in tension with the homogenising bodily practices of the armed organisations they work for, and Christine Sylvester's efforts with the artist Jill Gibbon (who infiltrates arms fairs to draw sketches) to grasp 'experience . . . that lies outside the rational' by 'thinking like an artist–researcher about war'.[68] The dialogue 'between the social scientists and artists' researching militarisation is two-way enough that *The Routledge Companion to Military Research Methods* included multiple artists in its final section, 'Senses', showing what aesthetic approaches could offer military research.[69] Its penultimate section, 'Experiences', had done the same for another of CMS's theoretical foundations – the social sciences' theorisation of embodiment.

What is Embodiment?

Embodiment, or the experiences and sensations of inhabiting a body, has conventionally been overlooked – as many feminists charge – by disciplines that pride themselves on the objective and scientific stance Donna Haraway termed the 'god trick'.[70] Embodiment is simultaneously intimately personal, so much that authors argue over how far one individual's experiences can ever fully be conveyed to another,[71] and undeniably social, since every person's body makes others ascribe them social identities. Some markers of social identity change over a lifetime (age, and often disability); some can be more flexibly controlled, with requisite 'body work',[72] than others; some are more vulnerable to being disbelieved (like trans people's gender identity, or ethnic and racialised minorities' nationality); blackness and other visible racialised differences force individuals to embody centuries-long legacies of structural racism on the surface of their body.[73] The experiences individuals have because of how they are embodied create their 'embodied knowledge', an idea which first became widespread in critical race scholarship and feminist theory before it empowered critical scholars to explain their own and others' affective relationships towards institutions of militarisation and war.

Literary studies and cultural history have, again, articulated links between war and embodiment which provided foundation for theorising embodiment in military research, as the sociologist Kevin McSorley acknowledged in his ground-breaking collection *War and the Body*.[74] The literary scholar Elaine Scarry famously emphasised war's purpose as being the destruction of bodies, though her position that physical pain both resists and destroys language has been contested as often as it has been taken up.[75] Cultural history's own embodied turn in the 1990s saw rehabilitation, disability and war wounds become central themes in the social and cultural history of the World Wars, especially with reference to disfigured and disabled veterans and to the condition then diagnosed as shell shock.[76] Ethnographers like Zoe Wool and Kenneth MacLeish do research with these veterans' counterparts today.[77] From feminist theory and the sociology of the body, meanwhile, military researchers have derived perspectives on embodiment, intimacy and sensation which connect the structures of world politics with 'the politics and sociality of bodies',[78] and individuals' 'felt, sensed, and experiential' notions of security,[79] theorising the individual as an *embodied* subject in international politics and war. Lauren Wilcox rejects security studies' conventional imagination of bodies as 'inert objects' by drawing on Judith Butler, emphasising that 'bodies are killed and injured, but also formed, re-formed, gendered, and racialized', in relation to each other, 'through the bodily relations of war'.[80] Militarisation thus acts on individuals as embodied subjects through how bodies are imagined and also how they are destroyed.

Acknowledging that military violence targets embodied individuals has been an especially radical move in IR, which Sylvester charges has historically ignored war's 'actual mission of injuring human bodies and destroying normal patterns of social relations'.[81] Both Sylvester's work on 'war as experience' and Swati Parashar's work on 'what . . . '"war bodies" know about international relations' seek to repair this from feminist perspectives, with Parashar also making a postcolonial critique of top-down analyses that theorise others' lives and conflicts from safe distances away.[82] Queer international relations' attention to bodily intimacy and sensuality, and to bodies which do not 'signify monolithically' within fixed categories, aligns with feminist enquiry to write embodiment into international politics in all its fleshy and psychic complexity:[83] hence Jesse Crane-Seeber's study of how military training harnesses the politics of recruits' desire to embody the ideal of militarised hardness, or Victoria Basham's reading of the hypervisibility of military women's supposedly 'weak and leaky' bodies.[84] Yet even some appropriations of feminist and queer phenomenology in IR have been disembodied, such as the argument that killing with drones (seemingly a difficult type of killing to fit into established hierarchies of military masculinities) 'queer[s] the experience of killing in war'[85] – an ostensible recognition of embodiment in war which is still detached from bodies being killed. As Ty Solomon notes, '[t]he fleshy materiality of the body becomes meaningful through language, yet the body's very corporeality exhibits forms of agency that often escape linguistic capture':[86] the study of militarisation has learned more from corporeal understandings of embodiment than from theoretical abstraction.

Critical military studies may even have led the way in bringing corporeality, fleshiness and embodied experience into the study of international politics, with one of its most important insights being acknowledgement that, as Sylvester argues, 'war is experienced through the body'.[87] This principle has enabled seeing both war and militarisation as 'embodied social practice', the central argument of *War and the Body*, a collection of applied approaches including phenomenology, ethnography, historical research, literary and visual studies to bodily experiences in the military and militarised imaginations of the body beyond it.[88] While military research had already engaged with embodied practice through John Hockey's sensory ethnography of infantry training and Marsha Henry and Paul Higate's study of everyday spatial practices in peacekeeping,[89] and McSorley himself had studied the 'emerging aesthetic regime of "somatic war"' in intimate media representations of troops' experiences in Afghanistan,[90] this volume interwove many strands of research into an 'embodied sociology of war'[91] – though did not take the further step of theorising it with reference to aesthetic politics as well. The conceptual conjunction of militarisation and embodiment it sparked off nevertheless creates ample space for incorporating such aesthetic approaches too, with what Synne Dyvik and Lauren Greenwood describe as the ambition to:

> stretch the concepts of militarism and militarization in directions that pay attention to its emotional, embodied, sensed, and corporeal manifestations . . . [and] recognize the ways in which processes of militarization are not always conscious, not always deliberate, but . . . 'something that is *felt*, as much as, if not at times more than, something that is explicitly *thought* about'.[92]

CMS's corporeal and experiential turn recognises the materiality of violence and injury, but also the full range of emotions in war and soldiering, including the more troubling yet well-attested ones of pleasure and joy.[93]

Methodologically, the most important resonance of embodiment in CMS is the call for researchers to be explicitly reflexive about their own embodied encounters with war and militarisation.[94] Here feminists, again, have led the way, including Parashar's reflections on negotiating her 'embodied "otherness"' as an Indian woman interviewing women who supported political violence in Kashmir and Sri Lanka.[95] All CMS scholars in close contact with militaries deal with embodied contradictions of 'negotiating a space between . . . two poles', knowing about the military without being co-opted by it.[96] Questions about how those with or without military experience 'know' the military are thus of particular methodological, political and ethical concern.[97] In a paper they first gave as a spoken dialogue, Sarah Bulmer, a civilian, and David Jackson, a veteran, plainly set out the stakes of 'claims "to know" the embodied experience of war and militarism', which even as of 2015 seemed often to miss the 'affective dimension' that really engaged with individual personhood and experience and that veterans like Jackson recognised.[98] Jackson also felt that framing topics such as military masculinities as a 'problem' pushed veterans away from research.[99] Their dialogic format, itself an aesthetic intervention, asked scholars to 'embrace, rather than erase, these multiple voices', emphasising that 'the *struggle* to articulate embodied experience is the key problem for research on war'.[100]

Elsewhere in CMS, scholars have used ideas about embodiment to theorise what Sylvester reminds us war is ultimately about – wounding and destroying bodies. Reflecting the character of early twenty-first-century warfare, CMS's continuum between studying representation and studying everyday military institutions juxtaposes imaginations of techno-scientific military futures and re-masculinised resilient military amputees with accounts of the embodied experience of recovery and caregiving after battlefield blast injuries, where survivors often distance themselves from what civilians and media project on to them.[101] And finally, scholars have confronted the reluctance of disciplines so concerned with war 'to deal with the destruction of the body' and its death:[102] the politics of which killed and dismembered bodies should be seen or hidden are the very politics of whose lives are, in Butler's terms, framed as grievable, killable or disposable in war.[103] While graphic images of acts and aftermaths of killing are circulated as shock, scandal or weapon, national war dead are typically commemorated through ritualised ceremony, with bodies hidden by caskets, monuments and flags, and media suggesting to national communities how they should feel about 'their' military dead.[104] This observation, like many others, suggests we cannot talk about embodiment without talking about aesthetics – aesthetics of how bodies appear and are represented, and aesthetics of sensory experience. In doing so, as this volume does, the intimate politics of militarisation come to the fore.

Aesthetics and Embodiment in Militarisation

The bridges between embodiment and aesthetics that help them work together in theorising militarisation already exist in the humanities and social sciences through the notions of emotion and affect – the very themes that led historians like Michael Roper towards their insights into the intimate politics of war.[105] If emotions are, as Emma Hutchison describes them, 'the conscious manifestation of bodily feelings', affect comprises even more 'nonconscious, noncognitive "inner states" and sensory experiences, including mood, disposition, and attachment.'[106] Distinctions between affect and emotion that preoccupy affect theorists matter less here than the fact they are both felt and shown through the body.[107] Emotions arise in response to what senses have perceived: that is, because some external stimulus, even just a trigger for remembering, has had aesthetic effects. Interpreting emotions and war, Linda Åhäll and Thomas Gregory suggest, thus requires an aesthetic consciousness and consciousness of embodiment at once:

> [W]e cannot make sense of war if we are unable or unwilling to pay attention to the sensual experiences of those affected . . . a nuanced understanding of emotions, affect and the somatic experience of the human body can only enhance our engagement with contemporary conflict and war.[108]

International politics research is thus now attending to the sensory dimensions of war and being in the military that humanities scholars have examined for some time. Here in the domain of 'sensuous' war might lie topics such as the soundscapes of battlefields, cities and bases in wartime Iraq;[109] the feeling of the heat and weight of armour for US troops there;[110] how trench warfare forced soldiers on the Western Front to rely on senses other than sight;[111] the 'overflowing' sensualities of pleasure and satisfaction which can be felt through both sexual sensation and the intensity of training and combat;[112] the way of feeling, sensing and perceiving Hockey had to develop in participant observation with infantry to describe the 'sensory work' of field exercises and patrol, or what he now calls 'an aesthetic of being in the field';[113] and in general 'the acquisition of particular militarised forms of sensation' in specific landscapes that constitutes military training, that is, the militarisation of the body within the military.[114] Theories of aesthetics and theories of embodiment are, therefore, rethinking 'militarisation' to foreground the intimate, everyday and sensuous encounters between individuals, the military and war.

Even refreshed, however, 'militarisation' is not without its critics. Without radically reassessing the relationship between the public, the military and the state, Marcus Schulzke questions whether good democratic civil–military relations might need some degree of militarisation: can the public really evaluate policy decisions about the military critically if they know less about it?[115] Other critiques go deeper into the structures of power undergirding and facilitating military violence and war. Maria Stern and Marysia Zalewski have expressed concern that 'familiar feminist fables' of militarisation might not transform gender relations enough because they arguably still rest on simple definitions of women and men based on sexual difference.[116] David Duriesmith, researching young men's Islamist networks in Indonesia, suggests 'militarisation' might not be globally applicable because these networks mobilise tropes of collective violence not linked to any formal tradition of soldiering for the state.[117] If 'militarisation' assumes Eurocentric concepts of the individual, violence and statehood, Duriesmith implies it cannot be simply transferred to the Global South, even if (as Pacific feminists have suggested) it might still help explain how Western imperialism and colonialism have altered gender relations in militarised sites like Okinawa.[118] Maria Eriksson Baaz and Judith Verweijen, meanwhile, argue most research on Africa misapplies 'militarisation', 'reproducing . . . troublesome imageries of "African" passivity and backwardness' by raising alarm about the military's influence over government rather than investigating everyday social practice as scholars of the Global North/ West more often do.[119] These deeper critiques should be addressed in any work reframing militarisation today.

An even more fundamental problem with 'militarisation', Alison Howell argues, is its unspoken assumptions about what relationships between individuals, states and violence scholars imagine as 'normal'. If militarisation is a process, was there ever a state of grace when politics, institutions or culture were not militarised? Studies of militarisation quite often imply those domains should return to that unmilitarised state. Yet, when today's global politics have already been historically shaped by settler colonialism, Europeans' enslavement of Africans, and structures of racism that spread worldwide, there is no 'unsullied' civilian political space – and where the law and police have already been mobilised to serve anti-Black and anti-Indigenous violence, the state's military and civilian arms have already collapsed together.[120] Even emphases on 'women's lives' and 'militarized masculinities' might fold 'analyses of race, Indigeneity, disability and coloniality' into gender too much.[121] Instead, Howell proposes conceiving of 'martial politics', a historical indivisibility of peace and war, where groups and individuals 'constituted as a threat to the nation's strength or civil order' have always been subject to the state's martial violence anyway.[122] These recent critiques of 'militarisation' force CMS to confront how it integrates the violence of racism and coloniality into the military and war.[123]

Accordingly, this volume thus not only combines the three conceptual lenses of militarisation, aesthetics and embodiment to demonstrate how deeply militarisation and resistance to it depend on an affective politics of the body – it does so by deliberately exploring a wider scope of contexts and experiences in its geographical coverage and in the range of organisations it explores. It traces the affective and embodied dynamics of militarisation not only through state militaries and their publics but also anti-colonial revolutionary movements, transnational insurgent terrorist groups, far-right youth movements and the companies that cater to them, non-governmental organisations (NGOs), artists and museums. It holds there is as much to learn about militarisation from Cuba, the Middle East, Croatia, Ukraine or Russia as from the UK, Australia or the USA. It begins, however, with where militarisation works on the body most intensively: embodied experiences of being, and becoming military, as represented through narrative and art.

Revisiting Hockey's foundational work on infantry training through current frameworks for theorising aesthetics and embodiment, Dan Evans begins the volume by spotlighting how basic training militarises the civilian body, through an autoethnographic narrative of joining the British Army Reserve in 2015. The immediacy of its writing confronts the reader from the outset with the disciplinary techniques through which training inculcates recruits with 'a soldier-like bearing', defined by military masculine norms which trainers contrast against both effeminate and disabled bodies. To encourage recruits to internalise this bearing, Federica Caso goes on to argue, requires cultural representations of the stoic, courageous and patriotic soldier, who has learned to control their emotions to rationalise killing and death. Yet war's emotional toll on the embodied mind, sometimes amounting to trauma, exposes the limitations of this ideal. Through studying the Australian war artist Ben Quilty's paintings of troops who served in Afghanistan, Caso suggests such tension is resolved through visual regimes of militarisation that create a politics of compassion towards the soldier – or rather towards the white male soldierly body, casting Indigenous and female bodies' suffering as subordinate, not to mention that of civilian and enemy victims of war.

Representations of soldiers' embodied, emotional experiences, this time through language rather than visual art, are also the subject of Catherine Baker's chapter on Svetlana Alexievich's composite narrative about female veterans of the Red Army, *The Unwomanly Face of War*. Alexievich's assembly of the testimonies she collected in 1978–83 (amid the fresh militarisation of the Soviet–Afghan War) into what purports to be a collective narrative of women veterans' experiences involves, Baker argues, a gendered moral aesthetics of the body. Drawing on disability studies and the social and cultural history of disabled veterans, the chapter suggests that Alexievich could not escape hegemonic Soviet scripts about disability and bodily normalcy even as she tried to de-normalise the Union of Soviet Socialist Republics' (USSR's) hegemonic masculine narratives of militarisation. While this historical example of using veterans' testimony to resist militarisation is mediated through literary intervention, the testimonies of anti-war Israeli veterans in Sorana Jude's chapter earn their truth claims by being presented as direct accounts of Israeli forces' violence against Palestinians. Like militarisation, Jude argues, military dissent too is an affective process: in this case, the testimonies collected by the Breaking the Silence organisation seek to transfer veterans' remembered emotions of shame and remorse on to the Israeli public, so they will press their government to end the occupation. Yet the testimonies' concentration on soldiers' distressing lived experiences, without constituting Palestinians as emotional subjects, seems to show the same gendered and racialised power relations that sustain the occupation even operate through these examples of military dissent.

The following three chapters emphasise militarisation's visual aesthetics, in the public (in)visibility of certain bodies and spectators' own embodied responses. Henri Myrttinen's study of posters and photographs of certain Lebanese war dead contrasts the 'hypervisibility' of fallen militia fighters regarded as martyrs with the invisibility of living disabled veterans, whose fates do not lend themselves to propaganda. While Myrttinen addresses still images bound to specific material sites, Jennifer Mathers considers the aesthetics of digital and viral images as well as the surprising militarisation of the non-human body in her chapter on animal images and the Russia–Ukraine conflict. The social media platforms facilitating the 'digital militarism' of states, armed groups and their transnational and diasporic audiences are, paradoxically, the same spaces that have further popularised the creation and sharing of ostensibly apolitical animal photographs inviting viewers to feel intimacy and warmth. When photographed in military settings and shared as memes, these animal images invite viewers to project sympathy from the animal on to a certain side's soldiers (and their nations): not only the human body can be militarised. Continuing the volume's examination of how affects travel between bodies through digital media, Daniel Møller Ølgaard uses examples from Islamic State (IS) online video production to explore embodied experiences of audiovisual spectatorship. Arguing that the transition from print and mass broadcast media to digital media has fundamentally altered how militarisation works on and through bodies, Ølgaard revisits Åhäll's 'dance of militarisation' to find the videos' affective force in how they address spectators as emotional beings, moved by the corporeal expressions and movements of the bodies that potential IS fighters are encouraged to want to become.

The affects of identification with a national and military collective, and the continuum between militarisation and political extremism, are also central to Catherine Baker's chapter on ultranationalist fashion in Croatia. The symbolic repertoire of the catalogue of T-shirts she analyses is grounded in a politicised interpretation of national military historical mythology but also shaped through transnational imaginative circuits, with influences including the visual cultures of the contemporary European far right and US pro-military apparel. While militarisation is inflected everywhere by specific gendered and racialised national frameworks, this chapter shows militarised imaginaries are simultaneously constructed through intertextual and transnational routes. Such was also the case, Jane Tynan argues, for images of the revolutionary masculinities deliberately cultivated by Fidel Castro, Che Guevara and their guerrilla army during the Cuban Revolution, which visualised them as heroic renegades and captured the international popular imagination in the 1960s, inspiring the visual identity of radical movements such as the Black Panther Party in the USA. The Panthers, whose critique of the US state as an institution structured around white supremacist violence is part of the tradition on which Howell draws, are the subject of Amy Abugo Ongiri's final chapter in this volume, showing how they became celebrated and memorialised as the embodiment of militarised resistance through iconic images of its male leaders, with a visual rhetoric achieving what de Certeau would call 'symbolic revolution' even though authorities neutralised their own militarised force.[124] Here, the struggle is not so much between militarisation and resistance as between ways of experiencing and representing Black masculinity in a context where confronting militarised state violence was already the rule in African American lives – suggesting, again, that when certain populations have always been the targets of state violence, 'militarisation' might be too limited a concept for understanding relationships between aesthetics, embodiment and military power.

Besides the different aesthetic practices and approaches these chapters discuss, and the historically specific settings they describe, the volume as a whole confronts a key aesthetic question: that of making sense of militarisation and embodiment through language, when the sensory complexity of war experience must be reduced into language to be understood through sight and/or sound. The work of producing affective responses in readers (or other media users) who have not been to war, or through the same war, can be thought of as an act of translation, with all the attendant politics of knowledge, difference and power.[125] Since processes of militarisation work transnationally, representations may even travel beyond their original linguistic area and still have aesthetic effects – such as IS videos or Lebanese martyr photographs reaching onlookers who do not speak Arabic, or Alexievich's writing becoming an artefact in Anglophone as well as post-Soviet understandings of war and gender. The linguistic boundary crossings these entail are messy and imperfect, but still part of how individuals surrounded by these transnationally circulating representations are experiencing war. This volume too must chiefly convey experiences of soldiering, spectatorship and other aspects of militarisation through language: even when a few key images help to visualise a chapter's subject matter, it is still through language – interacting with one's own memories and knowledge – that readers must interpret most of its understandings of what militarisation is and how intimately its aesthetic and embodied dimensions work.

These intimate and affective dimensions start, like this volume, with the soldier, and what the military expects of their bodies – which experiential testimony can communicate (as Evans and Jude illustrate), albeit in necessarily partial ways. But there is an intimate politics too in the aesthetic artefacts of militarisation, with which individuals form affective bonds – whether in paintings, photographs, digital images, T-shirts, uniforms or any other artefact that individuals view, hear, read, use, handle or wear. Artefacts which convey and/or contest processes of militarisation circulate through media using whatever technology is then available (Tynan and Ongiri point to photography, Ølgaard, Jude and Mathers to digital media, Myrttinen to street posters), while established art forms continue to be relevant (as Caso shows). As Ølgaard and Baker suggest, individuals invest these with meaning based on their own embodied subjectivity, memories and identities, but the affective associations thus generated can strengthen individuals' identifications with military projects to which they are already predisposed to relate – or impede them, as anti-militarist projects hope to do, even if (as Jude and Caso argue) they often fail to sufficiently expose the structures of attachments to military power. By showing the simultaneously aesthetic and embodied dimensions of attachments to militarisation, this volume demonstrates that an appreciation of the dynamics of spectatorship, participation and use in audiovisual, literary, digital and material culture is necessary to understand militarisation.

It also widens researchers' critical lenses towards where and why militarisation occurs. While state militaries decide what about war, military service and the bodies participating in or targeted by it they wish to normalise (and other less willed aspects may emerge through everyday social practice), non-state movements and insurgencies face choices about whether and how far to become militarised, allowing us to ask (like Tynan and Ongiri) what ends these choices might fulfil. Even Baker's Croatian case, where it seems to go without saying that the movement's iconography would be militarised, invites questioning *why* that should be so obvious – and in fact mythologised Croatian military history is just one stylistic ingredient of this ultranationalist visual culture, which also draws on the US gun lobby, football ultras and the transnational far right. The adoption of militarised bodily aesthetics by resistance movements may not necessarily be primarily intended to grow a militarised movement in action, even though it was in Tynan's Cuban case; sometimes, as Ongiri argues, it may be a symbolic move aimed at changing how a group or people see themselves. Yet even embodied aesthetic practices which did have a direct political goal in the Cuban context ended up effecting a transnational symbolic revolution in how radicals and the 1960s counterculture presented themselves.

This and many other examples in the volume demonstrates, finally, that processes of militarisation are transnationally shaped and also relationally produced: even if each set of processes primarily addresses a distinct national audience (or an audience defined by another collective referent, such as the transnational Islamist community hailed in Ølgaard's case), their aesthetic and embodied practices resound with other global audiences because they affect perceptions of and reactions to that military or movement. They also produce meanings that can be recirculated into other political, creative and commercial projects, as Tynan, Mathers, Ongiri and Baker all show. This becomes much more apparent once militarisation is studied across a geographically wider range of settings (where militarised masculinities research has, as in Myrttinen's example, begun to point the way) – and this in turn is necessary to draw better conclusions about whether the idea of militarisation is equally relevant or useful for contexts around the world.

Nevertheless, in so doing – and especially when exploring conjunctions of aesthetics and embodiment like those investigated here – we must be mindful of Åhäll's warning that the goal of researching militarisation is not simply to identify what is 'military-looking'; it is to perceive how people and societies are prepared for the idea of war, and which gendered and racialised social orders must be normalised to make that possible.[126] This deeper process is embodied because it depends on individuals' emotional reactions to the materiality and possibility of others' bodies. This deeper level of aesthetic perception is where militarisation operates most profoundly and where perhaps it can be contested most. While on a structural level the idea of societies *becoming* militarised is harder to support from critical perspectives that acknowledge how violence against certain targeted populations is worked into the fabric of the state, it is on this intimate and affective level where the concept of militarisation may have most to offer. Even if societies do not simply become more or less militarised, individuals' affective relationships to the military and the idea of war can dramatically change. It is on this intimate and everyday fulcrum that projects resisting militarisation so often exert pressure, and it is here where an understanding of the connections between militarisation, aesthetics and embodiment may be most valuable of all.

Notes

1. Synne L. Dyvik, *Gendering Counterinsurgency: Performativity, Embodiment and Experience in the Afghan 'Theatre of War'* (London: Routledge, 2017), 98.
2. Henry Alexander, 'Words and the War', *American Speech* 19:4 (1944): 276–80, 277.
3. Shaun Usher, 'Sin-Sationally, Mae West', *Letters of Note*, 19 September 2012. http://www.lettersofnote.com/2012/09/sin-sationally-mae-west.html.
4. Cynthia Enloe, *Bananas, Beaches and Bases: Making Feminist Sense of International Politics* (Berkeley, CA: University of California Press, 2014), xv, 215–21.
5. Linda Åhäll, 'Feeling Everyday IR: Embodied, Affective, Militarising Movement as Choreography of War', *Cooperation and Conflict* 54:2 (2019): 149–66.
6. Chris Rossdale, *Resisting Militarism: Direct Action and the Politics of Subversion* (Edinburgh: Edinburgh University Press, 2019).
7. Christine Sylvester, *War as Experience: Contributions from International Relations and Feminist Analysis* (London: Routledge, 2013), 4–5.
8. See Rachel Woodward and K. Neil Jenkings, 'Soldiers' Bodies and the Contemporary Military Memoir', in *War and the Body*, edited by Kevin McSorley (London: Routledge, 2013), 152–64.

9. Yuval Noah Harari, 'Scholars, Eyewitnesses, and Flesh-Witnesses of War: A Tense Relationship', *Partial Answers* 7:2 (2009): 213–28.

10. Synne L. Dyvik, 'Of Bats and Bodies: Methods for Reading and Writing Embodiment', *Critical Military Studies* 2:1–2 (2016): 56–69, 60.

11. Ibid., 58, 64–5.

12. See Matthew F. Rech and Alison J. Williams, 'Researching at Military Airshows: A Dialogue About Ethnography and Autoethnography', in *The Routledge Companion to Military Research Methods*, edited by Alison J. Williams, K. Neil Jenkings, Matthew F. Rech and Rachel Woodward (London: Routledge, 2016), 268–84, 281.

13. Cynthia Enloe, *Maneuvers: The International Politics of Militarizing Women's Lives* (Berkeley, CA: University of California Press, 2000), 262–71.

14. Jane Tynan, *British Army Uniform and the First World War: Men in Khaki* (Basingstoke: Palgrave Macmillan, 2013); Lucie Whitmore, 'Fashion Narratives of the First World War', PhD thesis (University of Glasgow, 2019); Matthew McCormack, 'Boots, Material Culture and Georgian Masculinities', *Social History* 42:4 (2017): 461–79.

15. Victoria Basham, 'Waiting for War: Soldiering, Temporality and the Gendered Politics of Boredom and Joy in Military Spaces', in *Emotions, Politics and War*, edited by Linda Åhäll and Thomas Gregory (London: Routledge, 2015), 128–40, 129.

16. See, for example, Rachel Woodward and Trish Winter, *Sexing the Soldier: The Politics of Gender and the Contemporary British Army* (London: Routledge, 2007); Vron Ware, *Military Migrants: Fighting for YOUR Country* (Basingstoke: Palgrave Macmillan, 2012); Adi Kuntsman and Rebecca L. Stein, *Digital Militarism: Israel's Occupation in the Social Media Age* (Stanford, CA: Stanford University Press, 2015).

17. Dyvik, *Counterinsurgency*, 11.

18. Julia Welland, 'Violence and the Contemporary Soldiering Body', *Security Dialogue* 48:6 (2017): 524–40, 527.

19. See, for example, Joanna Bourke, *Dismembering the Male: Men's Bodies, Britain and the Great War* (London: Reaktion, 1996); Elspeth Bösl, '"An Unbroken Man Despite Losing an Arm": Corporeal Reconstruction and Embodied Difference – Prosthetics in Western Germany after the Second World War (c. 1945–1960)', in *War and the Body*, edited by McSorley, 167–80; Zoe Wool, 'Attachments of Life: Intimacy, Genital Injury, and the Flesh of the U.S. Soldier Body', in *Living and Dying in the Contemporary World: A Compendium*, edited by Veena Das and Clara Han (Berkeley, CA: University of California Press, 2016), 399–417; Federica Caso, 'Sexing the Disabled Veteran: The Homoerotic Aesthetics of Militarism', *Critical Military Studies* 3:3 (2017): 217–34.

20. Suvrendrini Perera, 'The Craft of Killing: Trophy Bodies and Atrocity Aesthetics', *Critical Arts* 29:5 (2015): 658–75; Lilie Chouliaraki and Angelos Kissas, 'The Communication of Horrorism: A Typology of ISIS Online Death Videos', *Critical Studies in Media Communication* 35:1 (2018): 24–39.

21. Alison Howell, 'Forget "Militarization": Race, Disability and the "Martial Politics" of the Police and of the University', *International Feminist Journal of Politics* 20:2 (2018): 117–36.

22. Harvey Young, 'The Black Body as Souvenir in American Lynching', *Theatre Journal* 57:4 (2005): 639–57.

23. Kim A. Wagner, '"Calculated to Strike Terror": The Amritsar Massacre and the Spectacle of Colonial Violence', *Past and Present* 233 (2016): 185–225.

24. Sara Ahmed, *The Cultural Politics of Emotion*, 2nd ed. (Edinburgh: Edinburgh University Press, 2014), 4.

25. Tobin Siebers, *Disability Aesthetics* (Ann Arbor, MI: University of Michigan Press, 2010), 25.

26. Synne L. Dyvik, '"Valhalla Rising": Gender, Embodiment and Experience in Military Memoirs', *Security Dialogue* 47:2 (2016): 133–50, 136.

27. Swati Parashar, 'Discursive (In)Securities and Postcolonial Anxiety: Enabling Excessive Militarism in India', *Security Dialogue* 49:1–2 (2018): 123–35.

28. Amanda Chisholm and Joanna Tidy, 'Beyond the Hegemonic in the Study of Militaries, Masculinities, and War', *Critical Military Studies* 3:2 (2017): 99–102.

29. Maya Eichler, *Militarizing Men: Gender, Conscription, and War in Post-Soviet Russia* (Stanford, CA: Stanford University Press, 2011); David Duriesmith, *Masculinity and New War: The Gendered Dynamics of Contemporary Armed Conflict* (London: Routledge: 2017); Maria Eriksson Baaz and Maria Stern, 'Knowing Masculinities in Armed Conflict?: Reflections from Research in the Democratic Republic of Congo', in *The Oxford Handbook of Gender and Conflict*, edited by Fionnuala Ní Aoláin, Naomi Cahn, Dina Francesca Haynes and Nahla Valji (Oxford: Oxford University Press, 2018), 532–45; David Duriesmith and Noor Huda Ismail, 'Militarized Masculinities Beyond Methodological Nationalism: Charting the Multiple Masculinities of an Indonesian Jihadi', *International Theory* 11:2 (2019): 139–59.

30. Joanna Bourke, *Wounding the World: How Military Violence and War-Play Invades Our Lives* (London: Virago, 2014), 5.

31. Penny Summerfield and Corinna Peniston-Bird, *Contesting Home Defence: Men, Women and the Home Guard in the Second World War* (Manchester: Manchester University Press, 2007).

32. Bourke, *Dismembering the Male*; Graham Dawson, *Soldier Heroes: British Adventure, Empire, and the Imagining of Masculinities* (London: Routledge, 1994).

33. Rachel Woodward, *Military Geographies* (Oxford: Blackwell, 2004); Derek Gregory, 'The Everywhere War', *The Geographical Journal* 177:3 (2011): 238–50; Matthew Rech, Daniel Bos, K. Neil Jenkings, Alison Williams and Rachel Woodward, 'Geography, Military Geography, and Critical Military Studies', *Critical Military Studies* 1:1 (2015): 47–60.

34. Ines Prica, Lada Čale-Feldman and Reana Senjković (eds), *Fear, Death and Resistance: An Ethnography of War: Croatia 1991–1992* (Zagreb: IEF); Catherine Lutz, 'Making War at Home in the United States: Militarization and the Current Crisis', *American Anthropologist* 104:3 (2002): 723–35.

35. Victoria M. Basham and Sarah Bulmer, 'Critical Military Studies as Method: An Approach to Studying Gender and the Military', in *The Palgrave International Handbook of Gender and the Military*, edited by Rachel Woodward and Claire Duncanson (London: Palgrave Macmillan, 2017), 59–71, 60.

36. Ibid., 60–1.

37. Marsha Henry, 'Problematizing Military Masculinity, Intersectionality and Male Vulnerability in Feminist Critical Military Studies', *Critical Military Studies* 3:2 (2017): 182–99.

38. For this usage, see Robin Luckham, 'Armament Culture', *Alternatives* 10 (1984): 1–44, 1.

39. Enloe, *Maneuvers*, 3 (original emphasis).

40. Catherine Lutz, *Homefront: A Military City and the American 20th Century* (Boston, MA: Beacon Press, 2001).

41. Lutz, 'Making War at Home', 723.

42. Richelle M. Bernazzoli and Colin Flint, 'Embodying the Garrison State?: Everyday Geographies of Militarization in American Society', *Political Geography* 29:3 (2010): 157–66; see Rachel Woodward, *Military Geographies* (Oxford: Blackwell, 2004).

43. See Henry A. Giroux, 'The Militarization of US Higher Education after 9/11', *Theory, Culture & Society* 25:5 (2008): 56–82; Cynthia Enloe, 'The Risks of Scholarly Militarization: A Feminist Analysis', *Critical Military Studies* 8:4 (2010): 1107–11; Victoria M. Basham, 'Gender, Race, Militarism and Remembrance: The Everyday Geopolitics of the Poppy', *Gender, Place & Culture* 23:6 (2016): 883–96; Rachel Woodward, K. Neil Jenkings and Alison J. Williams, 'Militarisation, Universities and the University Armed Service Units', *Political Geography* 60 (2017): 203–12; Åhäll, 'Feeling Everyday IR', 149–50.

44. See Amanda Chisholm and Saskia Stachowitsch, 'Military Markets, Masculinities and the Global Political Economy of the Everyday: Understanding Military Outsourcing as Gendered and Racialised', in *The Palgrave International Handbook of Gender and the Military*, edited by Woodward and Duncanson, 371–85, 377; Reece Jones and Corey Johnson, 'Border Militarisation and the Re-Articulation of Sovereignty', *Transactions of the Institute of British Geographers* 41:2 (2016): 187–200.

45. Basham and Bulmer, 'Critical Military Studies as Method', 63.

46. Marsha Henry and Katherine Natanel, 'Militarisation as Diffusion: The Politics of Gender, Space and the Everyday', *Gender, Place & Culture* 23:6 (2016): 850–6, 850–1 (original emphasis).

47. Laura Shepherd, 'Militarisation', in *Visual Global Politics*, edited by Roland Bleiker (London: Routledge, 2018), 209–10.

48. Matthew K. Rech, K. Neil Jenkings, Alison J. Williams and Rachel Woodward, 'An Introduction to Military Research Methods', in *The Routledge Companion to Military Research Methods*, edited by Williams et al., 1–18, 3. For further definitions of militarism, see Anna Stavrianakis and Jan Selby, 'Militarism and International Relations in the Twenty-First Century', in *Militarism and International*

Relations: Political Economy, Security, Theory, edited by Anna Stavrianakis and Jan Selby (London: Routledge, 2012), 3–18; Bryan Mabee and Srđan Vučetić, 'Varieties of Militarism: Towards a Typology', *Security Dialogue* 49:1–2 (2018): 96–108.

49. Basham, 'Gender, Race, Militarism and Remembrance', 884.

50. Linda Åhäll, 'The Dance of Militarisation: A Feminist Security Studies Take on "the Political"', *Critical Studies on Security* 4:2 (2016): 154–68, 159.

51. Ibid., 160, 162 (italics removed).

52. Ibid., 158, 162.

53. John Berger, *Ways of Seeing* (Harmondsworth: Penguin, 1972).

54. Roland Bleiker, 'The Aesthetic Turn in International Political Theory', *Millennium* 30:3 (2001): 509–33, 511.

55. See, for example, Cerwyn Moore and Laura J. Shepherd, 'Aesthetics and International Relations: Towards a Global Politics', *Global Society* 24:3 (2010): 299–309; Aida A. Hozić, 'Introduction: The Aesthetic Turn at 15 (Legacies, Limits and Prospects)', *Millennium* 45:2 (2017): 201–5.

56. Bleiker, 'Aesthetic Turn', 524.

57. Rune Saugmann Andersen, Juha A. Vuori and Can E. Mutlu, 'Visuality', in *Critical Security Methods: New Frameworks for Analysis*, edited by Claudia Aradau, Jef Huysmans, Andrew Neal and Nadine Voelkner (London: Routledge, 2014), 85–117, 89. See Jacques Rancière, *The Politics of Aesthetics* (London: Continuum, 2004).

58. See, for example, Michael Shapiro, *Studies in Trans-Disciplinary Method: After the Aesthetic Turn* (London: Routledge, 2013), 30.

59. Anca Pusca, *Post-Communist Aesthetics: Revolutions, Capitalism, Violence* (London: Routledge, 2016), 2.

60. Anna M. Agathangelou and L. H. M. Ling, *Transforming World Politics: From Empire to Multiple Worlds* (London: Routledge, 2009), 97–9.

61. Åhall, 'Dance', 160.

62. Bleiker, 'Aesthetic Turn', 513.

63. Moore and Shepherd, 'Aesthetics', 308.

64. Megan Daigle, 'Writing the Lives of Others: Storytelling and International Politics', *Millennium* 45:1 (2016): 25–42, 26. See, for example, Annick T. R. Wibben, *Feminist Security Studies: A Narrative Approach* (London: Routledge, 2011); Laura J. Shepherd, *Gender, Violence and Popular Culture: Telling Stories* (London: Routledge, 2013); Woodward and Jenkings, 'Soldiers' Bodies and the Contemporary Military Memoir', 152–64; Naeem Inayatullah and Elizabeth Dauphinée (eds), *Narrative Global Politics: Theory, History and the Personal in International Relations* (London: Routledge, 2016).

65. Nicholas Mirzoeff (ed.), *The Visual Culture Reader*, 3rd ed. (London: Routledge, 2012); Lene Hansen, 'How Images Make World Politics: International Icons and the Case of Abu Ghraib', *Review of International Studies* 41:2 (2015): 263–88; Caitlin Hamilton and Laura J. Shepherd (eds), *Understanding Popular Culture and World Politics in the Digital Age* (London: Routledge, 2016); Andersen et al.,

'Visuality'; Roland Bleiker, 'Mapping Visual Global Politics', in *Visual Global Politics*, edited by Bleiker, 1–29.

66. See Alex Danchev, *On Art and War and Terror* (Oxford: Oxford University Press, 2009).

67. Santanu Das, *Touch and Intimacy in First World War Literature* (Cambridge: Cambridge University Press, 2005); Michael Roper, *The Secret Battle: Emotional Survival in the Great War* (Manchester: Manchester University Press, 2009).

68. Torika Bolatagici, 'Somatic Soldier: Embodiment and the Aesthetic of Absence and Presence', *Critical Military Studies* 2:1–2 (2016): 125–32, 126, 131; Jill Gibbon and Christine Sylvester, 'Thinking Like an Artist–Researcher About War', *Millennium* 45:2 (2017): 249–57, 252.

69. Alison J. Williams, K. Neil Jenkings, Matthew F. Rech and Rachel Woodward (eds), *The Routledge Companion to Military Research Methods* (London: Routledge, 2016).

70. Donna Haraway, 'Situated Knowledges: The Science Question in Feminism and the Privilege of Partial Perspective', *Feminist Studies* 14:3 (1988): 575–99, 581.

71. See Emma Hutchison, *Affective Communities in World Politics: Collective Emotions after Trauma* (London: Routledge, 2016); Sarah Bulmer and David Jackson, '"You Do Not Live in My Skin": Embodiment, Voice, and the Veteran', *Critical Military Studies* 2:1–2 (2016): 25–40.

72. See Debra Gimlin, 'What is "Body Work"?: A Review of the Literature', *Sociology Compass* 1:1 (2007): 353–70.

73. See Sara Ahmed, *Strange Encounters: Embodied Others in Post-Coloniality* (London: Routledge, 2000).

74. Kevin McSorley, 'War and the Body', in *War and the Body*, edited by McSorley, 1–32.

75. Elaine Scarry, *The Body in Pain: The Making and Unmaking of the World* (Oxford: Oxford University Press, 1985), 1–3.

76. See, for example, Bourke, *Dismembering the Male*; Ana Carden-Coyne, *Reconstructing the Body: Classicism, Modernism and the First World War* (Oxford: Oxford University Press, 2009); David A. Gerber (ed.), *Disabled Veterans in History*, 2nd ed. (Ann Arbor, MI: University of Michigan Press, 2012); Marjorie Gehrhardt, *'Gueules cassées*: The Men behind the Masks', *Journal of War and Culture Studies* 6:4 (2013): 267–81; Tracey Loughran, 'A Crisis of Masculinity?: Re-Writing the History of Shell-Shock and Gender in First World War Britain', *History Compass* 11:9 (2013): 727–38; Bösl, '"An Unbroken Man"'; Frances Bernstein, 'Prosthetic Manhood in the Soviet Union at the End of World War II', *Osiris* 30 (2015): 113–33; Suzannah Biernoff, *Portraits of Violence: War and the Aesthetics of Disfigurement* (Ann Arbor, MI: University of Michigan Press, 2017).

77. Wool, 'Attachments'; Kenneth MacLeish, 'How to Feel about War: On Soldier Psyches, Military Biopolitics, and American Empire', *BioSocieties* 14:2 (2019): 274–99.

78. Lauren B. Wilcox, *Bodies of Violence: Theorizing Embodied Subjects in International Relations* (Oxford: Oxford University Press, 2015), 2.

79. Laura Sjoberg, 'Centering Security Studies Around Felt, Gendered Insecurities', *Journal of Global Security Studies* 1:1 (2016): 51–63, 51.

80. Wilcox, *Bodies*, 2–5.

81. Christine Sylvester, 'War Experiences/War Practices/War Theory', *Millennium* 40:3 (2012): 483–503, 484.

82. Sylvester, *War as Experience*; Swati Parashar, 'What Wars and "War Bodies" Know about International Relations', *Cambridge Review of International Affairs* 26:4 (2013): 615–30.

83. Cynthia Weber, *Queer International Relations: Sovereignty, Sexuality and the Will to Knowledge* (Oxford: Oxford University Press, 2016), 3.

84. Jesse Paul Crane-Seeber, 'Sexy Warriors: The Politics and Pleasures of Submission to the State', *Critical Military Studies* 2:1–2 (2016): 41–55; Victoria M. Basham, *War, Identity and the Liberal State: Everyday Experiences of the Geopolitical in the Armed Forces* (London: Routledge, 2013), 75.

85. Cara Daggett, 'Drone Disorientations: How "Unmanned" Weapons Queer the Experience of Killing in War', *International Feminist Journal of Politics* 17:3 (2015): 361–79, 362.

86. Ty Solomon, 'Embodiment, Emotions, and Materialism in International Relations', in *Emotions, Politics and War*, edited by Åhäll and Gregory, 58–70, 66.

87. Sylvester, *War as Experience*, 5.

88. Kevin McSorley, 'Rethinking War and the Body', in *War and the Body*, edited by McSorley, 233–44, 236.

89. John Hockey, '"Switch On": Sensory Work in the Infantry', *Work, Employment & Society* 23:3 (2009): 477–93; Paul Higate and Marsha Henry, *Insecure Spaces: Peacekeeping, Power and Performance in Haiti, Kosovo and Liberia* (London: Zed, 2009).

90. Kevin McSorley, 'Helmetcams, Militarized Sensation and "Somatic War"', *Journal of War and Culture Studies* 5:1 (2012): 47–58, 48.

91. McSorley, 'Rethinking War', 237.

92. Synne L. Dyvik and Lauren Greenwood, 'Embodying Militarism: Exploring the Spaces and Bodies In-Between', *Critical Military Studies* 2:1–2 (2016): 1–6, 3, citing Kevin McSorley, 'Doing Military Fitness: Physical Culture, Civilian Leisure, and Militarism', *Critical Military Studies* 2:1–2 (2016): 103–19, 105 (original emphasis).

93. Julia Welland, 'Joy and War: Reading Pleasure in Wartime Experiences', *Review of International Studies* 44:3 (2018): 438–55.

94. See Catherine Baker, Victoria Basham, Sarah Bulmer, Harriet Gray and Alexandra Hyde, 'Encounters with the Military: Toward a Feminist Ethics of Critique?', *International Feminist Journal of Politics* 18:1 (2016): 140–54.

95. Swati Parashar, 'Embodied "Otherness" and Negotiations of Difference', in 'The Forum: Emotion and the Feminist IR Researcher', edited by Christine Sylvester, *International Studies Review* 13:4 (2011): 687–708.

96. Harriet Gray, 'Researching from the Spaces in Between?: The Politics of Accountability in Studying the British Military', *Critical Military Studies* 2:1–2 (2016): 70–83, 70.

97. See Baker et al., 'Encounters'; Sarah Bulmer and David Jackson, '"You Do Not Live in My Skin": Embodiment, Voice, and the Veteran', *Critical Military Studies* 2:1–2 (2016): 25–40; Stephen Atherton, 'Researching Military Men', in *The Routledge Companion to Military Research Methods*, edited by Williams et al., 243–55; David Walker, 'Putting "Insider-Ness" to Work: Researching Identity Narratives of Career Soldiers About to Leave the Army', in *The Routledge Companion to Military Research Methods*, edited by Williams et al., 256–67; Dyvik, 'Bats'; Nick Caddick, Alex Cooper and Brett Smith, 'Reflections on Being a Civilian Researcher in an Ex-Military World: Expanding Horizons?', *Critical Military Studies* 5:2 (2019): 95–114.

98. Bulmer and Jackson, 'Skin', 26.

99. Ibid., 27.

100. Ibid., 27 (original emphasis).

101. Cristina Masters, 'Bodies of Technology: Cyborg Soldiers and Militarized Masculinities', *International Feminist Journal of Politics* 7:1 (2005): 112–32; Caso, 'Sexing'; Wool, 'Attachments'.

102. Thomas Gregory, 'Dismembering the Dead: Violence, Vulnerability and the Body in War', *European Journal of International Relations* 22:4 (2016): 944–65, 949.

103. Parashar, '"War Bodies"', 622.

104. K. Neil Jenkings, Nick Megoran, Rachel Woodward and Daniel Bos, 'Wootton Bassett and the Political Spaces of Remembrance and Mourning', *Area* 44:3 (2012): 356–63.

105. On emotions in international politics, see Neta Crawford, 'The Passion of World Politics: Propositions on Emotion and Emotional Relationships', *International Security* 24:4 (2000): 116–56; Jonathan Mercer, 'Emotional Beliefs', *International Organization* 64:1 (2010): 1–31; Emma Hutchison and Roland Bleiker, 'Theorizing Emotions in World Politics', *International Theory* 6:3 (2014): 491–514; Emma Hutchison, *Affective Communities in World Politics: Collective Emotions after Trauma* (London: Routledge, 2016); Åhäll and Gregory (eds), *Emotions, Politics and War*.

106. Hutchison, *Affective Communities*, 16.

107. Welland, 'Joy', 450.

108. Thomas Gregory and Linda Åhäll, 'Introduction: Mapping Emotions, Politics and War', in *Emotions, Politics and War*, edited by Åhäll and Gregory, 1–14, 2.

109. J. Martin Daughtry, *Listening to War: Sound, Music, Trauma and Survival in Wartime Iraq* (Oxford: Oxford University Press, 2015).

110. Kenneth T. MacLeish, 'Armor and Anesthesia: Exposure, Feeling, and the Soldier's Body', *Medical Anthropology Quarterly* 26:1 (2012): 49–68.

111. Derek Gregory, 'The Natures of War', *Antipode* 48:1 (2016): 3–56, 9–11.

112. Welland, 'Joy', 447, citing Dyvik, '"Valhalla Rising"'.

113. Hockey, '"Switch On"'; John Hockey, 'The Aesthetic of Being in the Field: Participant Observation with Infantry', in *The Routledge Companion to Military Research Methods*, ed. Williams et al., 207–18, 215.

114. McSorley, 'Fitness', 108.
115. Marcus Schulzke, 'Necessary and Surplus Militarisation: Rethinking Civil–Military Interactions and their Consequences', *European Journal of International Security* 3:1 (2017): 94–112.
116. Maria Stern and Marysia Zalewski, 'Feminist Fatigue(s): Reflections on Feminism and Familiar Fables of Militarisation', *Review of International Studies* 35:3 (2009): 611–30, 625.
117. David Duriesmith, 'De-Centring "Militarisation" in the Study of Collective Masculine Violence', *The Gender and War Project*, 18 December 2017. http://www.genderandwar.com/2017/12/18/de-centring-militarisation-in-the-study-of-collective-masculine-violence/.
118. See Ayano Ginoza, 'R&R at the Intersection of US and Japanese Dual Empire: Okinawan Women and Decolonizing Militarized Heterosexuality', *American Quarterly* 68:3 (2016): 583–91; Teresia Teaiwa, 'Reflections on Militourism, US Imperialism, and American Studies', *American Quarterly* 68:3 (2016): 847–53.
119. Maria Eriksson Baaz and Judith Verweijen, 'Confronting the Colonial: The (Re)Production of "African" Exceptionalism in Critical Security and Military Studies', *Security Dialogue* 49:1–2 (2018): 57–69, 58, 65.
120. Howell, 'Forget "Militarization"', 118.
121. Ibid., 130.
122. Ibid., 130.
123. See Henry, 'Problematizing'.
124. Michel de Certeau, *Capture of Speech and Other Political Writings*, translated by Tim Conley (Minneapolis, MN: University of Minnesota Press, 1997), 11.
125. See Catherine Baker, 'Writing About Embodiment as an Act of Translation', *Critical Military Studies* 2:1–2 (2016): 120–4.
126. Åhäll, 'Dance', 160 (italics removed).

CHAPTER 1

Basic Training

Dan Evans

It's early January and I'm in a huge training area somewhere in the south of England. It's about 3 in the morning and we have pushed out of the harbour area on a night patrol. It's minus 6, pitch black and it's snowing. As usual, Cpl Donnelly is keeping a ridiculous pace and seems, to me at least, to be choosing the most obscenely difficult routes to traverse: it feels like we are continuously going uphill. My knees are fucked – completely black with bruising from throwing myself to the ground on the solid icy mud – I'm in so much pain I can no longer kneel so each time we halt I can't adopt the right firing position. Fuck it, I just crouch, he can't see me in this dark anyway. After we complete the first half of our 'mission' – picking up rations which the training team have hidden in a bush at the top of the hill (only a couple of miles but it feels like ten) – we head back towards the harbour area. I'm 2IC so I've got to attempt to appear to be quite switched on, but I'm so tired I'm not really conscious of what's going on – certainly not scanning for danger or keeping my rifle at a sensible angle to raise for firing as taught – I just keep my head down and concentrate on putting one foot in front of the other, assuming that it's so dark the Cpl won't be able to notice my lack of professionalism. I'm past caring now anyway, I hate this. I want to go home. After about a mile into the return journey we hit a big marsh. Donnelly hisses at me to 'go firm'. Fucked if I know what that means. Fuck it, let's just get back, I think. The rest of the section presses on, jumping silently and competently over a stream. My legs are too short and I fall short of the other side, cracking the ice and going up to my waist in icy water. Cunt! I yell. I then realise to my disgust that I've still got my spare thermals stuffed in my now sodden combat trousers because I was too lazy or forgetful to properly unpack earlier. No spare clothes now, you fucking mong. Donnelly runs up, incensed at the disturbance: 'Evans, what the fuck are you doing, I told you to go firm you little cunt.' I say I didn't know what it meant (the truth). He doesn't believe me and shakes his head in disgust. I know what he's thinking: fucking useless civvies, stupid TA bastards. I'm going to get cut from this course, I can feel it. We finally get back to the harbour area and ease our aching bodies into our shell scrapes. The shell scrape, which yesterday was a muddy quagmire, has thankfully frozen solid – shit to sleep on but better than sludge that gets in everything. As my basha buddy competently and silently sorts out his personal admin and beds down for some sleep, I'm nearly crying because my freezing fingers can't get my boots off to get my soaking trousers off, and I'm shivering so hard it feels like I'm having a fit, my teeth are going to wake up the whole section. We have to practice light discipline so I can't see anything, and of course I don't know where my spare combats are in my Bergan, which I can't fucking unzip, *again*. With my head fully inside my backpack lest anyone see how close I am to tears, I fumble round inside, testing one Ziplock bag after another – bags inside bags like Russian dolls as per packing instructions. Pants, socks, shirt, no sign of spare trousers. Cunt cunt cunt cunt. My fatigue is mixing with unprecedented levels of self-hatred and frustration at my performance, hatred of the army, hatred of myself, *what the fuck am I doing here?*

****

What am I doing here? What the fuck am I doing? The thought dominated my brain throughout basic training. My presence at this training establishment – although I was not aware of this at the time – can ultimately be traced back to what is known as the 'embodied turn' within international relations (IR), which, as the introduction to this volume makes clear, was a natural outgrowth of the 'aesthetic turn' within IR.[1] The aesthetic turn moves research away from the dominant positivist or 'mimetic' approach to IR and political theory, which seeks to 'objectively' capture 'world politics as it really is', or to learn 'facts about the real world'.[2] For Bleiker, and for feminist scholars such as Cynthia Enloe and Christine Sylvester, this narrow, empiricist view of the world tends to reproduce a 'masculine obsession with big heroic events' such as war, state summits and revolutions. This focus has 'dramatically narrowed the scope of inquiries into world politics', closing off vital areas and fields of enquiry as well marginalising certain actors and innovative *research methods* which might potentially allow us to obtain a greater and more nuanced understanding of the phenomenon.[3]

Central to the aesthetic turn is the recognition that 'politics' and 'international relations' are not just to be found and observed in 'the heroic domains of state action and high politics prescribed by existing scholarly conventions'.[4] Instead, these macro-level phenomena and their effects permeate and are observable in the everyday embodied experiences of 'normal people', as well as in art, literature, popular culture and poetry. Aesthetic scholars advocate the exploration of new research sites, groups and the adoption of a diverse range of methodologies in order to understand these new sites. Feminist scholars such as Cynthia Enloe foreshadowed this new approach. Enloe, for example, draws attention to the way international social forces are noticeable in hitherto neglected sites, such as sweatshops or brothels outside foreign military bases.[5] The feminist focus on liminal, marginalised groups and research sites reveals powerful insights into the international which would otherwise remain unnoticed, demonstrating the strength of the aesthetic turn as a *practical* methodology. Thus whilst there is certainly an ontological and epistemological dimension to the aesthetic turn, aesthetics also represents a new methodology which, as Bleiker writes, 'offers us possibilities to re-think, re-view, re-hear and re-feel the political world we live in. Aesthetics provides us with insights that we otherwise would not be able to gain.'[6] This is crucial: Bleiker reminds us that we study art and literature and everyday life not out of some postmodern sensibility or navel gazing self-indulgence, but rather because, on a *practical* level, studying these phenomena helps us to understand world politics in a way that would not be possible if we restrict our focus to grand actors and events, using only certain methodologies.

The Corporeal Turn within Critical Military Studies

The study of militarism and the military has fallen out of fashion within IR.[7] Instead, IR has become narrowly focused on 'why wars happen and how they end'.[8] It is not concerned with the events and phenomena which occur *between these two moments*.[9] This narrow focus has created a large gap in our understanding of how militarism and militarisation impact on society, particularly because military sociology as a discipline has historically been dominated by positivist thinking: much of the insights about war and the military have traditionally been written by sociologists who were themselves either serving military personnel or state officials. Any insights gleaned about the military were generally written for the benefit of the state and the military itself.[10] Military sociology therefore historically lacked a vital *critical* element. There has been, for example, little reflection on the methods used to study the military;[11] and military sociology has unsurprisingly historically focused on traditional field sites such as soldiering and the creation of soldiers; war itself; and the military–industrial complex. Recently, however, the aesthetic turn within IR has been mirrored within military sociology, as a new wave of scholars have begun to move beyond traditional positivistic ways of thinking and writing about war, the military and militarisation.[12] This new critical movement – centred around the journal *Critical Military Studies* – has introduced new (particularly feminist) perspectives on militarism and warfare, as well as new field sites and methodological innovations, including significant new *ethnographies* of militarism, building on the pioneering work of John Hockey.[13] As Christine Sylvester puts it:

> we should avoid privileging defence departments and military spokesmen as the ultimate experts on war. The strength of the new war studies approach is that it includes other places and potential power-holders or -losers in and through war, such as women combatants, curators of war-looted museums and rape victims.[14]

War, she continues, should be 'studied *up* from people and not down from places that sweep blood, tears and laughter away'.[15] Warfare and militarism can therefore be illuminated through exploring the 'exceptional condition' of soldiering and the everyday lives of soldiers;[16] the families and communities impacted and 'contaminated' by the violence of war;[17] and the militarisation of wider society.[18]

Within this new wave of military scholarship, numerous researchers have increasingly moved towards an *embodied* sociology of war and militarism.[19] If traditional military sociology has focused on the 'war machine' – the military as an *institution* – then the turn towards embodiment can be explained by Kenneth MacLeish's metaphor of soldiers themselves as *individual* 'machines': 'the soldier's body is the equipment and raw material for war, the most necessary and most carefully managed component of the good machine, or even the good machine itself in its most indivisible, cellular form'.[20] The human body is the most important piece of equipment within modern warfare: ultimately wars cannot continue without the presence of tens of thousands of such bodies.[21] And just as the human body is the raw material for war, so war (and indeed militarism) is experienced and reproduced *through the body*, 'through a panoply of embodied practices, movements, resonances and regimes of sensation' – smells, tastes, injury and the destruction of the body.[22] War is something that is *felt*, and it is therefore 'to the corporeal that we should turn in an attempt to develop a language to speak of its myriad violences and its socially generative force'.[23]

This chapter will add to this increasing body of work by detailing the affective experience of basic training and the insights this 'upstream journey'[24] provided into the nature of habitus formation within the British Army, and how bodies react to and are transformed by military training. Unlike more dramatic insights into the embodied experience of soldiering, however, this account of basic training mainly focuses on the banal, everyday ways that recruits learn what Stephen Atherton calls the *domestic* element of soldiering – the embodied routine and rhythm of barracks life. Atherton reminds us: 'just as the body and mind must be trained to fight when called upon, so it must be trained to eat, sleep and socialise in close company, and provide for the successful repro-duction of a military way of life'.[25] MacLeish's paradigmatic analysis of the biopolitics of warfare similarly points out 'even outside of combat, soldiering is a distinctly bodily undertaking, involving the disciplining, cultivating and monitoring of the body, the tedious chores of manda-tory exercise . . . being compelled to wakefulness at every hour of the day'.[26] This chapter is a reflection on a centrally important part of the author's own enactive ethnographic research[27] into life in the British Army reserve and the 'enduring modification of the bodily schema'[28] that basic training entailed.

Joining Up

I joined the Army Reserve in 2015 to conduct critical ethnographic enquiry.[29] The decision to actually *join* the military and to conduct covert research, rather than go through the extensive bureaucratic hurdles of conducting 'official' participant observation, was based on a number of factors. Central among these was a determination to conduct what Loïc Wacquant calls 'enactive ethnography', an immersive approach which advocates 'performing the phenomena' that is being studied.[30] Wacquant argues that a fertile method of understanding embodied phenomenon is to actually *acquire* these embodied skills and competencies – that is, the habitus of the phenomena under investigation – ourselves as research-ers. Whilst 'traditional' participant observation ethnography is of course also an embodied experience, Wacquant's enactive approach demands a further step for the researcher. I believed this method was particularly important given the uniquely embodied nature of warfare and soldiering. Ultimately I believed that this 'apprenticeship' would allow me to feel for myself the sensory, visceral nature of soldiering, something that I did not feel I could achieve as effectively as a participant observer. I undertook selection alongside my regular counterparts, spent three months attending training every Tuesday evening at my local barracks before beginning part one of my basic training, 'Phase One (Alpha)', which consisted of four residential weekends at a local barracks. A month or so after this I completed 'Phase One (Bravo)' at a regional training depot. This residential course lasted fifteen days and at the end I passed out as a trained reservist soldier. Throughout this period I continued to attend training every Tuesday evening as well as undertaking weekend training camps with my company.

A Soldier-Like Bearing

Recruits beginning Phase One (Alpha) are met with a large sign as they pass through the barrack gates. It reads 'You are now entering a British Army training establishment. From this point on, only the highest standards of behaviour and bearing are acceptable'. *Bearing.* The next morning, nervous and tired, we lined up on the parade square for our first drill session. The drill instructor demonstrates marching and turning at the halt in front of us. He tells us to 'walk confidently, in a soldier-like manner!'; 'Start moving like a fucking body of men!'; 'smart, *like a soldier!'*

What does a 'soldier-like bearing' mean? The move towards an embodied sociology of the military has largely focused on the sensual and visceral elements of the physical and masculine side of soldiering,[31] including tabbing,[32] breathing,[33] as well as the central experience of injury and the destruction of the body in war.[34] Basic training was something different, something perhaps more intangible and banal. As the recruit undergoes military socialisation, they must learn a whole array of everyday embodied competencies which occur alongside (or even before) the more dramatic facets of training (such as tabbing or 'fire and manoeuvre'), in the 'domestic' space of the barracks.

Pierre Bourdieu's concept of habitus can help us make sense of this issue of 'bearing' within the military. By habitus, Bourdieu refers to 'systems of durable, transposable dispositions, structured structures predisposed to function as structuring structures . . . the practices produced by the habitus are the strategy generating principles enabling agents to cope with unforeseen and ever changing situations'.[35] The habitus represents the internalisation by the individual of the structures of the external social world, represented outwardly by people's dispositions, or 'way of being'. But whilst the habitus refers to 'mental structures' or ways of thinking and acting, the habitus is also an embodied phenomenon. The mental structures of the habitus are also *inscribed in the body*. Bourdieu states that the bodily habitus 'is a permanent disposition expressed through durable ways of standing, speaking, walking, and thereby of feeling and thinking'.[36] The structures of a group are rooted in the body.[37] The embodied, physical manifestations of the habitus is called *hexis*.

It is hard to pinpoint exactly what a military habitus is, despite it being clearly central to becoming a soldier, and being continually talked about by instructors and officers throughout basic training. Indeed, 'bearing' is explicitly referred to in army training manuals.[38] Eyal Ben-Ari similarly identifies the distinct embodied nature of the military habitus, although he does not call it such:

> [an army identity] is readily evident in regard both to nonverbal behaviour – posturing, hunching of shoulders, or excessive preoccupation with guns and equipment – and verbal behaviour – free use of the imperative, barking words in a forceful manner, or the abandonment of politeness forms.[39]

MacLeish's masterful account of soldiers at Fort Hood also alludes to the embodied military habitus, both in terms of the muscle memory of soldiers on operations and their bearing in the domestic space: 'one starts to notice other things, none of them definitive but all of them common: dark, bug-eyed Oakley sunglasses, upright posture, a stiffness of carriage and gait, a neutral flatness of expression, and often a certain amount of muscular bulk'.[40]

Of course, there are different ways of 'bearing', different embodied competencies for different situations: on exercise, during drill, hanging round – outside the barracks and inside, on duty and off duty. It is therefore impossible to condense the whole array of embodied competencies into this chapter, or even to separate them artificially, given that each element is simply one component of the whole 'soldier-like manner' or intangible military habitus.

The distinction between a military bearing and civilian bearing was instilled right from my three-day selection. Here, as we disembarked our train, nervously shuffling around and looking lost in our ill-fitting suits, a huge sergeant emerged and began to scream at us as we started to amble towards him. 'Start fucking cutting about!', he yelled as we ambled over to him. 'Don't fucking walk!' Outwardly, then, a soldier-like bearing might simply seem to be standing up straight and moving fast, with a sense of purpose, never dawdling. It is simply defined as being the opposite of the embodied civilian habitus, which is slow, dawdling, soft. This focus on bearing continues into the ostensibly safe space of the classroom – 'sit up fucking straight!' – recruits cannot slouch, but must always be alert, focused. Following selection, I began attending Tuesday evening drill nights at my local barracks. In my first training session, I was briefed on how to 'brace up', how to come to attention, how to stand at ease, how to salute. Whole new ways of holding oneself. For weeks I slunk to the back of the platoon, out of sight, staring intently at the crisp creases on the combats of the soldier in front of me. Stand at ease, hands behind back, head facing forward, listening nervously for the command – Squaaad, ten . . . shun! – arms straighten, back braces, head raises up, left leg rises to the knee, slam it back down, hands by the sides. At ease. Attention. At ease. Stand easy. Dismissed – attention, right turn, march off the parade ground. For the first month of attending drill nights I would sweat profusely and turn bright red with embarrassment and frustration at simply not knowing how to move.

Drill represents perhaps the most obvious way of moving like a soldier. It is a central part of basic training because it forces recruits to shed their old civilian forms of movement and learn new, soldierly ways of moving and bearing (head up, back straight, sharp, crisp, exaggerated movements). Whilst almost universally resented by recruits as being 'pointless', it is used by the army as a way of inculcating military habits of discipline, unthinking obedience, and teamwork: move in sync on the parade square, move in sync on the battlefield. Drill is a deeply disorienting experience for recruits: these are not natural movements for civilians – one is forced to think about movements such as walking and turning which are pre-reflexive. Such is the difficulty in learning these new movements, drill is initially taught by the recruits calling out timings for every component of each basic movement – one, two three one! One two! This then progresses to Left, right, left, right, left, right leeeeeft. Crispness and sharpness of movement was rigorously enforced. 'Snap your fucking salute up!' 'Eyes . . . right!', 'not like that you fucking mong',[41] 'sort your belt out you cunt', 'stand up straight!', 'stand still!' and the constant, familiar exhortation: *'look like a fucking soldier'*. If backs and legs weren't straight they would be physically moved with the instructor's staff.

As Hockey makes clear, the body of the recruit is no longer theirs – it belongs to the state.[42] Our bodies are continuously inspected. Instructors stare at our faces, checking for signs of stubble, our fingernails, our hair-cuts. Beyond drill, recruits' physical movements are policed 24/7: through-out basic training, a recruit must march at all times when moving outside round the barracks. Recruits are distinguished in the training depot by their nervous marching and pained, worried faces, focusing on every ele-ment of their movement. The significance of marching everywhere cannot be understated: functional, everyday movement – getting from A to B – cannot be taken for granted by the recruit. There are few spaces or instances whereby a civilian bearing is permitted; every second of your movement and bearing has to be thought about.

Atherton notes how the army effectively subsumes 'feminised' prac-tices of homemaking by effectively using the banal, domestic routine of the barracks as a site of relentless discipline which reinforces military hierarchies.[43] Referring to Foucault, MacLeish notes how 'docile bodies are rendered productive', by being subjected to 'countless minute and technical compulsions'.[44] Every day after completing our daily tasks, whether classroom work, the firing range, drill or physical training (PT), we would begin the monotonous ritual of block jobs – frantically sweep-ing, mopping and wiping the floors, the toilets, walls, beds, windows and window sills. After these are completed, we iron and press our kit and polish our boots until the corporal bounds into our room, switches the light off and yells at us to get into fucking bed. Lockers, ostensibly a private space, are to be ordered and organised in a specific way: uni-forms hung up on this side, personal equipment on this side; boots polished and under the bed; Bergan and rest of personal belongings stowed away in the other cupboard neatly. Small mistakes by one indi-vidual, perhaps a bed not folded in the proper manner, lead to collective punishment – 'get on the fucking line' – the whole platoon sprinting onto the landing in pants and T-shirts to do press-ups and squats. Messy lockers are trashed by the instructors. Folded sheets ripped off the bed, items thrown out the window. 'Switching on' – the practice of height-ened sensory alertness and hypervigilance practiced by soldiers in com-bat zones (the militarisation of the senses) –therefore also occurs within the ostensible safety of the domestic space of the barracks.[45]

Uniforms and Kit

'What soldiers wear', as Jane Tynan notes, 'is central to the public image of the military'.[46] A soldier is distinguished in society by their uniform. It's what visually defines the soldier's role within wider society; reserv-ists from regulars; the British Army from other armies; regiments within the regular army, and so on. Uniform plays a central role in the recruit's journey from civilian to soldier and also plays a central role in learning a military habitus. As Bourdieu notes, aesthetics are physical manifestations of symbolic power and capital within a field, the expression of a privileged position within a particular social space.[47] Uniform is therefore an important aesthetic signifier of status and competence within the military, and functions to inculcate an awareness of military hierarchies and identity – both formal and informal – to the recruit. Throughout basic training, recruits are taught the dizzying array of ranks (which, as they are no longer worn on the arm but on the centre of the chest on British Army uniforms, are harder for recruits to identify). MacLeish's work with the US military similarly notes how human interaction in barracks entails 'eyes going to the chest' as soldiers determine the rank and value of the person they are engaging, which in turn determines the protocol for formal and informal interaction, which is of course governed by strict movements – saluting, bracing up – if speaking to senior ranks.[48] As he explains, 'rank entails a host of formal and informal interpersonal protocols – not just in terms of address ("Sir" for officers, the rank itself for NCOs [non-commissioned officers]) and gestures (salutes), but also posture, bodily disposition, and eye contact'.[49]

The military body in barracks therefore reacts in different ways to different people and contexts, and this is mediated by rank and uniforms. The recruit is always scanning for officers on the horizon in barracks, lest one commits the ultimate crime of not saluting. Recruits struggle to control their bodies – panicked recruits mistakenly salute corporals and sergeants, arms flying up to their heads as if a button has been pressed on a jack-in-the-box. Officer walks into a room – fuck, stand up as fast as you can. Recruits slouch around smoking, an officer appears out of nowhere – recruits fly to attention! Sir! We are always nervous when other ranks appear during lessons, or whilst marching across the parade ground to the mess hall: 'who's this cunt?' 'do we brace up, do we salute?' 'Fuck knows', we whisper to each other like ventriloquist's dummies. Because of our inability to memorise badges of rank, other forms of visual identification are more useful for recruits during basic training. One of these is colour:[50] recruits are defined by their dull green stable belts and generic black berets. NCOs are distinguished by their colourful regimental belts, distinct berets and other colourful insignia stitched onto their uniform such as brigade flashes. Next, badges of courses they have completed (e.g. parachute trained; commando dagger), small cotton patches which effectively convey status and hierarchies of competence and experience and mediate everyday interaction.

Beyond these formal hierarchies, uniform serves to distinguish the good soldier from the bad soldier. Indeed, uniform and aesthetics are explicitly linked to discipline and effectiveness by the army itself: according to an article on effective leadership by Field Marshal the Lord Bramall of Bushfield, reprinted by the Centre for Army Leadership in 2018, 'a generally dirty man and untidy man will almost certainly have poor self-discipline and require checking'.[51] Crisply pressed and ironed uniform and well maintained kit and webbing denoted military competence. Thus just as habitus is the underlying mental structure and dispositions its outward manifestation, in the army, appearance and bearing – both in terms of a particular way of holding oneself and the appearance of one's uniform – was the outward manifestation of a military habitus, of competence. That is, within basic training, there is no distinction between aesthetics (appearance) and embodiment (our ways of moving). The blurred lines between the uniform and the individual body was illustrated by our opening address by our platoon sergeant. He tells us in no uncertain terms that he dislikes civilians, he dislikes reservists. He tells us that you can spot reservists a mile off, 'scruffy, overweight, berets looking like shit, walking slowly, ambling, webbing looking like a bag of shit, fucking straps hanging off the fucking Bergan'. A 'soldier-like' bearing is therefore inextricably linked with the state of one's uniform and kit. The body is not distinguished from the uniform, but one and the same. Scruffy uniform, messy webbing with straps hanging off it – mong. Mess. Bag of shit. *Civvy*. Crisp uniform, perfectly organised webbing – switched on bloke.

Moreover, this obsession with uniform and appearance, and the harsh policing of the domestic routine which this necessitated – perpetual ironing, shining and pressing – was clearly bound up with the identity of the *British* Army specifically. Recruits were continually told that the British Army was the 'fucking best in the world, not just anyone gets to be a part' – and that this was deeply bound up with appearance, which incorporates both aesthetic turnout (neatness); and particularly disciplined forms of movement, inculcated through drill. The institutional obsession with neatness (enforced by harsh discipline and the relentless, ritualistic focus on drill, tradition and ceremony) demonstrated military competence and expertise – it was what marked the British Army out as unique. The *other* that this identity was constructed against was both us – reservists – but also Americans, Yanks, septics.[52] We were continually told how 'shit' 'the Yanks' were, and this was mainly bound up with their appearance, which naturally reflected their competence as soldiers: 'fucking state of the Yanks' – 'helmet straps hanging off', 'webbing a state', 'fat as fuck', 'scruffy useless cunts'.

My relationship with my uniform was terrible. It was uncomfortable, awkward. Attending my first drill night, my beret was on wrong and not shaped correctly, the other soldiers' berets were worn, their uniforms neatly pressed. The sergeant major roughly adjusted my beret on my head. My belt was on the wrong way round, the creases in my uniform weren't done properly. My combat trousers were not neatly tucked away at the bottom using twistys. My uniform did not fit, and therefore became prone to wrinkles and creases. This attracted the ire of the instructors on numerous occasions. Yet ironing was the least of my worries. MacLeish alludes to the interaction between uniform and body and the centrality of the uniform to everyday movement.[53] His respondents note how hard basic bodily movements are on deployment in the Middle East, and how helmets, heavy body armour and thick uniforms all contributed to this general misery. Uniform – basic dress – is thus used to signify competence and belonging within the domestic space of the barracks, but becoming soldierly is mainly to do with the management of the essential kit and equipment needed to function *beyond* the domestic space of the barracks. We were repeatedly told that the mastery of the domestic space of the barracks was an essential first step to being an effective field soldier: how are you going to fucking cope on operations under fire if you can't even keep your fucking locker clean? The popular image of the professional soldier on operations is of course not just combats and boots – formal drill dress – but a composite body covered in high tech kit, ready for war.[54]

Uniforms are above all functional: soldiers require it to store their ammunition, miscellaneous equipment like maps, flashlight, knives, lighters, water and rations – without uniform and kit the soldier cannot function effectively. For this reason, within the army, uniform is an extension of the body, and the recruit's mastery of uniform and kit is therefore an essential facet of the embodied nature of soldiering. Hockey's brilliant accounts of infanteering detail the endless drills and practices that infantry soldiers endure in order to make their movement and relationship with their weapon second nature or pre-reflexive.[55] The movement of the infanteer on the battlefield is mediated by kit – not just their weapon, but also webbing, Bergan, daypack, gloves, kneepads. Effective soldiering therefore depends on the mastery of these new appendages to the body. This is one of the most challenging elements of basic training. This inability to master my extended body – my kit – was central to my inability to become an effective field soldier. My hand-me-down webbing and Bergan felt entirely alien to me. My webbing hung off me limply; every time I taped up the straps like the instructors, they would come loose. When I moved I made a sound, my webbing flapping against my body, magazines rattling against each other in their pouch. Every time I reloaded a magazine, I could not do my ammunition pouch up swiftly or efficiently. Recruits could regularly be heard swearing and thrashing round in the dark, desperately trying to clip up an element of their Bergan, release a stuck zip. Rifle slings routinely got tangled in daysacks. We gathered round one another, pulling zips, untangling slings and checking each other's webbing pouches.

Going Sick

War is fought by men who are trained to use their bodies unthinkingly, to act like 'good machines'.[56] Soldiers are trained to fire their weapon, their ways of moving as individuals and within groups constantly worked on until these distinct ways of moving become second nature and essentially robotic and predictable, so they can be moved around by commanders to time. Military training focuses a huge amount of time on developing physical fitness and on developing unthinking embodied competencies.[57] This training places an enormous amount of stress on the body as it prepares for warfare. A central part of the recruit's journey to soldier is engaging in physical training – 'phys' – of a sort which deliberately pushes recruits to failure, and is designed to (literally) harden and condition the body to the physical demands of combat. Whilst preparing for basic training, recruits work on their mile and half run time and general physical fitness. Yet this cannot prepare you for the relentless physicality of soldiering, particularly the unique sensation of carrying heavy weight on your back over long distances. On top of loaded speed marches, we sprint up hills, run around the barracks, crawl on our bellies through mud, conduct regular strength training in the gym. Far worse than PT sessions is general military training: fire and manoeuvre and endless long patrols on frozen ground, interspersed with regular collective physical punishments (or 'beasting') for incompetence.

The intensity of the training affected unexpected places – fingers and hands became blistered, chapped and bloody. Feet blistered and bled. And, just like machines, recruits' bodies are routinely inspected, checked and subject to rudimentary maintenance. Feet – the most important part of the soldier's body – are regularly inspected for blisters or fungus. Recruits must constantly put talcum powder on their feet, and if your feet are falling apart, you put zinc oxide tape all over them. The regularity of exercise demands close attention to hygiene: we are told we must 'fucking shower every morning and every fucking night', because unclean sweaty bodies lead to infections. Sergeants sniff the air and rooms for any trace of bodily odour. Despite these maintenance checks, wear and tear injuries become routine during our training. Our knees turn purple with bruising from the constant contact with the frozen ground.

The relentless physicality of soldiering extends into the domestic space. MacLeish states that:

> beyond and before the extremes of combat, routine soldiering in garrison and during deployment can take a massive physical toll. In the service of the greater goal of combat and its exigencies, soldiers spend weeks, months, and years exercising, marching on rough terrain, lifting heavy loads, operating loud and dangerous equipment, performing repetitive tasks, climbing in and out of tanks and the back of trucks, sleeping on the ground, enduring heat and cold and the elements, eating miserable food, and going without sleep.[58]

Drill is intensely physical. Marking time – marching on the spot – was used routinely as a punishment by instructors, particularly if drill followed a PT session. Our shattered knees and feet slamming continuously into the concrete parade ground. The practice of standing still and tensing the body for long periods of time makes one dizzy and tired, especially when sleep deprived. It was fully expected that some of us would faint during our passing out parade. The ex-regular members of our platoon tried to teach us how to *appear* to be tense and upright whilst being relaxed, how to *appear* to be marking time intensely whilst actually gently tapping your feet on the floor. These older men had mastered how to 'cheat' using their bodies, an embodied facet of the widespread micro-rebellions that occur within the army. Block jobs are also deeply physical and clearly intended to be so – battered bodies are not allowed to rest, but made to kneel and scrub hard porcelain floors. Our platoon experiences 'slow death', the condition of being slowly worn out through the everyday grind of military work.[59]

Recruits who are struggling with injuries and aches are asked menacingly by instructors if they want to 'go sick' (and miss a day's PT). Those 'on the sick' go to the on-camp doctor and are either medically returned to their unit (RTU) or given painkillers or told to go and buy tape or strapping from the shop. Those who are not discharged attend PT sessions, but sit on the side in shame, watching the rest of us suffer. During speed marches and hill sprints, the platoon is always followed menacingly by a green army ambulance. We are told this is for our safety, but we all know that if we end up in that ambulance, whether through fatigue or injury, we have let ourselves and our regiment down. The instructors know this – the ambulance is used as a threat: 'if you want to quit, just quit, we've got an ambulance here for you'. During our tests, recruits who fall behind the rest of the platoon three times will be placed in the ambulance and will fail the course. As MacLeish points out, soldiering's innate masculinity is founded on 'connotatively manly practices', one of which is 'mastery over one's own sensitivity to pain and discomfort, and the suppression of care and empathy in order to be able to . . . inflict violence'.[60] Physical and emotional hardness is what separates soldiers from civilians.[61] Mark Burchell's account of Royal Marine basic training notes how the acceptance of bodily pain is a central pillar of the recruit's socialisation into a hypermasculine institution which celebrates aggression and violence.[62] The injured recruit is faced with a bind: we are repeatedly told we are being assessed not just for our physical attributes, but for our 'best effort' and mental toughness, the ability to keep going through pain barriers. Hardness and durability is central to military competence and proving oneself. Our PT instructors praise us – 'nails' 'solid' – for completing physical challenges, for gritting our teeth and keeping going. Our platoon sergeant notes with disgust that the other platoon has 'fucking birds' in it: he accordingly ramps up the intensity of our physical training, because being comparable to women is unthinkable. Our PT instructors encourage us by comparing us favourably to the other platoon, noting how many of them had 'gone sick', 'can't fucking handle it can they?' The other platoon (perhaps by virtue of containing two women) is effeminate, weak. We soon internalise the celebration of pain and exertion, and begin to feel pride in the physical punishment we can endure. In this milieu, going sick risks the ire and disgust of your instructor and platoon. On the other hand, recruits want to pass the course, and not caring for an injury may make it worse and risk being medically discharged. Most recruits opt for their own remedies: after PT or exercise, in the evening, older members of the training platoon spent significant periods of time stretching and desperately using foam rollers on aching limbs and taping up feet. We pop ibuprofens like sweets. Nonetheless, numerous recruits are medically RTU: they roll their ankles or their knees buckle during speed marches over uneven terrain. They get into the ambulance and are carted off, never to be seen again.

Basic training places recruits' bodies and minds under intense stress. On top of the aforementioned repetition injuries, the continuous and relentless pace of everything, the desire to maintain this 'soldier-like bearing' at all times is physically and mentally exhausting. In the training depot there is a café run by civilians. It is a space within the institution that is designed for soldiers and recruits to relax. It is good for their mental health, to sit down without being yelled at, to wear civilian clothes, to luxuriate in simple pleasures like a cup of coffee, a soft chair, a conversation. MacLeish notes the importance of civilian spaces within military institutions, arguing that the army's 'autocratic pastoralism', which largely extends to injuries and sickness, cannot meet the needs of many soldiers.[63] Given the overall feeling of terror and permanent nervous tension that is the defining feature of recruits' experiences in the domestic space of the barracks, these spaces serve a vital function within training depots: without such a space, recruit bodies and minds would break down completely, as indeed they often do anyway.[64]

The Ideal Military Body

After conducting an attack during our exercise, we have some spare ammo left over. Huddled round the centre of the harbour area, before a briefing, Cpl Donnelly puts his weapon on full auto and empties a mag into the hollows of the woodblock in a few seconds. We are in awe of him: his competence, how smoothly he handles his rifle, how easy he finds tabbing, how smart his webbing and uniform look despite living in the field, and his overall menacing, quiet demeanour. 'Fucking hard cunt', my basha buddy says later, the highest possible compliment.

When the habitus clashes with the field, the agent may feel like 'a fish out of water'.[65] In the case of the new recruit, this clash is deeply embodied, and perhaps all the more disorienting and upsetting for being so. The experience of the recruit is therefore that of an 'alienated body', defined by feelings of acute embarrassment and unease in one's own body.[66] The feeling of discomfort grew continuously, when continually confronted 'with the disparity between the ideal body and the real body, the dream body and the "looking glass self" reflected in the reactions of others'.[67] The 'looking glass self', the ideal military body, were the NCOs: lean men in their late twenties, veterans of numerous combat tours. They exemplified this cryptic phrase of a 'soldier-like bearing', that had previously seemed so abstract. In the midst of the muddy quagmire that was our training exercise area, where the recruit's weapons, boots and clothing were caked in thick mud, the NCOs' combats were clean and pressed, their webbing and berets perfect. They are alert yet relaxed. We are delirious with a lack of sleep and nerves. They glide over the terrain. The weapons drills that we clumsily attempt with shaking, freezing fingers, they do in mechanical, robotic and unthinking fashion, as naturally if the weapon was part of their body. Back in the domestic space of the barracks, they represented the intangible paradigm of a soldier-like bearing. They rarely spoke or smiled, and exuded menace. They were so comfortable in their uniforms, so at home in the barracks. Even the way they smoked was soldierly. The way in which these experienced soldiers carried themselves represented *ease*, which is the 'indifference to the objectifying gaze of others which neutralises its powers', born of a natural fit between the habitus and field. As Bourdieu puts it, embodied ease represents 'this self-assurance given by the certain knowledge of one's own value, especially that of one's body or speech, is in fact very closely linked to the position occupied in social space'.[68] Their ease represented the opposite of the alienated body.

Bourdieu explains how the mastery of embodied military movements creates a new mental state. His concept of *doxa* (or 'practical sense') refers to the unconscious, taken for granted sense of feeling at home in a field, a commonsensical acceptance of all the (arbitrary) rules and values of that field which feel, to the person socialised to the field, as natural as breathing. It is 'a relationship of immediate adherence that is established in practice between a habitus and the field to which it is attuned, the pre-verbal taking-for-granted of the world that flows from practical sense';[69] an 'undisputed, pre-reflexive, naive, native compliance with the fundamental presuppositions of the field'.[70] Perhaps more obviously in the army more than any other field, doxa – the pre-reflexive immanence of being perfectly at home in the field – is not a 'state of mind', but a *state of the body*:[71] here one can witness the *values of the field made body*. Practical sense, the perfect fit between habitus and field, is inscribed in the body of these experienced soldiers. Equally, Bourdieu argues that the doxa is inculcated *through* the body. He describes doxa as an 'enacted belief, which treats the body as a *memory pad*', and the body automation *'leads the mind unconsciously along with it'*.[72] For experienced soldiers, practical sense is inculcated by years and years of repetition of martial movements. For recruits, however, these embodied rules are unnatural and jarring.

Staying the Course

At the end of Phase One Alpha we were addressed by an officer of the Royal Lancers. He explained to us that the army was 'all a big game'. He exhorted us to 'learn the rules and just play the game'. His words echoed Bourdieu's claim that habitus inculcates an instinctive 'feel for the game'[73] in social fields where it fits.[74] As this chapter makes clear, the military habitus is deeply embodied, and learning these rules – these 'embodied competencies'– was hard. Prior to selection and attending basic training I had concentrated solely on running, passing my physical tests: the idea of army life that I had internalised from years of adverts and films was one purely based on masculine physical endurance, pain and toughness. I had not given a single thought to the daily embodied routine or the idea of living and moving in barracks: how to stand, walk and hold myself like a soldier, or how to speak like a soldier. My basic training was undoubtedly defined by pain and injury, yet it was also defined at least as much by the disorienting experience of attempting to cultivate this new 'bearing' within the confines of the barracks and coming to terms with the disciplined 'domesticity' of the barracks, which was similarly deeply embodied. Running was easy compared to the challenges faced in acting and becoming soldier-like.

Despite my general military incompetence, I did not get cut from the course, and passed out as a trained soldier. I could not shoot, march or look after myself in the field. Yet this uselessness was seemingly mitigated by me being a 'good lad' and possessing a pleasing amount of aggression and determination (which was ironically only produced by my aforementioned frustration at being incompetent). Moreover, despite my incompetence, I believe that I ticked some of the boxes in what a soldier is *meant* to look like and behave like, despite not being actually able to actually do my job. Perhaps being stocky, having tattoos, a skinhead, having the same regional class habitus as the instructors, all helped me look, sound and move like something approaching a soldier.[75] Another candidate – a good shot, good in the field, but possessed of an unfortunately awkward gait, somewhat effeminate with a pronounced lisp, and incapable of marching or lifting weights in the gym – got cut one day before our pass out parade, after his family had already arrived. This was an act of sheer spite by the training team, who could only have wished to humiliate and embarrass him by this timing. I have no doubt that his only crime was to not seem 'soldierly' in his overall bearing, despite his actual competence. This incident demonstrates that being a soldier ultimately remains highly gendered.[76] Despite claims that military culture is complex and open to non-masculine ways of being and moving,[77] the overall atmosphere within my platoon during basic training was certainly one of hypermasculinity, echoing other ethnographic accounts of military training. As Sarah Bulmer's account of lesbian, gay, bisexual and transgender (LGBT) sailors marching at Pride makes clear, soldiers can have non-normative sexualities or even have a non-military bearing in *private*, but non-heteronormative *public* performances or displays are absolutely forbidden from encroaching onto their military bodies, their military bearing and therefore the overall military aesthetic, which as aforementioned continually feeds back into the ideal of the military body.[78] Joe Glenton's account of army life similarly argues that women are 'tolerated' as long as they do not disrupt the notion of a masculine, heteronormative soldier-like bearing or indeed the sexist, even dangerous atmosphere of the barracks.[79] Being a soldier is implicitly always masculine, so in public one must be masculine. As we were told repeatedly during drill practice, there was to be no fucking 'mincing around'. In this environment, bodies which are not (hyper)masculine are seen as highly aberrant.

The methodological advances facilitated by the aesthetic and embodied turns should force IR to move beyond its traditionally narrow approach to warfare and militarism, and to focus on the everyday lives of those impacted by warfare and militarism which can tell us so much about 'the international'.[80] It is vital for scholars to remember that the war machine is comprised above all of individual soldiers who are its cogs and moving parts.[81] Ethnographic research, and in my view particularly enactive ethnography, can help us to understand how war and militarism are learned, reproduced and manifest in individual bodies, and should therefore remain a staple method of enquiry for military sociology as well as aesthetic approaches to IR and warfare more broadly. As Hockey brilliantly reminds us, studying the corporeal, embodied nature of military life represents a vital *foundational* analytic step in understanding war and militarism: the functioning of an organisation is dependent in the first instance on mundane, pre-reflexive habitual movements. It is upon these basic, embodied tasks that the work of an organisation – particularly the military – is ultimately built.[82]

Entering a new field is akin to learning a new language or game with its own 'grammar, rules and exercises, expressly taught by institutions expressly designed for that purpose'.[83] Recruits undergoing basic training are faced with a bewildering world with its own language, new rules, norms and beliefs. In the army this 'new language' is deeply embodied: the journey to becoming a trained soldier and finally acquiring the pre-reflexive practical sense of the institution (doxa) requires the continual repetition of new ways of moving and holding oneself until, as Hockey notes, the synthesis of knowledge and action come to pervade the soldier's very flesh;[84] until that which was formerly external and alien becomes pre-reflexive. This article illuminates how army recruits begin to learn these most basic embodied competencies – largely in the domestic space of the barracks – and the impact this has on them as individuals.

Notes

1. Roland Bleiker, 'The Aesthetic Turn in International Political Theory', *Millennium* 30:3 (2001): 509–33.
2. Ibid., 510.
3. Ibid., 518–19.
4. Ibid., 524.
5. Cynthia Enloe, *Bananas, Beaches, and Bases: Making Feminist Sense of International Politics* (London: Pandora, 1989).
6. Roland Bleiker, 'In Search of Thinking Space: Reflections on the Aesthetic Turn in International Political Theory', *Millennium* 45:2 (2017): 258–64, 260.
7. Synne L. Dyvik and Lauren Greenwood, 'Embodying Militarism: Exploring the Spaces and Bodies In-Between', *Critical Military Studies* 2:1–2 (2016): 1–6, 1.
8. Swati Parashar, 'What Wars and "War Bodies" Know about International Relations', *Cambridge Review of International Affairs* 26:4 (2013): 615–30, 617.
9. Ibid., 617.
10. Guy Siebold, 'Core Issues and Theory in Military Sociology', *Journal of Political and Military Sociology* 29 (2001): 140–59; Rachel Woodward and K. Neil Jenkings, 'Military Identities in the Situated Accounts of British Military Personnel', *Sociology* 45:2 (2011): 252–68.
11. Paul Higate and Ailsa Cameron, 'Reflexivity and Researching the Military', *Armed Forces and Society* 32:2 (2006): 219–33.
12. Catherine Baker, Victoria Basham, Sarah Bulmer, Harriet Gray and Alexandra Hyde, 'Encounters with the Military: Toward a Feminist Ethics of Critique?', *International Feminist Journal of Politics* 18:1 (2016): 140–54; Joanna Bourke, *Wounding the World: How Military Violence and War-Play Invade our Lives* (London: Virago, 2014).
13. Victoria M. Basham, *War, Identity and the Liberal State: Everyday Experiences of the Geopolitical in the Armed Forces* (London: Routledge, 2013); Helena Carreiras and Celso Castro (eds), *Qualitative Methods in Military Studies* (London: Routledge, 2013); Paul Higate, '"Switching On" for Cash: The Private Militarised Security Contractor', in *War and the Body: Militarization, Practice and Experience*, edited by Kevin McSorley (London: Routledge, 2013), 106–27; Kenneth T. MacLeish, *Making War at Fort Hood: Life and Uncertainty in a Military Community* (Princeton, NJ: Princeton University Press, 2013); Ken MacLeish, 'The Ethnography of Good Machines', *Critical Military Studies* 1:1 (2015): 11–22; Amanda Chisholm, 'Ethnography in Conflict Zones: The Perils of Researching Private Security Contractors', in *The Routledge Companion to Military Research Methods*, edited by Alison J. Williams, K. Neil Jenkings, Matthew F. Rech and Rachel Woodward (London: Routledge, 2016), 138–52. See John Hockey, *Squaddies: Portrait of a Subculture* (Exeter: University of Exeter Press, 1986).
14. Christine Sylvester, 'Experiencing War: A Challenge for International Relations', *Cambridge Review of International Affairs* 26:4 (2014): 669–74, 673.
15. Christine Sylvester, 'War Experiences/War Practices/War Theory', *Millennium* 40:3 (2012): 483–503, 484 (emphasis added).

16. MacLeish, *Making War*; MacLeish, 'Machines'.
17. MacLeish, *Making War*.
18. Bourke, *Wounding the World*.
19. Kevin McSorley (ed.), *War and the Body: Militarization, Practice and Experience* (London: Routledge, 2013); Kevin McSorley, 'Towards an Embodied Sociology of War', *The Sociological Review* 62:S2 (2014): 107–28; Dyvik and Greenwood, 'Embodying Militarism'.
20. MacLeish, 'Machines', 15.
21. MacLeish, *Making War*, 11.
22. McSorley, 'Embodied Sociology', 109.
23. Ibid., 108.
24. Charles Kirke, 'Postmodernism to Structure: An Upstream Journey for the Military Recruit?' in *Defence Management in Uncertain Times*, edited by Teri McConville and Richard Holmes (London: Frank Cass, 2003), 139–55.
25. Stephen Atherton, 'Domesticating Military Masculinities: Home, Performance and the Negotiation of Identity', *Social and Cultural Geography* 10:8 (2009): 821–36, 826.
26. MacLeish, *Making War*, 11.
27. Loic Wacquant, 'For a Sociology of Flesh and Blood', *Qualitative Sociology* 38 (2015): 1–11.
28. Loic Wacquant, *Body and Soul: Notebooks of an Apprentice Boxer* (New York: Oxford University Press, 2004).
29. The ethical implications of this decision and the significant problems I encountered as a result of this methodological approach are discussed further in Daniel Evans, 'Out of Depth in the Army Reserve: Methodological Lessons of an Enactive Ethnography', paper presented at Liverpool Management School Annual Ethnography Symposium, University of the West of England, 24–6 August 2016.
30. Loïc Wacquant, 'For a Sociology of Flesh and Blood', *Qualitative Sociology* 38 (2015): 1–11, 1. See also Loïc Wacquant, 'Carnal Connections: On Embodiment, Apprenticeship, and Membership', *Qualitative Sociology* 28:4 (2005): 445–74.
31. John Hockey, '"Switch On": Sensory Work in the Infantry', *Work, Employment & Society* 23:3 (2009): 477–93; John Hockey, 'On Patrol: The Embodied Phenomenology of Infantry', in *War and the Body*, edited by McSorley, 93–105.
32. John Hockey, '"Head Down, Bergen On, Mind in Neutral": The Infantry Body', *Journal of Political and Military Sociology* 30:1 (2002): 148–71.
33. Brian Lande, 'Breathing Like a Soldier: Culture Incarnate', *The Sociological Review* 55 (2007): 95–108.
34. MacLeish, *Making War*; MacLeish, 'Machines'; Zoe H. Wool, *After War: The Weight of Life at Walter Reed* (Durham, NC: Duke University Press, 2015).
35. Pierre Bourdieu, *The Logic of Practice*, translated by Richard Nice (Stanford, CA: Stanford University Press, 1990), 53.
36. Ibid., 70.
37. Ibid., 71.

38. Stephen Deakin, *Leadership: Proceedings of a Symposium Held at the Royal Military Academy Sandhurst*, Sandhurst Occasional Papers 18 (April 2014).
39. Eyal Ben-Ari, 'Masks and Soldiering: The Israeli Army and the Palestinian Uprising', *Cultural Anthropology* 4:4 (1989): 372–89, 378.
40. MacLeish, *Making War*, 40.
41. 'Mong' is an ableist slur in the UK, used to deride someone with learning difficulties, particularly used against people with Down's syndrome. Despite being controversial in the UK, it is routinely used within the British Army as a term for incompetent soldiers.
42. Hockey, *Squaddies*.
43. Atherton, 'Domesticating Military Masculinities', 827.
44. MacLeish, *Making War*, 12. See Michel Foucault, *Discipline and Punish: The Birth of the Prison*, translated by Alan Sheridan (New York: Vintage, 1979).
45. See Higate, '"Switching On"'; Hockey, 'Switch On'.
46. Jane Tynan, *British Army Uniform and the First World War: Men in Khaki* (Basingstoke: Palgrave Macmillan, 2013), 27.
47. Pierre Bourdieu, *Distinction*, translated by Richard Nice (Oxford: Routledge, Kegan and Paul, 1984), 49.
48. MacLeish, *Making War*, 38.
49. Ibid., 37.
50. See Xavier Guillaume, Rune S. Andersen and Juha Vuori, 'Paint it Black: Colours and the Social Meaning of the Battlefield', *European Journal of International Relations* 22:1 (2015): 49–71.
51. Field Marshal the Lord Bramall of Bushfield, 'Leadership the Green Jacket Way', Leadership Insight 5 (Sandhurst: Centre for Army Leadership, 2018), 2. https://www.army.mod.uk/media/2878/centre-for-army-leadership-leadership-insight-no-5.pdf.
52. British rhyming slang for Americans: septic tank – yank.
53. MacLeish, *Making War*, 38.
54. Ibid., 52.
55. Hockey, *Squaddies*; Hockey, 'Head Down'; Hockey, 'On Patrol'; Hockey, 'Switch On'.
56. MacLeish, 'Machines', 15.
57. Hockey, *Squaddies*.
58. MacLeish, *Making War*, 103.
59. MacLeish, 'Machines'. See Lauren Berlant, 'Slow Death (Sovereignty, Obesity, Lateral Agency)', *Critical Inquiry* 33:4 (2007): 754–80.
60. MacLeish, *Making War*, 17.
61. Ibid., 17.
62. Mark Burchell, 'An Anthropological Exploration of Discipline and Ritual Practices among the Royal Marines', PhD thesis (University of Bristol, 2011).
63. MacLeish, 'Machines', 17.
64. Harriet Gray, 'Domestic Abuse and the Public/Private Divide in the British Military', *Gender, Place & Culture* 23:6 (2016): 912–25.

65. Pierre Bourdieu and Loïc Wacquant, *An Invitation to Reflexive Sociology* (Chicago, IL: University of Chicago Press, 1992), 127.
66. See Bourdieu, *Distinction*, 204.
67. Ibid., 205.
68. Ibid., 204.
69. Bourdieu, *The Logic of Practice*, 68.
70. Ibid., 68.
71. Ibid., 68.
72. Ibid., 68.
73. Ibid., 66.
74. Gerry Veenstra and Patrick John Burnett, 'A Relational Approach to Health Practices: Towards Transcending the Agency–Structure Divide', *Sociology of Health and Illness* 36 (2014): 187–98.
75. The role of class within the military is an issue which requires significant further research.
76. Joe Glenton, *Soldier Box: Why I Won't Return to the War on Terror* (London: Verso, 2013), 24.
77. Regina F. Titinuk, 'The Myth of the Macho Military', *Polity* 40:2 (2008): 137–63; Aaron Belkin, *Bring Me Men: Military Masculinity and the Benign Façade of American Empire 1898–2001* (London: Hurst, 2012); Sarah Bulmer, 'Patriarchal Confusion?: Making Sense of Gay and Lesbian Military Identity', *International Feminist Journal of Politics* 15:2 (2013): 137–56.
78. Bulmer, 'Patriarchal Confusion?', 144–5.
79. Glenton, *Soldier Box*, 25.
80. Parashar, '"War Bodies"'.
81. MacLeish, 'Machines'.
82. Hockey, 'Switch On', 490.
83. Bourdieu, *The Logic of Practice*, 67.
84. Hockey, 'Switch On', 490.

CHAPTER 2

The Political Aesthetics of the Body of the Soldier in Pain

Federica Caso

This chapter explores the recent work of Australian artist Ben Quilty on combat fatigue and post-traumatic stress disorder (PTSD) collected in the exhibition, *After Afghanistan*. *After Afghanistan* presents a series of large-scale paintings of soldiers and veterans evoking the bodily imprints of combat fatigue and PTSD. The bodies are naked, in the grasp of sensations and emotions. The chapter argues that this work has an ambivalent relationship to militarisation whereby it proposes an alternative iconography of the modern soldier which seeds transformative potentials against the militarisation of the body; simultaneously, however, the iconography of the body of the soldier in pain has been co-opted as a militarising technology that silences opposition and contestation to war in the name of compassion towards the soldiers.

Overall, the chapter offers some considerations about the challenges and possibilities opened by representing the body of the soldier in pain in war art. In particular, it questions how far such visual representations are in fact able to exercise the agency they are often said to have. It is often assumed that representations of suffering soldiers are able to communicate the embodied consequences that war bears on those who fight and thus invite onlookers to question the ethics of how the state treats and provides for those it has sent to war. The chapter suggests that the very notion of visual images having agency is misconceived: when hegemonic public discourse is powerful enough to silence the processes of critical questioning that war art like Quilty's ostensibly invites, art is instead liable to become militarised.

I take militarisation to be the process of making war and war preparation a normal and desirable social activity.[1] In order to function as a soldier, that is, to be able to kill and be killed in the name of the state, a body must be militarised. This happens in basic training, where recruits are taught the rationalities of killing and death.[2] This requires fit and obedient subjects, but, above all, their ability to control their emotions. The militarisation of bodies relies on discursive and figurative representations of the stoic, courageous and patriotic soldier. Consider, for example, the iconic Australian painting ANZAC, The Landing, 1915 (1920–2), commissioned by the Australian War Memorial from artist George Lambert to memorialise Australia's first intervention in war as an independent nation. Australian soldiers are represented as brave in the face of danger. Some are dead, but the living are fearlessly advancing towards the enemy and regardless of the bullets and shrapnel. This image remarks the militarisation of Australia. The representation of this very Australian act of bravery sanctified the soldiers who demonstrated Australia's valour in war. It provided Australians with a visual reference of the birth of the nation, birth which is sanctioned by the blood spilled in war.

Militarisation, as certain scholars have already argued and this volume further shows, is linked to certain visual regimes.[3] These regimes are dynamic and highly adaptive, policed by powerful cultural institutions such as mainstream television and cinema, museums and art foundations. In Australia the most powerful cultural institution that mediates and polices visual regimes of militarisation is the Australian War Memorial (AWM), which was established by the end of World War I to memorialise Australia's intervention in war. There is consensus that the AWM is a major orchestrator of Australia's national identity, and that its war art programme significantly contributes to shape how Australians see themselves as a nation.[4] The records of the AWM do mention the psychological costs of war, and in 1942 official war artist Albert Tucker also famously painted a portrait of himself with glassy eyes typical of the so-called 'thousand-yard stare' of shell-shocked soldiers. Yet, the official historiography of Australia managed by the AWM framed the ability to overcome trauma as an emblem of national strength.[5] The militarisation of the nation was predicated upon the soldiers' ability to overcome the traumas of war and show the stoic and courageous characteristics of the militarised body. As I demonstrate in this chapter, today the narrative is different. With the work of Ben Quilty, the militarisation of Australian society has been linked to the seemingly demilitarised naked body of the soldier showing emotions that were supposed to be suppressed or put under control during basic training.

Following a more detailed presentation of the work of Ben Quilty and the exhibition *After Afghanistan*, the remaining of this chapter is divided into two parts. The first part articulates the commitment and intention of Ben Quilty to render combat fatigue and PTSD known to the wider Australian public through his art as a means of making institutions accountable for the wellbeing of soldiers. Here, I suggest that the artworks collected in *After Afghanistan* deploy the vulnerable body as a grammar of resistance against the militarisation of the body, and therefore harbour transformative potentials. The second part explains how Quilty's work has been co-opted into dominant narratives of liberal warfare that subtly effect the militarisation of society. I maintain that *After Afghanistan* has been made to function within a perilous politics of compassion that presents the soldier as innocent victim of war worthy of pity by civilians. Quilty's work is caught up into a narrative that reproduces hierarchies of suffering, and positions the suffering of the soldier above that of anyone else, civilians at home, civilian victims of war and enemy combatants. This part will also examine the racialised and gendered politics of compassion in the Australian context.[6] All the subjects of *After Afghanistan* are white or white-passing, and only one is female. While this reflects the identities of the soldiers Quilty met whilst in Afghanistan, I put representations of white male bodies in pain in perspective against the lack of representation of indigenous and female bodies in pain to demonstrate how the politics of compassion towards the soldier relies on casting the suffering of other bodies as subordinate. I conclude by offering some reflections about the challenges and possibilities of representing the body in pain. I consider questions of ethics and responsibility that we have when we look at images, especially those of suffering bodies.

Ben Quilty and *After Afghanistan*

Ben Quilty is one of Australia's most famous and respected contemporary artists. His work is overtly political. His artistic investigations have revolved around issues of the construction of toxic masculinity, Australian colonialism and postcoloniality, and their intersection with mortality, which he explores through a personal lens. Quilty openly recounts growing up in the suburbs of Sydney in the 1980s and flirting with death as a way to affirm his masculinity. Taking drugs, drinking alcohol and fist fighting were normalised, desirable and expected activities to bond with other boys. The artist reveals himself to have lost two good friends in these kinds of activities, one drowned when drunk and the other of pancreatic cancer. He juxtaposes these rituals of white Australian masculinity to Indigenous Australian rituals of initiation to manhood that involve a procedure lasting thirteen years.[7] Quilty has also explored his role as an Australian man of Irish descent in the European colonisation of Australia, by placing himself in his series of paintings about the colonial invasion collected in the exhibition *Inhabit* (2010), and has painted places where indigenous people were massacred during the invasion in *Fairy Bower Rorschach* (2012) and *Evening Shadows, Rorschach after Johnstone* (2012).

While by now Quilty's aesthetic politics are well known, the artist lets his paintings speak through affective contagion, that is, the ability to move the viewer. He has developed a captivating style that combines very large canvases, thick oil impasto and vibrant expressive colours. His paintings do not go unnoticed in a multi-artists' exhibition, but not because of the details of the form or their realism. Quite the opposite. Quilty can be said to impulsively only sketch his forms on the canvas by applying colours directly, a process that involves a certain degree of confidence in one's own abilities and skills. He has suggested that his way of painting is 'almost violent', in some ways

> mirror[ing] the attitude of the young male . . . We used to go out and get into fights and drive like absolute maniacs and knock things down as we drove along and that application of paint represents those kinds of ideas in another way.[8]

The impasto is applied with a palette knife to build up layers of colour, which, once dry, stick out of the canvas almost like small shiny waves that invite the viewer to touch them, or at least, observe them close up in their three dimensions. These lines and colours on large canvases are the backbone of the abstracted – but not yet abstract – forms that constitute the subjects of Quilty's art. They compose mostly stylised human figures and landscapes rendered with unnatural colours and often intersecting with skulls as metaphors for mortality and meaningless pursuits. The compositions are often allegorical in ways that require the viewer to look more than once and from more than one vantage point to read the artwork. As Quilty says, 'I enjoy the theatrics of forcing the viewer to move back from the enticing surface to see the more figurative imagery hidden in the paint.'[9]

In 2011, the AWM invited Ben Quilty to be an official war artist for Australia's military involvement in Afghanistan. Like Britain and Canada, Australia has a war art programme that was established in the course of World War I and through which artists have been commissioned to record the war for propaganda and memorialisation.[10] Initially, official war artists were treated and paid like soldiers, and at times war artists were actual soldiers.[11] More recently, especially since the end of conscription in 1972, the AWM has commissioned civilian artists to spend a limited amount of time (around three to six weeks) with Australian soldiers, thus creating a clearer separation between the military and the artists. The war art programme used to give strict directions to artists regarding the subject of their commissions, and some artists had their work rejected for not following them.[12] Artists now have more freedom to paint according to their sensibilities, and to choose the subject and focus of their representations. Considering Quilty's previous artistic interests, it comes as no surprise that he decided to paint soldiers, rather than landscapes, and to focus on their experiences of suffering.

Quilty has made public that the decision to take the AWM commission was not a light-hearted one. Joanna Bourke has remarked that '[w]ar licenses the militarization of art'.[13] And, indeed, we could add that war commissions licence the militarisation of the artist's body and mind. Ben Quilty has confessed that as a child he feared the possibility of being sent to war,[14] and has admitted that when the AWM approached him with the offer to go and paint in Afghanistan, he felt that it was a risk not worth taking.[15] Yet, the possibility of being close to soldiers in their own environment was an opportunity that he could not reject given his interest in masculinities and mortality. When considering the reasons why Quilty accepted the job regardless of his childhood fears and initial reservations, it is important to note that the commission comes with a significant cachet and remuneration. This is not to suggest that Quilty sold his artistic integrity by taking on the commission, but rather to lay out the challenges that artists face when art is a commodity and when museums are the sole holder of the power to name a person an artist.

A more relevant reason for the context of this analysis is Quilty's statement about his art as a civic commitment. In an interview publicly broadcast by the Australian Broadcasting Corporation (ABC), Quilty stated that: 'It is my duty as a citizen, and [therefore] as someone who sends these people [soldiers] over to Afghanistan to tell their stories the way it is.'[16] I stress this because it reveals the artist's intentions to bear witness to the stories of the Australian soldiers he met while in Afghanistan. And so he did. In a counter-memorial vein, Quilty painted the imprint of combat fatigue, deployment anxiety and PTSD on the body of eleven Australian soldiers. Whilst in Afghanistan, Quilty sketched the soldiers and took photos, but when he got back and was preparing the paintings for the AWM commission, he felt it difficult to convey the soldiers' experiences of war in the physical absence of soldiers. Therefore, he invited some soldiers he befriended in Afghanistan to his studio in Southern Highlands, New South Wales. He asked them to tell him more about their experience as soldiers and to choose a pose that encapsulated some of their feelings and emotions about their experiences in Afghanistan. He also asked them to pose naked. He said: 'I wanted [the soldiers] to be naked, showing not only physical strength but also the fragility of human skin and the darkness of the emotional weight of war.'[17]

The bare body was for Quilty a way to access and express the emotions associated with the experience of soldiering. The body sustaining emotions is, in fact, the main subject of the exhibition *After Afghanistan*. The majority of the artwork collected in this exhibition are portraits of soldiers across different ranks. Only one is female, and none of them can be identified as non-white. Most of the subjects are featured naked, in contorted poses. All portraits are characterised by a thick impasto of oil paint applied on the large canvas through broad brushstrokes and palette knife to build up layers of colour. There is no attempt to represent the details of the human form; rather, Quilty focuses on shadows and light. The end result is a human form that is sketched with colours, and while from a distance the viewer has a clear understanding of the subject that is represented on the canvas, this disappears with proximity. The human figures are positioned against dark or dull backgrounds of blue, grey and purple, and the final touches of light are rendered with intense bright colours such as red, orange and white. The use of colour does not aim at achieving realism, but at conveying psychological states of being such as fear, anxiety, sadness and resignation. The result is nothing but astonishing.

Affective Resistance to the Militarisation of the Body

The themes of combat stress and PTSD, as well as the iconography of the vulnerable naked body, that occupy the central stage of *After Afghanistan* are novel and defiant of conventional representations of soldiers in Australian war art. From Lambert's *The Landing* (1920–2) to Stella Bowen's *Bomber Crew* (1944), and more recently Jon Cattapan's *Looking Back (Baucau)* (2010), Australian soldiers have been represented in uniform and involved in war actions. As I have argued elsewhere, by the end of World War I, representations of bodies in uniform in Australian official war art were already being instrumentalised to construct a distinct Australian national identity independent and discrete from Britain.[18] Lambert, for instance, was famous for the historical accuracy and attention to detail of his paintings, but he put this aside when painting the uniforms of the Australian soldiers in *The Landing*. Lambert was aware of the sources which revealed that, on the day of the landing, Australian soldiers had been wearing peaked caps and sleeves rolled up to be more easily distinguishable from the Turks. Ignoring the sources, Lambert painted Australians wearing slouch hats (more readily associated with Australianness) as opposed to the British peak cap, and with sleeves down to give the impression of order and discipline, qualities for which Australian soldiers were not famous.[19] Quilty breaks with this iconography and instead presents the viewer with naked bodies imprinted by emotions. I suggest that this is not to reject Australian myths of the nation forged in war, but rather to revisit some of the implications this myth has on Australian soldiers. In Australia, the soldier in war has been made to signify the birth of the nation.[20] Because of this, the soldier is part of the Australian pantheon. As martyrs of the nation, soldiers are represented intact, either living or as dead spirits. Quilty brings in a different perspective, that of the bodily intact soldier, broken inside by war, which reveals that a nation forged in war cannot hide the fact that war is a traumatic experience etched on the skin of soldiers. If psychological trauma is recognised as intrinsic to war, and made visible through representations of the vulnerable (albeit intact) bare body, the myth of the stoic and emotionless soldier that dominates war narratives must be revisited to, at least, remove the social stigma and shame associated with soldiers showing emotions.

This is an act of resistance against the militarisation of the body of the soldier as merely an instrument of nation making or war policy. A person does not stop being human once they wear the military uniform, as Quilty emphasises by removing it. Quilty uses the vulnerable body not as a grammar of weakness, but of defiance of militarisation. Vulnerability is more readily noticeable in the naked body of Quilty's subjects. They have no weapons, armour or clothing to protect themselves, let alone others. They are exposed, vulnerable to violence that can be inflicted on them. Vulnerability is further conveyed by the exposure to the public eye of the re-emergence of emotions that were supposed to be suppressed or put under control at basic training. Quilty makes visible the body twisted in pain and the faces of soldiers darkened by sadness, sorrow and trauma. These bodies have nowhere to hide and are left with no other option but to share their emotions with the viewer, creating with them an intimate connection that transcends time and space. Judith Butler has remarked that being vulnerable is the very human condition that we seek to escape and deny because we have ascribed negative connotations to it. We have established that to be vulnerable is to be exposed to power.[21] Butler maintains that we are always already exposed to power, but also that this exposure is a precondition for agency.[22] The fact that we are all vulnerable in virtue of having a body means that we can be affected by others as much as we can affect others. For the soldier, to embrace their vulnerability means to accept mortality, but also the intense emotions that accompany the war experience. More than that, embracing vulnerability comes with agency. To show one's own vulnerability by posing for a notorious art project can be empowering for the soldier who no longer has to hide overwhelming emotions behind the mask of the stoic soldier, authorises other soldiers to do the same, and confront civilians with a different understanding of the soldier.

Stripping the soldier of the uniform is a subversive act. Uniform, as Dan Evans notes in this volume, both distinguishes the soldier in society and materially marks recruits' own journey from civilian to soldier as they acquire the appearance of the militarised body. The moment of receiving the uniform starts the process of shaping the recruit's body and mind into those of a soldier. David Morgan remarks that wearing the uniform is a crucial aspect of the embodiment of militarism. He states that '[t]he uniform absorbs individualities into a generalized and timeless masculinity while also connoting a control of emotion and a subordination to a larger rationality'.[23] And while the uniform disciplines the body of the soldier and submits it to the power and control of the military, it also confers a higher social status vis-à-vis civilians.[24] Removing the uniform undoes these processes. It shifts the generalised militarised masculinity back into individuality, as it is also remarked by the fact that none of the paintings of *After Afghanistan* has more than one person depicted in it. It also enables the resurgence of emotions and makes visible their imprint on the body before other people. Finally, it scales down the social status of the soldier to that of civilian, not as a demeaning act towards the soldier, but as a re-humanising process that exposes the fiction of the emotionless soldier. In other words, the iconography of the naked, feeling body represents the soldier as human again.

The Politics of Compassion and Militarisation

While the politics of Ben Quilty's paintings aimed at being subversive, they ended up reinforcing the dominant narrative of war and militarism. Once an image goes public, the author has little control over its use and the meanings it engenders. This was particularly true when Quilty handed over his artwork to such a discursively powerful institution as the AWM. In Australia, the AWM is an agenda-setting institution with significant social capital to lead the discourse of what being an Australian means. Being an Australian is to support the troops, those brave men and women who fight for the freedom of Australian society. This discourse is reproduced every year on ANZAC Day, on 25 April, a public holiday to commemorate the first military involvement in World War I as an independent nation. ANZAC Day is not only a war commemoration, but also the yearly re-enactment of the myth of the Australian nation born in war.[25] Within such a narrative of national identity, the soldier is elevated to a godly figure, and the state needs to be seen to be doing all they can to support them, for the integrity of soldiers is the mirror of the wellbeing of Australia's national identity. The images Quilty produced cast doubt on this: a doubt that needed to be addressed with a strong narrative of national support and compassion for the soldiers, as well as glorification of the artist who brought the issue of combat stress and PTSD to the attention of the Australian nation.

After Afghanistan has received an overwhelmingly positive response since it first opened in 2013: funding from the Department of Veteran Affairs enabled it to tour the country; the hub of Queensland art QAGOMA (Queensland Art Gallery & Gallery of Modern Art) bought one of Quilty's paintings through a fundraising campaign in 2014; two ABC shows on Quilty and his Afghanistan residency were broadcast in 2012 and 2013; and the online reviews of the touring exhibitions have been unilaterally positive.[26] Surely, the captivating Quilty-style of the artwork has played a major role in the success of the exhibition. However, politics also needs to be factored into it. As the presenter of the 2013 ABC show *Australian Story: On the Warpath*, Craig Reucassel, notes, within six months Quilty had gone from being an artist to an advocate for wounded soldiers.[27] Quilty has become vocal about the limited resources and will available to support wounded soldiers. He denounces the practice of discharging soldiers diagnosed with PTSD and depression as stigmatising. Soldiers discharged with PTSD, Quilty comments, feel dishonoured and lacking in support.[28] On his public Facebook page, Quilty calls for the Returned and Services League Australia (RSL) to be accountable for soldiers and veterans suffering from the emotional tolls of war. In the face of such stylistically powerful artworks and a controversially vocal artist, the AWM took actions to regain control over the narrative. It did so, I suggest, by promoting a politics of compassion towards the soldier that leverages national traumas that have no prospect of compensation or resolution.

First, however, I want to acknowledge the position of art historian Rex Butler, who has already suggested that the work of Ben Quilty lends itself to the operation and operationalisation of the modern rhetoric of war even though Quilty may not have meant it to do so. Butler blames the form of the artwork, which provides no context to reconstruct the background of the war in which soldiers were wounded.[29] This allows civilians to sympathise with the wounded soldier on a personal level without posing questions about war. He contends that *After Afghanistan* creates the illusion of offering an intimate insight into the lives of soldiers and their experience of war without really saying anything meaningful about it: no context, no reasons, no implications. As he puts it, the public success of *After Afghanistan* lies in the fact that it offers the viewer 'a way of avoiding any real encounter with the outcome of war, the public performance of responsibility without any of its real-world consequences'.[30] We can add that this distant proximity of the viewer to the soldier's experience of war is enabled by a focus on the body in pain as sole mediator of the experience of war.

The body in pain easily evokes compassion in the viewer. Compassion is an emotion that puts one in relation to the suffering of someone else by instilling a desire to alleviate that suffering.[31] It implies the existence of a privileged subject who is a spectator of the suffering of another person, as well as of a certain distance between the two. In order to be activated, therefore, the suffering body needs to be identified as a victim. When the soldier is successfully presented as victim, the desire to alleviate the suffering of the soldier takes the shape of unconditional support for the personal struggle of the soldier. The politics of compassion as an instrument of war to ensure public support for the troops has developed in conjunction with the strategy to embed journalists with the military. The practice of embedding journalists is controversial in its own right. On the one hand, it is a way of giving journalists access to dangerous warzones like Iraq mined with improvised explosive devices (IEDs). On the other hand, it is a strategy to control the flow of information starting from the production process.[32] Aside from this debate, however, it is undeniable that letting journalists train, eat and sleep with military personnel, and especially depend on them for their survival, inevitably enables personal relationships between journalists and soldiers to develop. Susan Carruthers documents how journalists embedded with US troops in Iraq soon started relying on soldiers' stories and experiences for their reporting, enabled by the official narrative that Americans 'deserved to admire their troops' professionalism'.[33] She comments that when war reporting relies on soldiers' experiences of being under threat by enemy sniper fire, explosions and rockets, it is easy to present the aggressors as victims of war.[34] In this way, embedded journalism has enabled a politics of compassion for the soldier to be the central concern of what civilians know, and want to know, about war.

War artists are embedded with the troops, and more than journalists, emotive sensibilities are the currency of their work. Quilty has deployed this currency with the intent of moving publics to make the government and the military accountable for the wellbeing of soldiers. However, the result has been that the AWM has mobilised the same currency to further pacify Australian publics around issues of war. This has been done by forcing a narrative about how Quilty's paintings reinscribe the bravery and courage of Australian soldiers. Representations of the suffering soldier serve as a reminder to Australians of the debt they owe to soldiers for protecting Australia's free way of life, and therefore ask people to curb negative private feelings to enable soldiers and publics to heal their grief without adding further challenges and difficulties to the process. The language of debt and reverence towards the soldiers is imprinted everywhere in the exhibition as well as in the exhibition merchandise such as the art guide and leaflets. The language of compassionate sentimentalism mobilised by the media and politicians on ANZAC Day, in other words, now has a visual mirror, thus making more authoritative the request to contain anti-war impulses in the name of respect for the soldiers.

Indeed, the image of the suffering body is particularly instrumental in making compassionate sentimentalism resonate louder. This is noticeable when considering the different popular and critical reception for the work of Quilty's fellow official war artists in Afghanistan and Iraq, Lyndell Brown and Charles Green. The still mundanity, silent contemplation and realism characteristic of Brown and Green's work have not been acclaimed in the same way as Quilty's abstracted and colourful bodies in pain. I maintain that the divergent approaches to representations of the body in these two exhibitions factor into differential receptions. The body Quilty depicts is uncanny, present and raw. It offers a different perspective on the soldier, accompanied by a salient political topic that has long been unaddressed publicly. It also fits into the politics of compassion towards the soldier that underpins modern warfare. The body in pain of Quilty's exhibition lends itself to the narrative that soldiers are victims of war, and therefore civilians owe them compassion. The work of Brown and Green offers none of this. The body is often absent in favour of dusty landscapes at sunset. When present, it is insignificant. It is not paying attention to the viewer, and at the same time, it demands no attention from them. There is nothing remarkable about the bodies of Brown and Green's war art. Faces are also rarely seen, thus foreclosing a point of identification for the viewer. The soldiers represented might be compassionate, as suggested by the normalised interactions between them and the local populations, but do not invite a politics of compassion towards the soldier.

In the Australian context the capacity of an image to evoke compassion as a precondition for success and popularity has to be understood within what Christina Twomey calls Australia's 'cultural obsession with trauma and victimhood'.[35] She contends that the Australian feminist movement which, at the end of the 1970s, used ANZAC Day as a bastion to protest against rape in war, has been a catalyst for the reinvigoration of a national narrative around support for the troops. The accusations of feminist activists that war was fomented by violent masculinity, and that war rape was a by-product of that, struck at the fragile masculinity of recently returned veterans who fought in the Vietnam War. Twomey puts this into a broader context in which PTSD had only just been recognised as a mental disorder which soldiers could appeal to in order to receive support as returned service people. The official recognition of war trauma immediately cast soldiers into the category of victim worthy of compassion,[36] which feminists were denying by refusing to see soldiers as victims in the way that mainstream culture was presenting them. This prompted a wave of unconditional support for veterans as well as of misogyny encapsulated in reported statements uttered at the press such as 'If it weren't [sic] for these guys these little bitches wouldn't even be here.'[37] More recently, Australia's cultural obsession with trauma and victimhood has manifested itself in the feeble inclusion of Indigenous soldiers who fought for the colonial state. Indigenous activists have been pressing the AWM to acknowledge the contribution of Indigenous people to the Australian history of warfare. In this context, Australia has demonstrated the will to embrace the trauma that settler institutions have perpetrated against those Indigenous people who wanted to enlist and fight in the Australian Defence Force but could not because of the ban against it, but has carefully cast Indigenous people who fought against European colonisers outside this history.

This is important to note because the visibility of gendered and racialised bodies create hierarchies of suffering. That is, compassion works differently across intersectional categories of identification. In the case of feminists protesting against rape in war, the white male veteran body has been privileged as a site of compassion, aided by images such as that of veteran Mike Lahey, who in 1985 interrupted a feminist protest against rape in war waving his prosthetic leg from the top of a truck, crying and shouting that the feminist protest made him feel inadequate.[38] The bodies of the feminist protesters were perceived to be invading a space, the ANZAC parade, dedicated to masculine bravery and courage. Their newly acquired status as victims enabled soldiers and veterans to discredit the intervention of feminists aimed at making visible the trauma of war rape. The feminist protesters had no images of raped bodies to accompany their protests apart from their own bodies, which were deemed insufficient to spark a politics of compassion vis-à-vis the male veteran body. Similarly, Indigenous activists demanding recognition of the contributions of Indigenous people in the Australian history of warfare, pre- and postcolonial, have been outsmarted by the AWM and the Australian National Archives which have collected visual evidence of Indigenous people fighting for Australia regardless of the ban, but have carefully cut out any image of Indigenous people fighting against European colonisers. Compassion can extend to the 'good' Indigenous citizen, the one who accepts and eventually assimilates into the settler colonial structures of power and governance.

Discourses of victimhood remove political accountability, leaving in its place compassionate sentimentalism that fuels militarisation by instantiating a passive civic posture. While the compassionate subject might mean well, oftentimes their compassion supports and conceals violence.[39] There are two main problems with the economy of compassion activated by representations of the soldier suffering from PTSD. First, compassion is an emotion that operates through moral grammars of good and bad. It is animated by moral narrations of suffering, which means that not all sufferings are worthy of compassion. Narratives of suffering soldiers activate a politics of compassion by positioning soldiers as good citizens whose service constitutes the debt that 'we' can never fully repay. Especially in societies with all-volunteer military service, those who do not serve are framed as having an outstanding debt towards those who do serve. This debt can be honoured only through unconditional support for those who serve. Second, scholars interested in the politics of compassion have noted that it leads to a passive civic posture, rather than to political activism, and to professing compassion in a declaration of one's own virtue and positive social engagement. It is a 'comforting move'[40] that reinstates the liberal position of the compassionate subject, as well as the position of victimhood of the soldier regardless of how they were involved in the commitment of violence. To feel compassion is to profess one's innocence in relation to the conditions that have caused suffering, and the unquestionable innocence of the subject of compassion.

The Body in Pain across Resistance and Militarisation

Representations of suffering bodies are never unproblematic. Elaine Scarry has articulated how pain destroys language, reducing the subject to a pre-linguistic state of moans and cries. Its language-destroying properties make pain difficult to represent discursively.[41] Following up on this, Elizabeth Dauphinée has noted that given the language-destroying nature of pain, visual representations are the only option left 'to point at the presence of the pain of others'.[42] Dauphinée explores a series of ethical problems that come about with this move, including that visual representations of the body in pain capture only the visual expressions of pain, and not pain in itself; they objectify, and at times beautify, the suffering of others; and they risk producing further distance between the viewer and the body in pain by becoming self-referential, that is, read for us, for our own pleasure, and to make us feel good about ourselves.[43]

The challenges to express pain through language articulated by Scarry, and the ethics of representing the body in pain suggested by Dauphinée, are important considerations that apply to the body of the soldier in pain too. Scarry has made a simple, but compelling point, that the central activity of war is to injure bodies, preferably opponents'.[44] With the emergence of national militaries, these bodies have been identified with soldiers. Soldiering bodies are legitimately injured in war; that is the nature of war. During the period when conscript militaries were the norm in international relations, militarisation consisted of borrowing the bodies of male citizens and claiming that they could be lawfully injured and killed in war for the security of the nation-state. This was accompanied by the articulation of the injured and scarred body around a rhetoric of pride and patriotism. As Joanna Bourke puts it in relation to changing understandings of the male body in Britain during World War I, the male body 'was intended to be mutilated'[45] and those injuries were seen as a sign of bravery and courage, as well as a proof of patriotism.[46] Less visible injuries and certainly psychological injuries did not carry the same cachet, as a demonstration of the power of visual representations to produce hierarchies of suffering.[47]

In post-conscription societies and with the development of discourses about human security, the body of the (white) soldier is no longer disposable and injurable. The soldier must be protected. Martin Shaw contends that, in modern warfare, safeguarding the life of Western soldiers is a priority, for popular democratic support for the war depends on that.[48] This means that images of suffering, injured or dead soldiers are less a symbol of national pride, as they were in conscription societies, and more a risk to the success of the military operation, if citizens were to withdraw their support. This explains why Quilty's paintings of suffering soldiers were met with significant institutional efforts to control the narrative about the government doing all it can to provide support for suffering soldiers, as well as to reinstate a rhetoric about pain being the epitome of soldiers' courage and bravery.

This framework poses important questions about the possibility to use the body, especially the body in pain, as a means for dissent or to contest war and militarisation. From military art representing battle scenes to more contemporary war art, the body of the soldier has been used to construct narratives of war and state the position of the nation in relation to it. Ben Quilty has used his position as official war artist to make an intervention into Australia's war narrative. His art about combat fatigue and PTSD was the starting point for his activism to demand accountability from institutions for psychologically injured soldiers. His stated position when producing the paintings was one of civic duty. Beside the theme Quilty raised and has been vocal about, I have suggested in this chapter that his work produces an affective form of resistance to the militarisation of the body activated by the act of figuratively stripping naked the body of the soldiers to show the imprint of overwhelming emotions and trauma. However, this dissenting position to militarisation has been co-opted into a narrative of sacrifice, redemption and compassion for the suffering soldier that silences contestation and deliberation about war. It has reinforced the idea that civilians have an undying debt towards soldiers.

To a certain extent, Quilty's activism has succeeded. The Australian authorities can no longer ignore the topic of PTSD when the wider population has been exposed to Quilty's paintings. These paintings, together with their topic, now hang in the halls of powerful cultural institutions like QAGOMA and the AWM and are discussed on broadcast television and social media. But the question of the relationship between this art and war remains. Quilty has said that his position as a war artist is not anti-war, and arguably, as an artist commissioned by the AWM, his position cannot be anti-war. This does not mean that he is pro-war, however. He has claimed to be 'filled with opinions about war and politics', but said that these are better told through his art rather than expressed in slogans and facile romantic positions.[49]

Other Australian war artists have expressed similar positions. Jon Cattapan, Lyndell Brown and Charles Green have all articulated the ethical condition of being an official war artist.[50] First, they note that war art has moved away from traditional understandings of memorialisation as a rhetorical exercise in nation building. War art increasingly functions as a counter-memorial, a way to show how national identity is constructed in relation to different positions as well as to contest national identity. This is particularly evident in more modern, if not postmodern approaches to war art. Second, they point out the seemingly diminished power of images to move people into action following the end of the Vietnam War, which they counterpoise to the paradoxical increase in attendance at war commemoration events such as the Gallipoli Dawn service on ANZAC Day.[51] Against this backdrop, they suggest that the position of war artist must be more sophisticated than simply being pro- or anti-war. They address the question of whether art can reshape public understandings of war. But these artists' intention is not to reshape public opinion by directing it to one side or the other. Rather, by reshaping public opinion they mean incentivising critical thinking. Their strategy has been to emphasise the stillness of the war experience, the waiting in the desert for action, and to remove the glamorous actions that we are so used to seeing in films and TV. They force the viewer to see the boredom and the mundanity of war, to revisit common understandings of war as action and heroism. In particular, they have taken the position of ambiguity that eschews dogma.

As I have suggested above, these artists represent the body as insignificant, and therefore their work did not lend itself to being appropriated by narratives of compassion that militarise society. Ben Quilty's use of the body in pain did, falling into the trap that seeing violence done to the body encourages sympathy for the victim. Certainly Quilty could have followed the path of those artists who, in order to avoid fetishising the body in pain, have represented its absence. A case in point is Melanie Friend's series *Homes and Gardens: Documenting the Invisible*, which features photos of houses of Kosovar Albanians who had been beaten and tortured by Serbian police in the mid-1990s. The silence, quietness and order of these spaces is juxtaposed against the testimonies of mistreatment and violence against their inhabitants.[52] But would have Quilty's work had the same popular impact, if he had removed the body? We cannot know, but we can speculate that given our cultural obsession with violence and the pain of others, the answer is most likely no. At stake is the removal of the stigma associated with PTSD and soldiers showing emotions.

There is also more than this at stake if we take on board Ariella Azoulay's insight that to look at a photograph, or an image, should involve watching it, that is, tracing the time and movement that are the background event of the photograph or image. She stresses that when the subject of the image is an injured body, reconstructing the background in which the injury happened is a civic duty, and not an exercise in aesthetic appreciation. She concludes that for one to realise this, one must grasp first that citizenship is not just a status but also a tool, if not an obligation to struggle against the injuries inflicted on others.[53] We cannot put the responsibility on the image itself. While there are certainly ethical considerations about images of bodies in pain objectifying the pain of others, the responsibility is not on the image. It is first on the artist and then on the viewer.

Artists have long fulfilled the social role of witnessing and conveying to an audience life experiences, even when these are not their own. Alex Danchev calls the artist a 'moral witness', for they have the moral duty to be truthful to what they are testifying in their art, and to move their audience's consciousness towards an encounter with their testimony. For Danchev, the artist is not an onlooker, but a conscious agitator. When the artist bears witness to life experiences, they become insiders of what they are witnessing, and have the responsibility of imaging the moral community that will receive their testimony.[54] And, if the artist is a moral witness of the suffering of others, as Danchev suggests, I propose that art can make the viewer into a 'modest witness' of that suffering. Donna Haraway proposed the figuration of the modest witness to underscore that they who witness do not need to make their observation a mirror for reality. For Haraway, there is no position from nowhere, and all views are situated in time, space, bodies and power relations. As situated, views are always partial and compromised. Thus, to be a modest witness is to be open to a dialogue and critical scrutiny that foreground accountability. It is to be able to recognise and subject to critique one's own position in the encounter with the other, especially the other in pain.[55]

The subject position of the modest witness is enabled by the mode of seeing that art engenders. Following Mieke Bal, Michael Shapiro contends that art can activate a process of 'slow looking'. Slow looking is a form of engagement with representations based on vision that encourages critical reflections in virtue of the time one can spend watching, decoding, encoding and questioning the ambiguities of what is represented. It is a mode of seeing that flips on its head the contemporary tendency of images to assault the viewer with pre-packaged emotions, moral connotations and characters.[56]

Images, Susan Sontag claimed, cannot repair our ignorance of the history and politics that caused the suffering of others.[57] We have devolved to images too much of our own responsibility as agentic viewers. The only thing that images can do is to ask us to pay attention, to reflect and to be curious enough to learn more. Scholars interested in the politics of images often ask if images have agency. On ethical grounds, I maintain that the answer to this question should be negative, not because images do not do something to the world – they do, in fact – but because the language of agentic images subtracts from the human responsibility to deal with the image ethically and politically. Drawing from this, I suggest that the question about the use of suffering bodies in war art and militarisation is not aesthetic, but discursive. Good art is art that makes the viewer question the image, the artist and the act of looking. Good art can feature bodies or not. But art, like any other image, is mediated through discourses. When the hegemonic discourse is so powerful that it silences the process of questioning and thinking critically, as in the case of Quilty's paintings, art is militarised.

Notes

1. Michael Mann, 'The Roots and Contradictions of Modern Militarism', *New Left Review* 162 (1987): 35–50, 35.
2. Cristina Masters, 'Bodies of Technology: Cyborg Soldiers and Militarised Masculinities', *International Feminist Journal of Politics* 7:1 (2005): 112–32; David Grossman, *On Killing: The Psychological Cost of Learning to Kill in War and Society*, 1st ed. (Boston, MA: Little, Brown and Company, 1995); Joanna Bourke, *An Intimate History of Killing: Face-to-Face Killing in Twentieth-Century Warfare* (London: Granta, 1999). See also Evans, this volume.
3. Federica Caso, 'Sexing the Disabled Veteran: The Homoerotic Aesthetics of Militarism', *Critical Military Studies* 3:3 (2017): 217–34; Rachel Whitworth and Trish Winter, *Sexing the Soldier: The Politics of Gender and the Contemporary British Army* (London: Routledge, 2007); Laura Shepherd, 'Militarisation', in *Visual Global Politics*, edited by Roland Bleiker (London: Routledge, 2018), 209–14.
4. D. A. Kent, 'The Anzac Book and the Anzac Legend: C. E. W. Bean as Editor and Image-Maker', *Australian Historical Studies* 21:84 (1985): 376–90.
5. Fiona Nicoll, *From Diggers to Drag Queens: Configurations of Australian National Identity* (London: King Street Press, 2001), 54.
6. See also Jude, this volume.
7. Helen Attrill, 'Ben Quilty: Education Resource' (Bendigo: Bendigo Art Gallery, 2014), 4. https://www.bendigoregion.com.au/sites/default/files/2018-08/Ben%20 Quilty%20Education%20Resource.pdf.
8. Ibid., 11.
9. Ibid., 13.

10. Laura Brandon, *Art and War* (London: I. B. Tauris, 2007).

11. Richard Travers, *To Paint a War: The Lives of the Australian Artists Who Painted the Great War, 1914–18* (Port Melbourne, Victoria: Thames and Hudson Australia, 2017), 115.

12. M. Hutchison, '"Accurate to the Point of Mania": Eyewitness Testimony and Memory Making in Australia's Official Paintings of the First World War', *Australian Historical Studies* 46:1 (2015): 27–44, 37.

13. Joanna Bourke, 'Introduction', in *War and Art: A Visual History of Modern Conflict*, edited by Joanna Bourke (London: Reaktion, 2017), 22.

14. *Australian Story: War Paint* (ABC, 3 September 2012, 00:00).

15. Laura Webster, *Ben Quilty: After Afghanistan* (Canberra: Australian War Memorial, 2014), 14.

16. *Australian Story: On the Warpath* (ABC, 25 March 2013, 01:00).

17. Webster, *Ben Quilty*, 22.

18. Federica Caso, 'The Body and the Militarisation of Western Societies: An Aesthetic Approach', PhD thesis (University of Queensland, 2019), ch. 4.

19. Travers, *To Paint a War*, 205; Peter Andreas Pedersen, *ANZAC Treasures: The Gallipoli Collection of the Australian War Memorial* (Crows Nest, NSW: Murdoch Books, 2014), 124.

20. Marilyn Lake, 'Mission Impossible: How Men Gave Birth to the Australian Nation – Nationalism, Gender and Other Seminal Acts', *Gender and History* 4:3 (1992): 305–22.

21. Judith Butler, 'Rethinking Vulnerability and Resistance', in *Vulnerability in Resistance*, edited by Judith Butler, Zeynep Gambetti and Leticia Sabsay (Durham, NC: Duke University Press, 2016), 12–27; Judith Butler, *Undoing Gender* (London: Routledge, 2004).

22. Butler, 'Vulnerability and Resistance', 25.

23. David H. J. Morgan, 'Theater of War: Combat, the Military, and Masculinities', in *Theorizing Masculinities*, edited by Harry Brod and Michael Kaufman (London: Sage, 1994), 165.

24. Jesse Paul Crane-Seeber, 'Sexy Warriors: The Politics and Pleasures of Submission to the State', *Critical Military Studies* 2:1–2 (2016): 41–55.

25. Lake, 'Mission Impossible', 311.

26. Rex Butler, 'Ben Quilty: The Fog of War', *Intellectual History Review* 27:3 (2017): 433–51, 442.

27. *Australian Story: On the Warpath*.

28. Ibid.

29. Butler, 'Ben Quilty', 442.

30. Ibid., 443.

31. Julia Welland, 'Compassionate Soldiering and Comfort', in *Emotions, Politics and War*, edited by Linda Åhäll and Thomas Gregory (London: Routledge, 2015), 115.

32. Carruthers, *The Media at War*, 2nd ed. (New York: Palgrave Macmillan, 2011), ch. 3 and 6.

33. Ibid., 229.

34. Ibid., 229.
35. Christina Twomey, 'Trauma and the Reinvigoration of Anzac: An Argument', *History Australia* 10:3 (2013): 85–108, 91.
36. Didier Fassin and Richard Rechtman, *The Empire of Trauma: An Inquiry into the Condition of Victimhood*, translated by Rachel Gomme (Princeton, NJ: Princeton University Press, 2009).
37. Twomey, 'Trauma', 101.
38. Ibid., 103–4.
39. Lauren Berlant, 'Introduction: Compassion (and Withholding)', in *Compassion: The Culture and Politics of an Emotion*, edited by Lauren Berlant (London: Routledge, 2004), 1–14.
40. Welland, 'Compassionate Soldiering', 119.
41. Elaine Scarry, *The Body in Pain: The Making and Unmaking of the World* (Oxford: Oxford University Press, 1985), 4.
42. Elizabeth Dauphinée, 'The Politics of the Body in Pain: Reading the Ethics of Imagery', *Security Dialogue* 38:2 (2007): 139–55, 141.
43. Dauphinée, 'Body in Pain'.
44. Scarry, *The Body in Pain*, 12.
45. Joanna Bourke, *Dismembering the Male: Men's Bodies, Britain, and the Great War* (London: Reaktion, 1996), 31.
46. Bourke, *Dismembering the Male*, 56.
47. Caso, 'Sexing'.
48. Martin Shaw, *The New Western Way of War: Risk-Transfer War and Its Crisis in Iraq* (Cambridge: Polity, 2005).
49. Webster, *Ben Quilty*, 8.
50. Charles Green, Lyndell Brown and Jon Cattapan, 'The Obscure Dimensions of Conflict: Three Contemporary War Artists Speak', *Journal of War and Culture Studies* 8:2 (2015): 158–74.
51. Ibid., 161.
52. Bourke, 'Introduction', 35.
53. Ariella Azoulay, *The Civil Contract of Photography*, translated by Rela Mazali and Ruvik Danieli (New York: Zone Books, 2008), 14.
54. Alex Danchev, 'Our Brothers' Keeper: Moral Witness', *Alternatives* 40:3–4 (2015): 191–200.
55. Donna J. Haraway, *Modest_Witness@Second_Millennium.Female Man©_Meets_ OncoMouseTM* (London: Routledge, 1997).
56. M. J. Shapiro, 'Slow Looking: The Ethics and Politics of Aesthetics', *Millennium* 37:1 (2008): 181–97.
57. Susan Sontag, *Regarding the Pain of Others* (London: Penguin, 2004).

CHAPTER 3

Svetlana Alexievich's Soviet Women Veterans and the Aesthetics of the Disabled Military Body: Staring at the Unwomanly Face of War

Catherine Baker

Aesthetics, embodiment and militarisation are perhaps never more closely joined than in the aesthetics of the military body disabled by war. The fundamental rationale of war, and the ultimate purpose of the institutions which fight it is, an interdisciplinary literature reminds us, the destruction of bodies.[1] Participants in war, and those who love them, do not just fear their death: they fear what condition war might leave their living bodies in. The mechanised and explosive means of destroying the body in modern warfare make war a matter of horrific injury even beyond what one armed body can inflict on another, or – to use the more sensory language that has come more naturally to cultural historians than disciplinary international relations[2] – a matter of mangling, roasting, poisoning, lacerating, dismembering and tearing limb from limb.[3] Indeed, Jasbir Puar now argues that both war and industrial capitalism require certain bodies to be marked out as 'preordained for . . . often targeted maiming', echoing Joanna Bourke's observation that the male body 'was intended to be mutilated' during the Great War.[4]

The disabled, maimed and disfigured body, moreover, looms large over the affective politics and psychodynamics of the body through which processes of militarisation work.[5] Against militarised representations of the health, strength, vigour and glamour military training and service bestows on bodies, experiences and representations of disabled veterans become embodied evidence of the other transformations war inflicts.[6] Anti-war art traditions in painting and photography, indeed, rely on images of horrifically wounded soldiers as much as civilian victims of war.[7] And yet disabled veterans' bodies can themselves be re-militarised, from the sacrificial spectacle that the French *gueules cas-sées* (World War I veterans with disfigured faces) represented in victory parades,[8] to the figure of the maimed US male veteran of Iraq/Afghanistan re-masculinised and re-eroticised through the twin technologies of 'sexually allusive' photography and 'techno-militarized' prosthetic limbs.[9] Physical disability and disfigurement are perhaps where the conjunction between militarisation, aesthetics and embodiment seems to become most uncomfortable: 'we' (the community of readers interested in all three things) are contemplating the aesthetics and embodiment, sometimes even the troubling yet seductive aestheticisation, of an activity which ultimately exists to tear bodies apart.

By investigating aesthetic practices of representing disability and disfigurement in Svetlana Alexievich's collection of interviews with women Red Army veterans, *The Unwomanly Face of War* (analysed here in its most recent English translation), this chapter argues the links between militarisation, aesthetics and embodiment must be anchored in the intersubjective aesthetics of disability. Asking what structures of feeling are projected on to disabled military bodies, and other bodies disabled in war, at any historical and political moment helps to establish what the aesthetics of both war and disability in those places and times have been: that is, how onlookers have been meant to feel on encountering the reality, imagination or thought of war-disabled bodies. The very question of how visible war-disabled bodies should be, on what terms, is both a psychically painful matter for those inhabiting them, such as thousands of facially disfigured World War I veterans who had to choose whether to hide their faces behind painted tin masks,[10] and a matter of wider cultural representation.[11] The answer is inflected by what impairments they have sustained, and socio-cultural perceptions of those; by each body's gendered, racialised, ethnicised and class-based signifiers of social identity; by which side they fought for, and what wartime violence (if any) they carried out. In the contemporary West, for instance, the re-empowered veteran amputee is almost hypervisible, while just as dead victims of coalition attacks and drone strikes are made ungrievable,[12] living but disabled civilian victims are concealed until activists inject their images into the public sphere.

Critical military studies (CMS) scholars including Zoe Wool, Ken MacLeish and Alison Howell have already studied troops' and veterans' embodied experiences,[13] and others are exploring figures of disabled veterans within wider socio-cultural militarisation.[14] Yet CMS aesthetic and cultural enquiry can integrate disability even further by drawing on disability studies' cultural and literary turn. Disability scholars like

Lennard Davis, Rosemarie Garland-Thomson, David Mitchell and Sharon Snyder view disability as the product of a social context structured by the construction and enforcement of bodily 'normalcy', turning material bodily impairment into socially constructed 'disability'.[15] War, creating large numbers of disabled veterans in social categories where disability pre-war was relatively rare, often creates crises in public imaginations of the body, potentially altering the gendered bodily politics of militarisation and resistance to it. Since most veterans of mass warfare have been men, studies of disabled veterans typically concentrate on post-war masculinities: yet states which have mobilised women for war also have to contend with the reality and figure of disabled female veterans – above all, perhaps, the Union of Soviet Socialist Republics (USSR), which in 1941–5 put more than 800,000 women on the front line. These women, and the public silence about their service, are the collective subject of Alexievich's *The Unwomanly Face of War*.

This chapter concerns Alexievich's book of 'documentary prose', based on interviews with Red Army women that she collected in 1978–83 and could first publish in 1985[16] – or, more accurately, the 2017 English translation of Alexievich's fourth Russian text. This more complex description foregrounds its complicated history of publication, revision and retranslation, the literary techniques through which Alexievich remediates the women's words, and the fact that I as a scholar am responding to a translation which has become an artefact of comparative literature, not to the original Russian.[17] Alexievich's winning the 2015 Nobel Prize in Literature led both to new Russian editions of her work and to the retranslation and reissue of her books in English. Hailed by reviewers as an 'extraordinary' account of Soviet women soldiers' experiences of total war,[18] the book is framed as a counter-narrative to official Soviet discourse of a glorious Great Patriotic War embodied by the heroism of men. Alexievich both asserts that 'the true *experience* of that conflict could be better grasped through the recollections of women combatants', which she selects and arranges to emphasise intimate and emotional detail, and uses those recollections to contest the idea of war as glorious, a myth in which the militarised Soviet system incorporated everybody.[19]

Alexievich's very title, indeed, already conveys a gendered moral aesthetics of war and embodiment. Its surface level plays on the famous gendered contrast between the male 'Just Warrior' and female 'Beautiful Soul', upsetting that binary because the reader knows it concerns women soldiers.[20] Though both the Russian and English titles contrast war to a womanly or woman's face, the Russian makes them separate domains

(*У войны не женское лицо* literally translates as *In War There Is No Womanly Face*) while the English collides them, inviting readers more directly to picture how war's unwomanly face might appear. Both in the title and throughout the text, this chapter argues, Alexievich organises her intervention against Stalinist and late Soviet layers of militarisation around the trope of disabling/disfiguring war injury preventing women from fully being women after the war. This trope amplifies what her interviewees (as remediated by her editorial work and their own remembering[21]) relate as their own fears during and after wartime, when it was commonsensically believed that disabled women would not be able to become wives and mothers as the Stalinist gender order expected[22] – roles already less accessible to former Red Army women just because they had served at the front.[23] Aesthetics and embodiment in this example of resistance to militarisation thus combine in two ways: firstly, the aesthetics of how (gendered) bodies would have looked, and how women feared their bodies would be made to look after disabling or disfiguring injury; secondly, the aesthetics of how Alexievich writes about bodies to activate readers' own embodied sense-memories or sense-imaginations. On both these levels, disability studies explains what is affectively at stake in aesthetic practices using the figure of the disabled veteran body.

Disability Studies and the Disabled Veteran Body

Disability studies, like other theoretical–activist approaches, collectively theorises the embodied knowledge many of its authors have acquired from lived experience and applies it for critical ends.[24] Against the so-called medical model of disability, treating impairments as individual defects to be cured, disability studies links 'the social meanings, symbols, and stigmas attached to disability identity . . . to enforced systems of exclusion and oppression', considering disability as socially produced.[25] Its own ways of knowing nevertheless always return to the materiality and lived experience of impairment, to bodily reality and physical as well as psychic pain.[26]

Embodiment and aesthetics, which this volume connects, are always already intertwined in disability studies. The literary scholar Lennard Davis has argued that 'disability is a cultural phenomenon rooted in the senses', since disability becomes meaningful when an observer perceives people to be disabled based on their deviation from bodily norms – of form, size, comportment, movement, symmetry and regularity itself.[27] So deep-rooted are ideas of what Garland-Thomson calls the 'normate' body that, theorists like Tobin Siebers suggest, they even inform how embodied identities based on race, gender, sexuality and class are marginalised and stigmatised.[28] Disability studies' cultural turn has questioned how literary and visual texts' representations of disabled characters and people 'enforce' (in Davis's words) the normalcy of the abled body. David Mitchell and Sharon Snyder, for instance, use the term 'narrative prosthesis' to explain how creators use disability in characterisation as 'a metaphorical signifier of social and individual collapse', showing (with an intentional play on words) that 'disability has been used throughout history as a crutch upon which literary narratives lean for their representational power, disruptive potentiality, and analytical insight'.[29] Disability studies thus offers reading practices which make sense of disability in literary and (audio)visual representations. But this cultural turn does not divert attention from disabled people's embodied experience and subjectivity – for it is the perceptions of disability and normalcy that nondisabled people have largely acquired from these representations which shape their reactions on seeing and encountering disabled bodies. Such perceptions thus shape the intersubjective psychological and affective dimensions of how disabled people experience their own embodiment, which Carol Thomas terms disability's 'psycho-emotional dimensions'.[30]

The psycho-emotional dimensions of disability do not just include the psychological effects of structural disablism which imposes physical and socio-economic barriers to what bodies and people can do, but also the barriers which create restrictions within individual selves, stemming from how others' reactions to their bodies have made them feel. These often embarrassing or humiliating everyday encounters can be theorised as an 'ontological invalidation . . . experienced at the point that the stranger reacts to the disabled person'.[31] This is especially the case for amputation and disfigurement, most severe among war's physical wounds.[32] Moreover, not just the stranger's gaze but (perhaps even more so) the loved one's gaze can inflict such psycho-emotional harm. The reintegration of the family unit around disabled veterans is thus a common subject of governmental and cultural anxiety when troops return, as social and cultural historians of war have shown.[33]

Disabled veterans' and bodies' complex relationships to wartime and post-war militarisation have been studied most extensively for World War I. The numbers of men who came home from war with such impairments, and the class differences between middle-class officers and the working-class men who in peacetime incurred them more frequently, left disabled veterans, their families and wider society renegotiating the aesthetics of post-war masculinities.[34] Drawing on disability studies scholars including Garland-Thomson and the historian Henri-Jacques Stiker, Ana Carden-Coyne argues that '[t]he mutilated body [of disabled veterans] offered visual evidence of the tragedy of war, searing it into cultural memory' and provoking an 'aesthetics of normalizing embodiment' in post-war Britain.[35] The hegemonic 'ideology of ability'[36] beneath the period's gendered and racialised constructions of masculinity is evident when Carden-Coyne describes the 'common reactions' of aversion or pity to disabled veterans, who 'literally embodied the [public's] fears of disabled people'.[37] Women, as constructed in literature, meanwhile 'often appear[ed] as the archetypal witnesses to the pain of war', as battlefield nurses or at home.[38]

Particularly terrifying, for soldiers and loved ones contemplating what they might suffer, as well as veterans, intimates and strangers witnessing what mechanised war did to flesh and bone, was facial disfigurement. Suzannah Biernoff argues that wartime and post-war British visual culture exhibited a 'visual anxiety and aversion' to veterans' facial disfigurement, contrasting with more common and happier depictions of veteran amputees.[39] Print, however, could depict their disfigurements in much more detail. Explaining why (as Biernoff argues) '[i]t was showing (and looking at) the disfigured face that was taboo' is an aesthetic question:[40] while reading text required picturing the injury in one's own mind, photography directly activated sight, confronting onlookers with a face which ideologies of bodily normalcy would not instantly resolve as such. While maxillofacial surgeons and prosthetic artists tried to find ways to 'humanise' the mutilated face, disfigured veterans lived with knowing their appearance had become frightful 'where there was once a handsome and welcome face' (as the *Manchester Evening Chronicle* wrote near the end of the war, calling the facially disfigured soldier's loss of identity 'The Worst Loss of All').[41] Contrasts in other combatant countries revealed that all militarised embodied aesthetics are nationally inflected. France's *gueules cassées*, for instance, received more collective public recognition than in Britain, while US media imposed 'visual quarantine' on disfigured veterans' images (besides a few exemplary recoveries) but turned the plastic surgeon into a hero of 'miraculous physical transformation' instead.[42]

The disfigured military body again became a cultural anxiety in countries heavily committed to the War on Terror, since advances in military medicine have increased the numbers of troops surviving extreme battlefield burns. Photojournalistic portraiture and documentary film dealt most with the aesthetics of disfigurement during these wars.[43] Nina Berman's award-winning 2006 photo-series 'Marine Wedding', taken for *People* magazine, depicted one such burns survivor, Marine Sgt Ty Ziegel, going about his everyday hometown life and marrying his fiancée. In Berman's wedding photograph, which *People* did not print, Ziegel stands in uniform with his earless, noseless head bowed.[44] His bride's expression, staring at the camera, seems to embody the uncertainty that (dominant aesthetics of disability make onlookers believe) it would be 'natural' to feel about resuming domestic and intimate roles towards someone whose appearance one has been culturally conditioned to find monstrous. Samantha Wehbi argues that Berman achieves a 'counter-hegemonic message' about US militarism by visualising how US wars have left young veterans' bodies – but that that message relies on a hegemonic message about disability itself, that is, that the disfigured face should be the 'exotic' object of the observer's stare.[45] A similar dynamic in Alexievich's evocation of disability and bodily destruction emerges once we consider Soviet constructions of disability and the history of disabled Soviet veterans.

Disabled Soviet Veterans after the 'Great Patriotic War'

No country involved in World War II had more returning disabled veterans than the USSR, or scarcer material resources to meet their needs.[46] The immediate Stalinist mythologisation of the war through the heroic conventions of 'socialist realism' resulted in 'silencing or denying' evidence of how much devastation war had caused, and disabled veterans or 'war invalids' were absent from official depictions of wartime or post-war life.[47] Soviet ideology constructed disability, or invalidity, in terms of (un)fitness for productive labour. The official figure of 2,576,000 disabled troops discharged before May 1945 (7.46 per cent of the Red Army's 1945 strength) itself concealed an unknown number of others who were not recorded because they could still resume their former jobs; the 'reconstruction' of war-disabled Soviet bodies, personally and socially, primarily concerned re-fitting them for work.[48] The problem Alexievich was contesting in Soviet public memory, however, also affects scholarly literature on Soviet veterans: the Great Patriotic War's disabled veterans have overwhelmingly been thought of as just men, although 800,000 women served on the front line.[49]

The estimated tens of thousands of disabled female veterans, doubly invisible in official Soviet discourse, are scarcely more visible in the social and cultural history, or even gender history, of late Stalinism. Historians have asked how disabled veterans negotiated the Soviet gender order, and how far (if at all) imaginations of the body were renegotiated after war's end; an almost exclusive emphasis on disability's intersection with masculinities, however, has compounded the erasure of disabled female veterans in Soviet society itself.[50] This erasure was widespread. Frances Bernstein, for instance, notes that the numbers of disabled, especially limbless, men needing reincorporation into Soviet society threatened a 'feminization' of the collective Soviet self, which had to be 'remasculinized' by reverting to pre-war gender norms: 'disability was perceived as a problem of men', and so was its solution.[51] This solution was engineered not just by erasing disabled men from monuments and victory parades (Red Army women suffered similar erasure) and massaging official disability statistics, but also through lauding new Soviet-made prosthetics, which (exemplifying the propaganda–practice gap) were only actually available to a few fortunate or well-connected amputees.[52]

In contrast to the contemporaneous rehabilitation of disabled veterans in the USA, which sought to restore disabled men as heads of families (involving wives/fiancées in the emotional labour of re-normalising disabled and disfigured male bodies[53]), Soviet ideology expected men to be reintegrated into 'the collective family' but not necessarily the domestic one.[54] Their 'mastery over feminized machines' mattered more than their recovery as potential husbands and fathers, despite the postwar demographic shortage of men, and despite the state's ambitions to increase the birth rate and preserve gender norms.[55] Veterans who publicly narrated their lives under Soviet rule internalised this ideology of rehabilitation through labour.[56] Bernstein only refers once to disabled women veterans, pictured doing 'strictly feminine pursuits such as sewing and knitting' in the few photographs of women wearing the famous 'Kononov arm':[57] disabling injury and rehabilitation, it would seem, were themselves part of the 'unwomanly' face of war.

Socialist realist aesthetics, too, adapted to the sheer number of returning disabled men, while writing out disabled women veterans. 'The new hero of Socialist Realist literature' in 1944–6, writes Anna Krylova, 'was physically and psychologically mutilated', representing men brought to emotional crisis by 'the seeming impossibility' of picturing themselves living 'normal family life'.[58] Offsetting these traumatised men were 'physically whole and psychologically integrated women', necessitating a 'silence about female trauma' to preserve the gendered binary between masculine war trauma and feminine nurture.[59] This version of the New Soviet Woman was not just 'Beautiful Soul' but also feminine 'soul-healer', requiring hard boundaries between the normative home and front.[60] The size of the ideological hole female veterans fell down is evident when Krylova notes that these novels' female characters who heal men had not been to the front, and that the few female characters who had been to the front are shown as unable to heal men.[61] Representing traumatised, disfigured and disabled female veterans when war disability was constructed as a masculine problem would have further upset late Stalinism's gender order.

A more realist war literature (including the oral historian Ales Adamovich, who inspired Alexievich), and war art, did however emerge after the Thaw.[62] One such artist was Gennadii Dobrov, whose drawings of disabled veterans in Soviet residential homes were completed in 1974–80 but only started being exhibited and published under glasnost. One, 'The Family', showed a male defender of Moscow and quadruple amputee in his wheelchair using a telephone with his wife behind him: the onlooker is told, but not shown, that she too lost her legs during the war.[63] Other drawings in Dobrov's 'War Autographs' series, rendered in heavily shaded dense black strokes, included a female Belarusian partisan who had lost both legs after being trapped in frozen marshland, and an unnamed woman 'with a burnt face' who had never been on the front line, but who had fainted into flames after hearing her husband had been killed in battle: Dobrov pictured her with a veil of sacking over her face, holding a cane and a bespectacled mask.[64] Unlike the facially disfigured men Dobrov shows face-on, the absence of any fleshly face – even a burned one – is here what forces the viewer's stare.

It was thus within a discursive space where official memory had concealed both disabled veterans and women veterans, and where everyday memory had largely turned against women veterans too, that Alexievich began interviewing female veterans in 1978.[65] Alexievich sought to recover women veterans' voices, but not necessarily to establish disabled female veterans as historical subjects. Her representations of women's own disablement were far outnumbered by narratives of women's and families' fears they would be disabled or disfigured, fuelled by social anxieties about what man would marry a disabled female veteran and how disabled women would fulfil their prescribed roles in Soviet society, or even meet their basic needs.

Disability and the Female Veteran in *The Unwomanly Face of War*

Svetlana Alexievich's 'documentary narrative' about women veterans, first published in Russian in 1985, was first translated into English in 1988 by the USSR's official English-language publisher Progress, was revised for three more Russian editions, then came to wider transnational attention after Alexievich won the Nobel Prize. The narrative, in Alexievich's characteristic style, comprises a composite of extracts from interviews she started collecting a year before the Soviet–Afghan War began. Her introduction, as presented in the 2017 English edition, frames the book as an act of recovery she was compelled to perform after growing up in a post-war Belarusian village, where women's voices carried the community's memory of war and occupation. Alexievich's search for women veterans' voices stems, she writes, from the gulf between a public culture where 'half of the books [in every library] were about the war', women veterans' public forgetting and shaming, and her remembered everyday life where 'stories of the war are told by women. They weep.'[66] Indeed, she introduces the book as an intervention into gendered ways of knowing about war itself:

> There have been a thousand wars – small and big, known and unknown. And still more has been written about them. But . . . it was men writing about men – that much was clear at once. Everything we know about war we know with 'a man's voice'. We are all captives of 'men's' notions and 'men's' sense of war.[67]

Besides what evidence it might give about women veterans' experiences, critics have importantly also viewed it as a historically situated text, written during the Soviet–Afghan War and challenging official memory of the Great Patriotic War in ways that (like Dobrov's paintings) could only be publicised more widely when glasnost began.[68] The women's testimonies, Krylova writes, convey this very tension between '[t]he pain of discursive erasure' and women's fears of admitting their veteran status amid 'the popular dissociation of family life and female front experience' in post-war Soviet society.[69] This dissociation extended to the shame attached to being a female veteran when gossip presumed front-line women would have been sexually promiscuous with men.[70] Alexievich's use of oral testimony sought to break the mould of official Soviet war discourse and the 'monolithic "Soviet" woman' at once,[71] while making the recuperative assumption (shared by much feminist oral history practice in the 1980s) that women interviewing women were especially equipped to uncover their subjects' emotional truths.[72] Aliaksandr Novikau, indeed, calls *Unwomanly Face* a paradigmatic illustration of Christine Sylvester's arguments about the centrality of emotional experiences in studying war.[73]

Women's perception, in Alexievich's epistemology, is clearly expected to offer 'a more "truthful" depiction of the war' than stories told by men.[74] Some responses to her work do, indeed, read her writing as direct journalistic access to her subjects' real words and feelings.[75] Specialists in (post-)Soviet literature emphasise, however, that Alexievich's books should be read as literary confections more than history (to the extent these are separate): Alexievich's technique of assembling extracts into 'choruses' or 'variations on themes' stitches them into a claim to represent a universal 'emotional history' of war,[76] and the scale of her editorial intervention is even clearer in her later book about young male veterans of the Afghan War (*Boys in Zinc*). Authorial revisions between that book's 1991 and 2013 Russian editions made the text noticeably less 'polyphonic' and more 'monochromatic', more like a single documentary truth claim.[77] Holly Myers describes Alexievich's aesthetic technique of threading repeated words and phrases through different monologues as an 'artistic manipulation'.[78] *Unwomanly Face* thus presents a (several-times-revised) story Alexievich wishes to tell about women veterans, not the stories women veterans told her.[79]

Although the metaphor of the face sits in the very title to connote war's corporeal and emotional toll on women, the material body in general, and disability/disfigurement in particular, have been less important in most responses to *Unwomanly Face* than the aesthetics of trauma. While Novikau observes that 'pain and suffering are the central topics of all Alexievich's books', this pain is psychic, not physical.[80] One extract highlighted by Daniel Bush, for instance, concerns a sniper who found a wounded female comrade with her legs 'so mangled that we were barely able to bandage her': the platoon saved her, although she had begged to be shot because 'Who will have any use for me in this condition?', and they found her in an invalids' home thirty years later when she had not even told her mother she was alive.[81] Alexievich comments in the 1990 edition that 'I physically feel the materiality of the pain living in this tiny woman in her old plaid wrap.'[82] This is the pain of the teller, not the sufferer, as in representations of disabled characters it can often be. Yet there is more to perceive about Alexievich's aesthetics of embodiment by applying Lennard Davis's observation that 'a disabilities studies consciousness' can alter readings not just of novels with disabled protagonists but any writerly text.[83]

The theme of disabling war injury and its bodily effects resonates through *Unwomanly Face* in two ways: depictions of witnessing the mutilated or burned bodies of others (sensory experiences which 'should' have been unbearable but women at the front still had to endure), and fears of suffering disability or disfigurement oneself. Both invoke an aesthetics of embodiment that does not concern disabled soldiers' and veterans' psycho-emotional experiences so much as onlookers', who typically encounter 'non-normate' bodies through a gaze conditioned to associate visible disability and disfigurement with fear and unease. Narrators' encounters with bodies robbed of their independence by amputation or rendered unrecognisable by severe burns become turning points for women's initiation into front-line war experience: the medical assistant who rallied against her fainting instinct on seeing her first wounded man, his thigh 'turned inside out' in a compound fracture; the nurse who did not tell her mother about assisting at 'unbearable' amputations, bloodied and carrying away heavy male legs 'like a baby', but instead reassured her she had warm boots and clothes; an infantry medic in her first battle at Sevsk, forced to bite off one man's arm by its remaining sinews so that she could bandage the rest of him at all.[84] All these accounts are, of course, Alexievich's edited narrative, not direct records of the women's words.

Fear of returning from the war 'crippled' or disfigured, likewise mediated through Alexievich's editing, also echoes through *Unwomanly Face*. The opening chapter, framed as testimonies by two snipers (including the story about the comrade who lost both legs saving a commander), also contains one woman remembering her mother's words after she came home 'gray-haired' and partially deaf aged twenty-one:

> I asked one thing of God, that if they disfigure you, better let them kill you.
> I went to the train station all the time . . . Once I saw a girl soldier there with
> a burned face . . . I shuddered – you! Afterward I prayed for her, too.[85]

An earlier passage in the account of Olga Yakovlevna Omelchenko, the medical assistant who fought at Sevsk, relates her company's chief of staff warning her away from the front: 'Let me at least transfer you to a medical unit. It's all very well if they kill you, but what if you're left without eyes, without arms? Have you thought of that?'[86]

The dread of being left alive but incapable, and socially unmarriageable, reverberated differently among troops depending on whether they were imagining their futures against scripts prescribed for Soviet fathers/husbands or Soviet mothers/wives. Intertwined ideologies of ability and sexuality meant that amputation and disfigurement were very widely assumed to be the end of individuals' intimate and sexual lives, therefore, heteronormatively, their social personhood.[87] Men, expected to fulfil themselves and feed their families through labour, feared destitution as an itinerant market vendor or being left to their mothers' care[88] – another medical assistant's testimony describes avoiding the market for years after the war because, among the men wheeling themselves around 'on homemade platforms', she imagined encountering a wounded lieutenant she had saved who had ordered her to shoot him instead.[89] The many women who, before departing for the front, had hoped to mature into motherhood also had to confront what it would mean, amid Stalinism's housing and food shortages, to be a permanently unmarried woman dependent on relatives. The loss of women veterans' pre-war future, Alexievich often implies, was at the heart of their tragedy: disability, in her composite narrative, sharpens the remediated contemporaneous fear that front-line service *itself* would make women unmarriageable, their reputations damaged by years spent among men.

Unwomanly Face's direct testimonies of disabled subjects, particularly *visibly* disabled subjects, are meanwhile scarcer. One tank battalion medical assistant was temporarily invalided to a Ukrainian village 'with [her] legs crippled' (the sympathy of the woman who hosted her, initially mistaking her for a boy due to her haircut and uniform, left her feeling 'so sorry for myself, and for mama. What am I doing here among men? I'm a girl. What if I come home with no legs?'), but recovered, the only girl from her village who survived.[90] An anti-aircraft artillery sergeant's testimony describes almost losing her feet to frostbite after a shrapnel wound trapped her in the snow: after six months in hospital, when the doctors wanted to amputate her leg above the knee, she planned to strangle herself with a towel, but an older nurse stopped her and the ward doctor lobbied for an experimental treatment that saved her from amputation the next day.[91]

The only extended testimony by a physically disabled female veteran belongs to Thecla Feodorovna Struy, an ex-partisan whose narrative begins by stating she had always believed Stalin and the Communists, and who had already been a Supreme Soviet deputy. Struy had suffered leg wounds in her last battle and frostbite when her German captors left the wounded in the snow. When the wounded prisoners from her unit escaped, her Party status entitled her to a rescue flight, which could not land until after her legs had been amputated in the field. Surgeons in the rear (one of whom had also lost his legs) performed four more re-amputations to excise a gangrene infection, and although '[a]t first [she] wept . . . [she] sobbed . . . [she] imagined how [she]'d go crawling on the ground', they praised her for being more stoic than any male patients and having 'never made a sound'.[92] Struy returned home after the war and became vice-chair of the district Party committee, in charge of visiting collective farms ('kolkhozes'). Struy's narrative distinguishes between the impairments of age and war-related disability when she emphasises:

[n]ow I walk poorly, because I'm old, but back then I ran around town and walked everywhere on foot. I ran around on my wooden legs; I travelled to the kolkhozes. . . . How happy I was then, though it was very, very hard for me to go from village to village. They would send me fifteen or twenty miles away, and sometimes I rode, sometimes I walked. I'd go somewhere through the forest, fall down, and be unable to get up. I'd steady myself against my bag, or cling to a tree, get up, and go on. And I received a pension, I could have lived for myself, for myself alone. But I wanted to live for others. I'm a Communist . . .[93]

Struy's narrative has itself been revised, between 1985 and 2004, when another Russian edition appeared.[94] In 1985, when reinscribing herself as a faithful Communist would actually have been closer to hegemonic public narratives about the war, the last sentences of the quoted passage instead ended 'I could have lived for myself. But I couldn't have stayed at home, I wanted to be useful. I wanted to be like everybody. I live here with my sister. They've built a house for us.'[95] The interview ended with Alexievich remarking on Struy's high ceilings and Struy saying they just seem so high 'because there are no children under them'.[96] Since this change runs counter to the direction Soviet censorship might have imposed, Galia Ackerman and Frédérick Lemarchand read it as 'an embellishment that makes the portrait of Thekla Struy more expressive: a Soviet woman proud of her past and, at the same time, fragile and dependent' – a motif repeated throughout the book to depict the composite veteran as 'a humble heroine who clings on to her past'.[97]

Even the older version of Struy's narrative, however, reveals how tightly the figure of the disabled female veteran is circumscribed. The only physically disabled veteran who (as constructed in the book) can speak of her post-war life is one whose public presentation of self has matched the post-war Soviet script for male veterans' resilience and rehabilitation as closely as possible, just like the disabled male veterans who 'fashion[ed] themselves as suffering but still striving subjects' while narrating their lives.[98] Women who suffered worse fates are only glimpsed in other women's stories, through lenses of pity or apprehension. While Struy did not become a mother, and (if living with her sister) probably did not marry, her post-war life was at least narratable in a socially and politically recognisable form. The text does not inform the reader whether any other interviewees lived with war disabilities, or how many other women silenced as disabled veterans *and* as women veterans even believed they had an intelligible subject position to be interviewed from.

Disability and disfigurement function in *Unwomanly Face* less to document disabled women's experiences, more to harness the reader's emotions in the service of Alexievich's resistance to the militarisation of Soviet society during her childhood and then the Soviet–Afghan War. The unwomanly face is, in part, the symbol of Alexievich's and her subjects' realisations that the glorious Soviet victory had had a darker side: 'for a long time I did not believe that our Victory had two faces – one beautiful and the other terrible, all scars – unbearable to look at'.[99] Combat itself transforms the face into something inhuman: Alexievich quotes Omelchenko saying that '[r]ight after an attack it's better not to look at faces; they're some kind of totally different faces, not like people usually have'.[100] Yet once we know the repeated motif is a deliberate aesthetic device for Alexievich, war's unwomanly face also becomes the agonised face of the soldier with the fractured thigh whom the nurse had to force herself to look upon as her transition into experiencing war, and the burned face of the girl soldier whose disfigurement, and its implications, haunted the sniper's mother until she came home. The identities of 'girl' and 'soldier', Alexievich suggests by including anecdotes where the categories clash, ought normatively to be incompatible, by virtue of gender combined with age: for girls imbued with Soviet mythology of war and duty to have fought en masse is depicted as a national catastrophe and inversion of the proper social order, militarisation's ultimate consequence.

Conclusion

The technique of representing war's effects through intimate sensory depictions of the war-damaged body, Alexievich hints in both *Unwomanly Face* and *Boys in Zinc*, is an aesthetic device aimed at making the reader feel war's horrific emotional consequences and thus to distance themselves from societal militarisation. A section of the introduction to *Boys in Zinc* presented as Alexievich's diary from visiting Kabul in 1988 directly opposes her to 'military socialism, a military country, military thinking . . . A human being cannot endure trials like this', and positions her writing as striving 'to reduce history to the human being'.[101] The body, its ordinariness and its dismemberment, are devices for harnessing the reader's imagination to this effect:

> All the physical details are important: the way blood changes in the sun, the human being just before he passes away. Life is incredibly artistic in itself and – cruel as this may sound – human suffering is especially artistic. The dark side of art. Just yesterday I saw them assembling the pieces of boys who had been blown up by an anti-tank mine.[102]

Ironically, the witnessing and representation of war-dismembered bodies is also the ground on which Alexievich (or the character she becomes in her narrative) has her own authority challenged by an Afghan War veteran. The threatening telephone call with which Alexievich introduces each chapter in *Boys in Zinc* comes from a voice representing himself as a veteran, speaking for his comrades.[103] The voice rejects her claim to write or know about war by appealing to what Yuval Harari calls 'flesh-witnessing',[104] an unshakeable moral authority born of direct embodied experience of war:

> Keep your hands off! My best friend, he was my brother, I brought him back from a raid in a plastic sack . . . The head separate, the arms and legs all separate . . . The skin ripped off him, like a wild boar . . . A butchered carcass . . . And he used to play the violin and write poetry. He could have written about it, but not you . . .[105]

Even if Alexievich has seen bodies in similar states, she has not had to witness a loved one's body so destroyed, and therefore – this figure or character implies – has no right to claim she knows war. The way Alexievich uses this dialogue (which she has 'imagined' in terms of incorporating it into literary narrative, even if it has originated in fact) to restate and justify her epistemology of writing about war is reminiscent of the 'imagined conversations with . . . authors' that Synne Dyvik writes of inventing while trying to make sense of how and why she researches military memoirs, which also claim authority through 'flesh-witnessing' of war.[106]

Alexievich's aesthetics of embodiment in her war narratives lie, however, not just in evoking sensory detail as emotional stimulus and literary device – a mode of perception that she suggests in *Unwomanly Face* is uniquely female,[107] even though the veterans' as well as mothers' testimonies in *Boys in Zinc* depend on it – but also in the motif of the physically disabled body, stripped of any social role after the self has experienced war. Witnesses' senses on the battlefield and civilians' senses at home are more important in these aesthetics than how disabled bodies themselves sense and perceive. As prose, her characters' testimonies about physical disability and disfigurement engage the senses through subtly different means from audiovisual film or still images of veterans whose bodies war has made non-normate. 'In literature', the disability scholar Ato Quayson writes, 'the disabled are fictional characters created out of language',[108] even when they represent real interviewees. The reader seeing, or sometimes hearing, these bodies described in language must picture their appearance in their own mind.[109] *Unwomanly Face's* lenses for understanding disabled women veterans' experiences, however, remain frames which were dominant in Soviet society: the resilient Party member, the unfulfilled potential mother and the pitiful reminder of war's toll. The sadness Alexievich tries to elicit through examples of disabled women unable to marry or have children seems a proxy, or a 'narrative prosthesis', for how she wants the reader to feel about the social fate of Red Army women writ large.

Disability studies thus illuminate the gender dynamics Alexievich constructs in the course of grounding her resistance to militarisation in the use of 'women's stories' of intimacy and grief to challenge the heroic narratives of men. They also reveal the socio-cultural and socio-economic anxieties surrounding the disabled female veteran, who even in Alexievich's collection speaks less than casualty figures would suggest she should. The experiences of Soviet women veterans disabled in World War II, and the anxieties mediated (in everyday life or in Alexievich's prose) through the symbol of the crippled or disfigured Red Army woman, are specific to Stalinist and late Soviet gender regimes and body politics, though have commonalities with experiences elsewhere. Indeed, perhaps even 'militarisation' as a concept might not fully describe how Soviet Communist ideology had always conceived of society as a collective whose members existed to do their sacrificial duty in revolution, shock work or war – another dimension, though a less racialised one, of where Alison Howell argues 'militarisation' falls short, that is, the implication that populations construed as threats to public health or order enjoyed a peaceful state before militarisation began.[110] Through the literary manipulation of testimony to sharpen its aesthetic effects, Alexievich's claim to give voice to Soviet women veterans frames itself as resisting this systemic militarism by appealing to women's experiences as truth. While Alexievich's imaginary collective subject amalgamates important differences in age, class, education, ethnicity and political background into one essential category of 'woman', her intervention against militarisation rests on an aesthetics of embodiment that did not trouble prevailing scripts about the disabled body, drawing the reader into staring at the unwomanly face of war.

Notes

1. Elaine Scarry, *The Body in Pain: The Making and Unmaking of the World* (Oxford: Oxford University Press, 1985); Joanna Bourke, *Dismembering the Male: Men's Bodies, Britain and the Great War* (London: Reaktion, 1996); Christine Sylvester, *War as Experience: Contributions from International Relations and Feminist Analysis*

(London: Routledge, 2013); Lauren B. Wilcox, *Bodies of Violence: Theorizing Embodied Subjects in International Relations* (Oxford: Oxford University Press, 2015); Jasbir Puar, *The Right to Maim: Debility, Capacity, Disability* (Durham, NC: Duke University Press, 2017).

2. See Sylvester, *War*, 66–7.

3. For example Bourke, *Dismembering*, 214.

4. Puar, *Right*, 65; Bourke, *Dismembering*, 31.

5. On these, see Jesse Paul Crane-Seeber, 'Sexy Warriors: The Politics and Pleasures of Submission to the State', *Critical Military Studies* 2:1–2 (2016): 41–55.

6. See David A. Gerber, 'Post-Modern American Heroism: Anti-War War Heroes, Survivor Heroes, and the Eclipse of Traditional Warrior Values', in *Disabled Veterans in History*, edited by David A. Gerber, 2nd ed. (Ann Arbor, MI: University of Michigan Press, 2012), 347–73, 352–9; Joanna Tidy, '(Re)Producing an (Anti)Military Masculinity: Popular Culture Representations of Gender and Military Dissent in the Figure of Ron Kovic', in *The Palgrave Handbook of Gender and the Military*, edited by Rachel Woodward and Claire Duncanson (London: Palgrave Macmillan, 2016), 509–24. See also Myrttinen, this volume.

7. Tobin Siebers, *Disability Aesthetics* (Ann Arbor, MI: University of Michigan Press, 2010), 37. See also Caso, this volume.

8. Julie M. Powell, 'About-Face: Gender, Disfigurement and the Politics of French Reconstruction, 1918–24', *Gender and History* 28:3 (2016): 604–22, 615–16.

9. Federica Caso, 'Sexing the Disabled Veteran: The Homoerotic Aesthetics of Militarism', *Critical Military Studies* 3:3 (2017): 217–34, 218, 223; David Serlin, 'Introduction', in *Phallacies: Historical Intersections of Disability and Masculinity*, edited by Kathleen M. Brian and James W. Trent, Jr (Oxford: Oxford University Press, 2017), 1–19, 1–5.

10. Marjorie Gehrhardt, '*Gueules cassées*: The Men behind the Masks', *Journal of War and Culture Studies* 6:4 (2013): 267–81.

11. Martin F. Norden, *The Cinema of Isolation: A History of Physical Disability in the Movies* (New Brunswick, NJ: Rutgers University Press, 1994); Gerber, 'Heroism'.

12. Judith Butler, *Frames of War: When is Life Grievable?* (London: Verso, 2009).

13. Kenneth T. MacLeish, *Making War at Fort Hood: Life and Uncertainty in a Military Community* (Princeton, NJ: Princeton University Press, 2013); Zoe Wool, *After War: The Weight of Life at Walter Reed* (Durham, NC: Duke University Press, 2015); Alison Howell, 'Resilience, War, and Austerity: The Ethics of Military Human Enhancement and the Politics of Data', *Security Dialogue* 46:1 (2015): 15–31.

14. Caso, 'Sexing'; Tidy, 'Dissent'; Laura Mills, 'Spectacle, Sport and Subjectivity: Aesthetic (Dis)Embodiment and the Invictus Games', paper presented at the International Studies Association Annual Convention, Baltimore, 22–5 February 2017.

15. Lennard J. Davis, *Enforcing Normalcy: Disability, Deafness, and the Body* (London: Verso, 1995); see Rosemarie Garland-Thomson, *Extraordinary Bodies: Figuring Disability in American Culture and Literature* (New York: Columbia University

Press, 1997); David T. Mitchell and Sharon Snyder (eds), *The Body and Physical Difference: Discourses of Disability* (Ann Arbor, MI: University of Michigan Press, 1997); Rosemarie Garland-Thomson, *Staring: How We Look* (Oxford: Oxford University Press, 2009).

16. Aliaksandr Novikau, 'Women, Wars and Militarism in Svetlana Alexievich's Documentary Prose', *Media, War & Conflict* 10:3 (2017): 314–26.

17. See Angela Brintlinger, 'Mothers, Father(s), Daughter: Svetlana Aleksievich and *The Unwomanly Face of War*', *Canadian Slavonic Papers* 59:3–4 (2017): 196–213; Daniel Bush, '"No Other Proof": Svetlana Aleksievich in the Tradition of Soviet War Writing', *Canadian Slavonic Papers* 59:3–4 (2017): 214–33. On comparative literature, see Emily Apter, *The Translation Zone: A New Comparative Literature* (Princeton, NJ: Princeton University Press, 2006).

18. For example Viv Groskop, 'The Unwomanly Face of War by Svetlana Alexievich Review: "A Monument to Courage"', *The Observer*, 23 July 2017. https://www.theguardian.com/books/2017/jul/23/unwomanly-face-of-war-svetlana-alexievich-monument-to-courage-soviet-women-war; Caroline Moorehead, 'The Unwomanly Face of War by Svetlana Alexievich Review: For "Filth" Read Truth', *The Guardian*, 2 August 2017. https://www.theguardian.com/books/2017/aug/02/unwomanly-face-of-war-svetlana-alexievich-review.

19. Heather J. Coleman, 'Svetlana Alexievich: The Writer and Her Times', *Canadian Slavonic Papers* 59:3–4 (2017): 193–5, 193 (original emphasis).

20. See Jean Bethke Elshtain, *Women and War* (New York: Basic Books, 1987), xii.

21. On the active re-production of narrative in military oral history interviews, see Alistair Thomson, *Anzac Memories: Living with the Legend*, 2nd ed. (Melbourne: Monash University Press, 2013).

22. On women's roles under Stalin, see Lynne Attwood, *Creating the New Soviet Woman: Women's Magazines as Engineers of Female Identity, 1922–53* (Basingstoke: Palgrave Macmillan, 1999).

23. Kerstin Bischl, 'Female Red Army Soldiers in World War II and Beyond', in *Gender in 20th Century Eastern Europe and the USSR*, edited by Catherine Baker (London: Palgrave Macmillan, 2017), 113–26, 121.

24. David T. Mitchell and Sharon Snyder, 'Introduction: Disability Studies and the Double Bind of Representation', in *The Body and Physical Difference*, edited by Mitchell and Snyder, 1–31, 5.

25. Tobin Siebers, *Disability Theory* (Ann Arbor, MI: University of Michigan Press, 2008), 3.

26. See Carol Thomas, *Female Forms: Experiencing and Understanding Disability* (Buckingham: Open University Press, 1999), 115–16.

27. Davis, *Normalcy*, 128.

28. Rosemarie Garland-Thomson, *Extraordinary Bodies: Figuring Physical Disability in American Culture and Literature* (New York: Columbia University Press, 1997), 8; Siebers, *Disability Theory*, 6.

29. David T. Mitchell and Sharon Snyder, 'Narrative Prosthesis', in *The Disability Studies Reader*, edited by Lennard J. Davis (London: Routledge, 2013), 222–35, 222, 224.

30. Thomas, *Female Forms*, 47.

31. Donna Reeve, 'Psycho-Emotional Disablism: The Missing Link?' in *The Routledge Handbook of Disability Studies*, edited by Carol Thomas, Nick Watson and Alan Roulstone (London: Routledge, 2012), 78–92, 80.

32. See Florentina C. Andreescu, 'Face and Facial Disfigurations: Self and Alterations of Self', *Psychotherapy and Politics International* 15:2 (2017): e1407.

33. See Ana Carden-Coyne, *Reconstructing the Body: Classicism, Modernism and the First World War* (Oxford: Oxford University Press, 2009); David A. Gerber, 'Heroes and Misfits: The Troubled Social Reintegration of Disabled Veterans in *The Best Years of Our Lives*', in *Disabled Veterans in History*, edited Gerber, 70–95, 74–6; Elsbeth Bösl, '"An Unbroken Man Despite Losing an Arm": Corporeal Reconstruction and Embodied Difference – Prosthetics in Western Germany after the Second World War (c. 1945–1960)', in *War and the Body: Militarisation, Practice and Experience*, edited by Kevin McSorley (London: Routledge, 2013), 167–80, 175–6.

34. Bourke, *Dismembering*; Carden-Coyne, *Reconstructing*; Powell, 'About-Face'.

35. Carden-Coyne, *Reconstructing*, 8, 74.

36. Siebers, *Disability Theory*, 8.

37. Carden-Coyne, *Reconstructing*, 4, 103; see Siebers, *Disability Theory*, 8.

38. Carden-Coyne, *Reconstructing*, 77.

39. Suzannah Biernoff, 'The Rhetoric of Disfigurement in First World War Britain', *Social History of Medicine* 24:3 (2011): 666–85, 666, 674.

40. Biernoff, 'Rhetoric', 671.

41. Ibid., 672.

42. Joe Kember, 'Face Value: The Rhetoric of Facial Disfigurement in American Film and Popular Culture, 1917–1927', *Journal of War and Culture Studies* 10:1 (2017): 43–65, 44–5.

43. Sharon Sliwinski, 'Face of Our Wartime', *Photography and Culture* 8:2 (2015): 233–41.

44. Suzannah Biernoff, *Portraits of Violence: War and the Aesthetics of Disfigurement* (Ann Arbor, MI: University of Michigan Press, 2017), 1.

45. Samantha Wehbi, 'Representing Disability and Disfigurement: Modes of Representation in Nina Berman's Photographs', *Disability Studies Quarterly* 32:1 (2012). http://dsq-sds.org/article/view/3035/3033; see Garland-Thomson, *Staring*.

46. Beate Fieseler, 'The Bitter Legacy of the "Great Patriotic War": Red Army Disabled Soldiers under Late Stalinism', in *Late Stalinist Russia: Society between Reconstruction and Reinvention*, edited by Juliane Fürst (London: Routledge, 2006), 46–61; Mark Edele, *Soviet Veterans of World War II: A Popular Movement in an Authoritarian Society, 1941–1991* (Oxford: Oxford University Press, 2008), 81–102; Ethel Dunn, 'Disabled Russian War Veterans: Surviving the Collapse of the Soviet Union', in *Disabled Veterans in History*, edited by Gerber, 251–71.

47. Sarah D. Phillips, '"There Are No Invalids in the USSR!": A Missing Soviet Chapter in the New Disability History', *Disability Studies Quarterly* 29:3 (2009). http://www.dsq-sds.org/article/view/936/1111.

48. See Fieseler, 'Legacy', 46–7.
49. See Anna Krylova, *Soviet Women in Combat: A History of Violence on the Eastern Front* (Cambridge: Cambridge University Press, 2010); Roger D. Markwick and Euridice Charon Cardona, *Soviet Women on the Frontline in the Second World War* (Basingstoke: Palgrave Macmillan, 2012); Bischl, 'Soldiers'.
50. See Bischl, 'Soldiers'.
51. Frances Bernstein, 'Prosthetic Manhood in the Soviet Union at the End of World War II', *Osiris* 30 (2015): 113–33, 115.
52. Ibid., 131.
53. Gerber, 'Heroes', 76.
54. Bernstein, 'Manhood', 131.
55. Maria Cristina Galmarini-Kabala, *The Right to be Helped: Deviance, Entitlement, and the Soviet Moral Order* (DeKalb, IL: Northern Illinois University Press, 2016), 186.
56. Maria Cristina Galmarini, 'Turning Defects to Advantages: The Discourse of Labour in the Autobiographies of Soviet Blinded Second World War Veterans', *European History Quarterly* 44:4 (2014): 651–77, 652.
57. Bernstein, 'Manhood', 129.
58. Anna Krylova, '"Healers of Wounded Souls": The Crisis of Private Life in Soviet Literature, 1944–6', *Journal of Modern History* 73:2 (2001): 307–31, 310.
59. Ibid., 310.
60. Ibid., 326.
61. Ibid., 326.
62. Bush, '"Proof"', 216–17.
63. Dunn, 'Veterans', 254.
64. Igor Shiryaev, 'The Sorrowful Artist Gennady Dobrov', *Different View*, 1 September 2014. https://web.archive.org/web/20140908021838/http://www.diff-view.com/the-artist-gennady-dobrov/.
65. Krylova, '"Healers"', 330.
66. Svetlana Alexievich, *The Unwomanly Face of War*, translated by Richard Pevear and Larissa Volonkhonsky (London: Penguin, 2017), xii.
67. Ibid., xiii.
68. Jeffrey W. Jones, 'Mothers, Prostitutes, and the Collapse of the USSR: The Representation of Women in Svetlana Alexievich's *Zinky Boys*', *Canadian Slavonic Papers* 59:3–4 (2017): 234–58, 237.
69. Krylova, '"Healers"', 330.
70. Ibid., 330.
71. Novikau, 'Women', 318.
72. See Sherna Berger Gluck and Daphne Patai (eds), *Women's Words: The Feminist Practice of Oral History* (London: Routledge, 1991).
73. Novikau, 'Women', 320.
74. Bush, '"Proof"', 216.
75. Anna Kadykało, 'The Afghan War (1979–1989) in the Cultural Memory of the Russians', *Cultural Analysis* 14 (2015): 48–85, 54.

76. Bush, '"Proof"', 217.
77. Holly Myers, 'Svetlana Alexievich's Changing Narrative of the Soviet–Afghan War in *Zinky Boys*', *Canadian Slavonic Papers* 59:3–4 (2017): 330–54, 346.
78. Myers, 'Narrative', 346.
79. Bush, '"Proof"', 227.
80. Novikau, 'Women', 323.
81. Bush, '"Proof"', 218–19. The 2017 translation renders the wounded woman's line 'I don't want to live like this', and includes the paragraph as part of Klavdia Grigoryevna Krokhina's story, though Bush ('"Proof"', 218) attributes it to Krokhina's friend Mariia Ivanova Morozova, and indeed a line on the previous page of the translation relates the speaker being addressed as 'Maruska' (a diminutive of Mariia), not a name derived from Klavdia: Alexievich, *Unwomanly Face*, 15–16.
82. Bush, '"Proof"', 219.
83. Davis, *Normalcy*, 43.
84. Alexievich, *Unwomanly Face*, 59, 62, 136.
85. Ibid., 10–11.
86. Ibid., 135.
87. See Anna Mollow and Robert McRuer, 'Introduction', in *Sex and Disability*, edited by Robert McRuer and Anna Mollow (Durham, NC: Duke University Press, 2012), 1–36.
88. See Edele, *Soviet Veterans*, 92–5.
89. Alexievich, *Unwomanly Face*, 155.
90. Ibid., 83.
91. Ibid., 107–8.
92. Ibid., 272.
93. Ibid., 273.
94. Galia Ackerman and Frédérick Lemarchand, 'Du bon et du mauvais usage de témoignage dans l'œuvre de Svetlana Alexievitch', *Tumultes* 32–3:1 (2009), 21–2. https://www.cairn.info/revue-tumultes-2009-1-page-29.htm.
95. Ibid., 17–19.
96. Ibid., 17–19.
97. Ibid., 25.
98. Galmarini, 'Turning Defects to Advantages', 653.
99. Alexievich, *Unwomanly Face*, xli.
100. Ibid., 135.
101. Svetlana Alexievich, *Boys in Zinc*, translated by Andrew Bromfield (London: Penguin, 2017), 16, 18.
102. Alexievich, *Boys*, 19–20.
103. Jones, 'Collapse', 242; Myers, 'Narrative', 339.
104. Yuval Noah Harari, 'Scholars, Eyewitnesses, and Flesh-Witnesses of War: A Tense Relationship', *Partial Answers* 7:2 (2009): 213–28, 214–15.
105. Alexievich, *Boys*, 23.
106. Synne L. Dyvik, 'Of Bats and Bodies: Methods for Reading and Writing Embodiment', *Critical Military Studies* 2:1–2 (2016): 56–69, 57, 64.

107. Alexievich, *Unwomanly Face*, xxi.
108. Ato Quayson, *Aesthetic Nervousness: Disability and the Crisis of Representation* (New York: Columbia University Press, 2007), 27.
109. See Carden-Coyne, *Reconstructing*, 74 (on war poetry).
110. Alison Howell, 'Forget "Militarization": Race, Disability and the "Martial Politics" of the Police and of the University', *International Feminist Journal of Politics* 20:2 (2018): 117–36, 118.

CHAPTER 4

Breaking the Silence: Embodiment, Militarisation and Military Dissent in the Israel/Palestine Conflict

Sorana Jude

This chapter studies the testimonies of violence published by the Israeli veteran organisation Breaking the Silence (Shovrim Shtika) and explores the role of embodiment as a means of military dissent within the Israel/ Palestine conflict. These testimonies represent aesthetic practices that describe the violent behaviour of the Israel Defence Forces (IDF) in the Occupied Palestinian Territories (oPt) and illustrate soldiers' embodied experiences of fear, shame, remorse or empathy for Palestinians during their military service under the occupation. Interested in the political power of emotions within military dissent, this chapter shows that the activism of Breaking the Silence (BtS) is in fact interweaved with the same ideas of power, hierarchy and violence that it seeks to challenge. It argues that dissenting military practices are fraught with contradictions, ambivalences and ambiguities that may actually reinforce, rather than destabilise, the militarised discourses that sustain the Israel/Palestine conflict. Despite the best efforts of this organisation in intervening in the dynamics of Israeli militarisation, the aesthetics of BtS activism show that military dissent draws on and discloses embodied experiences which reproduce military masculinity, validate militarism and may legitimise the further enactment of violence within the Israel/ Palestine conflict.

The organisation was established in 2004 by a group of Israeli veterans in order to warn the Israeli public about the moral deterioration of the military and society through the continuous deployment of the IDF in the oPt. It believes that confronting the Israeli public with Israeli soldiers' intimate military experiences will eventually lead the public to put pressure on the political leadership to end the occupation:

> We endeavor to stimulate public debate about the price paid for a reality in which young soldiers face a civilian population on a daily basis and are engaged in the control of that population's everyday life. Our work aims to bring an end to the occupation. While this reality is well-known to Israeli soldiers and commanders, Israeli society in general continues to turn a blind eye, and to deny what is being done in its name.[1]

Yehuda Shaul, a former infantry commander in the IDF, founded BtS after having served in the oPt during the Second Intifada (2000–5). The occupation, according to him, has a significant moral impact on Israeli society: 'We are in a very bad condition. It is almost a crime today in Israel to have empathy for the suffering of the other side, even though you are talking about women and children.'[2] Therefore, the testimonies published by BtS invite the Israeli society to reflect upon the moral implications of using the military as an instrument of occupation: 'Who are we as a society? The question is whether dropping all these bombs on families is something acceptable or not.'[3] For this organisation, emotional military experiences are instrumental in contesting the Israeli government's occupation policy and the society's indifference to the IDF's violence against Palestinians.

Embodied experiences of war like these become particularly significant through feminist approaches to international relations, which study emotions, bodies and war in order to challenge the disembodied language that characterises conventional studies of war.[4] Critical engagement with bodily experiences of war has revealed that emotions play an important role in soldiers' military life. This is particularly true about soldiers who, like the Israeli ones, interact daily with Palestinian civilians during their operations in urban spaces. Research on Israeli soldiers' frustration, confusion, fear or boredom shows that emotions influence their violent behaviour against Palestinians.[5]

Emphasising the idea of military dissent as an affective process, this chapter focuses on the political role of emotions embedded in and produced by BtS testimonies. It therefore builds on Sara Ahmed's argument that emotions are 'social and cultural practices' that 'do not reside in subjects or objects, but are produced as effects of circulation'.[6] Ahmed cautions that emotions, through their movement and accumulation, determine orientation towards some bodies and away from other bodies while differentiating between 'those that *can be* loved, those that *can be* grieved' and those that cannot, thus 'constituting some other as the legitimate objects of emotion' while disavowing the emotions of others.[7] In the BtS testimonies and in how they are presented to the Israeli public, the legitimate objects of emotion remain members of the Israeli military, not Palestinians.

The use of testimony as an aesthetic intervention against militarisation can be compared with the subject of the previous chapter in this volume (by Catherine Baker), Svetlana Alexievich's *The Unwomanly Face of War*. This collection of testimonies, albeit gathered by one writer rather than an activist organisation and arranged much more self-consciously into a single literary text, was also a use of written representations of embodied military experiences to make a personal aesthetic intervention against the militarisation of the society in which the editor(s) of the testimonies lived. By collecting, mediating and circulating soldiers' intimate experiences of military service with the aim of encouraging the Israeli public to engage in anti-occupation activism, the BtS testimonies of violence seek to make similar aesthetic interventions in the Israel/ Palestine conflict to those that Baker has argued Alexievich wanted to make in 1980s Soviet society, but with a more direct political objective.

The dissent expressed by BtS through using representations of soldiers' embodied experience as a form of activism is nevertheless, this chapter argues, still entangled with the militarised discourses that it aims to contest. In particular, it remains bounded by what Gada Mahrouse in her work on transnational solidarity activism refers to as 'contradictions and tensions related to whiteness, solidarity, privilege and power'.[8] The testimonies of violence published by BtS, contrary to their stated effect, ultimately reinforce the exceptionality and morality of the Israeli military by presenting soldiers as authoritative figures in speaking against the occupation, as individuals who are morally, emotionally and physically superior to Palestinians, and as reflective figures whose encounter with Palestinians has impact on their personal and military life.

This chapter is based on the archive of testimonies that is publicly available on the official website of BtS, which at the time of writing contained 665 testimonies collected into eleven booklets. They were analysed through a lens combining Feminist Critical Discourse Analysis with methodological investigations of emotions in international politics.[9] Feminist Critical Discourse Analysis combines feminist studies with Critical Discourse Analysis in order to investigate the gendered discursive practices that sustain power asymmetry in the social world. It also takes account of the intersections between gender, race, ethnicity, class, religion, sexuality or geography in showing the convergence between power and ideology in discourse.[10] To this end, this chapter regards Israeli testimonies of violence as discursive practices of military dissent and shows that the emotions 'expressed and communicated' in these testimonies reveal ideas about power, identity and hierarchy within the activism of BtS.[11]

This chapter thus contributes to a growing body of literature that analyses military experiences through aesthetic representations such as memoirs, films or digital representations in order to criticise expressions of militarism.[12] It argues that military dissent is an affective process, which mobilises and elicits emotions with the aim to end the occupation. By exploring the role of lived experiences within military dissent, this chapter develops our understanding of the entanglement between embodiment, aesthetics and militarisation. Showing that these aesthetic and affective practices may nevertheless reinforce militarised discourses has practical and political implications for the conduct of Israeli military dissent. It invites activists themselves to question their own privilege of speaking against the occupation, to recognise their activism draws on and reinforces militarism in Israel, and to acknowledge their dissent inadvertently rehearses the same gendered and racialised power relations that sustain the militarisation of Israeli society.

Although these many testimonies can be seen as relying on the same discursive logic, this chapter does not suggest that all their themes are completely identical. Instead, by interrogating their meaning within the context of military dissent, it proposes one analysis among possible ones. This chapter's reading of the testimonies highlights the discursive themes that construct an authoritative, self-reflexive and compassionate military figure within BtS testimonies, and then assesses the role of this figure in reinforcing the militarisation of Israeli society. The chapter concludes by addressing the political and practical significance of studying embodiment as a means of military dissent within the Israel/Palestine conflict. By exploring the entanglement between embodiment, aesthetics and militarisation within the activism of BtS, it argues that emotions mobilised and provoked through dissent may reinforce the militarised discourses that sanction violence and injustice within the Israel/Palestine conflict.

The Authoritative Figure of the Israeli Soldier

The testimonies published by BtS constitute the Israeli soldier as an authoritative figure, who possesses privileged access to the reality of the occupation. Capitalising on their prior presence in the oPt, soldiers provide extensive descriptions of the space in which they serve, their emotional experiences and the Palestinians they encounter during their deployment. A female sergeant describes her first tour of duty as follows:

> Just as we got there, you know, it really hits you. So we got there and I had to put on a ceramic bullet-proof, as far as I remember we rode a Hummer or Jeep, don't remember which, one of those large ones. We get there and I'm told, 'Come on out,' and I say: No way, I'm not coming out. 'Why?' Because I'm in Hebron, in the Territories, I'm not coming out. But I was excited with it all and thinking, wow, I'm seeing things that no one else gets to see.[13]

A sergeant provides a similar description of his military service at Erez checkpoint in the Gaza Strip:

> So you get there at 3 o'clock and there are thousands of people waiting, and a soldier yells in Arabic to open the door. Think about it, it's nighttime, and cold and stinking and everything there is made of concrete and metal. It looks like, I don't know how to describe it, horrible.[14]

Through testimonies that describe the space in which soldiers perform their military service and that offer representations of embodied experiences of fear, disgust, anxiety or uneasiness, BtS activists position themselves as experts who understand and explain the occupation to the local and international public. They assert authority to describe the immorality of the occupation and imply the credibility of their dissent. Therefore, these detailed sensory descriptions permit BtS to 'maintain a hierarchical positioning as experts, truth-tellers and the voices of reason'.[15] Similarly, Sara Ahmed insists that when 'narratives of proximity are *authorized as knowledge*' we witness a process of subjective formation through which the 'Western subject can *have* the difference and hence *knows* the difference'.[16] Within these authoritative narratives, Palestinians appear solely as background silhouettes, whose presence confirms activists' commanding knowledge about the occupation.

Due to their insistence on the lived experiences of military service, the Israeli soldiers' testimonies resemble military memoirs. Like military memoirs, soldiers' testimonies also claim that they communicate authentic embodied experience of military service to wider audiences.[17] Reflecting what Yuval Noah Harari has called the 'authority of flesh-witnessing' the reality of the occupation – the same authority claimed by the veteran who purportedly challenged Svetlana Alexievich's right to write about war discussed in the previous chapter – the soldiers' testimonies communicate the authenticity of military lived experience in order (BtS hopes) to end the occupation.[18] Also like military memoirs, however, the testimonies raise issues concerning the accuracy of the events presented and their production, circulation and consumption as representations of military life.[19]

BtS insists its testimonies provide a truthful representation of the violence of the occupation, and has stood up for their veracity during public debates about the testimonies' authenticity. In 2017, the Minister of Justice, Ayelet Shaked, launched an investigation against Dean Issacharoff, the BtS spokesperson, who had disclosed that he had assaulted a Palestinian during his military service in Hebron. After several months, the Israeli State Attorney Office concluded that the assault did not take place, thus portraying Issacharoff as a liar. Accusing the State Attorney of compromising the integrity of the organisation and failing to conduct a thorough investigation, BtS released a video showing Issacharoff assaulting the Palestinian, thus revealing that the prosecution had actually interviewed the wrong victim.[20]

Political elites are not the sole actors trying to restrict BtS's activism. Israeli right-wing organisations have increasingly launched a smear campaign against BtS in order to delegitimise its activism. In 2015, Im Tirtzu, an organisation that seeks to delegitimise Israeli left-wing and human rights organisations, accused BtS of supporting Palestinian terrorism.[21] Two years later, it was disclosed that Ad Kan, a right-wing group that supports the building of settlements in the West Bank, had hired an individual called Chaim Fremd to infiltrate BtS and secretly videotape its staff in order to sabotage their work.[22] These efforts to delegitimise the BtS activism indicate the growing influence of the right-wing and settler movement within the Israeli society and political sphere alike. Accepting that some criticism of BtS has been politically motivated, however, does not change the fact that these testimonies are their authors' personal perspectives on the reality of the occupation, created and selected for the purpose of ending the occupation. These testimonies filter reality and provide partial and selective representations of military service in order to express dissent. Yehuda Shaul argues that

> in a way Breaking the Silence operates in a very simple logic; you send us to do the job, we went there, we've done it, we're back, we're not going to tell you who to vote for, but there's one thing we demand – that you sit down and listen to what we've done.[23]

Therefore, these testimonies 'should be read not as innocent tales of reality but as strategic interventions' within the Israel/Palestine conflict in order to end the occupation.[24]

Although reflecting an intimate military experience, these testimonies are collectively edited and produced. They are collected through anonymous individual interviews and are crosschecked in order to ensure their accuracy: 'For every story we demand two eyewitnesses, we conduct an investigation [by speaking] with other soldiers, record conversations and verify with B'Tselem [the Israeli Information Center for Human Rights in the Occupied Territories] and other organizations.'[25] Nevertheless, some soldiers have agreed to disclose their identity in order to enhance the political impact of their activism.[26] A further layer of control affecting the testimonies is organisational censorship: BtS cooperates with the Israeli military in order to ensure testimonies do not disclose sensitive information, since members might face imprisonment if they break operational security rules,[27] and equally significantly, the IDF might welcome co-operation with the BtS in order to conduct its own investigations. For instance, the former IDF Chief of Staff, Gadi Eisenkot, has asked the military to work with BtS in order to investigate their claims that the IDF breached international law during Operation Protective Edge in the Gaza Strip in 2014.[28] Far from being individualised products, therefore, the testimonies are produced through an interactive process that involves a variety of actors: the Israeli soldier that testifies, the interviewer that asks questions during the testimony, the military institution, and other human rights activists.

Finally, yet significantly, these testimonies also go through a process of translation from Hebrew to English. Although these testimonies do not provide any information concerning the translation process, translators usually bring their own knowledge into the process of translation and interpretation since they approach a text through the lens of their own social position.[29] Translators attach meaning to the testimonies they engage with on the basis of their own experiences of the world while shaping them in such a manner in order to appeal to an English-speaking audience.

In order to elicit the attention of their English-speaking audience, most of the booklets circulated on the BtS website are preceded by an introductory text and by a map that represents the West Bank, the Gaza Strip or specific locations such as Hebron. The introductory texts provide a succinct presentation of BtS, highlight its mission to raise public awareness among the Israeli public concerning the impact of the occupation on Israelis and Palestinians alike, and provide background knowledge about the specific issues addressed in these testimonies. For instance, the booklet that addresses the Israeli Jewish settlers' violence in the West Bank introduces readers to settlers' violence against both Palestinians and Israeli troops, and exposes settlers' efforts to intervene in the military chain of command.[30] Interestingly enough, the booklet that addresses the Israeli soldiers' violence during Operation Protective Edge (2014) is the only booklet that includes photographic evidence, which shows the extensive destruction of the Gaza Strip in the aftermath of the military intervention.[31] Photographic evidence helps BtS to prove the authenticity of its testimonies, to tap into the growing international criticism against the Israeli military and to challenge the Israeli public's support for the military's interventions in the oPt. During the Operation Protective Edge, polls revealed that almost 91 per cent of Israelis supported the intervention and almost 85 per cent opposed a ceasefire while only 4 per cent opposed the war.[32] Visual representation may lead the Israeli public to question its support for the military and to enhance its criticism against the IDF's violent behaviour. These introductory texts contextualise the aims of the activism of BtS and give readers the opportunity to familiarise themselves with the structural violence of the occupation and its impact on Palestinians' everyday lives. In this way, readers are invited to express disapproval with the structural violence of the occupation even before reading the actual testimonies, an approach that is likely to enhance public support for BtS activism.

The Gendered Voice of Anti-Occupation Activism

Although the first testimony discussed in this chapter happened to be from a female soldier, the testimonies published by BtS are heavily gendered insofar as the majority of them are collected from male combat soldiers. By claiming that 'we're all ex-combat soldiers, in a way we've earned the right to speak out', BtS associates the authoritative nature of its testimonies with the soldiers' martial behaviour under the occupation.[33] For instance, a First Sergeant from the Kfir Brigade describes the Border Police's violence against Palestinians:

> They didn't give a damn, they go around breaking people's knees just like that. I remember once some Arab was caught throwing stones, they put his leg up against the wall as he lay on the ground and, boom, someone just stepped on his knee. No mercy.[34]

Similarly, a First Sergeant describes the military's extensive violence during Operation Protective Edge in the Gaza Strip:

> I remember that the level of destruction looked insane to me. It looked like a movie set, it didn't look real. Every house had a hole in the wall or a balcony spilling off of it, no trace left of any streets at all.[35]

The prevalence of the male voice within these testimonies indicates that the Israeli military is a male-dominated institution. Due to Israel's compulsory draft, women have served in the IDF since 1948. At first, they served in administrative positions but servicewomen have gradually moved into operational positions due to shortage in human power and pressures from feminist groups.[36] According to the IDF, the number of women serving in combat roles has increased significantly in the past several years. Whereas in 2012 the military recruited 547 female combat soldiers, it was reported that in 2018, 1,050 women joined combat units. However, women hold only around 7 per cent of combat roles.[37] It is estimated that women make up 32 per cent of the military and the majority of them serve in 'feminine' roles such as administrative positions, Hebrew language teachers or social workers.[38] Orna Sasson-Levy shows that women both accept and challenge the hegemonic masculinity of the Israeli military by incorporating 'masculine' traits in their behaviour, distancing themselves from assumed feminine traits or by trivialising sexual harassment.[39]

In 2009, BtS published a collection of testimonies from female soldiers, who had served either in combat or in support roles.[40] These testimonies indicate the complexity of women's role in the Israeli military. Female soldiers justify their violence against Palestinians as a means to gain recognition within the Israeli military. At the same time, the Israeli female soldiers' testimonies criticise the Israeli military's hegemonic masculinity by condemning the male soldiers' abuse against Palestinians, by identifying with the Palestinians they encounter, or by detailing instances of sexual harassment.[41] A First Sergeant insists that a woman has to demonstrate that she is 'capable' and 'a ball-breaker' in order to be accepted by her male peers.[42] Another sergeant condemns the failure of the Israeli military to investigate her male comrades' swift decision to kill a Palestinian boy despite evidence he did not pose any threat.[43] A third servicewoman describes male soldiers' violent behaviour against Palestinians during detention.[44] A former education officer condemns the constant humiliation and sexual harassment that she experienced while serving within the military.[45] Finally, yet significantly, a servicewoman discloses the shame she had experienced when she accompanied her unit in order to search a house in Hebron: 'I felt ashamed of the way we were behaving. I just wanted to die right then and there.'[46] Although both female and male soldiers' testimonies draw on the same martial language and privileged position in order to speak against the occupation, the servicewomen's testimonies indicate a profound relation between militarism, sexism and the violence of the occupation. Whereas female soldiers' violence against Palestinians may steam from a desire to be accepted by their male peers, these testimonies show servicewomen are both agents and victims of militarisation.[47]

Through their gendered configuration, these testimonies constitute dissent as a masculine act due to their reliance on symbols that denote masculinity: martial language, disclosure of their rank and combat experience (masculinised military symbols), and emphasis on violence against Palestinians.[48] The intersection between activism, militarisation and manhood rehearses 'the centrality and importance of militarism as a masculine ideology' in the Israeli military and Israeli society.[49] Dissenting military practices are ultimately quelled by hegemonic discourses that celebrate masculinity, militarism and martial violence.

The activism of BtS is not, however, shaped solely by gender, but rather by intersections between race, gender, ethnicity and class. Through its dissent, BtS idealises the Israeli model of citizenship that is based on the image of the combat soldier, which is largely drawn from the middle-class (white) Ashkenazi Jewish group.[50] It is estimated that the majority of the testimonies come from Israeli Jews that identify themselves as middle-class Jews, whereas 10–15 per cent of these testimonies come from Israeli Jews of different background.[51] The Ashkenazi Jews distinguish themselves from Mizrahi Jews, Oriental Jews of Middle Eastern origins, who have historically been relegated to a lower status in the Israeli military and Israeli society.[52] The Israeli movement of military dissent represents yet another sphere of activity within which Ashkenazi Jews assert their privileged position in the Israeli society. Speaking against the IDF and the occupation may not always be an option for Mizrahi Jews who perceive military service as an opportunity to gain a steady income and social recognition in Israel. Criticism of the military may result in jail time that could deprive Mizrahi Jewish families of significant financial resources.[53] Studying embodiment as a means of Israeli dissent as a reflection of the ethnic, racial and gendered hierarchies within Israel speaks to Marsha Henry's argument that intersectionality is a useful concept to reveal and question the power relations that are inherent to the construction of Israeli military masculinity.[54] Henry criticises Sasson-Levy and other scholars for failing to engage the role of race within the construction of Israeli military masculinity and to relate the inequalities that emerge within the Israeli military with the structural oppression of Palestinians.[55]

The engagement with Israeli military dissent responds to Henry's critique by showing that the activism of BtS is intertwined with discourses of superiority, power, gender, race and privilege that inform the construction of Israeli military masculinity and dominate the militarisation of

Israeli society. The insistence on soldiers' experiences of military service constitutes the IDF as morally and racially superior through their constant emphasis on soldiers' bodies and emotions in their testimonies to the detriment of Palestinians. Therefore, the reiteration of soldiers' experiences of military service shows that military dissent is infused 'by a racial logic and underpinned by a material system of white privilege' that permeates the Israeli military and Israeli society alike and, more significantly, has dire consequences for Palestinians living under the occupation.[56]

The Transformative Process of Military Service

The desire to raise awareness about the Israeli military's violence under the occupation is linked with some of the Israeli soldiers' sense of unease felt upon their return to civilian life. Yehuda Shaul insists that the end of his military service represented a moment of self-realisation: 'It's only when you take one step out and you see things from a different perspective, that's when you realize that something is wrong and we have to do something about it.'[57] Shaul and his comrades used the process of self-recovery in order to launch BtS as a means to interrogate the Israeli society's indifference to the violence of the occupation.

The Israeli soldiers' testimonies insist on the transformative impact that military service has upon their (prior) knowledge of the occupation. A female lieutenant from the Education Corps recalls that seeing a Palestinian man dying enabled her to acknowledge the moral corruption of the military: 'You simply see the tank shell coming and blowing him up. When you get out of things for a second it just doesn't make sense.'[58] Similarly, a male soldier who manned a checkpoint highlights that military service challenged his stereotypical beliefs about Palestinians and enabled him to become a better person:

> I kept hearing how they might shoot me, how they could hurt me from various spots in town. I see people who have nothing to do with all of that. I'd be in situations where – I don't know how else to put this – I'd disobey orders or something of that sort, just to be able to live with myself, doing the right thing at a given moment. Because anyone who decides that a certain place is out of bounds, or places a curfew so that people can't get out of their homes for over half a year, does not really know the situation on the ground the way we do, as soldiers who man the post and know these people.[59]

Military service becomes an opportunity to develop a humane attitude. By highlighting the discrepancy between those that decide about curfews and soldiers like himself who know the situation on the ground, the soldier insists that he knows and understands the Palestinians' experience of living under the occupation. The soldier's decision to disobey orders shows his privileged position to *'unmake the border between self and other'*.[60] Narratives of self-discovery like this, which celebrate individual transformation, ultimately sustain the exceptionality of the Israeli military. Soldiers envisage themselves as moral individuals who are ready to help Palestinians, yet disregarding their presence in the oPt is violent in itself.

Furthermore, these testimonies show the process of self-discovery is accompanied by an expectation of Palestinians' indebtedness to the Israeli soldiers for their appropriate behaviour. A soldier insists that 'you remember that actually you're in his favor, but you're not supposed to let him pass, and how dare he stand there in front of you proud and all'.[61] The soldier appears sympathetic to Palestinians' life under the occupation yet he arrogantly expects them to obey his commands. Another soldier insists that his urge to act violently is caused by Palestinians' lack of impatience:

> The [Palestinian] woman with the elderly mother is yelling in your face, and
> you yell at them all the time and you go crazy. So you start to raise your
> weapon, as if you're really going to do something with it.[62]

These narratives of proximity show the Israeli soldiers' effort to act as professionally as possible under the dire circumstances of the occupation. They show soldiers both acknowledge and disassociate themselves from the violence of the occupation by constructing Palestinians as sources of their ethical and unethical behaviour alike.

The Compassionate Figure

The Israeli soldiers' expressions of compassion for Palestinians indicate that their dissent blends with a racialising attitude. A soldier recalled the moment in which he felt compassion for a teenager who was punished by his father for having thrown stones:

> Usually the parents, [sic] start beating their kid up so you won't beat him up.
> He reminded me so much of my dad, really, I couldn't even look at him. I went
> over and said to him: 'Listen, I'm asking you, really, just take your kid and go.'
> You look at them, they have such a different culture, they behave differently,
> they live differently at home, everything. Then suddenly you see something
> that's so similar to you, to yours, even to your home, it was a real shock.[63]

A soldier who has served in Hebron describes a similar experience. He presents the occupation of a Palestinian house as a meaningful event that prompted him to imagine what he would have felt if his family had been subjected to such an invasive treatment:

> I thought what if someone were to burst into our house like that, entering through an upstairs window, and force my parents and my younger brother into one of the rooms and start interrogating us, searching the entrances and exits, and treating us so patronizingly.[64]

The subtle racialisation that accompanies expressions of compassion emerges as well within testimonies that portray Palestinians as pitiable and modest figures. A sergeant describes the distressing moment in which two Palestinian boys were arrested in front of their female relatives: 'Everyone is scared. Five soldiers, with guns, try to catch those two 13-year-olds who threw two stones. The mother was crying, the women were all in tears, the kids were shackled, taken into the jeep, scared.'[65] A female sergeant reinforces this representation by describing a disorderly moment from a checkpoint:

> They all rush in, shoving each other and falling all over each other and running forward to the first checking post. All I remember is that they looked really ragged and terribly poor, they always looked really miserable, holding these plastic bags, with some food for the day.[66]

The readers of these testimonies are invited to express empathy for the soldiers that serve under the occupation and to acknowledge their attempt to maintain their humanity even under the most strenuous situations. Gada A. Mahrouse criticises expressions of compassion in human rights activism like those presented by BtS because when 'activists succeed at drawing the attention of mainstream media or the Western public, it is usually the activists themselves, and not the site of conflict they are in, that become the focal points of the story'[67] – a further critical point to make about compassion besides Federica Caso's remarks in this volume about the silencing effects of compassion in some Australian war art. The Israeli soldiers' expressions of compassion enable the expropriation of the Palestinian painful experiences and represent, as Spelman has argued regarding the political dynamics of caring, 'a way of asserting authority over them to the extent that such feeling leaves no room for them to have a view about what their suffering means, or what the most appropriate response is.'[68] In contrast to their anti-occupation discourse, expressions of compassion cleanse Israeli soldiers' reputation and reconstitute them as 'white knights and victims', as moral individuals who are ready to help Palestinians, yet they are positioned within situations that constrain their actions.

The constitution of a privileged, reflective and compassionate military figure within the BtS testimonies reveals the entanglement between dissent, emotions and militarism within the Israel/Palestine conflict. Investigating Israeli soldiers' intimate experiences of military service as a means of activism indicates embodied experiences of military service may reinforce the same militarised discourses they aim to challenge. To this end, by revealing the way in which the activism of BtS is bounded by hierarchy, power and privilege, this chapter shows that the interlinkage between embodiment, militarisation and activism both shapes and compromises military dissent.

Dissent, (White) Privilege and Israeli Militarism

Alongside the soldier testimonies collected by BtS, a number of Israeli human rights organisations collect and disseminate Palestinians' narratives of the violence experienced under the occupation. For instance, B'Tselem (with whom BtS co-operates in verifying testimonies) has documented Israel's breaches of Palestinians' human rights in the West Bank, the Gaza Strip and East Jerusalem since 1989. The organisation insists on the military's failure to hold Israeli soldiers accountable for their violence against Palestinians, raises awareness about restrictions of movement which are imposed on Palestinians and exposes Israeli Jewish settlers' violence against them.[69] Yesh Din: Volunteers for Human Rights emerged in 2005 in order to map out the structural violence of the occupation and put pressure on the Israeli authorities to respect their obligations under international law.[70] The Association for Civil Rights in Israel (ACRI) was founded in 1972 with the aim of protecting human rights and civil liberties in both Israel and the oPt by holding the Israeli authorities accountable for injustices against Palestinians, Arab Jews, or refugees and migrants living in Israel.[71] Finally, yet significantly, other human rights organisations protect Palestinians' freedom of movement within the oPt. Whereas Gisha (founded in 2005) engages in public advocacy and provides legal assistance to Palestinians, Machsom Watch (founded in 2001) is a feminist movement, which monitors Israeli soldiers' behaviour and helps Palestinians to pass through checkpoints by acting as mediators between them and Israeli forces.[72]

By circulating Israeli soldiers' testimonies, BtS positions itself as a distinctive, privileged actor among these different non-governmental organisations that express dissent against the occupation. Their first-hand experience with regard to the violence of the occupation, their complex identity as perpetrators/witnesses/victims, and their reliance on a discourse of transformation in order to highlight the moral price that the Israeli society pays by maintaining the occupation, all show that BtS does not resemble any other organisation. Yehuda Shaul admits it is not easy to define his organisation: 'We don't really fit into the categories of "human rights organization", "anti-occupation organization", "peace group". I think that has a lot to do with who we are – we're all ex-combat soldiers.'[73]

The identity of the BtS activists as ex-combat soldiers raises interesting questions concerning their potential to contest the militarisation of Israeli society. Militarisation is a discursive, material and affective process through which military values, belief and presumptions naturalise the role of the military in a society thus demanding an extensive allocation of state resources for its purposes.[74] The Israeli compulsory military service followed by spells of reserve duty, the influence of military values and actors in the Israeli society, and the role of the military in enforcing the occupation, all demonstrate the militarisation of Israeli society and the relative acceptance of the IDF's extensive influence in the public and private sphere in Israel.[75] Despite its seeming effort to challenge the militarisation of Israeli society, BtS reveals the impossibility of detaching itself from the militarised discourse that it seeks to challenge, and indeed its aesthetic practices of military dissent draw on and reinforce the militarisation of Israeli society by reiterating the humanity and morality of the Israeli military. These features are captured in a phrase coined by the former British Colonel Richard Kemp, 'IDF is the most moral army in the world', a leitmotif that insists the Israeli troops act according to the highest moral and legal standards of military behaviour.[76]

This leitmotif of the military's morality and exceptionality has been reiterated through a familiar aesthetic military representation that has emerged within Israeli documentaries and films, which were produced in the early 2000s: the figure of a distressed and troubled soldier who is committed to acting as morally as possible during military service.[77] This aesthetic representation echoes the need to protect the Israeli soldiers' lives and humanises them at the expense of Palestinians who are either excluded or objectified within these representations.[78] In this respect, the circulation of this aesthetic representation reinforces the militarisation of

Israeli society insofar as it recalls the military's commitment to the highest moral standards and it contributes to the exclusions of Palestinians' narratives of violence.

Similarly, the activism of BtS risks reinforcing rather than ameliorating the racism underpinning the Israeli militarism insofar as it uses Palestinians' pain as a source of moral authority, reaffirming the (white) humanity and exceptionality of the Israeli military. Rather than challenging the militarisation of Israeli society, the aesthetic figure of the authoritative, self-reflexive and compassionate soldier reinforces the portrayal of the Israeli military as a conscientious institution. The testimonies in which Israeli forces appear as victims or as if aiding victims of violence reveal what Sherene Razack's critique of the racial politics of Canadian peacekeeping has described as 'a simplistic and colonial understanding of their role as being about helping those less fortunate, a charitable act that requires properly grateful recipients who must be seen as deserving'.[79] Carrying racialising features, these testimonies normalise the militarisation of Israeli society because the representation of Israeli military personnel as kind-hearted troops closes down a debate about their contribution and, in more general terms, Israel's contribution to Palestinians' suffering.

Despite the dynamics of militarism and racialisation within them, the role of these testimonies in contesting the increasing reliance of the IDF on digital technology in order to justify violence against Palestinians still cannot be denied. Adi Kuntsman and Rebecca L. Stein have criticised the Israeli militarisation of the digital sphere, challenging what was then a conventional assumption that digital technology carries an emancipatory influence in world politics.[80] For instance, in 2014 the IDF justified Operation Protective Edge in the Gaza Strip by circulating images on its official blog that alleged Hamas used mosques and Palestinian homes for military purposes.[81]

The ambivalent role of these testimonies in both challenging and reinforcing the militarisation of Israeli society is reflected further in the organisation's reliance on the traditional model of military masculinity, which is usually associated with combat, in order to address Israeli society's moral deterioration. BtS emerges as a heroic and virtuous organisation, which aims to save Israel from its immoral conduct: 'Israel is getting worse. We continue to build settlements. We increase our military rule over the Palestinians. Israel is not heading for a way out. We are digging ourselves in.'[82] Through this discourse, BtS activists emerge as saviours while Israel is feminised and constructed as an entity that needs to be rescued in order to recover its moral standing.

The use of militarised masculinity as a means to heal the Israeli nation has attracted the Israeli military's interest in co-operating with BtS. The testimonies of BtS have not only been used in order to conduct military investigations but have been instrumental as well in designing military pedagogical programmes. BtS contributes to Israeli military educational programmes by discussing with future recruits about morally problematic events that might occur during their military service.[83] The occasional co-operation between BtS and IDF shows the militarisation of dissent insofar as dissent is co-opted in order to reiterate the benign nature of militarised masculinity and to confirm the morality of the Israeli military. Erica Weiss shows that activists like BtS are aware of the moral implications of co-operating with the military in conducting investigations or designing educational activities for Israeli recruits. However, they acknowledge that their (former) military status ultimately plays a significant role in legitimising and disseminating their activism.[84] The aesthetic intervention of BtS activism within the Israel/Palestine conflict shows that militarisation of the Israeli society offers both opportunities and challenges in conducting military dissent from within a position of privilege.

The reconfiguration of militarised masculinity for the purposes of alleviating the moral deterioration of the Israeli military and society, and the readiness of the Israeli military to appropriate a more benign form of military masculinity for the purpose of representing itself as a moral institution, indicates the continuum between militarism and anti-militaristic activities in Israel. As a symbol of the porous boundary between militarism and anti-militaristic discourse within Israel, the authoritative, compassionate, self-reflective military figure indicates the limits of a militarised language in carrying effective criticism against the occupation and reflects the role of BtS in reinforcing the militarisation of Israeli society.

As a symbol of the hierarchies that inform militarisation, the activism of BtS raises questions with regard to the power of dissent within Israel's militarised society. The study of the militarised dissent of BtS illustrates Alison Howell's critique of the concept of militarisation, which assumes a distinction between the civil and military spheres, between war and peace, and implies a potential process of demilitarisation. In exchange, Howell proposes the replacement of militarisation with the concept of 'martial politics', a more appropriate illustration of the 'war-like relations' that are at the core of exclusionary liberal politics that shape our socio-political order.[85] The study of embodiment as a means of activism shows the importance of taking seriously the intersections between militarism and racism when engaging with militarised masculinity and, as Howell argues, with its violent colonial roots.[86] The Israel/Palestine conflict is rooted in colonial violence and the Israeli military (and its dissenting voices) are imbued with its colonial legacy. The assumed exceptionality of the Israeli military, its self-representation as a moral and benign force, and the privileged position of the Ashkenazi Jews (of European origins) within the military and civil spheres, all exhibit the lingering condition of the colonial past and remind us of the racial hierarchy that is inherent to Israel's colonial settler society.[87]

The entanglement between militarism, dissent and embodiment thus needs to be unpacked as this chapter has done in order to criticise the pervasiveness of the discourse according to which the IDF is supposedly 'the most moral army in the world'. By indicating the potential of aesthetic military dissent in reinforcing the same discourse that it seeks to interrogate, the chapter insists on the racialised and gendered power relations that sustain the militarisation of Israeli society and that manifest themselves even within anti-occupation activism. The reliance BtS places on representations of embodied experience as a means of dissent in fact reiterates the militarisation of Israeli society, by releasing the Israeli military from accountability for its violent behaviour within the oPt.

Conclusion

In arguing that the reliance of BtS on representations of soldiers' embodied experiences in pursuit of military dissent reaffirms the militarisation of Israeli society, this chapter neither seeks to dismiss the physical and psychological experiences of serving under the occupation nor deny that military service is a profoundly subjective experience. Rather, it captures the complexity and the limits of Israeli military dissent while underlining the contradictions and ambiguities through which the activism of BtS operates. By identifying the gendered and racialised relations of power that weaken their activism, this chapter argues for a continuous scholarly critique of military dissent and its role in both contesting and reaffirming militarisation. Rather than simply suggesting that military dissent always reinforces the same militarised discourse that it seeks to challenge, however, this research highlights the subtle patterns of power that might confine activism despite activists' best efforts and strategies to contest militarisation.

Although focused on BtS, this chapter invites scholars to continue the investigation of how dissent, emotions and militarisation intersect within other Western and non-Western countries as well. Joanna Tidy, for instance, has already shown the importance of studying the gendered politics of US veterans' dissent by cautioning that veterans' assumption of authority in speaking against military violence reinforces militarisation because their activism relies on the same martial discourse that sanctions the enactment of violence in the first place.[88] This chapter's intersectional perspective on the political role of emotions in military dissent develops Tidy's point further by making visible the concomitant operation of race, gender, ethnicity and class in sustaining the privilege of speaking against war, showing that the entanglement between embodiment, militarisation and military dissent is ultimately rooted in the structural violence and global inequalities that Marsha Henry argues should be at the centre of military masculinities research. The critical engagement with aesthetics, embodiment and military dissent within the activism of BtS provides the opportunity to criticise the gendered, classed, racialised and sexualised power relations that make up the hierarchies, differences and privileges that militarisation masks.

Studying the activism of BtS through a critical lens on militarisation, aesthetics and embodiment also, meanwhile, has practical and political implications for the organisation of military dissent in Israel, meaning that activists themselves should be invited to consider the way in which dissenting practices can, as Mahrouse argues, 'inadvertently reproduce the very relations they seek to disrupt'.[89] This chapter encourages military dissenting voices to be self-critical about their privilege in speaking against the occupation, their expressions of compassion about Palestinians, and to take account of Palestinians' aspirations of justice, dignity and conflict transformation without appropriating their lived experiences under the occupation. By acknowledging how the aesthetics of testimony and embodied knowledge can create implication in the same discourse of militarisation that military dissent protests against, activists may be better prepared to design alternative strategies of military protest that benefit Israelis and Palestinians alike.

Notes

1. Breaking the Silence, 'About'. https://www.breakingthesilence.org.il/about/organization>.
2. Yehuda Shaul quoted in Marian Brehmer, 'Interview with Yehuda Shaul', Qantara.de, 13 August 2014. https://en.qantara.de/content/interview-with-yehuda-shaul-the-treatment-of-the-palestinians-is-the-biggest-threat-to.
3. Yehuda Shaul quoted in Alistair George, 'Breaking the Silence: An Interview with Yehuda Shaul', International Solidarity Movement, 6 August 2011. https://palsolidarity.org/2011/12/breaking-the-silence-an-interview-with-yehuda-shaul/.

4. Carol Cohn, 'Sex and Death in the Rational World of Defense Intellectuals', *Signs* 12:4 (1987): 687–718.

5. Erella Grassiani, *Soldiering Under Occupation: Moral Numbing among Israeli Conscripts during the Al-Aqsa Intifada* (New York: Berghahn, 2013).

6. Sara Ahmed, *The Cultural Politics of Emotion* (Edinburgh: Edinburgh University Press, 2004), 8.

7. Ibid., 191 (original emphasis).

8. Gada A. Mahrouse, *Conflicted Commitments: Race, Privilege and Power in Solidarity Activism* (Montreal: McGill–Queen's University Press, 2014), 8.

9. Michelle M. Lazar, 'Feminist Critical Discourse Analysis: Articulating a Feminist Discourse Praxis', *Critical Discourse Studies* 4:2 (2007): 141–64; Maéva Clément and Eric Sangar (eds), *Researching Emotions in International Relations: Methodological Perspectives on the Emotional Turn* (London: Palgrave Macmillan, 2018).

10. Lazar, 'Analysis', 141.

11. Emma Hutchison and Roland Bleiker, 'Theorizing Emotions in World Politics', *International Theory* 6:3 (2014): 492–514, 506.

12. Synne L. Dyvik, '"Valhalla Rising": Gender, Embodiment and Experience in Military Memoirs', *Security Dialogue* 47:2 (2016): 133–50; Sara Helman, 'Challenging the Israeli Occupation Through Testimony and Confession: The Case of Anti-Denial SMOs Machsom Watch and Breaking the Silence', *International Journal of Politics, Culture, and Society* 28:4 (2015): 377–94; Yaron Peleg, '*Beaufort* the Book, *Beaufort* the Film: Israeli Militarism Under Attack', in *Narratives of Dissent: War in Contemporary Arts and Culture*, edited by Rachel S. Harris and Ranen Omer-Sherman (Detroit, MI: Wayne State University Press, 2013), 335–45.

13. Sergeant, Nahal Unit, 'Testimony 28', in *Breaking the Silence: Women Soldiers' Testimonies* (Jerusalem: Breaking the Silence, 2009), 46–7. http://www.breakingthesilence.org.il/wp-content/uploads/2011/02/Women_Soldiers_Testimonies_2009_Eng.pdf.

14. Sergeant, Erez Crossing Unit, 'Testimony 51', in *Breaking the Silence: Women Soldiers' Testimonies*, 74.

15. Mahrouse, *Conflicted Commitments*, 22.

16. Sara Ahmed, *Strange Encounters: Embodied Others in Post-Coloniality* (London: Routledge, 2000), 125 (original emphasis).

17. Rachel Woodward and K. Neil Jenkings, *Bringing War to Book: Writing and Producing the Military Memoir* (London: Palgrave Macmillan, 2018), 10.

18. Yuval Noah Harari, 'Scholars, Eyewitnesses and Flesh-Witnesses of War: A Tense Relationship', *Partial Answers* 7:2 (2009): 213–28. See Baker, 'Svetlana Alexievich's Soviet Women Veterans'.

19. Woodward and Jenkings, *Bringing War to Book*, 21–3.

20. David Martin, 'A New Twist in Israel's Case against "Breaking the Silence" and Dean Issacharoff', *DW*, 22 November 2017. https://www.dw.com/en/a-new-twist-in-israels-case-against-breaking-the-silence-and-dean-issacharoff/a-41487485.

21. Ruthie Pliskin, Amit Goldenberg, Efrat Ambar and Daniel Bar-Tal, 'Speaking Out and Breaking the Silence', in *Self-Censorship in Context of Conflicts*, edited by

Daniel Bar-Tal, Rafi Nets-Zehngut and Keren Sharvit (Cham: Springer, 2017), 243–68, 244; Raol Wootliff, 'Righty Im Tirtzu Faces Backlash Over "Foreign Agent" Clip', *The Times of Israel*, 16 December 2015. https://www.timesofisrael. com/im-tirtzu-faces-backlash-against-foreign-agent-clip/.

22. Mairav Zonszein, 'Breaking the Silence', *The Intercept*, 3 March 2019. https:// theintercept.com/2019/03/03/breaking-the-silence-israel-idf/.

23. Shaul quoted in George, 'Breaking the Silence'.

24. Lauren Greenwood, 'Qualitative Approaches to Researching Gender and the Military', in *The Palgrave International Handbook of Gender and the Military*, edited by Rachel Woodward and Claire Duncanson (London: Palgrave Macmillan, 2017), 89–104, 92.

25. Nir Hasson, 'Is There a Crack in the Israeli Army's Wall of Silence?', *Haaretz*, 8 July 2010. https://www.haaretz.com/1.5145719.

26. Peter Beaumont, 'Stories from an Occupation: The Israelis Who Broke Silence', *The Observer*, 8 June 2014. https://www.theguardian.com/world/2014/jun/08/ israel-soldiers-speak-out-brutality-palestine-occupation.

27. Hasson, 'Crack?'

28. Jerusalem Post Staff, 'IDF Chief Eisenkot Says He Welcomes Cooperation with Breaking the Silence', *Jerusalem Post*, 9 February 2016. https://www.jpost.com/ Israel-News/IDF-chief-says-he-welcomes-cooperation-with-Breaking-the-Silence-444335.

29. Bogusia Temple and Alys Young, 'Qualitative Research and Translation Dilemmas', *Qualitative Research* 4:2 (2004): 161–78, 164.

30. Breaking the Silence, *The High Command: Settler Influence on IDF Conduct in the West Bank* (Jerusalem: Breaking the Silence, 2017). https://www.breakingthesilence. org.il/inside/wp-content/uploads/2018/03/THC_Eng_210318.pdf.

31. Breaking the Silence, *This is How We Fought in Gaza: Soldiers' Testimonies and Photographs from Operation 'Protective Edge' (2014)* (Jerusalem: Breaking the Silence, 2015), 63. http://www.breakingthesilence.org.il/pdf/ProtectiveEdge.pdf.

32. Andrew Tobin, 'Poll: 85% of Israeli Jews Want to Keep Fighting', *The Times of Israel*, 31 July 2014. http://www.timesofisrael.com/poll-85-of-israeli-jews-want-to-keep-fighting/.

33. Shaul quoted in George, 'Breaking the Silence'.

34. First Sergeant, Kfir Brigade, 'Boom Boom', in *Children and Youth: Soldiers' Testimonies 2005–2011* (Jerusalem: Breaking the Silence, n.d.), 33. http://www. breakingthesilence.org.il/wp-content/uploads/2012/08/Children_and_Youth_ Soldiers_Testimonies_2005_2011_Eng.pdf.

35. First Sergeant, Infantry, 'Testimony 21', in *This is How We Fought in Gaza*, 63.

36. Orna Sasson-Levy, 'Feminism and Military Gender Practices: Israeli Women Soldiers in "Masculine" Roles', *Sociological Inquiry* 73:2 (2003): 440–65, 446.

37. Idit Shafran Gittleman, 'Female Service in the IDF: The Challenge of an "Integrated" Army', *Lawfare*, 28 February 2018. https://www.lawfareblog.com/ female-service-idf-challenge-integrated-army.

38. Sasson-Levy, 'Feminism', 445.

39. Ibid., 440–65.

40. Orna Sasson-Levy, Yagil Levy and Edna Lomsky-Feder, 'Women Breaking the Silence: Military Service, Gender, and Antiwar Protest', *Gender and Society* 25:6 (2011): 740–63, 741.

41. Ibid., 750.

42. First Sergeant, Border Patrol Unit, 'Testimony 1', in *Breaking the Silence: Women Soldiers' Testimonies*, 5.

43. First Sergeant, Border Patrol Unit, 'Testimony 8', in *Breaking the Silence: Women Soldiers' Testimonies*, 13–14.

44. Sergeant, 'Testimony 11', Erez Crossing Unit, in *Breaking the Silence: Women Soldiers' Testimonies*, 16–17.

45. Sergeant, Education Corps Unit, 'Testimony 19', in *Breaking the Silence: Women Soldiers' Testimonies*, 30–31.

46. Sergeant, Border Patrol Unit, 'Testimony 24', in *Breaking the Silence: Women Soldiers' Testimonies*, 39.

47. Edna Lomsky-Feder and Orna Sasson-Levy, *Women Soldiers and Citizenship in Israel: Gendered Encounters with the State* (London: Routledge, 2018), 2.

48. Noya Rimalt, 'Equality with a Vengeance: Female Conscientious Objectors in Pursuit of a Voice and Substantive Gender Equality', *Columbia Journal of Gender and Law* 16:1 (2007): 97–146, 126.

49. Ibid., 127.

50. Gal Levy and Orna Sasson-Levy, 'Militarized Socialization, Military Service, and Class Reproduction: The Experiences of Israeli Soldiers', *Sociological Perspectives* 51:2 (2008): 349–74.

51. George, 'Breaking the Silence'.

52. Adi Kuntsman, 'The Soldier and the Terrorist: Sexy Nationalism, Queer Violence', *Sexualities* 11:2 (2008): 142–70.

53. Tom Mehanger, 'Conscientious Objection is Yet Another Ashkenazi Privilege', +972, 14 May 2016. https://972mag.com/conscientious-objection-is-yet-another-ashkenazi-privilege/119307/.

54. Marsha G. Henry, 'Problematizing Military Masculinity, Intersectionality and Male Vulnerability in Feminist Critical Military Studies', *Critical Military Studies* 3:2 (2017): 182–99, 183.

55. Ibid., 190.

56. Sherene H. Razack, 'Stealing the Pain of Others: Reflections on Canadian Humanitarian Responses', *Review of Education, Pedagogy, & Cultural Studies* 29:4 (2007): 375–94, 389.

57. Shaul quoted in George, 'Breaking the Silence'.

58. Lieutenant, Education Corps Unit, 'Testimony 37', in *Breaking the Silence: Women Soldiers' Testimonies*, 57.

59. Anonymous, *Breaking the Silence: Soldiers Speak about their Service in Hebron 2001–2004* (Jerusalem: Breaking the Silence, n.d.), 24. http://www.breaking-thesilence.org.il/wp-content/uploads/2011/02/Soldiers_Testimonies_from_Hebron_2001_2004_Eng.pdf.

60. Ahmed, *Strange Encounters*, 124 (original emphasis).

61. Anonymous, *Breaking the Silence: Soldiers Speak About their Service in Hebron*, 40.

62. Lieutenant, Civil Administration Unit, 'You Feel Like One More Second and You'll Spray Them with Bullets', *Breaking the Silence* (n.d.). http://www.break-ingthesilence.org.il/testimonies/database/56815.

63. Anonymous, 'Testimony 96', in *Breaking the Silence: Testimonies from Hebron 2005–2007* (Jerusalem: Breaking the Silence, n.d.), 115. http://www.breakingthe silence.org.il/wp-content/uploads/2011/02/Soldiers_Testimonies_from_ Hebron_2005_2007_Eng.pdf.

64. Anonymous, *Breaking the Silence: Soldiers Speak About their Service in Hebron*, 21.

65. First Sergeant, Armored Corps, 'Jeans and a Red Shirt', in *Children and Youth*, 70–1.

66. Sergeant, Erez Crossing Unit, 'Testimony 51', 74.

67. Mahrouse, *Conflicted Commitments*, 71.

68. Elizabeth V. Spelman, *Fruits of Sorrow: Framing Our Attention to Suffering* (Boston, MA: Beacon Press, 1997), 70.

69. B'Tselem, 'About B'Tselem' (n.d.). https://www.btselem.org/about_btselem.

70. Yesh Din, 'About Us' (n.d.). https://www.yesh-din.org/en/about-us/.

71. Association for Civil Rights in Israel, 'Who We Are' (n.d.). https://www.english. acri.org.il.

72. Gisha 'About Gisha' (n.d.). https://gisha.org/about/about-gisha; Machsom Watch, 'About Us' (n.d.). https://machsomwatch.org/en/about.

73. Shaul quoted in George, 'Breaking the Silence'.

74. Catherine Lutz, 'Militarization', in *A Companion to the Anthropology of Politics*, edited by David Nugent and Joan Vincent (Malden, MA: Blackwell, 2007), 318–31, 320.

75. Meira Weiss, *The Chosen Body: The Politics of the Body in Israeli Society* (Stanford, CA: Stanford University Press, 2002).

76. Muhammad Ali Khalidi, '"The Most Moral Army in the World": The New "Ethical Code" of the Israeli Military and the War on Gaza', *Journal of Palestine Studies* 39:3 (2010): 6–23; Atilla Somfalvi, 'IDF Does More Than Any Other Army to Prevent Civilian Deaths', *Ynet*, 24 July 2014. https://www.ynetnews. com/articles/0,7340,L-4548821,00.html.

77. Raya Morag, *Waltzing with Bashir: Perpetrator Trauma and Cinema* (London: I. B. Tauris, 2013).

78. Joseph A. Kraemar, 'Waltz with Bashir (2008): Trauma and Representation in the Animated Documentary', *Journal of Film and Video* 67:3–4 (2015): 57–68, 65.

79. Sherene H. Razack, *Dark Threats and White Knights: The Somalia Affair, Peace-keeping, and the New Imperialism* (Toronto: University of Toronto Press, 2004), 30.

80. Adi Kuntsman and Rebecca L. Stein, *Digital Militarism: Israel's Occupation in the Social Media Age* (Stanford, CA: Stanford University Press, 2015).

81. Neve Gordon and Nicola Perugini, 'The Politics of Human Shielding: On the Resignification of Space and the Constitution of Civilians as Shields in Liberal Wars', *Environment and Planning D: Society and Space* 34:1 (2016): 168–87.

82. Shaul quoted in Brehmer, 'Interview with Yehuda Shaul'.
83. James Eastwood, *Ethics as a Weapon of War: Militarism and Morality in Israel* (Cambridge: Cambridge University Press, 2017), 220.
84. Erica Weiss, 'Struggling with Complicity: Anti-Militarist Activism in Israel', *Current Anthropology* 60:S19 (2019): S173–82, S175–7.
85. Alison Howell, 'Forget "Militarization": Race, Disability and the "Martial Politics" of the Police and of the University', *International Feminist Journal of Politics* 20:2 (2018), 117–36, 121.
86. Ibid., 120.
87. David Lloyd, 'Settler Colonialism and the State of Exception: The Example of Israel/Palestine', *Settler Colonial Studies* 2:1 (2012): 59–80, 67–9.
88. Joanna Tidy, 'Gender, Dissenting Subjectivity and the Contemporary Military Peace Movement in *Body of War*', *International Feminist Journal of Politics* 17:3 (2015): 454–72.
89. Mahrouse, *Conflicted Commitments*, 78.

CHAPTER 5

Death Becomes Him: The Hypervisibility of Martyrdom and Invisibility of the Wounded in the Iconography of Lebanese Militarised Masculinities[1]

Henri Myrttinen

Walking through the streets of Lebanese cities or driving through the countryside, one is confronted with diverse images of people: male and female models in advertisements living up to the latest conventional Western and/or Arab beauty standards; Christian and Shi'a holy men and the occasional Virgin Mary or Christian woman saint; revered Arab singers, both male and female; as well as international football heroes, powerful political leaders and their foreign, regional backers – these latter categories all being exclusively male. Depending on where one strolls or drives through, one might also encounter depictions of men – and very occasionally women – in uniform, sometimes armed and sometimes not, some looking serious, some laughing, some shy, some defiant. These are, for the most part, the war dead – though some military men (but not women) may be revered in a similar way even if they do not die on the battlefield, as discussed further below.

The pictures of the dead, of the martyrs,[2] mingle with those of the living, occasionally creating juxtapositions that at times seemed odd for me with my Western gaze. A photo of a recent casualty of the Syrian Civil War next to an advert with Lionel Messi touting Pepsi; a commemorative portrait of a Lebanese army officer on a wall, flanked by a poster in honour of the famed female Lebanese singer Fairuz (Nouhad Wadie' Haddad) on the one side and Ashoura flags depicting Husayn ibn Ali, grandson of the Prophet Muhammad, carrying a massacred child at the seventh-century Battle of Karbala on the other; a wall of photos of recent martyrs around the corner from a men's hair salon sporting adverts of metrosexual male models and the slogan (in English) 'between heaven and earth'. The walls are a palimpsest onto which memories of different wars – wars of the early Islamic age, the Lebanese Civil War, the wars with Israel, the Syrian Civil War – are projected, mingling with civilian messages. However, in spite of visiting Lebanon several dozen times and actively seeking out these posters of martyrs, I have yet to see any depictions of the visibly war-wounded or war-disabled. Even the dead, in these representations, are able-bodied.

This chapter seeks to explore the hypervisibility of some war dead in Lebanon and the general public invisibility of the war-wounded and disabled, who in fact should be more numerous than the dead. It arose from my own curiosity of walking around different quarters of Beirut but also of travelling in Shi'a areas in the south of the country and the Beqaa Valley bordering Syria, where walls, telephone poles and other surfaces are adorned with the recently fallen – but also with depictions of iconic martyrs of earlier wars. As engaging with militarised gender identities and the gendered after-effects of violent conflict is part of my everyday work of working for an international non-governmental organisation (NGO) on gender and peacebuilding, this piqued my interest – as did the invisibility of the war-wounded and disabled, which I was slower to pick up on, as I will explore further later on.

The martyr pictures of Beirut and Shi'a areas are, this chapter argues, a part of the broader visual and spatial landscapes and political imaginaries of Lebanon. They also form part of the necropolitics of the country, in which the dead, and the memories of them, are mobilised but where the dead also have a degree of political agency. The landscapes, imaginaries and necropolitics reflect the broader trends of social and political life in Lebanon: they are masculinised spaces, heavily determined by class, location, as well as sectarian and party affiliation.[3] I also argue that these are spaces which persons with disabilities – as in much of the rest of Lebanon – have difficulty accessing. The hypervisible dead are no longer of this world but not depicted as being visibly maimed, while those living with visible and invisible wounds and disabilities caused by the wars are invisibilised.

The photos of the martyrs are simultaneously public and very private. They are public announcements – perhaps even celebrations – of deaths but also more private, sombre, even touching expressions of mourning. The militarised masculinities which are depicted and constructed through the martyr pictures stand in stark contrast to Western preconceptions of militant Arab men and their masculinities but are also quite different from the more aggressive imagery used for example by Western militaries in recruitment campaigns or by radical right movements celebrating their nation's military.[4] On the other hand, those who live with the visible and invisible wounds of war remain mostly hidden in private spaces and the semi-private spaces of care facilities.

The findings presented here are based on my own observations and discussions since approximately 2014 with mainly Lebanese, Palestinian and Syrian civil society actors and academics, as well as desk-based research. Researching issues of war casualties is sensitive, and I was warned by my Lebanese colleagues to be especially careful about looking into issues around the war-wounded from the Syrian War, warnings I will return to later. As such, the research remained more superficial than I would have wished, presenting more an outsider's view rather than an insider's reading – in particular with respect to war veterans living with disabilities. I examine here primarily visual representations of militarisation, especially militarised masculinities, and the aesthetics related to their performance and embodiment. I contrast these both with the absence of war-wounded bodies as well as of their visual representations. I focus primarily on men and masculinities, as they are far more present than the very limited number of women in these representations, though I do highlight one particularly prominent case.

By militarised masculinities, I refer to the way in which persons in military and military-style organisations (such as political militias in this case) enact, perform and embody particular gender identities which fuse notions of masculinity and martial prowess. As a by now wide field of research has shown, militarised masculinities are not singular or straight-forward, and vary in their forms and performances historically, geographically and even within institutions, for example according to rank or role.[5] These performances of militarised masculinities involve particular aesthetics linked to both soldiering and imaginings of martial manliness, including in terms of dress (e.g. uniform or camouflage fatigues), accessories such as weapons or webbing, but also certain poses, postures, facial expressions, ways of walking and of talking.[6]

There are of course also forms of public commemoration in Lebanon other than the photographs and posters I examine here, such as statues, memorials, speeches or songs eulogising, remembering or mourning the dead. I decided to focus on the visualisations of mainly male martyrs here for a number of reasons. For one, I am personally interested in visual representations, especially in terms of what these convey about gendered expectations in conflict-affected societies.[7] For an outsider, these visualisations are also among the more accessible forms of commemoration, as compared to for example political songs which would only be sung on certain occasions or more personal memories.[8] The

martyr photos however also fit into a broader trend in Lebanese processes of remembering – and forgetting – violent conflict. Craig Larkin
identifies a 'post-war tendency that seems to favour visual representation over the more complex and contested narrative form' in the country.[9] That is not to say that these photos do not have a multiplicity of
meanings for different audiences. On the contrary, they simultaneously
and in part ambiguously convey personal and private messages (e.g. of
grief and longing); communal, sectarian and political messages; and act
as territorial markers which create mental boundaries that are reassuring
for some, threatening to others. They also visibly set the standards for
what celebrated, militarised masculinities should look like, conveying
notions of how masculinities should be performed and embodied in
times of war.

While the martyr pictures were easily accessible and hard to miss, the
opposite was true for disabilities and their depictions. That it took me
a while to even register their invisibility is an unfortunate reflection on
my own ableist biases up to that point of realisation, and beyond. As
with other social identity markers that have been historically and currently privileged and seen as the norm in much of Western thought, such
as male-ness or white-ness, able-bodiedness is embedded as the unarticu-
lated norm. The exclusions this creates for persons living with disabilities
often remain invisible to those, such as myself, who do not suffer the
consequences of these exclusions, barriers and invisibilisations.[10]

Background to Lebanon and its Wars

The visual landscape of Lebanon is not only one punctuated by visualisations of able-bodied men and women, as well as of consumer goods
and future real estate. It also abounds with party-political flags and
graffiti that echo the power structures of the 1975–90 Civil War (which
caused around 120,000–170,000 deaths and twice as many wounded)
and fissures caused by the Syrian Civil War.[11] Lebanon's cities continue
to bear the physical scars – pock-marked walls, derelict ruins, but also
memories of buildings that are no longer there – of both the Civil War
and the 2006 war against Israel. The wars and their aftermath still cast
their shadow over the political, social and geographical landscape. As
Larkin puts it:

> Although the topographical lines of confrontation have been dismantled,
> public spaces, shops and residential property are still often marked by com-
> peting political and sectarian emblems . . . identifying spheres of loyalty,

allegiance and ultimate territorial control. These signs, codes and symbols continue to impact on how Lebanese perceive themselves, distinguish others and inhabit their spatial surroundings. They contribute to a dynamic kaleidoscope of changing social and identity markers.[12]

The Civil War and its aftermath led to an increased segregation of space based on sectarian identity, interlinked with class, and a large part of the population continues to live with co-religionists, and the parties that evolved out of the sectarian militias of the Civil War continue to dominate politics. The approximately 480,000 Palestinians, who are refugees who fled Palestine mainly in 1948 and 1967 and their descendants, are mainly restricted to refugee camps. Both the country as a whole and the cities in miniature are a mosaic of areas defined by overlapping class and sectarian identities, often visually demarcated by flags and other visual markers such as political graffiti, street art and party flags. The kinds of persons on visual display also give a strong indication of what kind of an area one is in: depictions of bodies and faces seen in one quarter would not be seen in another – Iranian Ayatollahs here, stylised hipsters there; Saudi royalty here, underwear models there.

While the legacy of the three-decade Civil War continues to shape Lebanese society, its cityscapes and landscapes in multiple ways, remembering and commemorating the war has been somewhat dualistic. While private, family- and community-based sectarian memories of the war often remain strong, there has been little memorialisation of the Civil War in public.[13] According to Sune Haugbolle, however, the image of those who fought in the war as foot soldiers, the 'little militiamen', has slowly shifted over the years since the end of the war, in particular in the 2000s. After being initially generally blamed for the violence of the war and reckless behaviour, while simultaneously individual fighters were feted within one's own party-political and/or sectarian group, their overall image in public discourse now has gained more nuance, including discussions of their lack of agency, vulnerabilities and difficulties of adjusting to civilian life.

The outbreak of the Syrian Civil War, meanwhile, has also had major impacts on Lebanon. The country hosts at least 1.2–1.5 million Syrian refugees, and fighting has spilled over the border. Syrian opposition fighters and their families have at times used the border areas as a retreat area, leading to occasional military clashes, most notably in Arsal in 2014 between the Lebanese Armed Forces (LAF) and al-Qaeda-linked militants. Of most relevance to this chapter, however, is the involvement of Lebanese citizens as combatants in the Syrian Civil War. The exact number of Lebanese fighters who have fought in the war is unknown, as is which of the numerous factions they fought with, but extrapolating from the number of casualties, likely over 10,000 Lebanese have participated in combat. The most salient groups for this piece, and the ones I will focus on, are those that openly and publicly and visually commemorate the fighters who have fallen in Syria in Lebanon – Hezbollah and the Syrian Socialist National Party (SSNP).[14] Others, for example al-Qaeda-related groups, are more likely to celebrate their martyrs online and not publicly.

Hezbollah (literal translation: The Party of God) and the SSNP both fight on the side of the Syrian government of Bashar al-Assad. Hezbollah, which evolved out of the Lebanese Civil War, is by far the more significant military force of the two. It is simultaneously a political party that sits in the Lebanese government at the time of writing, an armed militia, a social welfare organisation, owner of a media empire and, allegedly, involved in licit and illicit multi-million-dollar businesses.[15] It primarily represents a part of the Shi'a population of Lebanon and has burnished its image both in Lebanon and in the broader Arab world through its military resistance against Israel, in particular in the 2006 war.[16] It is closely allied with Iran. The SSNP, on the other hand, is a secular, Lebanese–Syrian nationalist party dating back to 1932 that for decades was a rival of the Ba'athist party, led in Syria by Assad father and son, and was banned in Syria until 2005.[17] It also participated actively in the Lebanese Civil War. Hezbollah officially sent its fighting forces to Syria in 2013, and according to foreign estimates had lost around 1,700–1,800 fighters by May 2016, a number which has likely increased since combat activities have escalated since then.[18] The number of SSNP fighters, organised in the 'Eagles of the Whirlwind' militia, is estimated at 6,000–8,000, but information on them is scarcer.[19] The duration of its engagement in the Syrian Civil War, the number of casualties and the proportion of Lebanese amongst them could not be verified. However, as the combat role of the Eagles of the Whirlwind has become more pronounced, particularly in the south and west of Syria, the number of casualties has risen, and SSNP soldiers were among the dead and wounded in recent fighting in as-Suwayda against Islamic State in June–August 2018.[20]

Of the former Lebanese Civil War belligerent parties, the SSNP in Lebanon is among those which most prominently displays pictures of its martyrs from that war. In particular, it is pictures of Khaled Alwan, who conducted one of the first attacks against Israeli occupation forces in Lebanon, and Sana'a Mehaidli, one of the first, if not the first, female

Figure 5.1 A portrait of Musa as-Sadr by the Amal Party and 'Martyrs of the Lebanese Resistance', with Quran Surah, Al-Ahzab verse 23. Both posters by the Shi'a Amal Movement. Beirut, 2017 (photo: Henri Myrttinen)

suicide bomber globally, which are on display.[21] The posters are displayed around SSNP checkpoints and buildings, adorned with the 'red hurricane' logo of the party. Other parties also display Civil War dead, men and women, who are commemorated on posters, but often as litanies of photocopies of passport photos from the 1970s and 1980s in rows next to each other (Figure 5.1).

Framing the Martyr Pictures, As It Were

The visual commemoration of individual martyrs through photographs and posters is common across the region, whether among armed Kurdish opposition groups or in Palestine, Iraq or Iran. In Lebanon, they fit into a larger pattern of visual necropolitics, in which the political dead are not merely commemorated but have a degree of political agency. I use necropolitics not only in the original sense Achille Mbembe gave it, referring to the power to expose certain people (in this case the martyrs) to death, but also in the broader sense used by Finn Stepputat, as a corollary of sorts to biopolitics, including the governance of the dead by state and non-state actors as well as the political, beyond-the-grave agency of the dead.[22] This agency especially relates to particular 'potent dead', to borrow from the title of the book by Henri Chambert-Loir and Anthony Reid, and to what Craig Larkin calls 'living martyrs'.[23] These are figures, powerful after death, who become markers of identity but also urge the living to certain deeds. Photos of the assassinated Prime Minister Rafik Hariri (who was killed in 2005), for example, are photoshopped into political posters with his son, the current Prime Minister Saad Hariri, as if he were still alive and enjoying a jovial moment with his son, adding to the political gravitas of the latter. On the Shi'a side, images of the pensive face of the charismatic Imam Musa as-Sadr, who disappeared in 1978 while visiting Muammar Gaddafi, feed into and keep alive politically potent myths of vanished Imams and Shi'a martyrdom. On the Maronite side, charismatic ex-leader and martyr Bashir Gemayel also makes appearances from beyond the grave, including on posters of his likeness with the slogan 'he lives among us'.[24] Gemayel was controversially used in 2018 when his photo was displayed alongside anti-Syrian slogans on posters in the run-up to the parliamentary elections.

The current photos of martyrs in Lebanon draw on at least three visual legacies – those of the Lebanese Civil War, Palestinian martyr iconography, and the influence of the Iranian Revolution and its martyr depictions. Photographic depictions of martyrs became popular during the Lebanese Civil War and among the Palestinian groups fighting Israel. During the Iran/Iraq war with its mass casualties, a particular revolutionary Iranian style of martyr photos emerged, which may have been especially influential in the case of Hezbollah, given its close ties to the country and shared Shi'a culture.[25] The martyr photos fit into broader, established narratives of both secular and more religiously informed sacrifice (both Christian and Muslim), heroism, selflessness – and a call for others to follow their sacrificial example. Almost all of this sacrifice is coded masculine, and all of the few women martyrs whose pictures I saw on display died in the Civil War or as part of 'the Resistance' (against Israel). This in part reflects gendered recruitment patterns in the Syrian Civil War, where women's participation in combat is largely discouraged by all groups other than the Kurdish YPG (Yekîneyên Parastina Gel).[26]

The literal framing of the martyr photos, that is, not only what is in each picture as well as the martyr's photographs but also what is on display around them, gives further clues about the political and artistic influences as well as historical trajectories of Lebanese martyr iconography.

When it comes to Hezbollah, the intermingling of the Lebanese martyrs' causes with that of the Palestinians, with the Iranian revolution, but in part also with the historical marginalisation and discrimination as well as the mythologised struggles of the Shi'a, dating back to CE 680, is evident. The al-Aqsa Mosque in East Jerusalem acts as a nod to the Palestinian struggle, as in part do the Palestinian-style keffiyeh worn by some of the martyrs. Close to the martyr photos, on the same or opposite walls, one finds posters with Ayatollah Ruhollah Khomeini; Abbas al-Moussawi, the late co-founder of Hezbollah; the late Hezbollah Chief of Staff Imad Mugniyah; Hassan Nasrallah, current secretary-general of the party; and occasionally Moustafa Shahadeh.[27] Pictures of these men are at times combined on the same poster (see Figure 5.2), memorialising the dead while also giving political legitimacy to the living.

In Shi'a neighbourhoods, the use of Ashoura flags next to the photos helps to tie the deaths being commemorated to broader religious narratives of Shi'a sacrifice and martyrdom, going back to the events that led

Figure 5.2 From left to right: Imad Mugniyah, Hassan Nasrallah and Moustafa Shahadeh in front of a backdrop of the Al-'Abbās Mosque in Karbala (Iraq) and the Sayyidah Zaynab Mosque in Damascus (Syria). Poster opposite a wall with several martyr photos. Beirut, 2017 (photo: Henri Myrttinen)

to the founding of the branch after the Battle of Karbala in CE 680. These narratives of religious sacrifice, persecution and death are underscored by depictions, such as in Figure 5.2, of important and value-laden Shi'a shrines such as the al-'Abbās Mosque in Karbala (Iraq) and the Sayyidah Zaynab Mosque in Damascus, which have in recent years been sites of sectarian bombings by Sunni extremists. Thus a narrative arc is constructed between the founding of Shi'ism, recent sectarian killings and the sacrifice of the martyrs who died in Syria, for the greater cause of protecting their community. Narratives of unjustified suffering and targeting of the innocents are visible on some of the Ashoura flags, which depict children wounded and martyred at the Battle of Karbala with arrows through their bodies in a stylised fashion, carried by stoic, accusing adult men. These children on these flags were the only depictions of war-wounded that I came across. The secular SSNP, in contrast, frames its martyrs with political and nationalist rather than religious connotations (Figure 5.3). Images of the dead may be superimposed on to maps depicting the greater Syria which the party is fighting for and framed with political slogans.

Figure 5.3 Poster commemorating the SSNP 'martyr hero comrade' Mohammed Awad, killed in Syria on 27 December 2013. The slogan on the barrel translates as 'We are building a better community'. Beirut, 2017 (photo: Henri Myrttinen)

Figure 5.4 Martyrs of the Syrian War, two with Hezbollah emblems. Beirut, 2017 (photo: Henri Myrttinen)

Interestingly, given the martial context, it is not unusual for doves of peace to be incorporated into the framings of martyr photos, especially among the Hezbollah posters (see for example Figure 5.4). Texts accompanying the pictures tend to be matter of fact and undramatic, rather than aimed at arousing sectarian, political or nationalist fervour – even if their mere presence may act as a sectarian marker. Often, it is only the name of the martyr that is mentioned, and other information that is included mostly focuses on practicalities such as when funerals or commemorations are to be held. Unlike on those Western memorials for the war dead which are not collective, the Lebanese martyr posters tend neither include the place nor date of death. The Quranic verses which are added to some of the photos tend to focus on individual death and the afterlife, as well as sacrifice. The broader societal, historical and spatial framing discussed here sets the parameters within which the martyr photos can be, and are meant to be, understood. The pictures themselves however, with the styles they represent, add new dimensions of meaning which go beyond these parameters, including in terms of the embodiment and performance of militarised masculinities.

Martyr Style

Writing about martyr depictions in Iran during and after the Iran–Iraq War (1980–8), which also influenced Lebanese martyr depictions, Shahin Gerami describes the stereotypical martyr photo as follows:

> The martyr is a young, unmarried (virgin, innocent) man, fearless and strong. He is depicted with eyes cast forward to jihad and the blessed state of martyrdom. His hair is dark and held back with a bandana with Quranic inscriptions. If depicted in full figure, he wears white, the color of a coffin, while holding a gun.[28]

While there are similarities and Iranian influences in Lebanese martyr depictions, Gerami's stylised description of Iranian martyr pictures from the Iran–Iraq War applies only in part to the Lebanese martyrs.[29] While there are some recurring key elements, there is also considerable variation between the individual pictures. Commonly recurring elements are uniforms and weaponry (the weapon is often the iconic Russian AK-47 rifle, also known as the Kalashnikov, or variants of it, which also features in the Hezbollah logo). Taking a cue from Iranian iconography and the 1979 Iranian Revolution, some Hezbollah martyrs are depicted with the bandanas with Quranic inscriptions that Gerami mentions, and some wear keffiyeh around their necks. The latter are often symbolically linked to the Palestinian struggle but also, in the context, to – often 'youthful', masculine-coded – resistance and rebellion. Both the bandanas and keffiyeh are traditional accoutrements in the broader Middle East region for certain ethno-religious groups that gained new popularity and took on new, more politicised, more youth-oriented, militant and often masculinised meanings between the 1960s and the 1980s in a range of combatants and activists, including among Palestinian guerrillas and intifada activists, Iranian revolutionaries and soldiers, and militias in the Lebanese Civil War. That said, these appropriations may also have depopularised these accessories among other militiamen in Lebanon, given how linked Quranic headbands were to a revolutionary, Iranian political Shi'ism and given that left-wing Palestinian activism was the enemy of many Lebanese militias in the first decade of the war, which pitted Palestinian militias against especially Maronite forces and the invading Israelis but also the Shi'a Amal.

The martyr pictures are a product of their time and reflect trends contemporaneous with the photo, with haircuts, sartorial preferences and the types of poses deemed suitable for such an occasion. They also reflect private and personal agency even when the dead are being harnessed into the service of broader socio-political and military projects, which the dead – some more willingly than others – had signed up to.[30] The pictures are further pre-post-mortem performances in a sense: they were taken prior to death with the intent of showing a particular facet of the casualty's persona to the public after death. The range of emotions displayed and the quality of the pictures differ greatly: some men are serious, some determined, some smiling, some shy; some are more akin to quick passport photos; others clearly have effort and thought put into them. The overwhelming majority of my random sample of pictures showed friendly, shy or pensive men, though at times in uniform and armed, as well as a few in postures of focused determination and stoicism.

Instead of the anonymity, solemnity and patriotism of, say, European war memorials of the World Wars,[31] these were highly personal, at times delicate and individualised commemorations – albeit framed in broader social, political and at times religious narratives. The pictures one might expect given dominant Western stereotypes of Arab bloodthirsty, fanatic male fighters were missing completely, even if in part they were members of an organisation officially designated as a 'terrorist group' by the USA, no less.[32] Paul Amar has already critiqued the way in which Arab masculinities are often depicted in Western discourses as 'atavistic, misogynist, and hypersexual masculinities . . . and thus misrecognizing, racializing, moralistically-depoliticizing, and class-displacing emergent social forces in the Middle East'.[33] Furthermore, Western imageries of militarised masculinities, for example gung-ho, aggressive 'Rambos' or soldiers showing off their martial prowess, were also missing from the posters. When weapons are displayed, they tend to be shown with the barrel pointing downwards, rather than being pointed more aggressively at the camera, as would be the case for example in many Western military recruitment campaign posters.

Unlike the subjects of some of the similar martyr pictures on display in Palestine, for example, where martyrdom may have been more or less knowingly sought or factored in (e.g. by suicide bombers or commandos of Hamas and Islamic Jihad, or for that matter Lebanese suicide bombers of earlier eras), many of the Lebanese men going to Syria might also have had less of an expectation of death than their Palestinian counterparts when the photos were taken.[34] Whether or not expectations of death figured in the decisions of the fighters to strike a certain pose or choose a particular photo for a possible martyr photo while they were still alive can only be speculated upon, but the poses

Figure 5.5 Martyr pictures, commemorating Martyr Mujahid Mohammed Jawad Nasser Nasser (left) and Martyr Hussein Adnan Shaqeer (right). Beirut, 2017 (photo: Henri Myrttinen)

and expressions did tend towards the non-aggressive, amiable and approachable (Figure 5.5).

The highly visible commemoration of the late Lieutenant Colonel Rabih Kahil is in many ways a literally striking exception among the current visual memorialisations of martyrs. Kahil was a member of the LAF elite Commando Unit who had fought in the 2007 Nahr al-Bared operation against the Palestinian Fatah al-Islam group and in 2014 in Arsal against the al-Qaeda affiliated al-Nusra Front. His 'martyrdom', however, was not on the battlefield in Lebanon or Syria, but in a private dispute in 2015 over stopping on a civilian man's property. The verbal dispute escalated into a physical fight and in the end Kahil was shot, dying four days later of his wounds.[35] At the time of writing in 2018, he continues to be commemorated by an approximately 15 × 30 m poster on the side of a building in the centre of Beirut, next to the General Foaad Chehab flyover, one of the key throughways in the heart of the city (Figure 5.6). In 2016, the area surrounding the poster was akin to a shrine of worship, with numerous smaller posters of Kahil flanked by Ashoura flags and flower arrangements forming an ensemble on the nearby walls.

Figure 5.6 Commemorating Lieutenant Colonel Kahil. Shi'a Ashoura flag on the left. Beirut, 2017 (photo: Henri Myrttinen)

Behind and next to the larger-than-life poster of Kahil and the make-shift shrine of sorts, the predominantly Shi'a quarter's walls are replete with mostly A4-size paper posters of martyrs. Unlike Kahil, who likely died due to a flare-up of masculine egos and poor anger management in a civilian setting on a weekend in the Lebanese countryside, these less-celebrated martyrs died on the battlefields of Syria. In part, the public veneration of Kahil compared to the more low-key commemoration of Hezbollah and SSNP foot soldiers is due to his social status as a senior officer and public hero of the venerated LAF, who had fought against both Palestinian Islamists threatening the socio-political equilibrium in the country and Syrian infiltrators. The other martyrs, on the other hand, had died on foreign soil in a war that has deeply divided the Lebanese nation. Furthermore, the role of *wasta*[36] and social standing cannot be ignored in Lebanon: Lieutenant Colonel Kahil was a man of social sta-tus, a public persona and not a 'mere' foot soldier as were the men on the sheets of A4 paper, even if his pulling of rank may have escalated the events that led to his death. What is also notable in terms of the poses in which he is depicted is that they are, from a Western perspective, far more conventionally martial and in tune with notions of military masculinity than those of the (mostly) younger and less well-known men who died on the battlefield.

The individual martyr pictures display a comparatively broad range of representations of militarised masculinities, and the vast majority are ones that downplay aggression, opting for displays of other emotions instead. Even in death, however, class and *wasta* may determine the degree to which one is remembered in death, with the foot soldiers' paper photos quickly fading, being torn or plastered over and the commanders' and political leaders' heavy-duty plastic banners remaining pristine. However, even the fleeting visibility of the lower-ranked martyrs is more than what is given to the war-wounded and disabled.

Invisible War-Wounded

In stark contrast to visible commemorations of in particular Hezbollah and SSNP martyrs, as well as some deceased LAF members, the living-but-wounded casualties of war are publicly invisible in Lebanon, in real life and as visualisations. This is also the case for persons living with visible disabilities more broadly in Lebanon, and has social, practical and political reasons. While all of the dominant religions in the country stress the need for charity and kindness towards persons with disabilities, social realities and attitudes are in part quite different in practice. As in many other societies, persons living with disabilities in Lebanon do face a degree of stigmatisation, discrimination and may be seen as a source of social embarrassment.[37] Persons living with disabilities may also themselves avoid visibility due to an internalisation of such stigmas, but also out of a fear of encountering such attitudes in public, or wanting to avoid their opposite, pity.[38] Persistent stigma surrounds mental health issues and seeking psychological help as well, especially for men aspiring to live up to dominant norms of masculinity,[39] even if according to one study perhaps up to a quarter of the Lebanese population in 2008 suffered from war-related mental disorders.[40]

The ways in which disabilities are experienced often depend greatly on gender, on whether the disabilities are visible or not, and whether they are congenital or accident- or conflict-related.[41] Physical and mental disabilities can undermine war veterans' gendered sense of self as men, for example, as they are not able to live up to masculine-coded expectations of mobility, virility, economic and physical autonomy and agency. For some, however, war-related disabilities can also be a source of pride and identity, though this can also coexist with internalised stigma and shame.[42] The latter is particularly the case for physical, rather than mental, disabilities.[43] In the case of wounded Civil War veterans living in a Beirut care home studied by Julie Hartley, having a conflict-related rather than accident-related or congenital physical disability became an identity marker and source of pride which differentiated them from the other patients. Nonetheless, the patients still sought to avoid public visibility so as not to provoke pity or discriminatory behaviour.[44] For women former combatants, especially in cases such as Lebanon where women's direct involvement in armed combat is seen as a transgression of gender norms, conflict-related disabilities may, however, be an added source of stigma rather than pride.[45] This, however, has not been researched to any great length in Lebanon. What has also remained understudied in the Lebanese case and is of particular saliency to the visualisation (and lack thereof) of persons with disabilities are the gendered impacts on the sense of self of suddenly having to live with non-congenital, visible physical disabilities in societies which place a very high value on living up to societal expectations of external beauty and able-bodiedness, both for women and men.[46]

Apart from gendered social norms and attitudes, a further important factor in the invisibility of the war-wounded, in particular those with more severe disabilities, is the infrastructure of care in Lebanon and the lack of mobility for persons living with disabilities.[47] In my interviews, I was not able to establish the type of care that was available to Lebanese war-wounded from the Syrian Civil War and where it was being given, as this was regarded as being highly sensitive information. Several respondents speculated that the wounded might be treated outside Lebanon to keep them 'out of sight', so as not to affect morale among potential recruits and their families. However, drawing on Hartley's research, even those Lebanese war-wounded being treated in facilities in Lebanon remained mostly invisible to the rest of society, in part out of the veterans' own volition.[48] The lack of accessible transport options and ubiquitous mobility barriers also act to keep persons living with disabilities out of the cityscape.

The general lack of a visible presence in everyday life of veterans – or other persons – living with disabilities may be a contributing reason for them also not being memorialised in a visible manner.[49] Another might be general squeamishness about depicting or being exposed to visualisations of impairment and disability – what, as already noted in this volume's chapter on Soviet women veterans, Suzannah Biernoff called 'a culture of aversion' in reactions to visible disabilities in post-World-War-I Britain.[50] There is likely also a political factor at play, as the propaganda value of heroic, sacrificial death tends to be seen as being greater than that of war wounds and disabilities. The latter brings with it the risk of reducing rather than increasing morale and support for a war. Furthermore, the dead cannot express ambivalent feelings about their sacrifice any more – whereas the war-wounded can and do.[51]

While there are similarities with Iran and Lebanon when it comes to the visible commemoration of the war dead, there is a divergence here when it comes to the veterans with disabilities. In part due to the large numbers of veterans with disabilities from the Iran–Iraq War, disabled veterans in Iran have become a far more socially and politically visible group, one which has become active in a broader disabilities rights movement and which is publicly and visibly commemorated.[52] In contrast, they remain very much invisible in Lebanon, whether in person, in terms of visual representations, or as a social or political movement. The invisibility of the war-wounded and of their gendered experiences extends beyond their absence in Lebanese cityscapes and memoryscapes and the lack of visible commemorations, however. It is also reflected in the dearth of research on them, a gap which will hopefully be addressed in the future.

The invisibility of the Lebanese war-wounded is also in contrast to a growing trend in Global North countries as well as in some conflict-affected societies to visibly 'celebrate' them, or at least those amongst them who have been able to 'thrive' in spite of and because of their disabilities. This is especially the case for those physically maimed war veterans who are able to overcome their injuries and become athletically successful, for example in the Invictus Games. As Federica Caso argues, these veterans are not only 're-masculinized' as the ideal survivors but, for those fortunate enough to access such technologies, they may be 'techno-masculinized' through hi-tech protheses to 'embody a masculinity that is beyond the human'.[53] These avenues, whether one sees them as a necessary and laudable form of healing or as neo-liberal reassertions of militarised masculinities, remain, however, unattainable to the Lebanese war-wounded.

The multi-layered invisibility of the war-disabled and war-wounded in Lebanon raises a number of questions around able-bodiedness and stigmatisation of disability, of societal aversion and amnesia, but also of a bias in research that has largely not engaged with this demographic. In the Lebanese case, there is a particular gap in terms of examining the effects of conflict-related disability from a gendered perspective, and to examine what this means both for the individual's gendered sense of self and the broader societal understandings of what disabilities mean for, in this case, militarised masculinities and femininities. What is, however, literally visible is that dealing with death on the battlefield is politically and socially easier than dealing with the broken bodies and minds of war. Although the meanings attached to the deaths and their visualisations are not wholly unambiguous, they can still be slotted more easily into grand narratives of defence and sacrifice than war-related disabilities.

Conclusion

While the war dead, the martyrs of the various wars Lebanon has been involved with, are commemorated visibly in public spaces, the war-wounded and disabled remain largely invisible. The militias which the martyrs fought and died for seek to guide the meaning attached to their memorialisation, but the representations are more polysemic, allowing for different readings. As Mahmoud Abu Hashhash argues for Palestine, the posters of the dead celebrate martyrdom, their sacrifice for a greater common cause. The posters as well as their framing link this to greater political and/or religious narratives, and tie the individual deaths to broader struggles:

> Posters [of martyrs], created for local consumption and part of the daily visual environment, have a different role to play from that of the press and a different audience to address. The poster documents martyrdom; the press instead embodies the martyr in the context of agony, suffering and sadness triggered by his or her sacrifice of life. A martyr's poster containing written and pictorial information is an indirect obituary and at the same time a celebratory announcement of death.[54]

The same cannot be said for the war-wounded and war-disabled, who remain invisible for a range of reasons – stigma, fear of stigma, wanting to avoid pity and lack of mobility. In the case of the wounded from the Syrian War, there are also political risks associated with publicising their sacrifices, while the invisibilisation of Lebanese Civil War-wounded fits into a broader pattern of public amnesia around the war. The suffering of the war-wounded and disabled is thus not attached to similar broader public narratives of sacrifice and meaning-making as that of the martyrs.

Abu Hashhash argues that Palestinian martyr posters collapse the separation between public and private lives, between masculinities and femininities, between children and adults, and that in death the martyrs' lives are claimed and 'owned' by particular political parties and the Palestinian nation as a whole.[55] I would agree with this in part, but would argue that there is in fact more private agency involved in the depictions as well, both in Lebanon and Palestine. Unlike for example the vast majority of Iranian martyr pictures from the Iran–Iraq War which tend to use standard military ID photos, or the photos of Civil War-era martyrs in Lebanon, the Syrian Civil War-era ones are quite personalised in terms of demeanour, dress, haircut and messaging. The size and material used are reflective of economic means and social status of the dead and their families, with Lieutenant Colonel Kahil literally and figuratively towering above the rest. The photos of the martyrs fit into a broader visual necropolitics in Lebanon, whereby the politically potent dead remain visually present in the discourse of the living. In death as in life, however, the foot soldiers tend to remain foot soldiers. The impact of these pictures also differs depending on the beholder: for a friend or family member of the martyr, remembering the dead and their death in combat may evoke anguish, sorrow, pride and/or anger; for a supporter of the particular militia, it may symbolise honour and glory on the battlefield; for someone from a different sectarian or political background, the reaction may be one of seeing the poster primarily as a sign of territorial demarcation and political muscle-flexing. Rather than having a singular meaning, they convey a vast range of messages, often contradictory. While Craig Larkin suggests that the 'impulse towards a plural, differential and polysemic remembrance of the past . . . is best found through the safety of visual ambiguity and embracing diversity' in Lebanon,[56] the effect can also be one of segregation and underscoring of difference rather than embracing diversity – especially in the case of an issue as politically divisive as Lebanon's involvement in the Syrian Civil War.

In contrast to Palestine where there are more women martyrs – who, as Abu Hashhash argues, become masculinised in death – the Lebanese political arena of the visible dead remains a largely masculine space, again reflecting the world of the living.[57] The dead men's pictures reflect characteristics positively attributed to masculinities in Lebanon: they are able-bodied, sacrificed themselves for the communal good and showed agency. Apart from celebrated individual women such as Sana'a Mehaidli, women's role in the wars as well as the direct and indirect impacts of the wars on their lives remain invisible. While commemorating sombre deaths of the mostly male martyrs, these depictions paper over the physical, visceral ugliness and horror that was likely involved in many of the battlefield casualties, an aversion that the war-wounded could also evoke. Displaying the grim reality of war and its aftermath runs the risk of opening up discussions on the sense of the war itself and the potential futility of sacrifices made. The martyr photos hide the fact that the dead may not have wished to die for a greater cause, nor can they openly criticise the circumstances in which they died. The post-mortem political agency of the martyrs is of an ambivalent nature: they call upon the living to follow particular courses of action, but can no longer determine themselves what the message is that they are used to convey. As such, they are also hypervisible in the sense Paul Amar describes certain tropes of Arab masculinities: 'By hypervisible subjects I mean fetishized figures that preoccupy public discourse and representations but are not actually recognizable or legible as social formations and cannot speak on their own terms as autonomous subjects rather than as problems to solve.'[58]

However, I would also see a subtle questioning of the fetishised images of the male military martyr, of dominant notions of militarised masculinities at work in the photos. Rather than highlighting martial prowess and aggression, the depictions are for the most part of ordinary men, albeit in uniform and armed, of 'friendly war-fighters'.[59] The exception, once more, is arguably Lieutenant Colonel Kahil. The ordinariness and lack of martiality is underscored by the pared-down messages on most of the posters. These more nuanced understandings of masculinities at war may also help to open up spaces for discussions of male vulnerabilities, including openly discussing the mental, emotional and physical costs for those who returned alive, for their families and for the families of the martyrs. Given how contentious the Syrian Civil War is in Lebanese society, it remains to be seen whether there will be a similar kind of public amnesia as followed the Lebanese Civil War, and whether the 'little militiamen' who fought there will be cast in black and white terms. An opening up of these various discussions is fraught with political and social sensitivities, and will likely face powerful opposition.

The visualisations of the militarised masculinities and femininities of the martyrs are framed by the militias they fought for, but the personal touches allowed in the photos convey messages that go beyond notions of sacrifice or defiant resistance. The performances of militia masculinity are comparatively un-martial and unassuming, in particular when considering how Arab masculinities are often stereotyped in the West (but also to a degree in Lebanon) and how in particular Hezbollah is imagined by its detractors. This does, however, create a paradox between the depictions of the 'friendly war-fighters' from next door and the killings, maimings, sieges and other acts of violence these men had participated in – a paradox which theoretically could open up critical discussions, if there were space for this in Lebanon.

The luxury of researching and discussing these issues brings me lastly back to my own positionality. Although my access to former and current combatants and to the disabled of the Syrian Civil War was limited, my outside status gave me access that my Lebanese counter-parts often felt they did not have. My research also came with the free-dom but also the drawback of having a distance from local narratives of understanding the various conflicts and the various gendered identities and expectations at play. Instead, I came in with my own baggage of seeing and analysing what was in front of my eyes through particular lenses – lenses which, I noticed over the course of the research, had an ableist bias. This bias and lack of awareness towards disability was a product and reflection, I believe, of the way both the public narra-tives on conflict as well as the research on these narratives have often been centred on the able-bodied gendered performances of militarism among the living and on the representations of the dead. Fortunately, disabilities perspectives are increasingly being integrated into studies of the gendered performances, aesthetics and embodiments of militarism, giving important new insights into both the impacts of conflict-related disabilities on these as well as into the work that the processes of invisi-bilisation do, such as the perpetuation of sanitised, heroic narratives of war and sacrifice.

Notes

1. An early version of this paper was presented at the International Studies Asso-ciation's 58th Annual Convention in Baltimore, USA, 22–5 February 2017. I would like to thank Lana Khattab for her invaluable support with the research, the urban strolls and the chats over coffee in Beirut, and Suaad Ali Abdo for her help with translations.
2. In the context of Lebanon and the wider region, the term 'martyr' (*shahid* in Arabic, شهيد) can, but does not necessarily, carry religious connotations: see Mahmoud Abu Hashhash, 'On the Visual Representation of Martyrdom in Palestine', *Third Text* 20:3–4 (2006): 391–403.
3. While sect, often intermingling with party affiliation, is an important category of analysis in Lebanon, it is not necessarily the main factor and needs to be seen in relation to other power dynamics and identities: see Faten Ghosn and Sarah Parkinson, '"Finding" Sectarianism and Strife in Lebanon', *PS: Political Science and Politics* 52:3 (2019): 494–7.
4. See Catherine Baker, 'The Defender Collection: Militarisation, Historical Mythology and the Everyday Affective Politics of Nationalist Fashion in

Croatia', this volume; Paul Amar, 'Middle East Masculinity Studies Discourses of "Men in Crisis", Industries of Gender in Revolution', *Journal of Middle East Women's Studies* 7:3 (2011): 36–70.

5. See, for example, Frank Barrett, 'The Organizational Construction of Hegemonic Masculinity: The Case of the U.S. Navy', *Gender, Work & Organization* 3:3 (1996): 129–42; Paul Higate (ed.), *Military Masculinities: Identity and the State* (Santa Barbara, CA: Praeger, 2003); Regina F. Titunik, 'The Myth of the Macho Military', *Polity* 40:2 (2008): 137–63; Maria Eriksson Baaz and Maria Stern, 'Why Do Soldiers Rape?: Masculinity, Violence, and Sexuality in the Armed Forces in the Congo (DRC)', *International Studies Quarterly* 53:2 (2009): 495–518; Aaron Belkin, *Bring Me Men: Military Masculinity and the Benign Façade of American Empire, 1898–2001* (London: Hurst, 2012); Claire Duncanson, *Forces for Good?: Military Masculinities and Peacebuilding in Afghanistan and Iraq* (Basingstoke: Palgrave Macmillan, 2013); Amanda Chisholm, 'The Silenced and Indispensable: Gurkhas in Private Military Security Companies', *International Feminist Journal of Politics* 16:1 (2014): 26–47; Henri Myrttinen, Lana Khattab and Jana Naujoks, 'Re-Thinking Hegemonic Masculinities in Conflict-Affected Contexts', *Critical Military Studies* 3:2 (2017): 103–19; David Duriesmith, *Masculinity and New War: The Gendered Dynamics of Contemporary Armed Conflict* (London: Routledge, 2017); Guðrún Sif Friðriksdóttir, 'Soldiering as an Obstacle to Manhood?: Masculinities and Ex-Combatants in Burundi', *Critical Military Studies*, in press. https://doi.org/10.1080/23337486.2018.1494884.

6. See also Henri Myrttinen, 'Striking Poses: Notes on the Performances of Violent Masculinities in Conflict Situations', *NORMA: Nordic Journal for Masculinity Studies* 3:2 (2008): 133–49.

7. I explore my motivations further in Henri Myrttinen, 'Depictions and Reflections: Photographing Visualizations of Masculinities in Afghanistan and Democratic Republic of the Congo', *International Feminist Journal of Politics* 19:4 (2017): 530–6.

8. As has been noted by other foreign researchers in Lebanon, outside status also meant more access than many Lebanese feel they have. For Lebanese of other sects or political affiliations, martyr pictures act as a marker of a 'no-go zone' for them for fear that their outside status might be revealed and lead to serious repercussions. Being visibly a foreigner, and therefore outside the web of sectarian and political affiliations, allowed me, in the eyes of many of my Lebanese interlocutors 'to go where we would never dare to go' – though in a number of cases this was something of an exaggeration (see Craig Larkin, *Memory and Conflict in Lebanon: Remembering and Forgetting the Past* (London: Routledge, 2012)).

9. Larkin, *Memory*, 128.

10. See Tobin Siebers, *Disability Theory* (Ann Arbor, MI: University of Michigan Press, 2008).

11. For a history of the Lebanese Civil War and its background, see, for example, Robert Fisk, *Pity the Nation: Lebanon at War* (Oxford: Oxford University Press,

1990); Michael Johnson, *All Honorable Men: The Social Origins of War in Lebanon* (London: I. B. Tauris, 2001).

12. Larkin, *Memory*, 99.

13. See Sune Haugbolle, 'The (Little) Militia Man: Memory and Militarized Masculinity in Lebanon', *Journal of Middle East Women's Studies* 8:1 (2012): 115–39; Larkin, *Memory*; Julie Hartley, 'War-Wounds: Disability, Memory and Narratives of War in a Lebanese Disability Rehabilitation Hospital', in *War and the Body: Militarisation, Practice and Experience*, edited by Kevin McSorley (London: Routledge, 2013), 181–93.

14. Given the different political dynamics, I have not included the depictions of Palestinian martyrs in the Palestinian camps in Lebanon here. For an excellent historical overview of these, see Laleh Khalili, *Heroes and Martyrs of Palestine: The Politics of National Commemoration* (Cambridge: Cambridge University Press, 2007).

15. Matthew Levitt, 'Hezbollah's Procurement Channels: Leveraging Criminal Networks and Partnering with Iran', *CTC Sentinel* 12:3 (2019), 1–9. https://ctc.usma.edu/app/uploads/2019/03/CTC-SENTINEL-032019.pdf

16. See International Crisis Group, *Hizbollah's Syria Conundrum* (Brussels: International Crisis Group, 2017), 4. https://www.crisisgroup.org/middle-east-north-africa/eastern-mediterranean/lebanon/175-hizbollah-s-syria-conundrum.

17. While the Baathist party has historically supported pan-Arabism, the SSNP advocates for a Greater Syria that would encompass much of the so-called Fertile Crescent from Sinai to Kuwait and Iraq, including Lebanon, as well as Cyprus. Though secular in outlook, it reportedly recruits mostly Eastern Orthodox Christians in Lebanon, and its founder Antoun Saadé was himself Greek Orthodox.

18. International Crisis Group, *Hizbollah's Syria Conundrum*.

19. See Tracy Moran, 'Could a "Nazi" Party Soon Rule Syria?', *The Daily Dose*, 30 August 2016. https://www.ozy.com/fast-forward/could-a-nazi-party-soon-rule-syria/71156; Nour Samaha, 'The Eagles of the Whirlwind', *Foreign Policy*, 28 March 2016. https://foreignpolicy.com/2016/03/28/the-eagles-of-the-whirlwind/.

20. Leith Aboufadel, 'In Pictures: SSNP Forces Crack ISIL's Lines in Southeast Syria', *al-Masdar News*, 18 June 2018. https://www.almasdarnews.com/article/in-pictures-ssnp-forces-crack-isils-lines-in-southeast-syria/.

21. Khaled Alwan killed one Israeli soldier and wounded two in the so-called Wimpy Operation in 1982, named after the hamburger restaurant in downtown Beirut where the attack occurred, an attack which is often considered in Lebanon as the beginning of Lebanese resistance to Israeli occupation (see Larkin, *Memory*). Sana'a Mehaidli blew herself up in a car bomb attack against Israeli forces in Southern Lebanon at age sixteen in 1985, killing two Israeli soldiers and wounding twelve.

22. Achille Mbembe, 'Necropolitics', *Public Culture* 15:1 (2003): 11–40; Finn Stepputat, 'Governing the Dead?: Theoretical Approaches', in *Governing the Dead: Sovereignty and the Politics of Dead Bodies*, edited by Finn Stepputat (Manchester: Manchester University Press, 2014), 11–32.

23. Henri Chambert-Loir and Anthony Reid (eds), *The Potent Dead: Ancestors, Saints and Heroes in Contemporary Indonesia* (Sydney: Allen and Unwin, 2002); Larkin, *Memory*, 117–19, 157–63.

24. Larkin, *Memory*, 162.

25. See Shahin Gerami, 'Mullahs, Martyrs, and Men: Conceptualizing Masculinity in the Islamic Republic of Iran', *Men and Masculinities* 5:3 (2003): 257–74; Abu Hashhash, 'Visual Representation'; Khalili, *Heroes and Martyrs*.

26. Lana Khattab and Henri Myrttinen, '"Most of the Men Want to Leave": Armed Groups, Displacement and the Gendered Webs of Vulnerability in Syria' (London: International Alert, 2017). https://www.international-alert.org/sites/default/files/Gender_VulnerabilitySyria_EN_2017.pdf.

27. Both al-Moussawi and Mugniyah were killed in Israeli attacks, al-Moussawi in a missile strike in 1992 in Southern Lebanon and Mugniyah in a car bomb attack in Damascus in 2008 that has been attributed to the Mossad and the Central Intelligence Agency (CIA). Shahadeh was a founding member of Hezbollah and in charge of international operations, including allegedly the 1994 attack against the Jewish community centre in Buenos Aires and the 2012 bus bombing attack against Israeli tourists in Burgas, Bulgaria. He died of illness in 2014.

28. Gerami, 'Mullahs, Martyrs, and Men', 267.

29. Arguably, the description also only applies to some of the depictions of Iranian martyrs which are still, almost three decades after its end, prominent in Iranian cityscapes and often use military ID photos in which the soldier is in standard-issue uniform.

30. This is highly sensitive as it raises the resistance there might be, especially in the Shi'a community, to having to join or have sons, brothers, husbands join 'The Resistance', that is, sign up to fight in the ranks of Hezbollah. This has been cast by Hezbollah as an unquestionable call of duty. See also International Crisis Group, *Hizbollah's Syria Conundrum*.

31. See, for example, Jay Winter, *Sites of Memory, Sites of Mourning: The Great War in European Cultural History* (Cambridge: Cambridge University Press, 1995).

32. Jasbir Puar, *Terrorist Assemblages: Homonationalism in Queer Times* (Durham, NC: Duke University Press, 2007); Amar, 'Discourses'.

33. Amar, 'Discourses', 38–9.

34. While Palestinian suicide bombers and members of commando raids would at the very least be taking the very real probability of death into account before embarking on attacks, the same would not apply to martyred Palestinian civilians or those fighters killed in unexpected Israeli strikes.

35. A report for the Lebanon News Network has offered one detailed version of events ('Family Demands Killers of Military Hero Be Apprehended', *Lebanon News Network*, 30 July 2015. https://www.lebanonews.net/En/2015/07/30/family-demands-killers-of-military-hero-be-apprehended/) though other theories have also been floated. Elie Daou, the alleged shooter, was sentenced to six months in prison in 2018 for unintended manslaughter.

36. Personal, political and family connections and/or social capital which allow one to advance in a given situation.

37. Hiam Al-Aoufi, Nawaf Al-Zyoud and Norbayah Shahminan, 'Islam and the Cultural Conceptualisation of Disability', *International Journal of Adolescence and Youth* 17:4 (2012): 205–19; Hartley, 'War Wounds'.
38. See also Donna Reeve, 'Negotiating Psycho-Emotional Dimensions of Disability and Their Influence on Identity Constructions', *Disability and Society* 17:5 (2010): 493–508.
39. Interviews with Lebanese NGO service providers.
40. Elie G. Karam, Zeina N. Mneimneh, Hani Dimassi, John A. Fayyad, Aimee N. Karam, Soumana C. Nasser, Somnath Chatterji and Ronald C. Kessler, 'Lifetime Prevalence of Mental Disorders in Lebanon: First Onset, Treatment, and Exposure to War', *Public Library of Science Medicine* 5:61 (2008). https://doi.org/10.1371/journal.pmed.0050061.
41. Russell Shuttleworth, Nikki Wedgwood and Nathan J. Wilson, 'The Dilemma of Disabled Masculinity', *Men and Masculinities* 15:2 (2012): 174–94; Kharnita Mohamed and Tamara Shefer, 'Gendering Disability and Disabling Gender: Critical Reflections on Intersections of Gender and Disability', *Agenda* 29:2 (2015): 2–13; Jacqueline Moodley and Lauren Graham, 'The Importance of Intersectionality in Disability and Gender Studies', *Agenda* 29:2 (2015): 24–33.
42. Salih Can Açıksöz, 'Sacrificial Limbs of Sovereignty: Disabled Veterans, Masculinity, and Nationalist Politics in Turkey', *Medical Anthropology Quarterly* 26:1 (2012): 4–25; Hartley, 'War Wounds'; David Serlin, 'Introduction', in *Phallacies: Historical Intersections of Disability and Masculinity*, edited by Kathleen M. Brian and James W. Trent, Jr (Oxford: Oxford University Press, 2017), 1–24.
43. See also Joanna Bourke, *Dismembering the Male: Men's Bodies, Britain and the Great War* (London: Reaktion, 1996).
44. Hartley, 'War Wounds'.
45. Interestingly, the one woman respondent in Hartley's study sought to downplay her involvement in the militia which had led to her disability, casting herself as a civilian victim instead. How far this was due to gendered stigma or other reasons can, however, not be determined.
46. For comparisons with post-World War I Britain, see Bourke, *Dismembering the Male*; Ana Carden-Coyne, *Reconstructing the Body: Classicism, Modernism, and the First World War* (Oxford: Oxford University Press, 2009); Suzannah Biernoff, 'The Rhetoric of Disfigurement in First World War Britain', *Social History of Medicine* 24:3 (2011): 666–85. See also Catherine Baker, 'Svetlana Alexievich's Soviet Women Veterans and the Aesthetics of the Disabled Military Body: Staring at the Unwomanly Face of War', this volume.
47. Samantha Wehbi, 'The Challenges of Inclusive Education in Lebanon', *Disability and Society* 21:4 (2006): 331–43; Hartley, 'War Wounds'; Stephen Quillen, 'People with Disabilities in Arab World Face Struggle', *The Arab Weekly*, 2 April 2017. https://thearabweekly.com/people-disabilities-arab-world-face-struggle.
48. Hartley, 'War Wounds', 183.
49. On the visual memorialisation of conflict-related emotional and mental trauma, see Caso, this volume.

50. Biernoff, 'Rhetoric', 669.

51. Hartley, 'War Wounds', 190.

52. Megan Daigle, 'Gender, Disabilities, Conflict, and Peacebuilding', unpublished background paper (London: International Alert, 2018). In Turkey, meanwhile, the commemoration and bestowal of various masculine-coded benefits to the war-wounded tends to be more individual, but charged with nationalistic fervour: Açıksöz, 'Sacrificial Limbs', 10.

53. Federica Caso, 'Sexing the Disabled Veteran: The Homoerotic Aesthetics of Militarism', *Critical Military Studies* 3:3 (2017): 217–34, 219.

54. Abu Hashhash, 'Visual Representation', 391–2.

55. Ibid., 400–1. As a Palestinian interlocutor pointed out to me, this is also the case for the family members of martyrs, whose grief becomes public property and is expected to be expressed in particular ways.

56. Larkin, *Memory*, 128.

57. See Abu Hashhash, 'Visual Representation', 400.

58. Amar, 'Discourses', 40.

59. I borrow this term from the title of Torunn Laugen Haaland's study of perceptions of masculinities in the Norwegian military: Torunn Laugen Haaland, 'Friendly War-Fighters and Invisible Women: Perceptions of Gender and Masculinities in the Norwegian Armed Forces on Missions Abroad', in *Making Gender, Making War: Violence, Military and Peacekeeping Practices*, edited by Annica Kronsell and Erika Svedberg (London: Routledge, 2012), 63–75.

CHAPTER 6

Ginger Cats and Cute Puppies: Animals, Affect and Militarisation in the Crisis in Ukraine[1]

Jennifer G. Mathers

When civilians encounter depictions of soldiers displaying bonds of affection towards animals, the encounter sets in motion a process that triggers an affective response, engaging the audience at a fundamental, pre-conscious level and helping to create positive feelings towards the soldiers.[2] The definition of affect that Gregory Seigworth and Melissa Gregg provide fits very well with the phenomenon identified and discussed in this chapter: 'the name we give to those forces – visceral forces beneath, alongside, or generally other than conscious knowing, vital forces insisting beyond emotion – that can serve to drive us toward movement, toward thought and extension'.[3] At the same time, however, these almost instinctive forces do not act in a vacuum but interact with socially and culturally conditioned expectations to shape responses, whether those responses come in the form of attitudes, opinions or actions. This means, for example, that the affective response stimulated by depictions of soldiers with animals is also influenced by the audience's awareness of the military as a masculinised institution, as well as by its expectations that soldiers will engage in and (partly) be defined by gendered and racialised performances and discourses.[4] There will, therefore, be subtle differences between the view that the audience forms of a male soldier holding a cute puppy and that of a female soldier holding the same animal, although both responses may be positive. Audiences' views will also be influenced by which racialised categories they perceive the soldiers in the images to belong to, and how those gendered and racialised judgements intersect. For example, members of a community that perceives their state's military as hostile and a potential source of violence to themselves – especially those who have been historically and structurally targeted in the state's 'martial politics'[5] – are likely to have a very different response to an image of a soldier with a dog than citizens who regard the military as a protector of their values and their lives.

In general terms, though, there is something very appealing and emotionally satisfying in seeing or reading about humans sharing their lives with animals and enjoying their company; it tends to make the viewer or reader well-disposed towards the humans concerned, even in the absence of any other information about them, as the passage quoted below suggests:

> Most people seem to be born with an interest in animals, if not with an instinctive love for them. If you walk down the street with a fourfoot of any kind, almost everyone turns to look, and some of the children will even follow you. Of course, the element of curiosity is present, but there is also something finer and warmer than that. If the animal happens to be a particularly lovable one – a beautiful dog, for example, it at once changes your relationship toward almost everyone you meet. There is a bond of sympathy between you and people who a moment before were strangers.[6]

The emotion described here that is provoked by the fleeting encounter between the dog walker and other pedestrians – pleasure in the acknowledgement of a shared affection for dogs – changes the way that the humans regard each other, if only for a moment and even if they never meet again. But when the humans who are depicted with the animals are clearly identifiable as soldiers, that positive feeling translates into subtle changes in the way that the audience regard soldiers – not only the specific soldier in the image or the story, but soldiers and militaries more generally. This is especially the case when the animals concerned are from species that have been domesticated and are widely kept as household pets in civilian society, such as cats and dogs. When this process is repeated many times and distributed through a wide variety of media, it contributes to the broader phenomenon of militarisation.

Militarisation, as Linda Åhäll points out, is an everyday interaction, a normalisation of the presence of militaries, militarised bodies and militaristic ideas in civilian life and, through these interactions, a way of preparing civilians to accept the notion of war.[7] Militarisation involves the encroachment of the military institution into civilian life in a material sense as well as the acceptance by society that this encroachment is both acceptable and appropriate. In other words, it creates a blurring of the boundaries between what is distinctive and identifiable as military and what is not.[8] This chapter argues that when civilians see, for example, a photograph of a soldier holding a dog or playing with a cat, the viewer's sense of that distinction between military and not-military is blurred and confused by the transposition of a cosy, familiar scene from civilian life – a person spending time with their pet – to the world of national security, danger and war. Such images contribute to the creation of a narrative – even a brief one – about soldiers, militaries and wars, and thus to the production of feelings about these same things, since (as the introduction to this volume points out) recognising and exploring the ways that narratives produce feelings is essential in developing an aesthetic consciousness towards embodiment, militarisation and war.

This chapter's emphasis on the political significance of animals and the role that depictions of human–animal relationships can play in militarisation brings it into conversation with the rapidly growing literature on the post-human, particularly those elements of that literature that deal with relationships between humans and non-human animals. Research by scholars such as Donna Haraway emphasise the co-constitutive character of such relationships and the shifting, flimsy and constructed nature of the human–animal boundary.[9] Other researchers have taken concepts from the post-human literature and applied them to the specific case of animals in war, including Erika Cudworth and Steve Hobden, who emphasise the reciprocal nature of the human–animal military relationship, arguing that the character of war would have been very different without the participation of animals.[10] The argument in this chapter is that some state militaries rely on animals not only to help them win wars but also as a means of winning over hearts and minds. The audience targeted by these campaigns is first and foremost the state's own citizens, who must be persuaded to lend their support both for the level of military spending that the government decides is appropriate, and for the government's decisions to use the armed forces in support of political goals. State militaries are making use of more and more sophisticated ways of communicating their messages, including the internet and social media, and affective stories and images of soldiers with animals is a component of this phenomenon.[11]

The chapter starts with a short discussion of the wide range of roles that animals have played in wars, and the military work that they have done and continue to do that support the armed forces of countries around the world. It moves from a focus on animals as military instruments to a consideration of the development of bonds of affection by the human soldiers towards their non-human comrades, and then to a discussion of the affective power of the depiction of such attachments.

The chapter then compares the ways that Russia and Ukraine have sought to exploit this affective power since 2014 in order both to rehabilitate the reputations of their armed forces in the eyes of their own societies and to garner domestic support for their military operations: for Russia this is the occupation and annexation of Crimea, while for Ukraine it is the fight against Russian-backed separatists in the Donbas. In the case of Russia, the affective response has stayed mainly within Russian-speaking communities in the region, which can be attributed largely to the very culturally – and linguistically – specific ways in which Moscow distributes its messages. Ukraine has adopted a rather different strategy, including the use of English as a medium of communication in some of its social media accounts and the inclusion of hashtags that are commonly used. As a result, Ukraine has had greater – although still limited – success in reaching wider audiences.

Non-Human Animals as Indispensable Bodies in Wartime

The military use of animals in wartime has a long and varied history. Armies have typically used animals as instruments for waging war, deploying their strength, endurance and other specific abilities to compensate for human weaknesses and to enable soldiers, both individually and collectively, to accomplish tasks that would otherwise have been far more difficult, if not impossible. Perhaps the most common military use for animals has been as a means of transporting soldiers and equipment. Horses were used extensively in this context in Europe as recently as World War II, and continue to be valuable assets in locations where the condition – or absence – of roads makes motorised vehicles impractical.[12] Camels have served as military transportation in conflicts in the Middle East, including both World Wars.[13] Dogs were also used as draught animals in World War I, pulling cannons as well as performing other tasks such as carrying ammunition and providing transportation for military dispatches. The need to send reports and orders between commanders and front-line forces quickly over longer distances was filled by birds before the advent of telephones and other forms of communications technology, and some countries continue to retain the capability to use birds in this capacity.[14]

In addition to carrying out tasks that support military operations, animals have also been used as means to attack or harm opponents more directly. Armies have long used insects for this purpose, introducing agricultural pests to lay waste to crops that would otherwise sustain the enemy, spreading disease and even placing beehives in catapults during the Crusades.[15] Dogs were used by the Romans to track and round up escaping enemies and civilians fleeing their armies; this use of canines' keen sense of smell has also been used to locate, chase and aid in the capture of indigenous and enslaved peoples by colonising European forces since the fifteenth century – a practice that was adopted by slave-owners in the United States.[16] Elephants' sheer size, strength and crushing power has made them valuable military assets, especially in Asia, from ancient times to the late nineteenth century.[17]

The mirror image of using animals to cause harm to the enemy is the use of animals to protect one's own armies and to make their living and working conditions safer and more comfortable. The need to detect gas and other contaminants in the air was especially acute during World War I. Miners who were sent to the front to tunnel beneath enemy lines brought canaries with them to act as an early warning of air that was unsafe to breathe. Early submarine technology similarly posed dangers that were undetectable to human senses; each British submarine during World War I was reported to have carried three mice on board, whose distress at the effects of escaped gases would alert the sailors to the need to take action before they, too, were overcome by the fumes.[18] Dogs were used to detect landmines buried beneath the soil during World War II, and the practice of taking advantage of the canine sense of smell to identify hidden explosives has continued in the post-9/11 wars in Afghanistan and Iraq, made necessary by the extensive use of improvised explosive devices (IEDs) in those conflicts.[19] Pest control, especially the catching and killing of rats and mice, has been a vital task undertaken on land by both dogs and cats for hundreds of years, and at sea almost exclusively by cats.

The wartime work of animals has not been limited to the preparation for and conduct of military operations; animals have also been used to provide support of various kinds for wounded soldiers and veterans. The Red Cross used dogs during World War I to locate injured soldiers, while cages filled with songbirds were placed on ambulance trains and in military hospitals in the hope that their singing would cheer the wounded.[20] The reliance on animals to aid the rehabilitation of injured soldiers and disabled veterans continues, especially in light of greater awareness since the late twentieth century of the long-term effects of post-traumatic stress disorder (PTSD) on those who have been subjected to the physical and emotional violence of war.[21] When the horses of the 3rd US Infantry Regiment in Arlington, Virginia, are not needed for ceremonial duties, the regiment lends them as therapy animals to help in the rehabilitation of veterans who are re-learning how to walk following the loss of a leg.[22]

For the purposes of this chapter, even more significant than the practical uses that militaries make of animals to advance their war efforts are the development of strong bonds of affection by soldiers towards the animals with whom they share the dangers, hardships and boredom of war. There are many documented examples of soldiers feeling emotional attachments for their working animals, including expressions of concern for the animals' welfare and grief if the animals were killed. This is common in the relationship between soldiers and their military horses, although, as Louis DiMarco points out, we only have records of these bonds starting in the Napoleonic period, as this was the first time that a large proportion of soldiers were literate and included mentions of their affection for their horses in letters home.[23] An affecting story about the strength of soldiers' feelings towards their war horses is the experience of the 'walers'. During World War I, Australia sent more than 160,000 horses from New South Wales as part of that country's contribution to the war effort. The Australian soldiers developed particularly close bonds to their horses, which represented a link to the home that many of them did not have the opportunity to visit on leave during the war. As the Australian soldiers were preparing to return home after the war, they discovered that none of the walers would be returning with them; to save costs, the military authorities were planning to destroy the older animals and sell the younger ones to local buyers in the Middle East. The Australian soldiers so strongly objected to the abandonment of the young horses to new owners who might mistreat them that they organised quick, humane deaths by trained marksmen following a farewell that took the form of a day of races and a final bag of oats for each horse.[24]

Horses are not the only military animals to inspire affection in the soldiers who served in close proximity to them; soldiers' wartime letters and diaries are filled with anecdotes and mentions of the animals in their units or those that they encountered. Many of the animals adopted as unofficial mascots were pets or farm animals that were left behind when their owners were either killed in the war or fled as the conflict approached their homes, although some soldiers have had the opportunity to make pets of more exotic animals such as monkeys when they occupied cities with zoos. As Richard Van Emden points out, describing the animals that soldiers encountered and relating amusing stories about them gave soldiers a topic for their letters home that would not alarm or upset their families, while forming the relationships as well as writing about them provided ways of bridging the gap between the soldiers' own peacetime and wartime lives.[25] The humorous, self-deprecating tone of the excerpt below is typical of the way that soldiers wrote about their animal companions in war. Here Van Emden quotes from a letter written during World War I by Second Lieutenant Alexander Gillespie, of the 2nd Argyll and Sutherland Highlanders:

> Writing is difficult, for Sonia, the trench cat, is paddling about on my knees, and making herself into a living sporran. She has come from the ruined farm behind, I suppose, but she takes the change very philosophically, and is a sort of permanent housekeeper, who never leaves company headquarters in this dugout, but is handed over to each relieving regiment along with other fixtures, appearing in the official indent after the ammunition, spades, fascines, RE [Royal Engineers] material, etc, as 'Cat and box 1'.[26]

There are contemporary versions of this story in the accounts of American soldiers adopting stray dogs (and occasionally cats) in Iraq and Afghanistan during their deployments to those countries in the post-9/11 conflicts. The US Department of Defense policy against the feeding or adoption of strays has forced many animal-loving soldiers to conceal their new pets from commanders, while the successful efforts by some of these men and women to bring the animals home with them at the end of their tours of duty has been the subject of popular books.[27]

It is clear from the discussion so far that militaries and soldiers have relied upon animals for thousands of years to make a valuable contribution to waging and winning wars and to the ability of soldiers and veterans to cope with the physical and psychological trauma of war. But if we turn our attention from the details of the wartime relationships that soldiers have formed with animals and focus instead on the ways that these relationships are depicted and circulated, we are able to uncover and explore another – and far less-extensively researched – dimension to these bonds, as well as the uses to which they are sometimes put.

Animal Bodies and Human Bodies: a Closer Look at Affect and Militarisation

Reading a newspaper article about an American soldier serving in Iraq who adopted an abandoned puppy that becomes the pet and unofficial mascot of the unit, or seeing the reproduction of an old photograph of a British cavalry officer in World War I cradling the head of his dying horse, encourages the civilian reader or viewer to feel a sense of sympathy towards the soldier in the story or the image. Such stories and images are almost literally heart-warming – they establish a sense of fellow-feeling, a deep connection and approval of the protective and caring attitude displayed by the soldier towards vulnerable and appealing animals. The audience for such depictions feels certain things about that soldier because the soldier is demonstrating affection towards an animal. They would almost certainly feel differently – perhaps less positively, or positively but in a different way – towards that same soldier in the absence of the animal.

The positioning of animal bodies and soldiers' bodies together, sharing the same military and especially wartime setting, mimics a domestic scene of members of a family in their home with their pets. The presence of animals makes those militarised, wartime spaces seem home-like and encourages the audience to associate them at a subliminal level with home-like notions such as cosy, welcoming and safe. In other words, it triggers in the viewer or reader feelings that are precisely the opposite of the ones that civilians usually have towards war, which is typically felt to be hostile, dangerous and threatening. Indeed, some images of soldiers with animals appear deliberately to have set out to reproduce a home-like setting, such as a photograph from World War I that shows a group of US soldiers relaxing together while on leave in France: one is shaving, others are writing letters, reading newspapers or chatting to each other, while two soldiers in the centre of the shot are playing with a kitten.[28] Such depictions provide glimpses of those moments of friendship, affection and joy that, as Julia Welland's research reminds us, continue to exist even in wartime.[29]

These approving, positive feelings are not limited to the specific soldier in the story or the image; the affect encourages the viewing of a larger category of soldiers or indeed the military as a whole in a similarly sympathetic and connected light. This extension of the feelings thus provoked tends to be focused on 'our' soldiers and 'our' military, especially in wartime, when governments have a strong interest in maintaining morale and the enthusiastic support of civilian society for soldiers, the military and the war effort. By the same token, affective stories and images of soldiers with animals are rarely, if ever, part of wartime propaganda aimed at the enemy. A state at war wants its opponents to view the state's own soldiers as strong and formidable, not as soft and caring in their relationships with animals, and neither does the state want to encourage its own society to view the enemy's soldiers in such a light. It is no accident that similarly heart-warming stories and images of enemy soldiers with adorable animals tend not to be circulated until many years after the war has ended. It is possible to find sympathetic photos from World War I of German soldiers with animals (with a cat on the lap, with an arm affectionately around a dog) in the online photo archives of Allied nations.[30] Perhaps World War I is sufficiently far in the past, its causes seen as remote and not likely to be repeated, so that the descendants of these wartime enemies can safely view each other's ancestors in a more sympathetic light. This is in sharp contrast to the repugnance that was expressed at the surfacing of World War II photos of male and female SS guards laughing and enjoying themselves at a holiday camp.[31] In both cases, the wars are long over and those pictured are almost certainly dead. But the scale and nature of the war crimes committed by the Nazis are too enormous, too recent and have too much resonance with the rhetoric of some present-day white suprema-cist groups to risk triggering a sense of fellow-feeling with Nazi soldiers. In other words, the repudiation of any suggestion that SS guards should be regarded as ordinary people contains a tacit recognition that affect is both powerful and potentially dangerous if directed towards those who are deemed unworthy of sympathy.

Many of the images that we have of soldiers with animals were cre-ated for private communications – typically to record a wartime affec-tionate relationship between soldier and animal, either as a keepsake for the soldier or to be sent to the soldier's family, perhaps with a letter reassuring them that all was well and to demonstrate that the soldier had found some companionship amidst the hardships and dangers of war. Photographs in the late nineteenth and early twentieth centuries were often printed on stiff cardboard and were sometimes written on in the form of a postcard. There is an example of such a military postcard in the collection of the US National World War I Museum: a German officer is shown in uniform mounted on his horse, in front of a house where a cat sits on the doorstep. On the reverse the officer has written a short letter to his family, drawing his young son's attention to the pres-ence of the cat.[32] Early photographs of soldiers and animals were taken by professional photographers, usually in studios but often in front of backdrops that mimicked a wartime or military setting, such as the pho-tograph of the Australian World War I soldier solemnly holding a kitten in the crook of his arm as he stands in front of a backdrop depicting a military tent.[33] Other photographs were taken in the field, and although were clearly posed, were evidently intended to depict scenes from the everyday life of the soldier. In this category are the many photos we have showing World War I soldiers in or near a trench and either holding or positioned next to cats or dogs, as well as sailors from both World Wars with their ships' cats or kittens, which are sometimes shown sleeping in tiny hammocks with one or more sailors looking on.[34] There are also photographs that depict animals in military settings without any accompanying humans – many of these show ships' cats, often posed on or poking their heads out from inside the barrels of massive ships' guns.[35]

There are many examples of both formal and more casual photographs of soldiers and sailors with animals from other wars of the late nineteenth century (including the US Civil War and the Second Boer War), the twentieth century (especially World War II but also the Vietnam War and the Korean War among others) and contemporary conflicts.[36] As photography has become a more familiar practice and cameras more widespread, states at war have increasingly used heart-warming images of soldiers and animals to accompany morale-boosting anecdotes that are provided to the press, ensuring that such depictions do not remain the exclusive preserve of private remembrance and communication. During World War I, photographs and drawings of soldiers and animals – typically horses or dogs – were reproduced in mass-circulation publications such as Britain's *Daily Mail* newspaper, with very sentimental captions and accompanying stories.[37] The construction and relaying of inspiring stories about the adventures of animals during World War I (and the British soldiers who served with them) was undertaken by Ernest Harold Baynes. Baynes was given extensive access to serving and former soldiers, sailors and officers to gather material for his 1926 book *Animal Heroes of the Great War*, which is also the source of the quotation in the introduction to this chapter. In 1943, Britain introduced the Dickin Medal as an award for animals who demonstrate gallantry and devotion to duty in wartime, with the first award going to three pigeons serving with the Royal Air Force.[38] The publicity generated by each awarding of the medal ensures that the affective response in (particularly domestic) audiences is renewed. American journalists reporting on US soldiers serving overseas during World War II made 'mascot photography' or 'buddy photography' a staple of the photographs they sent back home with their stories. As L. Douglas Keeney puts it, 'Photos of "buddies" – soldiers and their dogs – conveyed to the people on the home front that their boys, in spite of the horrors they faced, were still boys.'[39]

If anything, present-day media outlets are even more aware of the affective power inherent in depicting the bodies of animals in military spaces than their predecessors, as well as the popularity of such depictions with the consumers of media. It has become commonplace for newspapers, television channels and magazines, as well as their corresponding websites, to feature upbeat stories and images that depict the affection that soldiers or veterans feel for the working animals, pets and mascots they have encountered in war zones. These are the sorts of feel-good, human interest stories that might provide the closing item on a news broadcast or be included in the lifestyle section of a newspaper. As we have already seen in this chapter, publishers have discovered that they can sell books about soldiers forming bonds with the animals they encountered in post-9/11 Afghanistan and Iraq.

State militaries and military alliances have, in turn, become much more sophisticated and systematic about creating such stories and images themselves. In addition to providing this material to external media outlets, militaries use their own websites, YouTube channels and social media accounts as part of their strategies to ensure that their messages reach wider audiences.[40] Research into this 'digital militarism' of the early twenty-first century reveals the extent of the use of digital media by both ordinary soldiers and by the public relations arms of state militaries. As Kuntsman and Stein argue, these practices extend 'militarized culture into social media domains often deemed beyond the reach of state violence'.[41] Uplifting stories and images of soldiers and animals are just one category of messages that are conveyed through digital militarism, but they may be among the most effective in persuading audiences to develop positive opinions of military forces and wartime goals precisely because of the emotional punch that they pack. The popularity of animal images on the internet and social media in general also means that the animal-related messages created by state militaries can travel far beyond audiences in their own nation-states. The spread of a short video clip showing part of Chile's annual military parade in Santiago in September 2018 provides an illustrative example. In the clip, members of the Chilean national police force's canine corps are shown marching with their human handlers. But while male police officers marched with adult dogs, the procession was led by female police personnel who carried 45-day-old golden retriever puppies in specially designed pouches. The video was posted on the main Reuters Twitter account and also picked up on by the websites and social media accounts of other broadcasters such as Sky News, Fox News, *Newsweek* and the BBC. Responses to the tweet were posted in a variety of languages, with many of those who replied in English expressing the wish that other military parades would include dogs and puppies, while one that suggested more Americans would have been receptive to Donald Trump's proposal of a military parade to mark Independence Day celebrations on the Fourth of July if only the USA would follow Chile's example and place cute puppies in prominent positions.[42]

Even a brief exploration of the images that have been posted on the official social media accounts of some Western militaries during 2018 reveals that the practice of sharing affective depictions of soldiers with animals is becoming both fairly common and increasingly sophisticated. Posts to these accounts (that is, Twitter, Instagram and Facebook) frequently use hashtags that are widely used in the civilian social media space, such as #MondayMotivation, #inspiration or #ICYMI ('In Case You Missed It'), which greatly increases the chances of such posts being noticed, liked and shared by civilian users. When images of soldiers and animals are posted by these accounts, the posts also often include a hashtag that will make the post more widely visible, especially hashtags that mark some animal-related occasion. On 26 August 2018, the British Army posted a short video of a young female private featuring her work as a dog handler in Afghanistan which included the hashtag #NationalDogDay.[43] National Dog Day was also marked by a post from the North Atlantic Treaty Organization (NATO) which included a short video about Mali, described as a hero dog who had saved lives while serving with the British Army in Afghanistan.[44] Cats are also popular subjects of social media posts that feature soldiers with animals. In July 2018 the Massachusetts National Guard posted the image of a kitten in the pocket of a soldier's camouflage uniform with the hashtag #AllAmericanPetPhotoDay. In the closely cropped shot, only the kitten's head and one of its arms is visible, along with a man's hand petting the young cat. This simple gesture links a display of human affection for a pet with the military's role of providing protection for the weak and vulnerable.[45]

Affective images and stories about the close bonds that soldiers have developed with animals in wartime or during military service have become a common currency in news media and social media alike, with state militaries in the West putting considerable effort into getting those depictions circulating as widely as possible. Both visually and emotionally appealing, these are stories and images that are easy and enjoyable to share on social media, which thousands upon thousands of people do on a daily basis, probably without ever asking themselves why these military institutions are trying so hard to get them to associate soldiers and war with cuddly pets. Turning from the practices of Western military institutions to those of Russia and Ukraine, we can see some continuities, especially in the use of depictions of soldiers and animals to provoke an affective response, first and foremost within their own societies, of sympathy and admiration for the armed forces. There are some distinct differences, however, both between the actions taken by the militaries of Russia and Ukraine, and when comparing strategies adopted in Western Europe and North America with those pursued by Moscow and Kyiv.

Cats, Dogs and Soldiers in Military Operations in Crimea and the Donbas

Military operations in Ukraine since the spring of 2014 have been accompanied by very explicit attempts by both Moscow and Kyiv to exploit affect through the creation and promotion of carefully chosen images of soldiers with animals, almost exclusively with cats and dogs: domestic pets who have found themselves in an area of military operations but who have had the good fortune to be rescued, looked after or otherwise placed under the protection of soldiers. Quite apart from any recent societal disapproval of the two militaries sparked by their behaviour during these operations, the armed forces of both countries have reputations that have been tarnished over many years by well-founded allegations of corruption, the callous treatment of young conscripts and professional incompetence.[46] The promotion of charming images of soldiers with adorable animals is an aspect of wider efforts to rehabilitate their images, primarily in the eyes of their own societies, although for Ukraine there is a distinct outward-facing dimension to this campaign of affect which is almost certainly linked to Kyiv's efforts to gain membership in international organisations such as NATO and the European Union.

Cats have been closely associated with Russia's deployment of 'polite people' (or 'little green men' as they are described in the West) to Crimea in February 2014, as well as with the ways that this event has been officially commemorated. Russia deployed troops wearing uniforms without any identifying national insignia to Crimea shortly after the former Ukrainian president Viktor Yanukovych fled Kyiv and Ukraine, abandoning his presidency in the face of political pressure from opposition parties backed by sustained popular protests. Initially Moscow denied that Russia had sent the soldiers, although the Russian president Vladimir Putin later admitted that the troops were Russian. The phrase 'polite people' to describe these soldiers was coined by a Russian blogger, partly as a joke, but was quickly seized upon by Moscow to emphasise the contrast between the previous reputation of Russian troops – poorly trained and lacking in discipline and manners – and this new army comprised of *polite* people, who are professional in all respects and always courteous to civilians.

During the initial deployment, the Russian soldiers were welcomed by those local civilians who supported the transfer of the Crimean

peninsula from Ukraine to Russia, and the troops quickly became magnets for selfie-takers.[47] Numerous photographs were posted on social
media accounts that showed local civilians posing next to one or more
of these anonymous soldiers, sometimes handing flowers to the uniformed men, but in several others the soldier in the photo is holding
a ginger tabby cat. The presence of a ginger cat echoed a previous incident, also shared widely on social media, when a soldier caught and
returned a feline of this colour to a young boy who had evidently lost
his pet. The image of that moment (or, more likely, the image of that
moment as re-enacted for the camera of the TASS photographer) has
been reproduced extensively in the Russian news media.[48] The return of
the cat nicely encapsulated the image of restraint, professionalism and
benevolent protection that the Russian Ministry of Defence wanted to
project, and the link between cats and the Crimean military operation
has been cemented in the popular imagination in Russia, Crimea and
the separatist areas of the Donbas. The return of the cat is memorialised
by a statue in the Siberian city of Belogorsk.[49] Another statue celebrating
the polite people was erected in the Crimean city of Simferopol; this
statue depicts a soldier standing next to a young girl, and by their feet
is a seated cat.[50] The Russian model-making company Zvezda has produced a set of 'polite people' toy soldiers. The box features a photograph
of a ginger cat sitting next to a group of soldiers, while the collection of
models in the box includes a cat.[51] The phrase *Vezhlivii Lyudi* ('polite
people' in Russian) together with the silhouette of a soldier with a cat
at his feet has been picked up by Russian commercial companies and
printed on T-shirts and car stickers. Badges embroidered with the 'polite
people' phrase and the soldier and cat image have been adopted unof-
ficially by many separatist units fighting in eastern Ukraine.[52]

But in spite of the success in spreading this particular, positive message about Russian soldiers to Russian-speaking communities in the
region, the association of the Russian military with ginger cats has
barely extended beyond Russians and those who study the country.
Perhaps the return of the ginger cat is too obscure and contextually
specific to resonate with wider audiences, who might themselves not
be very receptive to a sentimental story involving the controversial
annexation of Crimea. Another factor that might have restricted the
ability of this highly visual episode to travel is the content and style of
Russian military social media accounts, which tend towards the official and rather bland. The images posted are usually very serious, carefully composed shots of weapons and equipment, training exercises,
parades and formal meetings. The text is almost always in Russian and

the hashtags they use are factual and specific to the military. There seems to be little space in the world of Russian military social media for content that is whimsical, sentimental or heart-warming.

Ukraine, meanwhile, has been engaged in efforts to associate its armed forces with cats and dogs in general, rather than invoking a distinctive memory. The manner in which Ukrainian state actors, including the military, conduct their social media campaigns is very different from their Russian counterparts. Several social media accounts affiliated with the government (including that of Ukraine's former President Petro Poroshenko) and the armed forces post photos of soldiers with animals (usually cats or dogs) or photos of animals in military encampments in the Donbas region. Such posts are interspersed with more formal photos and text that demonstrate the professionalism and combat-readiness of the Ukrainian military, together with their frequent interactions with NATO, such as meetings between senior officials and joint training exercises. For the most part, these social media efforts are aimed squarely at Ukrainian audiences; the text is almost always written in Ukrainian, and, when hashtags are used, they are also Ukrainian. Kyiv regards the conflict in the Donbas as one that poses an existential threat to the country, and the government is clearly using social media as one way of trying to persuade Ukrainian society to lend its wholehearted support to the war effort. This includes invoking affective images and stories of soldiers with animals.

In addition to efforts to tug at the heartstrings of Ukrainian civilians by depicting soldiers demonstrating their affection and caring towards animals, there are some distinctly gendered dimensions to these posts. The photos of soldiers and animals posted by the Ukrainian Ministry of Defence Twitter account 'Defence of Ukraine' (@DefenceU) are accompanied by very different styles of commentary depending on whether the soldiers pictured are male or female. Where the soldier is a man, the text usually describes the animal–human relationship in terms that suggest the humans and non-humans are comrades in arms, such as the tweet posted in March 2018 captioned 'true friends' that accompanied a photo of a male soldier holding a cat,[53] or the photo of a male soldier with two puppies that was posted the following month with the comment 'real friends'.[54] By contrast, in February 2018 the same account posted a photo of a woman soldier holding a black cat with the caption 'fluffy helpers',[55] leaving ambiguous whether the description referred to the cat (and other animals) or the cat and the woman together. A similar tweet was sent on 11 April 2018 with a photo of puppies held in a woman's arms with the text 'little helpers',[56] again not making it

clear whether women soldiers are regarded as diminutive, appealing creatures who are there to help soldiers fulfil their military duties
or as full soldiers in their own right. This ambiguous messaging was
reinforced by posts from Poroshenko's official Twitter account, which
posted photos of male soldiers posing with dogs under captions that
praised the soldiers pictured for their heroism and remark on their courage and the pride that Ukrainians must feel about their actions.[57] In contrast, the former President's Twitter account posted a photograph of a
woman soldier holding a puppy on 7 March 2018 to mark International
Women's Day, accompanied by text that praised the kindness, love,
joy and warmth of women who symbolise all that is best in life and
expressed the sentiment that with such women, Ukraine will soon win
the war against its enemies.[58] These suggestions that Ukrainian civilian
and military authorities might not take the country's women soldiers
entirely seriously is consistent with the ongoing struggles for acceptance
that women in the Ukrainian armed forces have experienced.[59]

While much of the social media output from Ukrainian government
and military accounts is aimed primarily at domestic civilian audiences,
there is an exception: a dedicated Twitter account, 'Ukrainian army cats
and dogs' (@UAarmy_animals), which normally posts several photos
a day with short captions in English praising the relationship between
the soldiers and their non-human companions. In addition to posting
in English, @UAarmy_animals also uses hashtags that can easily be
found by civilian social media users. This account typically posts photos
of soldiers with one or more animals but also quite frequently tweets
images of cats and dogs in military settings without any humans visible
in the shots. So, for example, we might see a photo of a cat sleeping
among weapons, ammunition or grenades, or a dog sitting in an apparently empty camp or at a lookout position.[60] The placement of cats and
dogs in these wartime locations could be jarring and disturbing – and
for some who view these images they might be, prompting concerns
about the vulnerability of these animals who have the misfortune to
live in a war zone, but it is clearly not the perception intended by those
who operate this account. @UAarmy_animals provides a steady stream
of positive messages about the cheerful, everyday heroism of Ukraine's
armed defenders who combine patriotism and courage with a touching
demonstration of compassion towards local pets who were presumably
abandoned when their owners fled the conflict zone. The presence of
these animals in military spaces also encourages us to see those spaces
as cosy and home-like. Cats in particular are renowned for their desire
for comfort and enjoyment of pleasure; at a subliminal level, we are

conditioned to regard any place that a cat is willing to sleep as welcoming and comfortable.

In many respects the @UAarmy_animals Twitter account represents a rather basic attempt to influence English-language social media users. The English text is often awkwardly phrased and words are sometimes misused or misspelled. Every post uses the same hashtags in the same order: #army #Ukraine #cats #war #soldier #cat #freedom #pet #pets. It would appear that someone involved in running the account has calculated that #cat is a more popular hashtag than #dog, although it is disconcerting to see images of dogs under the hashtag #cat. With a little over 2,000 followers as of June 2019, the direct reach of the account is limited, although its followers do include English-speaking journalists who are in a position to disseminate the images and impressions created by the posts. Despite its limitations, the account's very existence and manner of functioning suggests a strategy to engage audiences in Western Europe and North America with a positive and upbeat message about the Ukrainian war effort. This is in keeping with Kyiv's explicit goal of gaining membership in major Western international organisations, especially NATO and the European Union.

Conclusions

Exposure to affective depictions of soldiers with animals, especially with domesticated animals such as cats and dogs, encourages civilian audiences to view soldiers, militaries and even the aims of war with sympathy and approval. Witnessing the affection that a soldier feels for a working military animal, a mascot or an abandoned animal adopted as a pet helps to soften the image, not only of that specific soldier but also of the military as a whole. How can we fear or dislike a soldier who is holding a kitten or giving a loyal dog a friendly pat? At the same time, the caring and protective attitude that the soldier displays towards the animal echoes the stance that state militaries are expected to adopt with respect to members of civilian society. Perhaps one reason for the persistence of affecting narratives and images of soldiers and their wartime animal friends lies in this mirroring of soldier–animal and idealised soldier–civilian relationships.

Appealing depictions of soldiers with animals also invoke cosiness and domesticity, even in otherwise inhospitable wartime settings, further blurring the boundaries between military and civilian spheres. Such images provide personal glimpses into the everyday lives of soldiers that are distinct from the grand scale and spectacle of public, staged events such as the military parade and are an example of the emotional and intimate politics of militarisation that are discussed in the Introduction to this volume. This process of militarisation has taken on a new and more intimate tone in the social media age, when the civilian–military boundary being crossed is one that leads directly into the everyday activity of checking Facebook, Twitter and Instagram accounts on a phone, tablet or laptop. As Laura Shepherd writes, 'To see the military on a Facebook feed, alongside photos from a family party and updates from friends, brings the military as an actor into the private lives of citizens in a previously unimaginable way.'[61]

The combination of heart-warming depictions of soldiers with animals with social media would seem to be a golden opportunity for militaries to create and spread ever more appealing and attractive messages ever more widely, and some states (such as Britain and the USA) appear to be doing precisely this. The examples of Russia and Ukraine, however, provide instructive reminders about the continuing importance of contextual specificity in processes of militarisation. All images and messages are not equally appealing to all audiences, even those involving cuddly, adorable animals. Perhaps one of the pre-requisites for successful militarisation is a certain degree of sympathy – or, at least, the absence of hostility – towards the state that controls the military, as well as towards the military itself. This may explain why some states, like Russia, find that their particular soldier-with-animals narrative simply does not translate well across cultural and linguistic boundaries, or that it is not powerful enough to overcome a prevailing sense of anger at their policies, such as the annexation of Crimea. Other states, like Ukraine, may struggle to exert a wider influence for other reasons, such as the need to focus primarily on audiences that are closer to home, and may also lack the English language fluency and the familiarity with social media's rapidly changing practices to establish themselves firmly using these platforms. Militarisation is above all a set of social processes which operate and resonate quite differently depending on the time, place and the people concerned.

Notes

1. The inspiration for the topic of this chapter came in part from a lecture given by Emeritus Professor Martin Alexander at Aberystwyth University, which later appeared in print as Martin S. Alexander, 'War and its Bestiality: Animals and Their Fate During the Fighting in France, 1940', *Rural History* 25:1 (2014): 101–24.

2. The affect described here is stimulated in societies where developing and demonstrating affection towards animals is encouraged and regarded as admirable.

3. Gregory J. Seigworth and Melissa Gregg, 'An Invention of Shimmers', in *The Affect Theory Reader*, edited by Melissa Gregg and Gregory J. Seigworth (Durham, NC: Duke University Press, 2009), 1–28, 1.

4. On this point, see Synne L. Dyvik, *Gendering Counterinsurgency: Performativity, Embodiment and Experience in the Afghan 'Theatre of War'* (London: Routledge, 2017), 23. I am grateful to Catherine Baker for pointing this out.

5. Alison Howell, 'Forget "Militarization": Race, Disability and the "Martial Politics" of the Police and of the University', *International Feminist Journal of Politics* 20:2 (2018): 117–36.

6. Ernest Harold Baynes, *Animal Heroes of the Great War* (London: Macmillan, 1933), 3–4.

7. Linda Åhäll, 'The Dance of Militarisation: A Feminist Security Studies Take on "the Political"', *Critical Studies on Security* 4:2 (2016): 154–68, 160, 162.

8. See Cynthia Enloe, *Does Khaki Become You?: The Militarization of Women's Lives* (London: Pandora, 1988), 9–10; Laura Sjoberg and Sandra Via, 'Introduction', in *Gender, War, and Militarism: Feminist Perspectives*, edited by Laura Sjoberg and Sandra Via (Santa Barbara, CA: Praeger, 2010), 1–16, 7.

9. Donna J. Haraway, 'Cyborgs to Companion Species: Reconfiguring Kinship in Technoscience', in *The Haraway Reader*, edited by Donna Haraway (London: Routledge, 2004), 295–320, 300; Donna J. Haraway, 'A Manifesto for Cyborgs: Science, Technology, and Socialist Feminism in the 1980s', in *The Haraway Reader*, edited by Haraway, 7–46, 10.

10. Erika Cudworth and Steve Hobden, 'The Posthuman Way of War', *Security Dialogue* 46:6 (2015): 513–29, 514.

11. For discussions of some of the ways that state militaries use the internet and social media, see: Adi Kuntsman and Rebecca L. Stein, *Digital Militarism: Israel's Occupation in the Social Media Age* (Stanford, CA: Stanford University Press, 2015); Rhys Crilley, '"Like and Share Forces": Making Sense of Military Social Media Sites', in *Understanding Popular Culture and World Politics in the Digital Age*, edited by Caitlin Hamilton and Laura J. Shepherd (London: Routledge, 2016), 51–68.

12. R. L. DiNardo and Austin Bay, 'Horse-Drawn Transport in the German Army', *Journal of Contemporary History* 23:1 (1988): 129–42; Nigel Allsopp, *Animals in Combat* (London: New Holland Publishers, 2014), 8, 45–6.

13. Allsopp, *Animals in Combat*, 30–1; Cudworth and Hobden, 'Posthuman Way of War'.

14. Tony Allen, *Animals at War 1914–1918* (York: Holgate Publications, 1999), 33–7; Allsopp, *Animals in Combat*, 19.

15. Jeffrey A. Lockwood, *Six-Legged Soldiers: Using Insects as Weapons of War* (Oxford: Oxford University Press, 2009); on the military use of bees, see also Lisa Jean Moore and Mary Kosut, 'Bees, Border and Bombs: A Social Account of Theorizing and Weaponizing Bees', in *Animals and War: Studies of Europe and North America*, edited by Ryan Hediger (Leiden: Brill, 2013), 29–44.

16. Gervase Phillips, 'Technology, "Machine Age" Warfare, and the Military Use of Dogs, 1880–1918', *Journal of Military History* 82:1 (2018): 67–94, 68.

17. Konstantin Nossov, *War Elephants* (Oxford: Osprey Publishing, 2008).

18. Allen, *Animals at War*, 39.

19. Robert G. W. Kirk, 'In Dogs we Trust?: Intersubjectivity, Response-Able Relations, and the Making of Mine Detector Dogs', *Journal of the History of the Behavioral Sciences* 50:1 (2014): 1–36; Allsopp, *Animals in Combat*, 55–9.

20. Allen, *Animals at War*, 33. On physically disabled veterans, see Baker, 'Svetlana Alexievich's Soviet Women Veterans', this volume; Myrttinen, this volume.

21. See, for example, Myra F. Taylor, '"Nudging Them Back to Reality": Towards a Growing Public Acceptance of the Role Dogs Fulfill in Ameliorating Contemporary Veterans' PTSD Symptoms', *Anthrozoos* 26:4 (2013): 593–611.

22. Allsopp, *Animals in Combat*, 86–7.

23. Louis A. DiMarco, *War Horse: A History of the Military Horse and Rider* (Yardley, PA: Westholme, 2008), 217.

24. Ibid., 321–2.

25. Richard Van Emden, *Tommy's Ark: Soldiers and their Animals in the Great War* (London: Bloomsbury, 2010), 7.

26. Ibid., 88.

27. See, for example: Jay Kopelman and Melinda Roth, *From Baghdad with Love: A Marine, the War, and a Dog Named Lava* (Guilford, CT: Lyons Press, 1999); Christine Sullivan, *Saving Cinnamon: The Amazing True Story of a Missing Military Puppy and the Desperate Mission to Bring Her Home* (New York: St Martin's Press, 2009); Terri Crisp with Cynthia Hurn, *No Buddy Left Behind: Bringing US Troops' Dogs and Cats Safely Home from the Combat Zone* (Guilford, CT: Lyons Press, 2013).

28. 'Black and White Photograph of American Soldiers Relaxing While on Leave from the Front', 2018.30.94, National World War I Museum Online Photo Collection. https://theworldwar.pastperfectonline.com/photo/54C250FE-1C96-4F4B-8F86-385423354201.

29. Julia Welland, 'Joy and War: Reading Pleasure in Wartime Experiences', *Review of International Studies* 44:3 (2018): 438–55, 439.

30. See, for example: 'German Soldier Seated with a Cat and Two Dogs', Q93874, Sulzbach Herbert Collection, Imperial War Museum. https://www.iwm.org.uk/collections/item/object/205337209; 'Black and White Photograph of a Group of Germany Military Officers. Officer on the Right is Playing with a Small White Dog', 2012.54.18.89, National World War I Museum Online Photo Collection. https://theworldwar.pastperfectonline.com/photo/BA7B6B61-4865-49C2-94B5-937219338258.

31. John Donoghue, 'Solahütte: The Auschwitz Holiday Camp for the SS', *Sunday Express*, 26 February 2015. https://www.express.co.uk/news/history/560416/Solah-tte-Auschwitz-holiday-retreat-SS-Nazis-rest-recreation.

32. 'Photo-Postcard from Karl Rosendahl to His Child, Friedel', 2014.27.60, National World War I Museum Online Photo Collection. https://theworldwar.pastperfectonline.com/photo/23DF6AF7-15FE-4560-A94E-279623442847.

33. 'Studio Portrait of JG Harrison Who Has Not Been Further Identified, Holding a Kitten', DA16537, Australian War Memorial online collection. https://www.awm.gov.au/collection/C1050066.

34. See, for example: 'Sailors Surround the Ship's Cat "Convoy" Asleep in a Miniature Hammock on Board HMS HERMIONE, Gibraltar, 26 November 1941', A6410, Admiralty Official Collection, Imperial War Museum. https://www.iwm.org.uk/collections/item/object/205185505; 'Sailmaker JW BRIGHT, of Kraaifontein, Cape Province, South Africa, Has Made a Miniature Hammock for His Cat Trinco', A24419, Admiralty Official Collection, Imperial War Museum. https://www.iwm.org.uk/collections/item/object/205156299.

35. See, for example: 'The Mascot Cat of the Royal Navy Battleship HMS QUEEN ELIZABETH Walking Along a 15 Inch Gun', Q13781, Ministry of Information First World War Official Collection, Imperial War Museum. https://www.iwm.org.uk/collections/item/object/205248928.

36. For a selection of such images that covers much of the period since the invention of photography, see Kerry McDermott, 'The Real Dogs of War: Intimate Images Show "Soft" Soldiers Caring for the Animals Who Have Helped Them Through the Ages', *Daily Mail*, 31 December 2012. https://www.dailymail.co.uk/news/article-2255374/The-real-dogs-war-Intimate-images-soldiers-caring-animals-helped-them.html.

37. Van Emden, *Tommy's Ark*; Allen, *Animals at War*, 8.

38. Ben Johnson, 'The Dickin Medal'. https://www.historic-uk.com/HistoryUK/HistoryofBritain/The-Dickin-Medal/.

39. L. Douglas Keeney, *Buddies: Men, Dogs and World War II* (Osceola, WI: MBI Publishing Company, 2001), 10.

40. On this point see Crilley, '"Like and Share Forces"'.

41. Kuntsman and Stein, *Digital Militarism*, 6.

42. Reuters, 'Gang of puppies steals the show at Chilean military parade', Tweet, @*Reuters*, 20 September 2018. https://twitter.com/reuters/status/1042855915848785920.

43. British Army, 'Private Jones, a military working dog handler currently serving in Afghanistan, explains her role in the NATO mission in support of Afghan security and development', Tweet, @*BritishArmy*, 26 August 2018. https://twitter.com/BritishArmy/status/1033647745947463680.

44. NATO, 'Not all heroes wear capes', Tweet, @*NATO*, 26 August 2018. https://twitter.com/NATO/status/1033649732047065088.

45. Massachusetts National Guard, 'The OCP uniform offers Soldiers deep cargo paw-cats', Tweet, @*TheNationsFirst*, 11 July 2018. https://twitter.com/TheNationsFirst/status/1017109400237068289.

46. On the reasons for the poor reputations of the two militaries and recent reform efforts, see: Deborah Sanders, '"The War We Want; the War That We Get": Ukraine's Military Reform and the Conflict in the East', *Journal of Slavic Military Studies* 30:1 (2017): 30–49; Bettina Renz, *Russia's Military Revival* (Cambridge: Polity, 2018).

47. Tara Brady, 'Selfskies from the Frontline: People of the Crimea Pose Up with the Masked Russian Invaders', *Daily Mail*, 3 March 2014. https://www.dailymail.co.uk/news/article-2571799/Shocking-pictures-people-Crimea-taking-SELFIES-Russian-masked-gunmen-Ukraine-teeters-brink-war.html.

48. Natal'ya Galimova, 'Mi idem v Rossiyu. Kak – ne znayu', *Gazeta.Ru*, 12 March 2015. https://www.gazeta.ru/politics/2015/03/11_a_6503589.shtml.

49. Daisy Sindelar, 'Russia Unveils Monument to "Polite People" Behind Crimean Invasion', *Radio Free Europe/Radio Liberty*, 7 May 2015. https://www.rferl.org/a/russia-monument-polite-people-crimea-invasion/27000320.html.

50. 'Crimean Authorities Honor Russian Troops with "Polite People" Monument', *Sputnik News*, 11 June 2016. https://sputniknews.com/russia/201606111041176683-crime-authorities-polite-monument.

51. Many online shops sell this set of Zvezda models, such as Scalemates.com. https://www.scalemates.com/kits/965295-zvezda-3665-polite-people#.

52. Roland Oliphant, 'Ukraine Crisis: The Meaning behind Badges and Symbols of the Conflict', *Daily Telegraph*, 26 February 2015. https://www.telegraph.co.uk/news/worldnews/europe/ukraine/11436081/The-meaning-behind-symbols-of-the-Ukraine-conflict.html.

53. Ministry of Defence of Ukraine, 'Virni druzi', Tweet, *@DefenceU*, 5 March 2018. https://twitter.com/DefenceU/status/970569672188887040.

54. Ministry of Defence of Ukraine, 'Spravzhni dryzi', Tweet, *@DefenceU*, 17 April 2018. https://twitter.com/DefenceU/status/986498391407513600.

55. Ministry of Defence of Ukraine, 'Pukhnasti nomichniki', Tweet, *@DefenceU*, 28 February 2018. https://twitter.com/DefenceU/status/968823335965593601.

56. Ministry of Defence of Ukraine, 'Malen'ki pomichniki', Tweet, *@DefenceU*, 11 April 2018. https://twitter.com/DefenceU/status/984317426820091904.

57. See, for example, photos and messages posted on Twitter by @poroshenko on 3 June 2018 (https://twitter.com/poroshenko/status/1003509651269455872) and 11 July 2018 (https://twitter.com/poroshenko/status/1017014626171736066).

58. Petro Poroshenko, 'Zhinka – simvol us'ogo naikrashchogo v nashomu zhitti', Tweet, *@poroshenko*, 7 March 2018. https://twitter.com/poroshenko/status/971622103098195969.

59. For more on Ukraine's women soldiers, see Tamara Martsenyuk, Ganna Grytsenko and Anna Kvit, *Invisible Battalion: Women's Participation in ATO Military Operations* (Kyiv: Ukrainian Women's Fund, 2016). http://eca.unwomen.org/en/digital-library/publications/2016/08/invisible-battalion-womens-participation-in-ato-military-operations-in-ukraine.

60. See the @UAarmy_animals Twitter account. https://twitter.com/UAarmy_animals.

61. Laura J. Shepherd, '"Social Media, Gender, and the Mediatisation of War": A Reply', *Global Discourse* 7:2–3 (2017): 348–52, 350.

CHAPTER 7

Embodying War, Becoming Warriors: Media, Militarisation and the Case of Islamic State's Online Propaganda

Daniel Møller Ølgaard

The success with which the so-called Islamic State (IS) organisation managed to conquer the global imagination with a gory yet savvy online propaganda campaign remains noteworthy, even with the movement currently on the brink of defeat. The unprecedented amount of people who travelled to Iraq and Syria from all over the world to join the organisation, the string of violent attacks carried out in Europe by IS sympathisers or militants returning from the Syrian–Iraqi battlefield, and the increasing concern about online propaganda among both the public and politicians encourage reflection on the Janus-faced nature of digital and social media as both an intimate space and part of the war machine.[1] Whereas existing research on online propaganda has focused predominantly on digital and social media as tools of radicalisation or as resources for disseminating information that challenges state sovereignty, this chapter analyses such media platforms as new spaces for the promotion and normalisation of war and violence, where the aesthetic affordances of digital and audiovisual technologies create new possibilities for militarisation.[2] Specifically, the embodied and aesthetic sensibilities of spectators that are addressed by IS's propaganda, but also the embodied dynamics of how spectators might respond to them, are distinctive features of how war is experienced on and through digital media, revealing possibilities for promoting military action for insurgent groups like IS who do not have the communicative capacities that state militaries do.[3]

In examining digital and social media as new spaces of militarisation, the chapter engages with an already extensive field of literature in critical military studies (CMS) that examines the aesthetic and sensuous dimensions of militarisation.[4] Such an approach entails a shift in analytical focus from the content of texts, images or videos to the wide range of senses and practices involved in providing meaning to these forms of representation. Rather than analysing the cultural impact of texts, images or videos from the top down, this chapter thus emphasises the multiple and situated practices involved in making sense of media. It begins from an 'embodied reading' of Islamic State's online propaganda video 'Flames of War' in which I employ my own ethnographic imagination to uncover the affective sensibilities involved in everyday experiences of war on and through digital and social media. In this context, it is important to note that while, as a young man and a skilled digital media user, I resemble the intended target of IS's online propaganda, I also differ from this group in other, crucial aspects. For one, I do not share any form of sympathy with militant Islamist movements nor with their worldview in general. Moreover, I am not religious, much less a Muslim, although, as has been pointed out by others, neither were a considerable amount of IS sympathisers and recruits before affiliating themselves with the organisation.[5]

Of particular interest in my embodied reading of 'Flames of War' are moments where I felt my neck hairs stand up or my stomach churning, where I experienced breathlessness, registered a tingling sensation in my chest, or similar. The purpose of an embodied reading of these affective intensities is not to provide evidence of the embodied effects of media but rather to use these as a point of departure from which to examine how digitally mediated experiences of war promote and normalise war and military action in the intimate contexts of the everyday. I am inspired here most notably by Synne Dyvik's embodied readings of soldier memoirs as 'flesh-witness accounts' of wartime experiences and Susanna Hast's work on the aesthetics and embodiment of trauma, which not only examines the role of the body in war but also expresses the results of that research corporeally and aesthetically through the author's own songs about the war in Chechnya from the point of view of a civilian 'outsider'.[6] In more general terms, an embodied reading of war and militarisation thus involves some form of personal engagement with one's affective and emotional sensibilities in the form of critical reflections – whether written or performed – through which one attempts to fuse one's own life with the often distant worlds one studies. To read and sense with the body is thus to read and sense through the experience of affective intensities, without separating thinking from sensing. Neither Dyvik nor Hast, however, deal specifically with the aesthetics of digital and social media, despite these platforms' prevalence in the contemporary world as spaces for experiencing and knowing about war. In extending these authors' work to digital media, the chapter offers a critical reconsideration of militarisation that is attentive to how war and violence are embodied through corporeal dispositions and affective sensibilities, emphasising how such processes intersect with the sensory affordances provided by digital and social media.

In addition to the interpretative possibilities described above, an embodied reading also poses a number of epistemological challenges. Of these, two seem particularly important to address at the onset. The first challenge, as Catherine Baker argues in this volume and elsewhere, relates to the 'translation' of corporeal sensations into writing which inevitably reduces the complexity of such experiences.[7] As a consequence, an embodied reading risks 'overstepping into appropriation'.[8] This raises valid concerns about the power of the researcher in establishing normative forms of truth at the cost of alternative readings. Yet, while these are important concerns to keep in mind, if scholars such as myself who have never experienced or witnessed military violence are to ever understand how war works on and through bodies we must also try to *imagine* how war feels. And to share this knowledge with others we have to translate those embodied feelings into words – even if these words might often seem insufficient.

The second epistemological concern relates more closely to the ability of an embodied reading of IS online propaganda to produce knowledge about the affective qualities of digital media. As a young, white man born and raised in Denmark who uses digital and social media on a daily basis, one could certainly argue that I fit the mould of a potential IS recruit, though in other equally important aspects I also differ from the primary audiences of IS's online propaganda. These include language, class and religious belief. The concern is that these differences makes it impossible for me, as a researcher, to imagine how such audiences experience and embody online propaganda content. But while I did not bring the same sympathies to my viewing of IS's online propaganda as the organisation's intended audience is likely to have done, it is worth noting that individuals who travelled to the Syrian battlefield and expressed sympathy for IS came from all over the world, including Denmark and other affluent Western countries. A substantial amount of IS propaganda videos, including the video which is the subject of this chapter, 'Flames of War', indeed targeted people such as myself; people who had been born and raised in the West, did not speak Arabic, and had only relatively recently gained an interest in militant Islam.[9] So although I was evidently not influenced by IS propaganda in the same way as viewers who became supporters or joined IS as a result, an embodied reading of 'Flames of War' grounded in my particular positionality as a spectator thus still has something valuable to say about the affective potential of online propaganda, precisely because such artefacts need to produce meaning across both geographical and socio-economic/socio-cultural boundaries. This is particularly the case for IS propaganda, since IS's strategy was to appeal transnationally to sympathisers who would travel to the Middle East and join its envisaged Islamic state: indeed, the promotion and normalisation of IS's claim that it constituted a state military defending the sovereign territory of the Caliphate against an external enemy encapsulated the organisation's particular brand of militarisation.

Militarisation, as this chapter understands it, can be seen as a set of seemingly mundane processes that occur in the intimate settings of the mediatised everyday. The ways – that is, the aesthetic practices – in which such processes work on and through bodies have been fundamentally altered, this chapter argues, by the transition from broadcast media to a digital media ecology, fuelled by the spread of the internet and smartphones. This context informs the chapter's embodied reading of IS's propaganda film 'Flames of War', paying attention to the aesthetics of how its visual and sonic representations addressed viewers' affective sensibilities – especially the role of particular images and sounds in facilitating a *felt* – or embodied – sense of intimacy with IS's self-declared war against the West. The affective potential of 'Flames of War' is mobilised, the chapter argues, through the networked interactions made possible by digital and social media, demonstrating how aesthetic practices which depend on embodied representations of fighters and embodied reactions by viewers were used as processes of militarisation by a transnational militant movement like IS.

Militarisation and Media

It is no longer contentious to claim that war is increasingly being conducted on and through media.[10] Nor is it particularly novel to say that social media, computer games and popular culture is increasingly employed in the pursuit of militarism.[11] Today, soldiers go to battle armed with smartphones, and the public back home increasingly follow their efforts by sharing, 'liking' and commenting on still and moving amateur images of war via platforms such as YouTube, Facebook and Twitter.[12] So while digital and social media provide intimate spaces in which to connect with friends, such media platforms are also sites of militarism and militarisation that allow both military and civilian users to promote (or challenge) war and military practices of violence in novel and largely unexplored ways.

To understand how war is normalised and promoted on and through digital media, this chapter engages with and extends Linda Åhäll's work on militarisation, which emphasises the everyday and embodied politics of processes that normalise the military and war.[13] As opposed to mainstream definitions of 'militarism' and 'militarisation', which tend to define these concepts in relation to the promotion of military action and the military institutions of nation-states, Åhäll examines the everyday interactions and encounters that underpin the normalisation and promotion of war.[14] In doing so, Åhäll's work resonates with the work of a growing number of scholars in CMS. Notable examples include Victoria Basham, who shows how the 'communities of feeling' which emerge around the Royal British Legion's Annual Poppy Appeal invite the public to remember and celebrate the military sacrifice of soldiers whilst forgetting the violence and bloodiness of actual warfare; Joanna Tidy, who examines how military charity food brands participate in a 'nostalgic rehabilitation' of the British military; and Kevin McSorley, who analyses how the appropriation of military training programmes in civilian forms of exercise performs a 'repurposing and rearticulation of collective military discipline'.[15] All these seemingly mundane practices form part of what Åhäll, drawing on Cynthia Enloe, describes as the 'dance of militarisation'.

In defining militarisation as a dance – in other words, as choreographed forms of collective movement – Åhäll emphasises the ways in which the political and the corporeal are entangled, especially in relation to the production and circulation of emotions and affects that constitute or mobilise militaristic forms of political subjectivity. In doing so, Åhäll emphasises that processes of militarisation do not just involve militaristic shows of strength by states and their institutions but can also involve seemingly mundane events that 'can be found anywhere in the everyday'.[16] This everyday includes the many spaces where individuals watch online videos on computers, tablets and smartphones. Analysing militarisation as collective, choreographed forms of movement through an embodied reading of online propaganda thus entails an attention to how individuals or groups of individuals become associated with military organisations or take on military characteristics without necessarily becoming military-looking by putting on a uniform or carrying a weapon.

Thinking about militarisation along these lines opens up an analytical engagement with sensory meaning-making beyond words, providing a necessary vantage point for understanding how affective sensibilities – which we make sense of through experience – come to act as the conduit for processes of militarisation.[17] Conceiving of 'affects' as the embodied or felt intensities that pass between bodies, as Sara Ahmed also does, means that bodies can be seen as mediators of affects, and affects themselves as properties of the spaces in which bodies interact.[18] The concept of 'dance' is helpful in highlighting the role of affect in this context, precisely because it 'puts focus on how bodies move us through non-verbal communication' and draws attention to militarisation as subtle, embodied and sensory processes through which the idea of war is embodied.[19]

This 'dance' of militarisation, as Åhäll formulates it, already acknowledges some of the role of media by showing that, when media frame war as an event worthy of our emotional engagement, they invite their audience to be moved by the heroics of war and, as a result, media audiences are often unknowingly enrolled in a dance of militarisation via the circulation of media content that mobilise such affective sensibilities.[20] Yet, although Åhäll positions television and mass media as cultural spaces in which the aesthetics of militarisation circulate, her work is concerned with how affects circulate via different channels (including but not limited to media) rather than with devices and platforms themselves. In itself, it thus does not account for how the proliferation of the internet and smartphones, as well as the emergence of social, interactive platforms such as Facebook and YouTube, have reshaped how processes of militarisation work on and through bodies.

It is hardly contentious to say that the proliferation of digital and social media is changing both how wars are fought and how they are perceived. What Andrew Hoskins and Ben O'Loughlin have referred to as 'broadcast wars'[21] took place in a media ecology comprised of discrete organisations, dominated by large audiences and international news coverage and driven by satellite television; the contemporary digital media environment is characterised instead by a diffusion and fragmentation of media centres and audiences. The newness of digital media in this context lies in the forms of intimacy and immediacy its platforms generate. While the embedded 'liveness' of television was and is a feature of the medium itself, the forms of intimacy and immediacy generated by and through twenty-first-century portable online media devices are features of a dynamic network of shiftable, mutable relations, involving and connecting audiences in new ways through interactive media activities such as commenting, 'liking', retweeting or hashtagging. As Hoskins argues, this 'sociotechnical flux' has even become a 'principal shaper of the 21st century [through] the medial gathering and splintering of individual, social, and cultural imaginaries, increasingly networked through portable and pervasive media and communication devices'.[22]

How, then, does the dance of militarisation unfold on and through digital and social media? Our contemporary world's increasingly digital culture seems to be characterised first and foremost by an intensification and saturation of audiovisual media content. In 2010, 50 per cent of data circulated online already consisted of audiovisual objects, and by 2020 analysts estimate that it will rise to as much as 91 per cent.[23] This proliferation of audiovisual media content changes the structural division between spectators and the wars they watch via media because we do not read images in the same way that we read texts; when we experience images, we *feel* them, and we do so in ways that are significantly different from the way we experience words.[24] In this sense, the prevalence and saturation of audiovisual media in digital culture can be said to qualitatively transform everyday experiences of war, since, as Nicholas Mirzoeff argues, while 'the body stubbornly refuses to be in more than one place at once, a networked visuality [allows] a measure of real-time global experience'.[25]

Two concepts seem to describe the socio-political possibilities afforded by a networked visuality. First, the saturation and intensification of digital media and audiovisual content has given way to a growing sense of 'hyperconnectivity' among media users; a condition defined by increasing levels of 'individual, social, and cultural dependency on media, for maintenance, survival, and growth'.[26] Today, media platforms and devices are increasingly the locus of the interactions, both social and economic, of which everyday life consists – from paying bills to arranging dates and maintaining friendships. Second, our contemporary condition is also characterised by the emergence of a 'hyperimmediacy' where, instead of being passive viewers, we are encouraged to interact with both media content and with other media users in cyberspace.[27] For example, Facebook's social media feed combines representational forms such as text, photographs and GIFs within an interactive platform that allows users to 'remediate' content. In this sense, digital and social media defy traditional conceptions of audiences as passive bystanders. The socio-political effects of this are obvious: digital and social media allow us to be 'present' in ways that defy physical limitations. More importantly, the affective sensibilities of connectivity and immediacy afforded by digital visual media, as this chapter argues, are qualitatively transforming the task of promoting and normalising war.

A distinctly *digital* dance of militarisation is thus best described as the bridging of war and the everyday to the point where they are indiscernible in both space and time through the affective sensibilities fostered by hyperconnectivity and hyperimmediacy, where these affective intensities circulate through media with performative effects that might come to underpin processes of militarisation. To understand how digital audiovisual content can address the affective sensibilities, and how such videos' movement across the digital terrain of online platforms can mobilise and actualise their affective potential, this chapter begins from what I term an embodied reading of IS's propaganda video 'Flames of War'.

Embodying War: Aesthetics and Affect

In September 2014, the Islamic State's English-language media channel, Al-Hayat Media Centre, published an hour-long propaganda video aptly titled 'Flames of War'. The video, as well as a number of gruesome execution films published around the same time, emerged as an integral part of IS's communicative efforts to cement its name and purpose globally.[28] For while the actual effects of the video on its intended audiences are difficult to establish, 'Flames of War' quickly became a powerful example of the power of the internet and social networks – spearheaded by emotional filmmaking and propelled by both social and traditional media – to create a self-sustaining narrative of IS's war.[29]

Understanding 'Flames of War's ability to make militancy, war and violence sensible to an increasingly global and heterogeneous audience, as IS online propaganda aimed to do, requires what I am terming an embodied reading that follows Sarah Bulmer and David Jackson's approach to making sense of the affective vitality of political subjects – subjects who can only ever be partially known through the fragments provided by experience, which is by its nature embodied.[30] As already noted, an embodied reading is relevant in this context because it allows researchers to critically reflect on their own sensuous experiences of the world they are studying and how these might relate to the embodied experiences of others. While fragmented, such an approach thus allows us to grasp what is not immediately apparent from the visual rhetoric of the film: namely how 'Flames of War' represents war and violence as an *embodied* form of knowledge – not as something that one reflects on but something that one *feels* or senses innately and immediately.

My embodied reading of 'Flames of War' begins around the six-minute mark of the one-hour video where a number of individuals are presented through a visual juxtaposition of group shots and face-ups. These, we are told by the narrator, are the *mujahedeen* who have travelled from all over the world to defend the caliphate. Unlike many of the organisation's online propaganda videos, it is not IS's gory spectacles of violence that is emphasised here. Instead, it is the faces – laughing, smiling or gazing thoughtfully into the distance – of the organisation's self-proclaimed holy warriors who address the viewer. I emphasise this scene because it is representative of a wider theme in IS propaganda that seeks to portray and valorise everyday life in the caliphate which stands in stark contrast to the organisation's spectacular displays of beheadings and violence that have received most of the traditional media outlets' attention in the West.

The prominence of facial aesthetics in 'Flames of War' is noteworthy from an embodied perspective because much research suggests that we privilege images containing faces to other images – and that we do so because humans have both a capacity and a tendency to imitate the gestures, movements and bodily expressions of other bodies.[31] The affective potential of the face as an aesthetic device is best described, in this context, as a specific form of 'affective entrainment' or interpersonal correspondence that is both 'rapid, automatic and unconscious'[32] and which addresses the human subject as an affective being who will be moved by the figure of the other.[33] Facial aesthetics can thus be said to intensify the affective experience of 'Flames of War' because they possess an inherent, perhaps even primordial, force that invites our gaze and evokes our interest.

Moreover, the level of (embodied) experience on which the aesthetics of the face capture viewers' attention is more than just preconscious. As Jenny Edkins argues, faces are also sites of empathy that evoke or promote a felt sense of interconnectedness to others, and facial aesthetics can thus be said to intensify mediated experiences of the emotional life of distant others.[34] As Edkins argues: 'When we look at a photograph of a face, we tend to search the image for some indication of what the person depicted is thinking or feeling, or what sort of person they are.'[35] In this sense, through the prominence of facial aesthetics, 'Flames of War' can be said to enable viewers to ponder on the emotional life of the mujahedeen and promote a felt sense of interconnectedness with a suddenly not-so-distant war and its warriors.

Such an argument finds support in the work of Manni Crone. Based on ethnographic fieldwork in extremist environments in Denmark, Crone shows that aspiring militants are not looking 'for authoritative (religious) *speech*' but 'for living or dead models, who embody the life they want to live – specific ways of behaving, dressing, protesting, kill-ing'.[36] To this end, Crone identifies digital/visual media platforms such as YouTube and Instagram as new platforms for making war and vio-lence sensible and palpable to aspiring militant subjects who, devoid of the first-hand experience of war, 'govern[s] himself [*sic*] by consult-ing YouTube-videos from conflict zones and militant environments'.[37] By repeatedly screening videos or images from war zones, as Crone argues, 'the life and death of the mujahideen come to permeate the sensory horizon of the viewer in such a way that [they] become part of the present'.[38]

My embodied reading of digital experiences of war cannot only focus on visual signs, however. Equally important is the role of sound. Watching 'Flames of War', I was particularly taken by the prevalence of nasheeds – an Arabic genre of songs characterised by rhythmic forms of chanting, usually about Islamic beliefs, Arab history or similar – which provide the video with a persistent, repetitive sonic backdrop. The sonic backdrop provided by nasheeds is interesting here not simply because of the words that are spoken in these songs but because of the rhythms they reiterate and the bodily responses that these reiterations engender at the site of viewers. For while the lyrics of the nasheeds in the video are inaccessible to me, as a non-Arabic speaker their untranslated sound still has an embodied effect I can examine. Indeed, in this, my linguistic limitations are similar to the relatively large number of IS militants and sympathisers who do not speak Arabic, but still formed part of the audi-ence for IS propaganda.[39]

Literature on the micro-sociological formation of crowds, which describes how the constitution of group subjectivities happens at the level of rhythmic resonance as much as spoken interaction, helps to explain how the rhythms of nasheeds and the bodily responses they engender become involved in processes of militarisation. From this per-spective, a seemingly mundane event such as the act of singing in uni-son 'coordinates breathing and eventually the heartbeats of the singers come to accelerate and decelerate in sync with one another', so that in '[m]oving together, we are moved together'[40] – and affects circulate between bodies in the 'dance' of militarisation Åhäll describes.

Particularly instructive in understanding the link between sound, embodiment and synchronicity in militarisation is John Protevi's work on the affective underpinnings of how a violent group ethos is formed through military training, which (as Dan Evans has already shown in this volume) is designed to instil in recruits the 'embodied competen-cies' of how soldiers are supposed to act, move and appear. Protevi describes how the rhythmic chanting soldiers perform while marching come to function as a bodily technique that enable soldiers to bypass their cultural and somatic inhibition to killing.[41] According to Protevi, the rhythmic chanting of racialised slurs substitutes personal identities with a group-based identity, which enacts the violent ethos of the military and repeatedly dehumanises the enemy in the process.

The affective and embodied aspects of rhythms are also drawn out by Randall Collins's work on social interactions. Sport events, street parties and other crowd occasions are rich affective spaces where rhythms pulse through assemblages of bodies; similarly to military marches, such 'interaction rituals', as Collins terms them, are best described as contexts 'in which participants develop a mutual focus of attention and become entrained in each other's bodily micro-rhythms and emotions'.[42] This also resonates with recent research in neuroscience that suggests that affectively attuned bodies are 'more likely to share objects of attention, to show concern for each other, to cooperate, identify with one another, and even to think alike'.[43]

The significance of the use of nasheeds in 'Flames of War' can thus be said to relate to how they attune or 'entrain' physically disparate viewers – sonically and rhythmically – across space and time. For an illustrative example of this, think of yourself in a collective event such as a concert, a football match or indeed a military parade. In such contexts, our actions and expressions are entrained or attuned to those we observe around us; that is to say that we continually analyse and react to the collective mood of the crowd through the rhythms we hear as well as the movements we observe. This explains why, as the crowd grows louder and the rhythms intensify in strength, suddenly and without us quite realising it, we start to sing along, raise our fists, or even jump up and down: 'These are physical reactions, carried out by us to be sure', as Erik Ringmar argues, 'yet, they are in a sense not ours [but] the reactions of a shared, public body.'[44]

By addressing the affective sensibilities of viewers through images and sounds that seek to move them and make them move together with the images and sounds on the screen, 'Flames of War' exemplifies how IS's online propaganda can be said to facilitate a *felt* sense of intimacy with the organisation's war against the West. The question, then, is how this affective potential is translated into thought and action through the video's circulation online. Alongside an embodied reading of the affective potential of online propaganda, therefore, one should also consider the infrastructures of digital and social media along which these affects travel in order to understand the embodied aesthetics of militarisation in the digital realm.

Becoming Warriors: Circulation and Interaction

The importance of the communicative infrastructures provided by the internet to IS is underlined, as Roxanna L. Euben notes, by the fact

> that those most likely to be drawn to [IS] are between 18–29 years old and that, within this age range in the Global North alone, 89% are active online, 70% use social networks daily, and spend 19.2 hours per week online.[45]

It should come as no surprise then that – at the height of its powers between September and December 2014 – IS was supported by more than 46,000 active Twitter accounts with an average of 1,000 followers each, often tweeting and retweeting about IS propaganda in both Arabic and English.[46] In addition to this, IS programmers created so-called Twitter bots that, upon being installed by supporters, automatically shared content posted by the organisation, thus increasing the circulation and reach of its online propaganda.[47] Together, these are the basic components of what many have called IS's online recruitment machine which also employed professional filmmakers, journalists, editors, photographers and IT professionals.

Against this context, 'Flames of War' can not only be analysed as a media object in and of itself, but must also be seen as a node in a wider network of media centres, devices and users through which IS produced and published digital propaganda content to English-speaking audiences on a regular basis during the organisation's most successful period around 2014.[48] Put differently, 'Flames of War' not only works on and through bodies at the site of the individual; the individual is always already part of a circulatory logic of hyperconnectivity and hyperimmediacy through which individuals are enlisted in Åhäll's 'dance' of militarisation in the intimate spaces of the everyday. While videos such as 'Flames of War' address the affective sensibilities of viewers, it is in this wider digital media ecology in which the video circulates that these potentialities are mobilised. The place of affects in this ecology is well explained by Sara Ahmed, who argues that our affective and embodied reaction to images and other cultural objects do not originate in some perceived affective power of the object in and of itself; instead, cultural objects become 'sticky' only as a consequence of their movement between bodies.[49] As Ahmed puts it, 'affect does not reside positively in the sign or commodity but is produced only as an effect of its circulation' and, in this sense, images and other cultural objects 'increase in affective value as an effect of [their] movement', so that 'the more they circulate, the more affective they become'[50]

The political potential of affects and their transnational circulation on and through digital media is also illustrated through the work of Ty Solomon. Spurred by an interest in the transnational spread of protests across Egypt and Tunisia during the so-called Arab Spring, Solomon shows how amateur videos containing visual and audible signs such as 'Tunisia' or 'Peace' came to carry both meaning and affect through their online circulation and remediation by protesters and supporters alike. As one Egyptian protester put it: 'This is what freedom *feels* like . . . it was impossible to rally like this before, but today I knew I had to come out. This is our Tunisia.'[51] As Solomon subsequently argues, the 'visual power' of the civilian forms of visual activism that flooded Twitter, Facebook and YouTube during the Arab Spring thus seemed to involve 'affective factors that exceeded rationality'.[52] Certainly, to the protester quoted above, it was a seemingly inexplicable and unqualified *feeling* of freedom engendered by the online circulation of videos of protests in Tunisia that made the protests in Egypt meaningful.

Solomon's account of the generative capacity of affects in the spread of political action across geographical and cultural borders is a good starting point for describing how the circulation of affects normalise and promote war in the intimate contexts of the mediatised everyday. A Facebook post reproduced by *The Guardian* in June 2014 shows an image published by an unknown member of Islamic State depicting a bloodied hand, presumably belonging to the man who posted the image, with the caption 'My first time!'[53] More important than the image and its caption, however, is the discussion that takes place in the comments section next to the image. Writing in English supplemented by Arabic loanwords – a linguistic style often adopted by Islamist sympathisers from English-speaking or non-Arabic backgrounds – initial comments seem to sarcastically identify the blood as that of a goat or a sheep before, finally, another user profile intervenes with the question 'killed a *kaafir*!? [Arabic for non-believer]' Ironically, this question seems to complete the indexical signification of the image, as the following comments all enact it, mutually confirming that the blood is indeed that of a *kaafir* who has died at the hands of the Islamic State. While gruesome, the indexical signification of this image is an example of how online platforms involve viewers and transform those who interact with digital images into vicarious participants in what the image shows. This is particularly evident in the prominence of words of praise or absolution – 'sins are gone IN SHA ALLAH' – and of encouragement – 'first of many'.

In examining this seemingly insignificant social media post, we see how the online circulation of an image and the interactivity that social media platforms facilitate come to provide users with a sense of connectivity and immediacy. In the context of militarisation, we might thus say that digital/visual media enables the dance of militarisation to move and choreograph disparate bodies inasmuch as war and violence are increasingly materialised through the online circulation of affects in the mediatised everyday. As Judith Butler has suggested, it is the ability of such affective sensibilities to transgress and travel between subjects and objects that allows them to participate in processes of materialisation through which the surfaces and boundaries of bodies and their worlds are formed and maintained.[54] Through the insertion of audiovisual content into patterns of digitally networked circulation and interaction is what enables the affective intensities engendered by 'Flames of War' to participate in the materialisation of IS's self-declared war against the West – or, put another way, the digital logic of how affects circulate enables 'Flames of War' to facilitate an online 'crowd', which might be disembodied in the sense that no bodies are actually physically co-present but where the salience of war and violence is very much felt by the embodied subjects experiencing and performing these interactions. It is exactly in the materialisation of this shared, public body that the idea of war enters the intimate settings of the mediatised everyday, where militancy, violence and war become corporeally and collectively felt. At such a level of embodied immediacy, it is easy to imagine that it might take just a few clicks with the mouse or a few taps on the touch-screen for viewers to place themselves in the digitally mediated contexts they experience.

Taken together, we might thus say that digital and social media have transformed the methods through which processes of militarisation work on and through bodies in two particular ways. First, digital and social media have fundamentally altered the structural division between sender and receiver imposed by earlier forms of mass media, through the dual logics of 'hyperconnectivity' and 'hyperimmediacy'. The digital spectators of the present are encouraged to interact with mediated events – and it is through such forms of vicarious participation that war is allowed to enter the intimate contexts of the mediatised everyday. Second, the ability of digital and visual content to circulate the globe in endless and repetitive patterns of dissemination both broadens and intensifies the affective power that any image or video might have in and of itself, since such technologies radically speed up circulatory patterns of reception and reaction, heightening affective and interpersonal relations through online forms of interaction. So while the experience of digital and visual media address the embodied and affective sensibilities of specific audiences, these responses are mobilised only through their networked circulation. My embodied reading of 'Flames of War' thus demonstrates how the emergence and proliferation of digital and social media has created new possibilities for promoting military action for insurgent groups like IS – not only by providing a new space for the publication and circulation of aesthetic representations that address the embodied and affective sensibilities of viewers but also by creating a new embodied dynamic through which spectators might respond to and interact with them.

Conclusion

This chapter has looked at the affective and embodied underpinnings of the aesthetics of militarisation in the context of digital and social media. It argues that the emergence and proliferation of digital media allows for the idea of militancy, war and violence to become normalised through mediated interactions in which war enters the everyday in two specific steps. First, online forms of media content such as 'Flames of War' address viewers' affective sensibilities and seek to facilitate a felt sense of intimacy with IS's war on the Syrian–Iraqi battlefield through a distinctly *digital* dance of militarisation. Second, the affective potentials and intensities generated through this digital dance of militarisation are mobilised through an increasingly networked form of visuality, as aesthetic representations travel the interactive infrastructures of the internet and facilitate the emergence of online crowds that might come to participate in the promotion and normalisation of war and organised violence. Together, these conclusions draw the contours of a framework for the study of aesthetics, embodiment and militarisation that encourage scholars to pay attention to the affective and embodied dimensions of digitally mediated processes of militarisation as they occur in the intimate settings of the everyday.

Notes

1. A recent United Nations (UN) report claims that more than 25,000 people from more than 100 different countries have joined IS, primarily as a result of IS's 'cosmopolitan' use of social media and digital propaganda. See Patrick Kingsley, 'Who is Behind Isis's Terrifying Online Propaganda Operation?', *The Guardian*, 23 June 2014. https://www.theguardian.com/world/2014/jun/23/who-behind-isis-propaganda-operation-iraq.

2. See, for example, Simone M. Friis, '"Behead, Burn, Crucify, Crush": Theorizing the Islamic State's Public Displays of Violence', *European Journal of International Relations* 24:2 (2018): 243–67; Roxanna L. Euben, 'Spectacles of Sovereignty in Digital Time: ISIS Executions, Visual Rhetoric and Sovereign Power', *Perspectives on Politics* 15:4 (2017): 1007–33. On online propaganda more widely, see also Manni Crone, 'Religion and Violence: Governing Muslim Militancy through Aesthetic Assemblages', *Millennium* 43:1 (2014): 291–307, 297; Xander Kirke, 'Violence and Political Myth: Radicalizing Believers in the Pages of Inspire Magazine', *International Political Sociology* 9:4 (2015): 283–98.

3. That is not to say that digital and social media do not also provide opportunities for state militaries. For a study of how state militaries have used digital and social media to promote war and military action, see for example Adi Kuntsman and Rebecca L. Stein, *Digital Militarism: Israel's Occupation in the Social Media Age* (Stanford, CA: Stanford University Press, 2015).

4. See for example, Richelle M. Bernazolli and Colin Flint, 'Embodying the Garrison State?: Everyday Geographies of Militarisation in American Society', *Political Geography* 29:3 (2010): 157–66; Kevin McSorley (ed.), *War and the Body: Militarisation, Practice and Experience* (London: Routledge, 2013); Kevin McSorley, 'Towards an Embodied Sociology of War', *The Sociological Review* 62:S2 (2014), 107–28; Linda Åhäll and Thomas Gregory (eds), *Emotions, Politics and War* (London: Routledge, 2015); Synne L. Dyvik and Lauren Greenwood, 'Embodying Militarism: Exploring the Spaces and Bodies In-Between', *Critical Military Studies* 2:1–2 (2016): 1–6.

5. In a recent report, researchers conclude that a large number of young Dutch men and women who did not have a Muslim family background made their way to Syria and Iraq to join IS. While converts make up less than 2 per cent of the Dutch Muslim population, they made up 14 per cent of Dutch jihadi volunteers or 280 individuals. The share of converts among the ranks of German jihadists was similar: 12 per cent. And among French recruits, the number of converts made up 23 per cent of the total recruits: Bart Schuurman, Peter Grol and Scott Flower, 'Converts and Islamist Terrorism: An Introduction' (The Hague: International Centre for Counter-Terrorism, 2016), 9. https://www.icct.nl/wp-content/uploads/2016/06/ICCT-Schuurman-Grol-Flower-Converts-June-2016.pdf.

6. Synne L. Dyvik, 'Of Bats and Bodies: Methods for Reading and Writing Embodiment', *Critical Military Studies* 2:1–2 (2016): 56–69, 58; Susanna Hast, *Sounds of War: Aesthetics, Emotions, and Chechnya* (Bristol: E-International Relations, 2018). https://www.e-ir.info/publication/sounds-of-war-aesthetics-emotions-and-chechnya/.

7. Catherine Baker, 'Writing about Embodiment as an Act of Translation', *Critical Military Studies* 2:1–2 (2016): 120–4, 121; Catherine Baker, 'Svetlana Alexievich's Soviet Women Veterans and the Aesthetics of the Disabled Military Body: Staring at the Unwomanly Face of War', this volume.

8. Baker, 'Embodiment', 121.

9. See, for example, Charlie Winters, *The Virtual 'Caliphate': Understanding Islamic State's Propaganda Strategy* (London: Quilliam, 2015); Euben, 'Spectacles'; John M. Berger and Jonathon Morgan, *The ISIS Twitter Census: Describing and Defining the Population of ISIS Supporters on Twitter* (Washington DC: Brookings Institution, 2015).

10. Jesper Strömbäck and Frank Esser, 'Mediatization of Politics: Transforming Democracies and Reshaping Politics', in *Mediatization of Communication*, edited by Knut Lundby (Berlin: De Gruyter Mounton, 2014), 375–403; Andrew Hoskins and Ben O'Loughlin, *War and Media: The Emergence of Diffused War* (Cambridge: Polity, 2010).

11. Carl Boggs and Tom Pollard, 'Hollywood and the Spectacle of Terrorism', *New Political Science* 28:3 (2006): 335–51; Kuntsman and Stein, *Digital Militarism*; Nick Robinson, 'Militarism and Opposition in the Living Room: The Case of Military Video Games', *Critical Studies on Security* 4:3 (2016): 255–75. See also James Der Derian, *Virtuous War: Mapping the Military–Industrial–Media–Entertainment Network*, 2nd ed. (London: Routledge, 2009).

12. Kari Andén-Papadopoulos, 'Body Horror on the Internet: US Soldiers Recording the War in Iraq and Afghanistan', *Media, Culture & Society* 31:6 (2009): 921–38.

13. Linda Åhäll, 'The Dance of Militarisation: A Feminist Security Studies Take on "the Political"', *Critical Studies on Security* 4:2 (2016): 154–68; Linda Åhäll, 'Feeling Everyday IR: Embodied, Affective, Militarising Movement as Choreography of War', *Cooperation and Conflict* 54:2 (2019): 149–66; see also Cynthia Enloe, *Maneuvers: The International Politics of Militarizing Women's Lives* (Berkeley, CA: University of California Press, 2000).

14. For example, Laura Shepherd defines militarism as 'the belief that the most appropriate solution to a problem or response to an event is the military one', and militarisation as 'the process by which beings or things become associated with the military or take on military characteristics': Laura J. Shepherd, 'Glossary', in *Gender Matters in Global Politics: A Feminist Introduction to International Relations*, edited by Laura J. Shepherd, 2nd ed. (London: Routledge, 2015), xxii–xxviii, xxv; for a similar definition, see also Annika Kronsell and Erika Svedberg, 'Introduction: Making Gender, Making War', in *Making Gender, Making War: Violence, Military and Peacekeeping Practices*, edited by Annika Kronsell and Erika Svedberg (London: Routledge, 2012), 1–18, 5.

15. Victoria Basham, 'Gender, Militarism and Remembrance: The Everyday Geopolitics of the Poppy', *Gender, Place & Culture* 23:6 (2016): 883–96; Joanna Tidy, 'Forces Sauces and Eggs for Soldiers: Food, Nostalgia, and the Rehabilitation of the British Military', *Critical Military Studies* 1:3 (2015): 220–32; Kevin McSorley, 'Doing Military Fitness: Physical Culture, Civilian Leisure, and Militarism', *Critical Military Studies* 2:1–2 (2016): 103–19, 103.

16. Åhäll, 'Dance', 161.

17. As Catherine Baker notes in the introduction to this volume, what matters in this context is not the ontological distinctions between affect and emotions discussed in much work on affect theory but, rather, the fact that such affects and emotions are both felt and performed by the body. For a thorough discussion of

affect see, for example, Nigel Thrift, *Non-Representational Theory: Space, Politics, Affect* (London: Routledge, 2007), 222.

18. Sara Ahmed, 'Affective Economies', *Social Text* 22:2 (2004): 117–39.

19. Åhäll, 'Dance', 162; See also Manni Crone, 'Radicalization Revisited: Violence, Politics and the Skills of the Body', *International Affairs* 92:3 (2016): 587–604, 600–1.

20. Åhäll, 'Dance', 165.

21. Hoskins and O'Loughlin, *War and Media*, 15–18.

22. Andrew Hoskins, 'The Mediatisation of Memory', in *Mediatization of Communication*, edited by Lundby, 661–80, 662.

23. Jessica Jacobs, 'Listen with your Eyes: Towards a Filmic Geography', *Geography Compass* 7:10 (2013): 714–28.

24. See, for example, Rune Saugmann Andersen, Juha A. Vuori and Can E. Mutlu, 'Visuality', in *Critical Security Methods: New Frameworks for Analysis*, edited by Claudia Aradau, Jef Huysmans, Andrew Neal and Nadine Voelkner (London: Routledge, 2014), 85–117, 101.

25. Nicholas Mirzoeff, 'Invisible Empire: Visual Culture, Embodied Spectacle and Abu Ghraib', *Radical History Review* 95 (2006): 21–44, 22.

26. Hoskins, 'Mediatisation', 662.

27. Ibid., 662–3.

28. Euben, 'Spectacles', 1008.

29. The *Daily Mirror* newspaper in the UK even described the video as 'the latest effort in a propaganda battle between Islamic State and the West that is being played out as much online as it is on the battlefield': Sam Rkaina, 'Islamic State Releases Propaganda Film Warning "the fighting has just begun"', *The Daily Mirror*, 20 September 2014. https://www.mirror.co.uk/news/world-news/islamic-state-releases-propaganda-film-4295302.

30. Sarah Bulmer and David Jackson, '"You Do Not Live in my Skin": Embodiment, Voice, and the Veteran', *Critical Military Studies* 2:1–2 (2016): 25–40.

31. Thrift, *Non-Representational Theory*, 237.

32. Andrew A. G. Ross, *Mixed Emotions: Beyond Fear and Hatred in International Conflict* (Chicago, IL: University of Chicago Press, 2013), 22.

33. See also Ben Anderson, *Encountering Affect: Capacities, Apparatuses, Conditions* (Farnham: Ashgate, 2014), 46–7.

34. Jenny Edkins, *Face Politics* (London: Routledge, 2015). See also Baker, 'Svetlana Alexievich's Soviet Women Veterans'.

35. Edkins, *Face Politics*, 13.

36. Crone, 'Religion and Violence', 297 (original emphasis).

37. Ibid., 299.

38. Ibid., 304.

39. According to Mathieu Guidère, IS have stated that they are inspired by the language politics of the 'Hebrew state' that allowed people with Jewish backgrounds from all over the world – regardless of their language – to settle in Israel: see Michael Erard, 'ISIL Isn't Merely Tolerant of People Who Speak Languages Beside Arabic; It Needs Them', *Quartz*, 4 August 2016, <https://qz.com/746731/isil-isnt-merely-tolerant-of-people-who-speak-languages-besides-arabic-it-needs-them/>.

40. Erik Ringmar, 'How the World Stage Makes its Subjects: An Embodied Critique of Constructivist IR Theory', *Journal of International Relations and Development* 19:1 (2016): 101–25, 109; see also Björn Vickhoff et al., 'Music Structure Determines Heart Rate Variability of Singers', *Frontiers in Psychology* 4 (2013): 334.

41. John Protevi, 'Affect, Agency and Responsibility: The Act of Killing in the Age of Cyborgs', *Phenomenology and the Cognitive Sciences* 7:3 (2008): 405–13, 410–11.

42. Randall Collins, *Interaction Ritual Chains* (Princeton, NJ: Princeton University Press, 2004), 47.

43. Ringmar, 'World Stage', 109.

44. Ibid., 117 (emphasis added).

45. Euben, 'Spectacles', 1009.

46. Berger and Morgan, *ISIS Twitter Census*, 2–3.

47. Ibid., 24–5.

48. See, for example, Winters, *The Virtual 'Caliphate'*.

49. Ahmed, 'Affective Economies', 120, 119–24.

50. Ibid., 120.

51. Ty Solomon, 'Ontological Security, Circulations of Affect, and the Arab Spring', *Journal of International Relations and Development* 21:4 (2018): 934–58, 948 (emphasis added).

52. Ibid., 945.

53. Kingsley, 'Isis's Terrifying Online Propaganda Operation'.

54. Judith Butler, *Bodies That Matter: On the Discursive Limits of 'Sex'* (New York: Routledge, 1993), 9.

CHAPTER 8

The Defender Collection: Militarisation, Historical Mythology and the Everyday Affective Politics of Nationalist Fashion in Croatia

Catherine Baker

In 2018, the record-breaking Croatian football team that reached the men's World Cup final played mostly in a strip that contrasted with the colours many spectators expected: the black and midnight-blue chequerboard of their reserve kit, transposing Croatia's famous red and white checks into a darker palette, which when compressed into long camera shots or small smartphone screens looked all-black. This departure from Croatia's traditional blue reserve kit with red-and-white chequerboard details, familiar from past tournaments' iconic images, appeared dramatic and unusual, as its designers at Nike intended: the Croatian captain Luka Modrić, in Nike's press release, described it as 'daring, confident and tough; characteristics that also describes [sic] the spirit of our team'.[1] At home, however, all-black also had potential historical and ideological connotations which only activated for onlookers who already knew that struggles over the memory of the collaborationist Independent State of Croatia (NDH) of 1941–5 and its black-uniformed 'Ustaša' militia have been contentious in Croatia ever since Croatia's war of independence from Yugoslavia. The anti-nationalist journalist Drago Pilsel, for instance, wrote on Facebook: 'I don't cheer for people wearing black. End of story.'[2] The politics of militarisation in Croatia, in other words, gave black different connotations – which the aesthetic and embodied dimensions of fashion, and of identification with the nation and its military, help to explain.

The dynamics of militarisation in Croatia are simultaneously the dynamics of ethnonational homogenisation, permeating into everyday life, that characterised the public culture of the 1991–5 'Homeland

War' and institutionalised an official patriotism which turned the war of independence into a new founding myth.[3] Indeed, 'retraditionalization' of Croatian politics and society around nationalism after the Yugoslav federation collapsed and Franjo Tuđman's Croatian Democratic Union (HDZ) won Croatia's multi-party elections in April–May 1990 was (as elsewhere in postsocialist Europe) also a patriarchal reaction:[4] politics and media were strengthening a binary of women as 'the passive body to be protected' and men as 'the nation's active agent and soul, ever ready to protect and defend' strengthened even before the war.[5] The 'gendered narrative of war and nationhood' that defined symbolic national bodies (e.g. maternal, victimised or armed bodies) ethnically was, Dubravka Žarkov argues, the Croatian (and Serbian) media's chief representational strategy in creating the Self/Other stereotypes that legitimised violence during the war.[6]

After Croatian forces held out against the Yugoslav National Army (JNA) and defeated the parastate that claimed one third of the republic's land as Serb, the myth of a hard-fought and glorious defensive war also became embedded in post-war culture, through the national commemorative calendar and constant political and media appeals to the memory of the war.[7] This collective myth (that is, a story a society tells to explain its history, not an untruth) expresses many veterans' and civilians' sentiments but, societally, has been said to impede critical reflection about war crimes committed by Croats.[8] The war's sacralisation has arguably also created a climate where young people are less likely to question sympathetic interpretations of the NDH[9] – causing regular moral panics in liberal and left-wing media when groups of teenagers are photographed in crowds (e.g. at live performances by the patriotic musician and war veteran Marko Perković Thompson) wearing black T-shirts and giving Ustaša salutes.

The intertwining official and pseudo-countercultural forms of militarisation that have made this possible are the product of postsocialist ethnonationalism but also of transnational imaginative circuits (or what Robert Saunders and Vlad Strukov call 'popular geopolitics feedback loops'[10]) along which practices and representations flowing into Croatia are adapted. Among these are the US culture of unofficial apparel celebrating guns and the military; rock and metal music subcultures; football ultras' visual cultures; and changing practices on the European far right. By tracing how national and transnational imaginaries of history, combat and masculinity are combined by a T-shirt company catering to young people who identify themselves with Croatian patriotism and against the Left, this chapter shows that militarisation harnesses imaginations which are simultaneously aesthetic and embodied, charged with the intertwined affordances of identifying with the nation and with the gender order of a militarised public sphere.

Fashion and Style: The Aesthetics of Embodying Militarisation

Militarisation, as this volume argues, operates in aesthetic and embodied dimensions simultaneously. Militarisation is aesthetic because the practices, representations and techniques through which it occurs engage the senses; it is embodied because so many of the imaginaries it mobilises involve the body, such as the spectacles of the gendered national body in trained motion that are produced through drill.[11] Moreover, militarisation is simultaneously aesthetic and embodied because the senses' engagement with practices and artefacts of militarisation evokes powerful emotions (thrill, awe, pride, longing and fear to name a few) which are produced and experienced through the body, often before the individual is even fully cognisant of what they have felt and why.[12] These are the 'pathway[s]' along which Emma Hutchison argues emotions 'acquire a collective dimension', continually reproducing nations and other groups as *affective* political communities.[13] One specific aspect of how aesthetics and embodiment converge in militarisation's affective politics is particularly important for this chapter: how processes of militarisation shape and play on individuals' imaginations and aspirations about how they desire their body to socially appear, that is, the same imaginations of the body and identity driving fashion.[14]

Scholars of militarisation including Cynthia Enloe have, indeed, pointed to civilian fashion's fascination with military aesthetics to illustrate how militarisation works in everyday spheres where the public would not normally expect to encounter ideas about the taken-for-grantedness of the military.[15] The appearance of details adapted from military uniforms on civilian mass-produced consumer clothing or exclusive haute couture, for Enloe, perfectly illustrates how '[m]ilitarization and the privileging of masculinity are both products not only of amorphous cultural beliefs but also of deliberate decisions . . . Camouflage patterns or epaulettes appear on fashionable clothes because some designers made a profit-making fashion choice.'[16] Indeed, dress history shows this is a long tradition: British menswear manufacturers including Burberry appealed to World War I customers by advertising their overcoats as the trench officer's choice,[17] and Georgian bootmakers made the long top-boot (derived from equestrian military jackboots) and eponymous Wellington boot, which emphasised the length of the leg and thus the 'natural' authority of the elite men who wore them, 'part of the outdoor uniform of the patrician man' as eighteenth-century Britain was renegotiating gender and citizenship.[18]

Through such circuits, official and unofficial military embodied practices and civilian appropriations of military style combine to shape perceptions of militarised bodies as desirable, and to imply what gendered, class-based, racialised and ethnicised ideals a desirable body should fulfil.[19] The military, an institution in need of legitimacy, needs the public to desire their nation to have strong, respected and well-funded armed forces; among those it targets as potential recruits (especially young men), it needs them to desire to undergo the bodily transformations military training and service will enact in them.[20] These bodily desires will have been formed by citizens' gazes towards representations of militarised bodies in advertising and media as much as (often more so than) first-hand encounters with the military. Simultaneously, militaries also need wider society to perceive the embodied traits of military belonging as desirable, so that potential soldiers' families, friends and lovers are more likely to endorse recruits' choices about joining and re-enlisting.[21] The affects militarised fashion mobilises are thus part of the economy of fantasy and desire which charges the relationship between individuals, militaries, nations and states.[22] Fashion's militarisation, for Laura Shepherd, thus epitomises how *visual* practices are part of the militarisation process'.[23] Appreciating the convergence of aesthetics and embodiment in militarisation, moreover, permits deeper engagement with how fashion's pleasures and affordances interact with imaginaries of the military.

Visual research methodologies such as those already applied to militarised fashion by the fashion historian Jane Tynan sharpen our understanding of militarisation by focusing on how its visual dynamics interact with public and personal identifications with gender, class, race, ethnicity and nation.[24] Fashion designers' militarised allusions vary in how (in)directly they evoke their nation's or another's actual military, and both vagueness and specificity can elicit different identifications from wearers along or across collective identity boundaries (does an item seem to reference 'one's own' military/nation, 'someone else's', or 'no one's in particular' at all?). The most diffuse allusions are colours or decorations which have become so abstracted that they probably connote an abstract 'militarity' rather than referencing a specific military, although as innovations in military clothing (as when the British Army adopted khaki between the 1880s and 1902) they were themselves historically, socially and culturally situated decisions.[25] Other allusions reference particular national militaries more specifically, on a continuum that may range from parodic to authentic (and how designers, wearers and onlookers each classify a garment or a bodily practice might vary too). The 'US Army' patches on so many ('men's' and 'women's') parkas and olive or camouflage jackets, for instance, carry at least latent traces of the 1960s countercultural appropriation of army surplus as well as the transnational mystique the US military began creating around itself during the early Cold War.

These more nationally specific militarised allusions invite buyers and wearers to make acts of sincere or ironic identification with symbols of a national military that may or may not be 'theirs'. They mobilise the pleasures of identification and social recognition that give fashion its imaginative charge. The affective politics of nationalism itself, however, might suggest those pleasures operate differently depending on whether wearers feel they are performing attachments towards their nation or another (inflected in each case by their lived experience and individual sentiments towards those nations). The flags and stylised 'US' insignia frequently rediscovered by mass-market fashion connote the wearer's own nation to an American, and the most thoroughly mythologised military in the contemporary world to a wearer who does not identify themselves with the US political community. Designers, sellers, wearers and onlookers negotiate the potential meanings and identifications of symbolic references between each other, and do not always agree, or even always recognise symbols, garments or practices as invested with the same national significance. The national and cross-national identifications enabled by militarised fashion are, generally, contingent, performative and often ironic. This chapter, however, analyses T-shirts designed and manufactured by a Croatian company (here called Defender Hrvatska[26]) which address a politically defined subset of one ethnonational community: Croats who sympathise with irredentist claims to territory in Bosnia-Herzegovina, reject the legacies of Yugoslav state socialism and are likely to accept the Ustaše as part of Croatian national military tradition. The national, ideological and subcultural identifications that Defender invites customers to make reveal how it constructs a contentious ideal of national military masculinity as normal and natural, and how broader processes of societal militarisation in Croatia have laid foundations for it.

Militarisation, Historical Mythology and Identification with the Nation Inside and Outside the Far Right

The affective circuit of militarisation behind these examples of politicised, militarised and gendered fashion in Croatia occupies a blurred area between a US militarised culture of apparel celebrating the military and first responders (through constructions of militarised heroism

that often incorporate civilian uniformed services by evoking their sacrifices on 9/11, while pledging military retribution against terrorists and
exhorting civilians to support the troops) and the culture of mocking
politicised allusion that characterises style on the contemporary German
far right. The allusive symbolic repertoire of the apparel that youth in
Germany buy to express sympathies with the far right is a consequence
of German prohibitions on displaying fascist symbols, which designers
evade by obliquely referencing Nazi/white nationalist slogans and citing the longer German and Nordic historical and mythological past. The
nationalism scholar Cynthia Miller-Idriss, researching contemporary
German far-right fashion's visual and embodied culture, perhaps comes
closer than any study yet to explaining the synthesis of aesthetics and
embodiment that gives identifications with nationalism and militarism
their affective charge.

Miller-Idriss observed the embodied aesthetics of far-right German
nationalism having already theorised 'everyday nationalism' (with Jon
Fox), emphasising the 'actual practices' through which individuals 'engage
and enact (and ignore and deflect)' ideologies of nationalism and nationhood.[27] This occurs through routine talk, everyday decision making,
everyday use of national symbols, and consumption habits which express
and constitute national difference. Since nationalism and militarism are
interdependent, of course, this framework also spotlights militarisation
and the everyday.[28] Two extra steps, however, give Miller-Idriss more
insights into how aesthetics and embodiment combine in these processes.
One is greater attention to the aesthetics of the body, which mediate the
pleasures of identifying with militarised projects; the second is locating
aspiration (that is, desire) as the affective dynamic behind feelings of
national belonging. These allow her to explore how designers and wearers of far-right apparel use a 'fantasy of Nordic heritage' to produce identification with the German nation, and one they emphatically racialise
as white.[29] This narrative is specific to the German far right but illustrates
a wider point about national historical mythology: all myths of nationhood shape the national imaginary by 'integrat[ing] factual elements
into imagined pasts', creating narratives about a shared national history
which define and explain the nation's identity today.[30] Even if national
regeneration – and the demonisation of those blamed for national catastrophe or victimhood – characterises far-right imaginations in particular,[31]
all national myths offer idealised depictions of the nation's past, present
and future, 'hold[ing] a promise of an alternative existence to which a
nation can, or should, aspire'.[32]

If the affects of national identification can be expressed as collective desires (composed of many individual desires) to embody an image one identifies with and thus strives to become, nationalism turns out to involve surprisingly similar affective circuits to those mediating individuals' relationships with fashion, advertising or audiovisual media. Feminists rethinking notions of the spectatorial gaze have argued that individuals' gazes towards fashioned bodies in advertising (and everyday life) involve identifications with those bodies or what the individual takes them to represent, and aspirational desires to embody what they do take them to represent by being seen as somehow resembling them. Indeed, fashion facilitates many of the embodied practices through which spectators extend the pleasures of identification with stars and characters beyond the moment of viewing, into everyday life.[33] The cultural historian Graham Dawson found the same process at work in men's and boys' identifications with British 'soldier heroes' (though did not enquire about other genders).[34] This unexpectedly intimate politics of nationalism has implications for how we conceive of the affects of militarisation, which equally mobilise relationships of identification and desire.

Many of the desires shaped and sustained by militarisation are intimately bound to the nation. Nations' own gender orders and historical mythologies, perhaps more than anything else, distinguish military imaginaries from each other; many points of aspirational identification in almost any pantheon of national heroes are individuals and archetypes who embodied military masculinities, and repertoires of heroes are almost entirely military on the far right. Fully understanding how these meanings are produced in practice also requires ethnographic or focus-group research such as the interviews Miller-Idriss conducted with German youth 'in and around the far right scene'. Exploring what associations wearers and others project on to the symbols and references of this clothing, and how much historical background to them they indeed know,[35] is essential for completing the circuit and illustrating how fashion acquires its affective meanings in embodied practice, but beyond this chapter's scope. Even systematically analysing the Defender collection's images and narratives in the context of wider Croatian memory politics and historical mythology, however, lets inferences be drawn about what masculinities its designers place within the shared national past. In this as in more official accounts of Croatian history, the shared national past is heavily militarised.

Militarisation and War Memory in Croatia
since the 1990s

The length of Croatian historical and cultural traditions, and the continuity of sovereignty between the medieval Croatian kingdom and today's Republic of Croatia implied in the notion of 'state right', is a shared Croatian historical narrative across the political spectrum. Arriving on the Adriatic side of the Balkan Peninsula during the great wave of Slavic migration (CE 6th–8th centuries), the Croats were among several peoples whose societies became kingdoms, converted to Catholicism during the early Middle Ages and were recognised by the Pope. The medieval Croatian kingdom, especially the reigns of Tomislav (925–8, first King of Croatia), Petar Krešimir IV (1059–75, whose campaigns grew Croatia to its fullest extent) and Dmitar Zvonimir (1075–89, killed by his own conspiring nobles), represent the 'golden age' of independence in Croatia's national past. Although the Croatian Crown passed to the Hungarian kings in 1097, the terms of an 1102 treaty kept the Croatian crown autonomous and preserved the assembly of nobles from which today's Croatian parliament derives. These provisions continued when Hungary became a Habsburg crownland in 1526 amid repeated Habsburg–Ottoman warfare in south-east Europe, the background to myths of nations standing 'at the bulwark of Christianity' absorbed by nationalisms in Croatia and other central/south-east European countries. The 1102 union was the origin of 'state right', by which the Croat people (*narod*) can claim to have exercised sovereignty over Croatian territory even while under foreign rule, thus deserving independence in 1991.[36]

The most contentious aspects of Croatian history, where far-right and official national narratives diverge, involve the twentieth century. Although Yugoslavia's unification in December 1918, after Austria–Hungary collapsed in World War I, ostensibly realised Croats' national self-determination, many Croats in practice experienced this Yugoslavia (ruled by the former Serbian monarchy), as Serb domination, causing constitutional crises that made the authorities create an autonomous 'Croatian Banovina' (expanding into Bosnia-Herzegovina) in 1939. In April 1941, the Axis powers invaded Yugoslavia and installed Ante Pavelić, the head of the fringe ultranationalist Ustaše, as leader of the NDH (encompassing most of Bosnia and Herzegovina, but without Istria, which Italy had been occupying since World War I, or prime Dalmatian territory that Fascist Italy kept for itself). Some Croats supported the collaborationist regime and others joined the Communist Partisan resistance, which mobilised in June 1941.

Two sites symbolise Croatia's clashing ideological memories of World War II: the NDH concentration camp at Jasenovac, where 83,145 people were killed in the NDH's genocide against Serbs, Jews and Roma,[37] and the field outside Bleiburg in Austria where Partisans executed at least 20,000–30,000 Croat, Slovene and Serb collaborators in May 1945 after British troops had handed them over.[38] Competition over the sites' relative death tolls characterised the exchanges of historical revisionism that broke out in mid-1980s Yugoslavia and were already ongoing in Croat and Serb diasporas. The period between 1941 and 1945 thus produced divisive historical legacies within Croatian national memory as well as between Croats and Serbs (since Croat anti-Communist narratives demonised Croatian Partisans as agents of another illegitimate Serb-dominated regime, despite their leader Josip Broz Tito being half-Slovene half-Croatian, and despite Yugoslav Communism affirming Croatia as a republic[39]). The 1991–5 war, in contrast, offered the opposite, or so its memory in Croatian public culture makes it seem: a heroic narrative of the nation standing together against the aggression of Serb paramilitaries and a Yugoslav army under Slobodan Milošević's control, defending the Republic of Croatia's territorial sovereignty and creating a new national founding myth.

Tuđman's use of the Homeland War as a myth of national origin still structures Croatian public memory today, which arguably has become even more militarised since Tuđman's death in 1999. Annual commemorations of the war's key anniversaries, including the fall of Vukovar (November 1991) and the victorious Oluja offensive (August 1995), restate the notion today's public have lessons to learn from the heroism of the wartime 'branitelji' ('defenders' – the standard word for this war's Croatian veterans), invite public gratitude for their sacrifice and reinscribe the war as a modern national golden age.[40] Yet the myth of the 'Homeland War' edges easily into, and in Tuđman's hands certainly threatened to become, a problematic 'national reconciliation' that wiped clean 1941–5's historical slate by equating Ustaša and Partisan guilt, and by diverting attention from war crimes Croats committed in the Homeland War.[41] These included massacres such as paramilitaries' killing of 100 Serb civilians near Gospić in October 1991, 250,000 Serbs being forced from their homes during Oluja, and Tuđman's support for Bosnian Croat separatists during the Bosnian war who desired a monoethnic Croat parastate, 'Herceg-Bosna'. At the largest imagined extent of Croat 'integralism', Herceg-Bosna would have covered all the Croatian Banovina's (and the NDH's) territory in Bosnia-Herzegovina. The strategy of ethnic cleansing necessary to remove non-Croats from

Herceg-Bosna involved atrocities such as the massacre of 116 Bosniak civilians at Ahmići in April 1993, and the International Criminal Tribunal for the Former Yugoslavia (ICTY) judged it a 'joint criminal enterprise' in May 2013.[42]

Although almost all national histories and mythologies involve war as an institution and the military as an organisation,[43] the militarised versions of Croatian public memory which have become dominant through repeated ceremonial and everyday commemoration hold that Croatia has been especially 'forged in war'.[44] The organised veterans' movement, which in the late 1990s coalesced to oppose Tuđman from the right, appeals to comrades' collective sacrifices and the memory of Croat war victims in order to make moral claims about matters that far exceed veterans' (under-resourced) welfare and therapeutic needs, including Serbs' minority rights in Croatia, Croatian/Serbian cultural contacts, and the ICTY's (lack of) legitimacy to prosecute Croats for crimes committed in a defensive war. Its members have ascribed themselves, and politicians have granted them, a role as guardians of memory that collapses the figure of the veteran to men most like them.

This hegemonic veteran figure has become embodied in Croatian popular culture by the singer Marko Perković Thompson, who turned professional in 1992 after recording a song on the front line about defending his home village ('Bojna Čavoglave' ('The Čavoglave platoon')). Thompson has devoted himself exclusively to themes of wartime heroism, national history, political crisis and Catholic revivalism since the late 1990s.[45] While his music ostensibly addresses the nation as a whole, it in fact (as one or two songs on each album show) employs a heavily politicised narrative that blames 'Communists' in league with Croats' historic enemies for Croatia's social and economic crises today. Several of his songs contain phrases alluding to slogans used by the NDH, or in one case the name 'Herceg-Bosna'.[46] Indeed, it is through the introduction of 'Bojna Čavoglave', an iconic and aggressive wartime song that the state broadcaster initially refused to play,[47] that many young Croatians encounter the Ustaša salute of 'Za dom spremni' ('For the Home – ready!') and are invited to see it as an unfairly stigmatised part of national history, which some of the Croatian right defends as an old Croatian battle-cry.[48]

The Croatian extreme right's visual (and musical) cultures therefore have some themes in common with the German far right, most troublingly a willingness to rehabilitate the memory of troops on the Fascist side in World War II. The movement certainly seems to belong to the same networks of transnational style: the German far-right fashion label Thor Steinar, which designs clothes 'laced with sophisticated codes relying on historical, colonial, military and Norse mythological references' (often integrating its graphics and script subtly into clothes that use militarised elements like camouflage print just like high-street brands),[49] has been available in Croatia since at least 2012, and is among Croatian football ultras' favoured labels.[50] Yet an important contextual difference is that mainstream imaginations of German national identity (and German law) reject the German far right's historical narratives, while the major premises of the Croatian far right's narrative, including the 'myth of the Homeland War', are shared with public narratives that have been hegemonic in Croatia since 1991.[51] This compatibility between far-right and official narratives is closer to variants of patriotic discourse in the USA post-9/11.

Official and far-right narratives generally disagree, however, on the NDH's place in the national past and whether Herzegovina should be part of today's Croatian nation-state. Yet even then, slippage has occurred: Tuđman famously offered a remarkably low total for the number of victims of Jasenovac in a historical opus he published before becoming president; his close émigré associates did openly rehabilitate it, and supported the Herceg-Bosna entity.[52] The current Croatian president, Kolinda Grabar-Kitarović, has distanced herself from rehabilitation of the Ustaše by stating she finds the 'Za dom spremni' cry 'unacceptable',[53] but has been noticeably closer than her post-Tuđman predecessors to the revisionist HDZ Bosnia-Herzegovina leader, Dragan Čović, and both spoke at the ceremony marking the seventieth anniversary of Bleiburg in May 2015.[54] Thompson's 1999 song 'Lijepa li si' ('How Beautiful You Are'), listing 'Herceg-Bosna' equally to other regions in lyrics praising the beautiful Croatian homeland, is part of the Croatian Navy choir's patriotic song repertoire and was sung to an audience including Grabar-Kitarović and the HDZ prime minister Andrej Plenković (who both sang enthusiastically) in May 2017 at a ceremony commemorating the founding of the Croatian armed forces.[55] The blurred space between celebration of the regular military and celebration of paramilitarism and extremism is the context in which Defender designs, and customers wear, its fashion.

Militarisation and the Politics of Symbol in the Defender Collection

Within the Croatian integralist right's visual culture, the Defender collection exemplifies how repertoires of symbols and images combine into particular interpretations of national historical mythology, and shows how easily Ustaša symbols can be assimilated into a broader narrative of historical continuity and masculine military heroism, more directly in fashion than in writing. The strategy of projecting interpretations of a contemporary conflict back into the past, implying the nation fought the same enemies then for the same reasons, was noticed by political anthropologists across the Yugoslav region during the 1990s wars.[56] The 'myth of the Homeland War' as historical grand narrative accordingly frames the nation's ancient, medieval and more recent wars, kings, soldiers and irregular fighters as equally involved in a defiant struggle to defend the Croats and their historic territory against foreign enemies and internal traitors. This narrative has been made hegemonic and common sense in contemporary Croatia when applied to the regular military in the 1990s and figures of historical consensus. Yet on the far right it equally includes the collaborationist Ustaše, on the grounds that they were fighting the Communist partisans and the Serb expansionist Četniks. Defender's repertoire of images illustrates this more contentious continuum in practice.

The stages of Miller-Idriss's visual analysis, 'decoding' the historical and mythological references in far-right clothing (including catalogue images) and grouping them into 'symbolic codes',[57] can also be applied to the Defender collection. The visual elements carrying most symbolic meaning in this collection are the people and objects depicted, the historical periods they appear to convey, the content and typeface of any text, and one of T-shirts' most basic features – colour. In military contexts, colour choices for uniforms, insignia, equipment and built structures form part of battlefields' (and militaries') 'societal imaginaries'.[58] Even once mechanised warfare shifted the rationale of military uniform from bright colours to camouflage, colour has remained a 'semiotic resource' that makes statements about individual and collective wearers of uniforms:[59] Croatian US-surplus woodland uniforms during the Homeland War, for instance, symbolised a national and military identity constructed as more modern, democratic and Western than the plain drab olive uniforms of the JNA.[60]

The politics of colour and the military in Croatia also illustrate probably the most contested way in which militarised associations of colour transfer symbolic resonances into civilian fashion. In Croatia, like Germany or Italy, the fact that elite fascist troops from that nation wore (heavily aestheticised) black uniforms has left the colour with enduring ideological connotations.[61] By wearing black uniforms and choosing the slogan 'Za dom spremni' on forming in June 1991, the militia of the Croatian Party of Right (HSP), known as the Croatian Defence Forces (HOS), put themselves in continuity with the Ustaše, ostensibly to intimidate their Serb opponents.[62] Black T-shirts and hoodies are, of course, also elements of transnational subcultural style in scenes not defined by political ideologies (rock, metal, mixed martial arts (MMA)) or even defined against the far right (anarchism, Antifa).[63] Yet, again as in Germany, the polysemy of black provides designers and wearers with useful ambiguity – as it arguably did for Thompson, whose uniformly wore a black T-shirt (and St Benedict medallion) on stage until his 2007 tour, when he began wearing stone-grey and olive green, apparently so as not to present an 'Ustaša' image so readily in photographs.[64] Surrounding elements and other embodied signals about the wearer and their context influence whether or not an onlooker will perceive far-right 'meaning' in a black T-shirt.[65] Of the seventy-seven T-shirt designs for sale on Defender's website in July 2018, forty-one were only available in black and fourteen more were in black plus other colours (a further five were out of stock but photos suggested used to be sold in black). Black T-shirts dominated the collection, with twenty-seven designs available in white, eleven in 'desert brown', and twelve in grey and 'military green'. Colours made fashionable by association with military uniform were therefore strongly represented in Defender's range.

Grouping the represented symbols into themes reveals what aspects of national identity these T-shirts' designers chose to emphasise. More than half (thirty-nine) reference recent or distant national history, thirty-nine directly reference masculinity by picturing a male figure, and twenty-four reference Catholicism by picturing a cross, medallion or saint (including one with a St Benedict medallion's two faces on front and back). Unlike the German repertoire, none references white nationalism, though ten contain aggressive anti-Communist or anti-Left messages (and one transfers the numbers '1312', a US far-right numeric code denoting the anti-authoritarian slogan 'All Cops Are Bastards',[66] into 'All Communists are Bastards'). Four reference 'Za dom spremni', but only one reprints it (a shirt with HOS insignia and 'Za dom spremni' motto). Others allude to it: 'za' and 'spremni' in brush-script letters with a cartoon house in between; 'ZDS 1991' in two chunky white rows laid out like RUN-DMC's band logo (again attaching the slogan to the beginning of the Homeland War, not the Ustaše); one reading 'za dom' ('for the home') in a US-style athletic font and 'sveti spremni mrijeti' ('ready to die for the sacred [home]') in gothic script. A large capital U (the device on the Ustaša emblem) appears on only two shirts, once with 'Ultras' underneath and once laid out as the chemical symbol for uranium. None features a perfectly reproduced Ustaša symbol or Pavelić's face, though more crudely designed T-shirts showing these are often available from market vendors selling Ustaša paraphernalia. Like the Thor Steinar wave of far-right brands, the Defender collection distinguishes itself from cruder competitors with more sophisticated design, and does not directly reproduce the most extreme symbols, yet uses graphical cues that let viewers perceive affinities with them.

Text descriptions under certain images suggest the designers too were aware of certain symbols' sensitivity, including the contentious version of the Croatian chequerboard emblem with a white square (rather than red) at top left. The 'red first' version is on the state flag adopted in December 1990 and was on the emblem (though not the flag) of the Socialist Republic of Croatia within Tito's Yugoslavia, of which today's Croatia is constitutionally a continuation. The 'white first' version appeared on the NDH flag (which had the Ustaša 'U' and four-pointed knotwork symbol on its upper left), on HOS's insignia and on the wartime 'Herceg-Bosna' flag. Although red-first and white-first were more interchangeable before the twentieth century (for instance, the Croatian coat of arms tiled on to the roof of St Mark's Church in Zagreb's old town is white-first), the NDH's use of white-first and its preservation among anti-Communist émigrés gave it political connotations in the early 1990s which only strengthened with time.[67] In the Defender collection, nineteen T-shirts contain white-first emblems (sometimes combined with other images, or as a warrior's shield) and eleven contain red-first emblems, suggesting designers may expect the white-first version to be more appealing (the inner neck label, however, is red-first). One design, with the chequerboard inside a four-pointed knotwork border, is available in both variants.[68] Its description shows the designers expect their customers to understand the different political connotations:

> Although the white-first field, on our coat of arms, has absolutely nothing disputable about it, and we too know our own history and rights very well, and we possess serious academic literature which not one single court can destroy . . . some of our friends have still expressed discomfort about going out in public or to work in such a t-shirt.
>
> For that very reason we have also made an extra version with a red-first field, because the last thing we would want is for anyone to have problems at work or in their neighbourhood because of our products.
>
> And especially because those problems can only occur as a result of ignorance of the facts . . . one of those facts is that the white-first field was NEVER banned, not even during the time of Communism in Yugoslavia!! Of course there is proof for this claim as well, not to mention the rooftops and vaults of our churches, though they alone should be proof enough . . . Whether the field is red or white first, that is completely the same and equally ours.[69]

This appeal invites site users to feel belonging to an unjustly persecuted, tightly bonded community that the company is nurturing by offering a choice of shirt.

Exploring individual images' composition in more depth, meanwhile, helps to reveal the collection's gendered imaginary of the Croatian national and military past. The syncretism that blends seventh-century warriors, medieval knights and contemporary soldiers into one presentist expression of the Croatian martial spirit (which politicians and media subscribe to when they call present-day troops 'vitezovi', or 'knights') is reproduced both across the collection and in some individual designs. References legible as medieval,[70] usually knights or historic crosses, appear on nineteen shirts, while thirty-six carry modern references, including ten that allude to immediately before, during or after World War II.[71] Others mark themselves as modern by featuring firearms or hand grenades, or football ultras (including two dedicated to 'Against Modern Football'[72]). Surprisingly only nine directly reference the 1990s conflict, including two with versions of HOS insignia and one dedicated to three Croat soldiers and a Frenchman who died defending Vukovar: customers are told this design was created in co-operation with a small far-right group founded in Split in 2012.[73] Another is laid out with white text at top and bottom and states in Croatian 'From cradle to grave, I am proud of my father', over a drawing of a toddler in hat, coat and dummy holding on to the leg of a figure in woodland camouflage fatigues, with a Croatian Army shoulder-patch as background image on the left. Both the son/father relationship and the text layout's resemblance to a digital meme suggests the target customers are the generation young enough for their fathers to have fought the war.

One design named 'Mi Hrvati' ('We Croats'), the words of a common patriotic slogan chanted at football matches and Thompson concerts, illustrates the syncretic mythologisation of Croatian military masculinities by placing three armed figures against the background edged with a Croatian 'pleter' and the slogan 'Mi Hrvati' underneath (placed on a tattoo-style ribbon, using Papyrus font).[74] One is a bare-chested axeman dressed in furs and a winged helmet, with a braided moustache; one is a bearded knight in chainmail and a cape holding a battered sword and a thick, scratched shield with the Croatian chequerboard (white-field-first); the third is a soldier in a camouflage jacket and dark beret (plus a just-visible white-first chequerboard badge), holding a machine-gun, with a rosary (an accessory which wartime journalists made an iconic symbol of Croatian volunteers[75]) around his neck. Read left to right, they create an evolving timeline of national military masculinity across three glorious ages of the nation's past. The description explains these are '[t]hree ages of us Croats' struggle [borbe] and development': 'the barbarian age before and during the time when the Croat name came to today's homeland' (the seventh century), '[t]he medieval knight [who] stands for Christianisation and kings on our territory', and 'our branitelji, all those to whom we owe today's freedom'. The discourse of gratitude for the soldiers' wartime sacrifice, echoing US patriotic formulations, has been embedded into Croatian public culture through two decades of politicians' ceremonial rhetoric and by the Oluja anniversary officially being named Homeland Thanksgiving Day ('Dan domovinske zahvalnosti').

Women are all but absent from this patriotic imaginary as they are from the repertoire of patriotic songs by Thompson and similar musicians, where the only women appearing are aspects of the Virgin Mary, a folkloric spirit called the Fairy of Velebit and the occasional martyr. Only one shirt depicts a female figure, who is indeed the Mother of God. Defender does offer women a few shirts, but only fourteen of the seventy-seven designs: none references weapons, violence or 'Za dom spremni' except one shirt with two crossed swords behind King Zvonimir's crown and another with the HOS badge. The sole design available for women only is a grey wolf howling at the moon, which could belong in a women's rock collection irrespective of the country. Women, the repertoire suggests, might sometimes wish to express closeness to a beloved man by wearing a symbol he has earned, but are not expected to identify with the more extreme and active pursuits of the community Defender constructs as its audience, such as street-fighting, football fandom or military combat.

Finally, the collection also reveals some of the intertextual and even transnational circuits through which militarised imaginaries are constructed. One is the same interrelationship between militarisation, nationalism, fashion and popular music that comes into play through how Thompson (who endorsed Defender in 2013) has used T-shirts' colour and pattern on stage and in press photography to reinforce his veteran identity and his persona's connection to national military tradition. Thompson has modelled three of their shirts (a logo T-shirt with a red Croatian trefoil and a grey tribal band; a royal blue polo shirt with a Chi-Rho badge; and the T-shirt with the Virgin Mary etching).[76] Defender's and Thompson's thematic repertoires unsurprisingly have much in common: the fusion of the medieval and contemporary military past; anti-Communism; Catholicism as a source of national regeneration; masculine homosociality; and apparent yet deniable references to NDH symbols.

Other imaginative circuits extend outside the nation. A white T-shirt with an Eiffel Tower drawing and the letters '#CRO' filled with the Croatian tricolour suggests it was designed for customers to wear in solidarity with the victims of the 2015 Paris attacks: what inferences onlookers might draw about Islamist terrorism, migrants' responsibility for the attacks or even about Bosniak religious nationalism in Bosnia-Herzegovina, cannot be stably read from the T-shirt, but will manifest when they see the design alongside others in the catalogue or among other clothed bodies in a crowd. Two shirts carry English-language slogans more commonly associated with US gun lobby bumper stickers ('In Glock We Trust' and '8 reasons to get out of my way. . . and 1 more in the chamber'), neither with any Croatian national insignia. The least localised of all is a graphic of a skull wearing a dog-tag and a camouflage helmet, smoking a cigar, over two crossed rifles and a spray of broad green leaves, with an ace of spades stuck into the helmet band. The background shows more skulls dissolving into grey smoke. On closer inspection, the top two skulls wear Vietnamese-style conical hats. The ace of spades, dog-tag and cigar all connote images of US soldiers in the Vietnam War as remediated by 1980s Hollywood cinema.[77] Why these three designs appear in the collection, again, cannot be known from their public presentation: yet viewing the collection as a body of symbols links its imagination of Croatian militarism to the reassertion of masculinity through militarism and gun rights activism in the USA, an identification that has been expressed more through visual than textual representations of Croatian soldiers ever since the Homeland War.[78]

Conclusion

Understanding the politics of militarisation, nationalism and symbol through the lens of fashion, especially the allusive strategies through which designers and wearers create spaces to identify with integralist narratives of national identity, explains why Pilsel and the Facebook users who agreed with him perceived politicised connotations in the black Croatian reserve kit. Defender Hrvatska did not invent turning the black T-shirt as subcultural rock style into an assertion of ethnonational and ideological belonging; that practice was well-established by the early 2000s as soon as young people attending concerts like Thompson's began being photographed as crowds and Croatian journalists began commenting on the visual effect of this sea of black at events charged with national sentiment.[79] The aesthetics of how militarisation, nationalism and ideologies of masculinity intertwine through fashion explain this specific case, but also reveal the place of imaginations of the body within militarisation.

Fashion, a simultaneously aesthetic and social practice, is charged with the affects of desiring to be recognised as something with which wearers individually and collectively identify – the same aspirational drives that charge both nationalism and militarisation. If nationalism can become so taken-for-granted and so strongly emotionally experienced through reproduction in everyday practice, militarisation, too, is most effective in the everyday. The power of this everyday level of militarisation in the wider civilian world is that its manifestations are made particularly difficult to recognise – and therefore to contest – because they are bound up with pleasurable emotions that civilians rarely associate with war: the thrill of watching a powerful jet plane,[80] the pride of cheering a ceremony that connects you with what you imagine your nation's shared history to be,[81] or even the domestic comfort of pouring ketchup from a Forces-themed bottle or tapping into the shell of a veterans' fundraising egg.[82] It is no coincidence that sociologists can just as easily discuss 'banal nationalism' and 'banal militarism', or 'everyday nationalism' and 'everyday militarism': nationalism and militarism are not just parallel, they are already intertwined.[83] What binds them together is a gender order where hegemonic national masculinity is inseparably informed by representations of a nation's military masculinities, while the military's own everyday practice measures soldiers – of all genders – against ideals of how to embody *that nation's* military masculinities.

The myth of the national–military past conveyed by the Defender collection, revealed through employing an aesthetic approach to its representations and understanding the embodied affects its wearers might anticipate and experience, unfolds within the historical mythology that has structured Croatian public culture since independence. The possibilities it creates for wearers to perform knowing yet deniable celebrations of the Ustaša movement and its salute is counter to the state's declared stance on the NDH, yet the state and mainstream media have created a space with few discursive obstacles to the normalisation of the Ustaše as part of the national military past. The 'game-playing' strategy of ultranationalist fashion in Croatia, as in Germany,[84] lets its symbols operate in a space where the onlooker's inability to unambiguously determine what they refer to is the rationale for them existing at all. Yet in Croatia the historical narratives of the far right slip into what many more of the public would consider 'common sense' with much more ease, because of how the official Homeland

War myth has itself so successfully militarised public and commemorative culture. This myth, with Tuđman's 'national reconciliation' woven in, is a grand narrative which can all too easily be projected back on to the Ustaše, as if they had been fighting for the same goals as the 1990s' already-idealised 'defenders'. Beneath the ambiguity of individual symbols, exploring fashion's convergence of aesthetics and embodiment reveals how both official and far-right forms of militarisation operate through individuals' imagined identifications with a gendered mythologised national past.

Notes

1. 'Check It: Croatia's New Kits Are Bold and Beautiful', *Nike News*, 21 March 2018. https://news.nike.com/news/2018-croatia-national-team-collection.

2. Drago Pilsel, 'Ne navijam za ljude u crnoj boji. Kraj priče', Facebook, 21 June 2018. https://www.facebook.com/drago.pilsel/posts/10155619696625878.

3. See Lada Čale Feldman, Ines Prica and Reana Senjković (eds), *Fear, Death and Resistance: An Ethnography of War* (Zagreb: IEF, 1993); Dubravka Žarkov, *The Body of War: Media, Ethnicity, and Gender in the Break-Up of Yugoslavia* (Durham, NC: Duke University Press, 2007); Dejan Jović, *Rat i mit: politika identiteta u suvremenoj Hrvatskoj* (Zagreb: Fraktura, 2017).

4. Biljana Bijelić, 'Women on the Edge of Gender Equality', in *Democratic Transition in Croatia: Value Transformation, Education, Media*, edited by Sabrina P. Ramet and Davorka Matić (College Station, TX: Texas A&M University Press), 276–99, 277.

5. Carol S. Lilly and Jill A. Irvine, 'Negotiating Interests: Women and Nationalism in Serbia and Croatia, 1990–1997', *East European Politics and Societies* 16:1 (2002): 109–44, 113.

6. Žarkov, *Body*, 45.

7. Tamara Banjeglav, 'Conflicting Memories, Competing Narratives and Contested Histories in Croatia's Post-War Commemorative Practices', *Politička misao* 49:5 (2012): 7–31.

8. Jović, *Rat*.

9. Snježana Koren, 'Twentieth-Century Wars in History Teaching and Public Memory of Present-Day Croatia', *Studie sulla Formazione* 2 (2015): 11–32.

10. Robert A. Saunders and Vlad Strukov, 'The Popular Geopolitics Feedback Loop: Thinking Beyond the "Russia against the West" Paradigm', *Europe–Asia Studies* 69:2 (2017): 303–24, 305.

11. See Evans, this volume.

12. See Emma Hutchison, *Affective Communities in World Politics: Collective Emotions after Trauma* (Cambridge: Cambridge University Press, 2016), 101.

13. Hutchison, *Affective Communities*, 19.

14. See Joanne Entwistle, *The Fashioned Body: Fashion, Dress and Modern Social Theory*, 2nd ed. (Cambridge: Polity, 2015), 138.

15. Laura J. Shepherd, 'Militarisation', in *Visual Global Politics*, edited by Roland Bleiker (London: Routledge, 2018), 209–14, 213.
16. Cynthia Enloe, *Maneuvers: The International Politics of Militarizing Women's Lives* (Berkeley, CA: University of California Press, 2000), 33.
17. Jane Tynan, *British Army Uniform and the First World War: Men in Khaki* (Basingstoke: Palgrave Macmillan, 2013), 119–23.
18. Matthew McCormack, 'Boots, Material Culture and Georgian Masculinities', *Social History* 42:4 (2017): 461–79, 473, 478.
19. Jane Tynan, 'Military Chic: Fashioning Civilian Bodies for War', in *War and the Body: Militarisation, Practice and Experience*, edited by Kevin McSorley (London: Routledge, 2013), 78–89, 87.
20. See Jesse Paul Crane-Seeber, 'Sexy Warriors: The Politics and Pleasures of Submission to the State', *Critical Military Studies* 2:1–2 (2016): 41–55.
21. Enloe, *Maneuvers*, 168.
22. See Anna M. Aganthangelou and L. H. M. Ling, *Transforming World Politics: From Empire to Multiple Worlds* (London: Routledge, 2009), 31.
23. Shepherd, 'Militarisation', 213 (emphasis added).
24. See Tynan, 'Military chic'; Tynan, *British Army Uniform*; Tynan, this volume.
25. See Tynan, *British Army Uniform*, 30–2.
26. This chapter uses a pseudonym for the company firstly in order not to advertise it, and secondly to make the chapter less discoverable by internet users searching for the brand (an extra layer of defence against online harassment). URLs from its website have been shortened using a link shortener. The first word of the company's real name is also an English noun with which customers buying clothing with Croatian national symbolism would identify.
27. Jon E. Fox and Cynthia Miller-Idriss, 'Everyday Nationhood', *Ethnicities* 8:4 (2008): 536–63, 537–8.
28. On militarisation and the everyday, see Richelle M. Bernazzolli and Colin Flint, 'Embodying the Garrison-State?: Everyday Geographies of Militarization in American Society', *Political Geography* 29:3 (2010): 157–66; Lorraine Dowler, 'Gender, Militarization and Sovereignty', *Geography Compass* 6:8 (2012): 490–9; Victoria M. Basham, *War, Identity and the Liberal State: Everyday Experiences of the Geopolitical in the Armed Forces* (London: Routledge, 2013); Marsha Henry and Katherine Natanel, 'Militarisation as Diffusion: The Politics of Gender, Space and the Everyday', *Gender, Place & Culture* 23:6 (2016): 850–6; Linda Åhäll, 'Feeling Everyday IR: Embodied, Affective, Militarising Movement as Choreography of War', *Cooperation and Conflict* 54:2 (2019): 149–66.
29. Cynthia Miller-Idriss, *The Extreme Gone Mainstream: Commercialization and Far-Right Youth Culture in Germany* (Princeton, NJ: Princeton University Press, 2017), 82.
30. Miller-Idriss, *Extreme*, 83. See Anthony D. Smith, *Myths and Memories of the Nation* (Oxford: Oxford University Press, 1999); Duncan S. A. Bell, 'Mythscapes: Memory, Mythology and National Identity', *British Journal of Sociology* 54:1 (2003): 63–81.

31. See Roger Griffin, 'Staging the Nation's Rebirth: The Politics and Aesthetics of Performance in the Context of Fascist Studies', in *Fascism and Theatre: Comparative Studies on the Aesthetics and Politics of Performance in Europe, 1925–1945*, edited by Günter Berghaus (New York: Berghahn, 1996), 11–29, 12–13.

32. Miller-Idriss, *Extreme*, 83.

33. See Jackie Stacey, *Star Gazing: Hollywood Cinema and Female Spectatorship* (London: Routledge, 1994), 159.

34. Graham Dawson, *Soldier Heroes: British Adventure, Empire, and the Imagining of Masculinities* (London: Routledge, 1994).

35. Miller-Idriss, *Extreme*, 19.

36. Ivo Žanić, 'The Curse of King Zvonimir and Political Discourse in Embattled Croatia', *East European Politics and Societies* 9:1 (1995): 90–122.

37. Stipe Odak and Andriana Benčič, 'Jasenovac – a Past That Does Not Pass: The Presence of Jasenovac in Croatian and Serbian Collective Memory of Conflict', *East European Politics and Societies* 30:4 (2016): 805–29, 808.

38. David Bruce MacDonald, *Balkan Holocausts?: Serbian and Croatian Victim-Centred Propaganda and the War in Yugoslavia* (Manchester: Manchester University Press, 2002), 170–1.

39. Vjeran Pavlaković, 'Flirting with Fascism: The Ustaša Legacy and Croatian Politics in the 1990s', in *The Shared History: The Second World War and National Question in Ex Yugoslavia*, edited by [unnamed] (Novi Sad: Centar za istoriju, demokratiju i pomirenje, 2008), 115–44.

40. Banjeglav, 'Memories'.

41. Antonija Petricusic, 'Nation-Building in Croatia and the Treatment of Minorities: Rights and Wrongs', *L'Europe en formation* 3 (2008): 135–45, 141.

42. Predrag Dojčinović, 'The Shifting Status of *Grand Narratives* in War Crimes Trials and International Law: History and Politics in the Courtroom', in *Narratives of Justice in and Out of the Courtroom: Former Yugoslavia and Beyond*, edited by Dubravka Žarkov and Marlies Glasius (Cham: Springer, 2014), 63–88, 77–9.

43. Siniša Malešević, 'Nationalism, War and Social Cohesion', *Ethnic and Racial Studies* 34:1 (2011): 142–61; John Hutchinson, *Nationalism and War* (Oxford: Oxford University Press, 2017).

44. Marcus Tanner's paperback history of Croatia has this subtitle: Marcus Tanner, *Croatia: A Nation Forged in War*, 3rd ed. (New Haven, CT: Yale University Press, 2010).

45. See Catherine Baker, *Sounds of the Borderland: Popular Music, War and Nationalism in Croatia since 1991* (Farnham: Ashgate, 2010).

46. Neven Barković, 'Daliću, Modriću i ostali: poslušajte zašto je Thompson problem', *Index*, 23 July 2018. https://www.index.hr/vijesti/clanak/dalicu-modricu-i-ostali-poslusajte-zasto-je-thompson-problem/2013123.aspx.

47. Svanibor Pettan, 'Music, Politics, and War in Croatia: An Introduction', in *Music, Politics, and War: Views from Croatia*, edited by Svanibor Pettan (Zagreb: IEF, 1998), 22.

48. See Dario Brentin, 'Ready for the Homeland?: Ritual, Remembrance, and Political Extremism in Croatian Football', *Nationalities Papers* 44:6 (2016): 860–76, 863. Elements of the salute had been used by Nikola Šubić Zrinski (leading troops against Ottoman forces in 1566), Josip Jelačić (who added a call-and-response rhythm) and the composer Ivan Zajc (in his 1876 opera about Zrinski), but the exact 'Za dom spremni' formulation was the Ustaša regime's work: Brentin, 'Ready?', 863.

49. Miller-Idriss, *Extreme*, 2.

50. Gordan Duhaček, 'U centru Zagreba dućan s neonacističkom i "ustaškom" modom!', *Tportal*, 19 March 2012. https://www.tportal.hr/vijesti/clanak/u-centru-zagreba-ducan-s-neonacistickom-i-ustaskom-modom-20120318; Benjamin Perasović and Marko Pustapić, 'Football Supporters in the Context of Croatian Sociology: Research Perspectives 20 Years After', *Kinesiology* 45 (2013): 262–75, 268. Its current Croatian importer comments on the brand's 'hiding [of] many details, forbidden and untold tales based on Nordic mythology and glorious ages of history' in copy explaining its exclusivity to the Croatian streetwear consumer: 'Thor Steinar', Vandal Shop (no date). http://www.vandalshop.hr/brandovi/thor-steinar.

51. Jović, *Rat*, 37.

52. Ivo Goldstein and Slavko Goldstein, 'Revisionism in Croatia: The Case of Franjo Tuđman', *East European Jewish Affairs* 32:1 (2002): 52–64, 53; Dojčinović, 'Status', 79.

53. 'Kolinda Grabar-Kitarović: pozdrav "Za dom spremni" je neprihvatljiv', *Dnevno*, 10 September 2017. https://www.dnevno.hr/vijesti/hrvatska/kolinda-grabar-kitarovic-pozdrav-za-dom-spremni-je-neprihvatljiv-1061090/.

54. Amra Čusto, 'Bosnia-Herzegovina and the Cultural Memory of Bleiburg', *Politička misao* 55:2 (2018): 111–30, 116–17.

55. Sven Milekić, 'Croatian Leaders Sing Praises for Herzeg Bosna', *Balkan Insight*, 30 May 2017. http://www.balkaninsight.com/en/article/croatian-leaders-sing-praises-for-herzeg-bosna-05-30-2017.

56. See Ivan Čolović, *The Politics of Symbol in Serbia: Essays in Political Anthropology*, translated by Celia Hawkesworth (London: Hurst, 2002); Ivo Žanić, *Flag on the Mountain: A Political Anthropology of War in Croatia and Bosnia-Herzegovina, 1990–1995*, translated by Graham McMaster and Celia Hawkesworth (London: Saqi, 2007).

57. Miller-Idriss, *Extreme*, 195–201.

58. Xavier Guillaume, Rune S. Andersen and Juha Vuori, 'Paint it Black: Colours and the Social Meaning of the Battlefield', *European Journal of International Relations* 22:1 (2016): 49–71, 53.

59. Ibid., 55.

60. Reana Senjković, 'Image of the Warrior', *Narodna umjetnost* 33:1 (1996): 41–57, 42.

61. See Rory Yeomans, 'Cults of Death and Fantasies of Annihilation: The Croatian Ustasha Movement in Power, 1941–45', *Central Europe* 3:2 (2005): 121–42, 138–9.

62. Pavlaković, 'Fascism', 129.

63. See Maple Razsa, *Bastards of Utopia: Living Radical Politics after Socialism* (Bloomington, IN: Indiana University Press, 2015), 41–3.

64. At his concert celebrating the twentieth anniversary of Oluja in August 2015, Thompson wore a camouflage-print T-shirt with a regular Croatian Army patch on one arm and HOS's emblem on the other, signalling he placed both forces' veterans in the same community of honour.

65. See Miller-Idriss, *Extreme*, 200–1.

66. Ibid., 58.

67. Alex J. Bellamy, 'Reclaiming the Croatian Flag', *Rethinking History* 3:3 (1999): 324–8.

68. The triple-stranded knotwork pattern, or 'pleter', is a symbol of Croatian tradition dating back to early medieval stone monuments, often used as a border in patriotic graphic design: Reana Senjković, *Lica društva, likovi države* (Zagreb: IEF, 2002), 20–2.

69. 'Prvo Crveno'. https://bit.ly/2zELrev.

70. See Andrew B. R. Elliott, *Medievalism, Politics and Mass Media: Appropriating the Middle Ages in the Twenty-First Century* (Cambridge: Boydell Press, 2017), 10.

71. This includes the 'U' or 'Za dom spremni' references above, except 'ZDS 1991', which both does and does not reference 1941–5. One features the German MP 40 submachine pistol used by the Ustaše, and another is a propaganda image called 'Rob nikada!' ('Never a slave!'), depicting its bare-chested, fair-haired soldier with a torn uniform and flag, clutching his rifle with a wounded arm, as the ideal of Ustaša masculinity. Two commemorate Frane Tente, a young Croat from an Ustaša family who survived Bleiburg and died in prison in 1948 after replacing a Yugoslav flag with a Croatian one outside Split. Another calls Tito a 'vampire' with his portrait inside a crossed-out red circle, and one of the site's four eagle and coat-of-arms designs is described as inspired by Hrvatski Orlovski Savez (the Croatian Eagle Association), a Catholic youth organisation founded in 1923 in opposition to the Yugoslav 'Sokols' ('Falcons'): see Sandra Prlenda, 'Young, Religious, and Radical: The Croat Catholic Youth Organizations, 1922–1945', in *Ideologies and National Identities: The Case of Twentieth-Century Southeastern Europe*, edited by John R. Lampe and Mark Mazower (Budapest: CEU Press, 2006), 82–109.

72. This fan movement against corporate football is not far right, but occupies 'an ambiguous position which could be associated with anti-capitalist right and/ or left-wing perspectives': Andrew Hodges and Paul Stubbs, 'The Paradoxes of Politicisation: Fan Initiatives in Zagreb, Croatia', in *New Ethnographies of Football in Europe: People, Passions, Politics*, edited by Alexandra Schwell et al. (London: Palgrave Macmillan, 2016), 55–74, 69.

73. 'Heroji'. https://bit.ly/2zFHqGB.

74. 'Mi Hrvati'. https://bit.ly/2DHGt4s.

75. Senjković, *Lica društva*, 220–9.

76. 'Marko Perković Thompson za [Defender] Hrvatska', 8 July 2013. https://bit.ly/2DHGuFy.

77. See Susan Jeffords, *The Remasculinization of America: Gender and the Vietnam War* (New York: Wiley, 1989).
78. Senjković, *Lica društva*, 188–9.
79. For example Lenka Gospodnetić, 'Thompson i Hrvati', *Slobodna Dalmacija*, 17 September 2002.
80. See Matthew F. Rech and Alison J. Williams, 'Researching at Military Airshows: A Dialogue about Ethnography and Autoethnography', in *The Routledge Companion to Military Research Methods*, edited by Alison J. Williams et al. (London: Routledge, 2016), 268–84.
81. See Angharad Closs Stephens, 'The Affective Atmospheres of Nationalism', *Cultural Geographies* 23:2 (2016): 181–98.
82. See Joanna Tidy, 'Forces Sauces and Eggs for Soldiers: Food, Nostalgia, and the Rehabilitation of the British Military', *Critical Military Studies* 1:3 (2015): 220–32.
83. See Tanja Thomas and Fabian Virchow, 'Banal Militarism and the Culture of War', in *Bring 'Em On: Media and Politics in the Iraq War*, edited by Lee Artz and Yahya R. Kamalipour (Lanham, MD: Rowman and Littlefield, 2005), 23–36.
84. Miller-Idriss, *Extreme*, 53.

CHAPTER 9

Images of Insurgency: Reading the Cuban Revolution through Military Aesthetics and Embodiment

Jane Tynan

Transnational histories of insurgency are growing. The increased emphasis on transnational aspects of political violence have challenged traditional understandings of insurgency as a form of militarism internal to the state.[1] Few studies, however, draw attention to how insurgency is shaped by aesthetics and embodiment. The aesthetic turn in international relations has generated new research on material and visual cultures of militarisation, but there is less understanding of how this impacts patterns of resistance in revolutionary contexts, that is, how social actors resist, rebel and revolt against political authority. In this chapter, I examine how ideas of 'revolution' can be read through images and self-presentation techniques. Here, the visuality of the Cuban Revolution is brought into focus, first through its strategies of urban guerrilla warfare and then through its nation-building programmes. How did rebel leaders embody the revolutionary spirit, and did the circulation of images of insurgency enlist people to a participatory revolution? Further, did the revolution consolidate and circulate specific kinds of images and embodiments of military masculinities?

Since the nineteenth century, Cuba has had many periods of economic, political and social change, and these 'crises have been characterized by strong ideas about renewal, progress, development, social justice, national vindication, and independence'.[2] In 1511 the Spanish established themselves on the island and for the next two centuries it acted as a gateway to the region, making Havana a significant commercial location. Since the island's indigenous population was small, the Spanish colonisers met their demand for labour by importing enslaved Africans. Slavery would only be abolished in 1886, and Afro-Cubans continued to experience discrimination and segregation after that.[3] A short period of British occupation in the late 1700s gave Cubans a taste of freedom from Spanish taxation policies, while strengthening trade relationships, an episode that prompted interest in wider political change. When Spain's empire fell in the early 1800s, it was the USA that sought to develop commercial interests on the island, not least because slavery was still widely practiced there.[4] By the mid-1800s, the drive for abolition and independence led to various attempted rebellions, culminating in the Cuban War of Independence in 1895–8. Afro-Cubans played an influential role in this war, but the Negro Rebellion in 1912 saw their own demands for equality with Cuba's white population denied.

The discourse that formed around Cuba's struggle for independence once slavery had been abolished in 1886 was inspired by the activism and writings of Cuban intellectual José Martí, who sought exile in various countries including Spain, Mexico and the USA before eventually returning to Cuba. Martí was a key figure in the intellectual movement for independence and he advocated education and free speech as key to the development of Latin America. Martí founded the Cuban Revolutionary Party (PRC), uniting various separatist factions and in 1895 Cuba's War of Independence began with uprisings across the island, which became the Spanish–American War. When a peace treaty was signed in 1898 it became clear that the peace was a victory for the US rather than Cuban revolutionaries; in 1899, the USA formally began a military occupation of Cuba.

By the 1920s, growing public frustration that the ideals of independence had not been fulfilled led to a complex period of upheaval. Fulgencio Batista came to power, first from 1933–44 bringing peace and prosperity and then from 1952–9 as a US-backed dictator, until rebel forces dramatically deposed him. On 26 July 1953, an anti-Batista activist named Fidel Castro led a group to attack Moncada army barracks in Santiago de Cuba, a disaster that saw many of them, including Castro, sent to jail. Disastrous though it was, the Moncada attack did make a case for revolution and became symbolic of Cubans' struggles, so much so that rebel forces adopted the name 'the 26 July Movement'. Following an amnesty for all political prisoners, Castro and others fled to Mexico to plot their return to Cuba. In November 1956, Castro and eighty men, including an Argentinian doctor called Ernesto 'Che' Guevara who had come to Cuba to join rebel forces, staged an insurgency against Batista. Other revolutionary groups supported them, including the University of Havana's student group, Directorio Revolucionario Estudiantil, who in 1957 attacked the presidential palace in an attempt to assassinate Batista. The informal group Revolutionary National Action, led by Frank País, was also strategically important to support Fidel Castro's forces in its use of cell-based structures and guerrilla tactics. It was this military strategy that ensured success for the January 1959 insurrection. Extensive political support and the social networks of the 26 July Movement were also critical to uniting a political coalition of groups to overthrow Batista.

The '26 July' commanders, soldiers and rank and file came to embody the 1959 revolution, even though the insurgency was supported by a wider anti-Batista front. A discourse emerged from the insurrection that gave form to the revolutionary Cuban citizen, who came to embody the characteristics of those who fought for independence: as Julia Sweig writes, 'the guerrilla *foco* came to be cast as the formative experience of the revolutionary, the womb that gestated the "new Cuban man."'[5] If the efforts of guerrilla fighters were perceived to have won Cuban independence, the identities they laid claim to gained currency in the post-revolution period. The revolution had a masculine image, not because it excluded women, who were on the front lines shaping the process of revolution, but because they were not conspicuous as combatants in battles such as the Sierra Maestra.[6] This 1958 battle saw a group of 300 rebels led by the Castro brothers defeat Batista's 10,000-strong army. From 1953 an estimated 5 per cent of guerrilla fighters were women, most of whom were mobilised as students.[7] In common with many similar insurgencies since the start of the twentieth century, women had key roles, but usually as non-combatants: they formed women-only groups, played strategic roles as liaisons, distributed propaganda, raised funds and smuggled information. Women clearly participated in the Cuban Revolution in various ways, but the struggle created images that were distinctly masculine, suggesting 'the central role played by gendered imagery and discourse in the revolutionary process'.[8] This discussion considers why a discourse emerged in media reports, photographs, in accounts from the rebels themselves and throughout popular culture to frame the revolution as a masculine enterprise. The distinctive aesthetic that emerged in visual images of the revolution and in evidence in the self-presentation techniques of the rebel army offer insights into how these events were later interpreted and understood.

Ernesto 'Che' Guevara, through his image, in particular, became a transnational figure thanks to the Cuban Revolution. In fact, his participation and military leadership in the revolution not only concerned Cuba, but also represented a Marxist view of how poor and working-class solidarity might be forged across the developing world. Guevara inspired, and continues to inspire, those interested in developing social structures based on egalitarianism, transnational social justice, liberatory education and anti-imperialism (including the Black Panther Party in the USA, whose own iconic aesthetic is the subject of the next chapter in this volume[9]). The ways in which Guevara's image has been circulated and appropriated in popular culture in Europe and North America will be discussed later. What is clear is that Guevara himself was convinced that identity could be formed and re-formed through events. His specific dispositions in youth, central to his idea of creating the new man or woman (*el hombre nuevo*), betrayed his belief that institutions could only change through the transformation of subjectivity.[10] His awareness of the role of subjectivity in social transformation highlights how studies of aesthetics and embodiment offer critical insights into the revolutionary project. He saw the value of instilling a desire for change on every level, which not only meant creating new images of the future, but also involved 'making' new kinds of people. While a focus on aesthetics and embodiment is important when considering how any kind of military identities are formed, in a revolutionary context like the Cuban Revolution it is critical: in revolutions, the functions, meanings and circulation of images, ideas and bodies all exist in opposition to hegemonic structures of power, and thus revolutionary ideologies about bodies, and how they might be militarised, necessarily involve an aesthetic sense of how those bodies will need to be transformed in order to break down the structures that the revolutionaries oppose. The revolution is often itself a creative and improvised project. Many of the rebel leaders, including Guevara, improvised revolutionary masculinities; this chapter considers the significance of these identity positions, how they emerged as part of a visual culture, and asks whether their construction was a political or a creative act.

Revolutionary Masculinities

Studies of masculinity emphasise its instability and contingency. The philosopher Judith Butler highlights gender as a performance, a being in process, but one constrained by the 'various forces that police the social appearance of gender'.[11] While the notion of performance might suggest free expression, for Butler gender scripts work within a rigid regulatory frame. Thus, the range of acceptable masculine social roles is 'determined within this regulatory frame and the subject has a limited number of "costumes" from which to make a constrained choice of gender style'.[12] This is further enforced in military culture, which normalises a narrow range of masculine identities within its structures. This tendency towards gender normativity is evident in the representation of social relationships that make up military institutions.[13] The military, represented as a masculine institution, does not offer the opportunity to express a range of masculine identities beyond those enshrined in military culture. Masculine unity is one of the most pervasive fictions in military discourse, neatly perpetuated by images of a uniform military masculinity.[14] This uniformity speaks of power and control exercised through a binary construction of gender, but also through the demand to conform to heterosexual ideals. Images are critical to perpetuating gender fictions. Hegemonic masculinity, a term used to describe how particular groups of men legitimate and reproduce their power through relationships of dominance, is powerfully represented by images of uniformed military men.[15] Revolutionary masculinities, though, upset this image of unity and uniformity, both visually and in terms of subjectivity. How then are military bodies imagined and created to embody social roles in a revolutionary struggle?

A very distinct form of military masculinity is created within revolutionary struggle. If dominant masculinities are framed by patriarchal capitalism, do men taking up revolutionary struggle give up masculine privilege? If men engaging with ideas of anti-imperialist revolution act them out through insurgent forms of military action, does this behaviour necessarily depart from normative military masculinities? What does it mean when whiteness and masculinity dominate the representation and embodiment of a revolutionary struggle? What is clear is that the social appearance of masculinity is meaningful to how histories of war are played out. According to the historian Joanna Bourke, men's bodies were, in World War I, produced by material forces that 'affected not only the shape and texture of the male body, but also the values ascribed to the body and the disciplines applied to masculinity'.[16] Thus, the performance, the experience of 'being' a soldier, is critical to understanding how military conflict shapes people.[17] Whatever material forces affect the shape of the male body is, therefore, also critical to understanding the nature of the conflict. So too is the absence or marginalising of other kinds of gendered and raced bodies. Revolutionary masculinities owe much to normative embodiments of military masculinity, but there are significant ways in which they can also be disruptive and deviant.

How particular versions of military masculinity circulate is of interest, but so too is the paradox of revolutionary masculinities, whereby military identity is defined both by power and by dissent. Insurgents might engage with some myths of militarism consistent with patriarchal norms, but insurgents are forced through the circumstances of the conflict itself to creatively interpret masculine tropes. History in revolutionary contexts is made from below, and often recreated from the remnants of disestablished structures. For Bourke, it was the material reality and experience men had of conflict, rather than its coded representations, which determined the destiny of the male body. Uniform, one of the techniques by which these disciplines are applied to men's bodies in military conflicts, is a technique to mobilise key elements in the myth of bodily masculinity.[18] Insurgents are under particular kinds of pressures to create their own myths of military strength and to contest the disciplinary power of state armies. While state soldiers might engage in micro acts of embodied resistance to uniform codes, insurgents are inventing and improvising military identities through the specific conditions of the conflict. A critical part of that is the creative construction of the combatant civilian. A visual culture that exalts revolutionary masculinities engages with complex military identities. Revolutionaries are simultaneously defined by patriarchal power, but also by its undoing; they are equivocal about modernity but also seek to build new social structures.

The power of images coming out of Cuba in the 1950s and 1960s lay in their communicative quality and transnational potential. The events of the revolution ignited social transformations which had been common to various anti-imperialist struggles in earlier decades, in Ireland, Bengal and Palestine, where the success of insurgencies owed much to strategic alliances formed between urban and rural people. Nationalism in the colonial world had forged localised protest with a strong ideology: 'Colonial "nationalism" was therefore an expression of a dual focused rhetoric . . . no successful protest movement was made without ideology and without peasant support.'[19] National liberation had to be invented, which could not be achieved by military strategy alone, but relied upon the manipulation of symbols, ideas, material objects and even bodies. Victory was dependent upon the peasantry and the bourgeoisie coming together to foster nationhood, and so too would it be in Cuba. Guevara explained this in very material terms in a speech he made on 27 January 1959 in Havana:

> We were a group of city people who were thrown into the Sierra Maestra, but were not part of it . . . Little by little the peasants' view toward us began to change . . . The shift in the peasants' attitude translated into the incorporation of palm-leaf hats into our ranks, as our army of city folk was becoming transformed into an army of peasants.[20]

Guevara sought to articulate the revolutionary spirit as one where subjective experience for peasants became incorporated into the actions of the rebel army, while also demonstrating how urban rebels could learn from citizens who lived in the Cuban countryside. Through references to embodiment, he articulated how the raising of consciousness manifests in the revolutionary transformations of the body. The notion of incorporation is particularly powerful in revolutionary contexts because non-state actors are forced to hide and often find it useful to adopt a civilian image. Guevara used an example of peasant adornments infiltrating military units to signal how the conflict was a transformative event that made guerrilla fighters and civilians become one. As the introduction to this volume suggests research on aesthetics and embodiment exposes how the intimate politics of militarisation operates.

Guevara's *foco* theory of guerrilla warfare, whereby a vanguard sought the support of workers and peasants through their fast-moving attacks in the countryside, exploited uncertainty. What distinguishes insurgents from regular forces is their capacity for surprise attacks, which necessarily involves some skill in camouflage and disguise; this kind of warfare is thus characterised by an equivocal attitude to uniform on the part of revolutionaries.[21] Guerrilla warfare embodies the energy and vision of peasant rebellion combined with the ideology of modern revolution.[22] In another part of the same speech, Guevara explains that the peasant was the 'invisible collaborator who did everything that the rebel combatant could not'.[23] He articulates something important here about how guerrilla warfare works, by highlighting the strategic reliance on invisibility, disguise and transformation.

In the Cuban countryside, invisibility, or the capacity to create illusion, had been critical to the guerrillas' military strategy. When rebel leaders came into view, however, they had a distinctive appearance. More often they were white, male charismatic leaders with a raw appearance and informal attitude representing a new kind of image for revolutionary socialism, particularly in Latin America. The notion that revolution constructs new forms of masculine power had already been evident in how the Bolsheviks, during the Russian Revolution, had 'invented an entirely new lexicon for gender and masculinity'.[24] Significant in the Cuban context is the extent to which revolutionary military identities had to be improvised through the lived reality of conflict, illustrated by Fidel Castro's description of his comrade Camilo Cienfuegos (Figure 9.1):

> One sure thing is that Camilo became legendary, among other things because of that medium-brim Stetson hat, which was the most distinguished headpiece in the whole Rebel Army, and not just because of the way it evoked a Tombstone sheriff. There simply wasn't a hat or cap like it in Cuba. Nor boots, whether they were tall or short.[25]

Figure 9.1 Robert A. Paneque and Camilo Cienfuegos. Bayamo, February 1959 (photographer unknown). Wikimedia Commons: https://commons.wikimedia. org/wiki/File:Robert_A._Paneque_y_el_Comandante_Camilo_Cienfuegos,_en_ Bayamo,_febrero_de_1959.jpg

Castro lovingly describes Cienfuegos's clothes in ways that revere a particular version of masculinity, one reminiscent of the cowboy or renegade, or the outsider prepared to be unconventional. Part of a familiar discourse that elevates heroic masculinities in time of war, Castro's exaltation of his comrade places a curious emphasis on dress and body. More significant, though, are the ways in which the Cuban Revolution gave new impetus to established ideas of what constituted a soldier hero.[26] Castro cites his creative approach to dress as evidence of Cienfuegos's revolutionary militarism. By focusing on the body and its adornments Castro places value in the role of dress to constitute military identity, and in particular hints at its distinctive power in unconventional warfare. With the instability of masculinity in mind, improvised military identities such as these reflect the creativity rebel soldiers brought to the work of 'fashioning' their bodies. Various models of identity adopted by the rebels were communicated verbally, textually and in visual images, which contributed to the widespread mythologising of the rebel army. Unlike the conventional images of military men that had been established by the modern appearance of state armies in the first half of the twentieth century, those of Cienfuegos, Castro and Guevara displayed less concern with an appearance of masculine unity. The rebels departed from the ideal that had been embraced by the US Army in World War II, and were instead more interested in the dynamics of visibility and invisibility; creating illusion was critical to the guerrillas' military strategy, but rebel leaders also at times saw the value of being conspicuous. A new vocabulary for masculinity was evolving through the circumstances of the struggle itself.

In fact, the very notions of military heroism, traditionally framed by British colonial narratives to express power and dominance, were being reinvented by the architecture of the conflict in late 1950s Cuba. In its more traditional forms, the soldier hero is ordained by a Christian God, represents a sovereign state, and ideally embodies the gentlemanly state through a convincing image of a 'civilizing force'.[27] In both colonial and anti-colonial military action, bodies can be fashioned to legitimise extreme actions, and the uniform's abstraction from violence is what allows it to authorise the use of violence while maintaining an image of fashionable progress. Impeccably uniformed, formally presented, white and sexually restrained, the gentleman soldier embodied colonial power and its claims of superiority. The gendering of adventure and its imaginative connection with imperialism endured in various regions up to the twentieth century as the 'modern adventure tale is imbued with the imaginative resonance of colonial power relations underpinned by science and technology'.[28] Graham Dawson claims that these images, which had energised imperial adventure, were by World War I redundant and by this time the soldier, his struggles and contradictions laid bare, had become a figure of irony, as exemplified by T. E. Lawrence; the characteristic soldier hero of the new century was a secular figure, often an irregular, and was more likely to be a guerrilla fighter on the margins of the conflict.[29] Dawson was describing dynamics with British imperialism, but how might this be significant to the colonial imaginaries at work in Cuba, which were Spanish and then American? What he does highlight is the extent to which the myth of a unified military masculinity was breaking down in the early twentieth century under the pressure of new kinds of warfare. Less concerned with morality than the pleasures of adventure, the popular soldierly ideal was changing just as the notion of heroism itself underwent transformation. By this time, as Dawson suggests, distinctive outsider qualities had become a desirable form of military masculinity in various regions, due partly to the prevalence of anti-colonial struggle. Whatever outsider qualities the Cuban rebels had, though, and however much they sought to craft an alternative military masculinity, their bodies were presented as distinctly white, male and heterosexual.

Exaltation of physicality and fearlessness were common to both traditional and modern forms of military heroism. The Cuban Revolution saw military masculinities emerge that were oppositional and secular. Further, the motivations of combatants were consistent with a form of militarism that arose from anti-colonial struggle. The new soldier hero embodied not a sovereign gentlemanly state but its rupture. These revolutionary masculinities were the product of the imagination, but also arose from the experience and reality of conflict. When Arminio Savioli, a reporter for the Italian newspaper L'Unità, sought to interview Fidel Castro in 1961, he witnessed a group of guerrilla fighters entering the El Caribe nightclub in the Havana Libre Hotel in the early hours of the morning. His description of the all-male group, which included Castro, is revealing of the ways in which the physical presence of the Cuban rebels inspired onlookers: 'Five athletic silhouettes in uniform, with pistols on their waists and small submachine guns on their shoulders, came in in complete silence (the carpet eliminated any noise made by the boots), sat around a table and ordered Coca Cola.'[30] As is clear from Castro's description of Cienfuegos, the rebel leadership gave themselves special status through their creative approach to military clothing, but particularly striking in Savioli's account is his willingness to observe beauty in these men's bodies. Clearly star-struck by Castro, Savioli admires his physique in the half-darkness of the club, when he recalls 'I recognized the heavy and slightly round shoulders, the tall size and the black, Renaissance-like beard of Fidel Castro.'[31] In both Castro's detailed description of Cienfuegos's clothes and Savioli's sketch of Castro, there is a sense that the circumstances of the revolution allow men to take pleasure in observing male physical beauty. These homosocial narratives, however, did not translate into progressive views on same-sex desire in revolutionary Cuba. In fact, between 1959 and 1980 there was a particularly repressive attitude towards what were considered the visible hallmarks of male homosexuality.[32] While the outsider qualities of Cuban rebels were conspicuous, they were constructed within a frame of normative military masculinities that valorised heterosexuality and whiteness.

Images of military men work to mythologise the actions of particular soldiers. How then did ideas of heroism, common to various forms of military masculinities, operate in the context of the Cuban Revolution? As instigators of an anti-colonial war, the Cuban rebels were less interested in being viewed as a civilising force and instead saw themselves as agents of social transformation who sought to encourage creative rather than conformist styles of citizenship. Once the soldier became a figure of irony, a new kind of popular militarism emerged through the way in which the rebels fashioned themselves and, in turn, how this was then represented in photography and poster art. These images accommodated many of the characteristics of anti-colonial struggle: the misunderstood outsider, the irregular soldier or the guerrilla. Invisibility was critical to the identity of the guerrilla; accounts of the rebel leadership suggest that a capacity for camouflage was ideally complemented by charisma and physical beauty. Castro's description of Guevara's military appearance draws attention to the rebels' blatant disregard for uniformity and the ways they sought to transform and mutate:

> And everywhere he went, Che descended the airplane steps in his baggy olive-green uniform, never mind that it was American Army Infantry clothing that Batista's army wore until their defeat, his shirt regularly hanging out of his pants, his boots tied only halfway up his calves, sporting a black beret sometimes and not others, his spare beard with those gaps under his sideburns where his beard refused to grow and his hair meticulously combed at times, and other times glowing freely like Prince Valiant's pageboy.[33]

A tendency to move in and out of focus contributed strongly to the magical persona of what appeared to be the typical Cuban revolutionary fighter. As Castro's description implies, Guevara's capacity to transform from guerrilla to leader, when the situation demanded it, contributed to his success as a new kind of revolutionary. As with other anti-colonial struggles from World War I onwards, the dynamics of the revolution demanded an equivocal attitude to uniform and a new kind of physical presence. Guevara's bodily transformations, his metamorphoses from meticulous soldier to shabby rebel, his tendency to choose when and how to wear his beret, reflect ideas about fashion as an expressive and adaptive force that is 'transitory, mobile and fragmentary'.[34] Fashion in this context, however, is not about the consumption of apparel, but instead represents the everyday work of making the self. Guerrilla fighters in this context used the instability and mutability of identity to maximise military effectiveness.

These shifts between civilian and military identities reflect how anarchic bodies shaped events in the Cuban Revolution, through the strategic use of camouflage, disguise and bodily transformation. When translated into the language of popular entertainment, informal kinds of military appearance quickly evoke the idea of the heroic outsider. Further, these forms of casual militarism suggest that the unique pleasures of adventure are available to men prepared to be outsiders and renegades as they move through the countryside on an unauthorised, and often dangerous, quest for freedom. This is not to suggest that visual culture drove the popularity of the Cuban Revolution, which in the USA has been attributed to the influence of journalists and scholars, but many narratives that emerged from the conflict were reliant upon images such as one favoured by news editors at the time, who delighted in calling the rebels Castro's *barbudos*, or 'bearded ones'.[35] Uniform is one of the techniques by which discipline can be applied to men's bodies in military conflicts; indeed, it is one of the 'costumes' available to men who conform to a narrow range of masculine identities. Castro adopted uniform for the discipline and control it gave his troops, but over time he also saw the value of improvising military identities, which made war experience pivotal to how Cuban revolutionary citizens came into being. His equivocal attitude to uniform is evident in his own words:

> Nothing mattered, nonetheless, as long as the uniform's cloth was olive-green. You could add all of whatever pockets, buttons, zippers, epaulets and pleats you could think of to the basic cloth. So, with an olive-green uniform, a cigar in your mouth and an assigned task, you were invested of all the powers the Revolution gave you.[36]

When his rebel army crafted a military appearance, Castro appeared to value creativity above discipline. He was flexible about what might constitute a military masculinity, and, as his description suggests, it was one capable of yielding to events and circumstances. Photographs taken by Reverend David W. Havens in the first week of January 1959 offer a glimpse of what passed for military garb for the rank and file.[37] In one photograph, a large group of young men in fatigue uniform, some bearded, others clean-shaven, point their guns at the camera. The shabbily dressed men have uniforms, in a sense, and the drab colour and cut of the loose-fitting shirts suggest that they are likely to be US infantry uniforms. Many also wear the field cap, but there is little effort to conform to a uniform style. In another photograph taken by Havens, an unknown reporter engages two rebels in conversation, both men in fatigues, one matches his uniform with a top hat while the other prefers to wear a beret.[38] Other photographs featuring women revolutionaries show they adopt the same air of casual militarism. The impression is of a ragtag army of cheerful civilians unaccustomed to military life, playfully styled to look like a military unit. Other photographs taken by Havens depict women guerrillas who wear a combination of civilian and military clothing and also men mixing with ordinary Cubans, their unmilitary appearance amplifying the sense that on the street combatants were often indistinguishable from civilians.

Though Castro was not interested in enforcing a strict uniform policy, for him the use of olive green was his nod to military discipline. He was fetishistic, however, about the cigar, which for the rebel leadership at least was a key signifier, and became central to his idea of what constituted the Cuban revolutionary masculinity. Castro was vocal on the masculine pleasures of cigar smoking, and boasted that even during the Bay of Pigs invasion in April 1961, when counter-revolutionary militants surrounded the island, he would have sent Cuban cigars to the White House if the press secretary had asked for them. In his view, the cigar mediated and deepened male bonds:

> Cigar-smoking is a bond that doesn't fail the powerful . . . Oh, to slowly roll a puff of smoke over my tongue, meditating on it, because meditating on smoke when you're the one in power – preferably ruling with an iron fist – has been the experience of very few men.[39]

He delighted in making personal gifts of Cuban cigars to foreign dignitaries: for him, this symbol represented and embodied masculinity in ways that he knew were resonant. He may have appeared to be casual about uniform but he was also very aware of the currency of male privilege for the purposes of diplomacy.

There are many photographs from the period featuring prominent women fighters such as Vilma Espín Guillois (Figure 9.2), and various images also show women in uniform interacting with Fidel Castro. A feature of the revolution was the priority given to gender equality, but this was often a tactical weapon, which in a new Cuba was unsustainable, partly due to the potency of images and ideas about revolutionary military masculinities.[40] Of the available photographs of women – many fewer than those images featuring exclusively men – their military uniforms are clearly modelled on the garb worn by male fighters. Women too concocted a military image by mixing uniform with civilian fashionable clothing, and their outfits often included olive green fatigues, boots and military caps. It was not the first time that women were forced to mimic a version of militarism created by men for men. But when Celia

Figure 9.2 Raúl Castro, Vilma Espín Guillois, Jorge Risquet and José Nivaldo Causse in Tumba Siete, 1958 (photographer unknown). Wikimedia Commons: https://commons.wikimedia.org/wiki/File:Raúl,_Vilma,_Jorge_Risquet_y_José_Nivaldo_Causse.jpg

Sánchez prepared to enter Santiago de Cuba with Fidel Castro alongside the rebel army to declare victory it was not the usual olive green tunic and trousers that she wore but the 26 July uniform 'and a cloth cap, perched on the back of her head so the bill stood up'.[41]

Sánchez, like the male rebels, sought to craft an image that mythologised the revolutionary struggle; here her clothing was a device used to re-enact key battles, but she also engaged with the present through contemporary fashionable styles. A particularly captivating image by photographer Alberto Korda shows Castro and Sánchez engaged in conversation, him with his signature cigar and her holding a cigarette.[42] They are both uniformed but the distinct styles they adopt suggest a desire to highlight gender difference. Images such as these reflect how rebels and their photographers used style to signify rebellious bodies but when women fashioned themselves as feminine it held specific connotations. Women in uniform made compelling images, precisely because of their transgressive qualities, incorporating as they did both masculine and feminine aspects. Despite the interest they could attract, there is also a strong sense that women in uniform would always be subordinate in military terms to their male counterparts and had to contend with the reality that the image of military men would dominate the memory of the revolution – much as it dominated the memories of other wars and conflicts discussed in this volume where women had also fought.[43]

Castro might have been casual about uniform but he was also very concerned with crafting a revolutionary image that referenced aspects of military masculinities. The rebels were anarchic bodies shaped by events in the Cuban Revolution, so they were bound to fashion their own informal and unauthorised military appearances. Castro's 'gendered tactics' describe his use of gender transgressions, such as women taking on traditionally masculine tasks, to provide evidence of the urgency of revolutionary struggle.[44] His narrative suggested that the revolution was so compelling that *even* women took up arms. As I have shown, rebels had various embodiments, but it is also clear that a narrow range of masculine styles were pre-eminent. Hegemonic masculinities were raided to create dominant Cuban revolutionary images; although they were less likely to rely on the rigid aesthetics of uniformity, they did opt for the traditional military olive green for their loosely regimented uniforms. Castro's rebels were selective in their use of normative masculinities, and while leaders sought to subvert symbols such as the phallic cigar, they rejected the imperialist connotations of gentlemanly soldiering, signified by the perfection of regulation uniform. For Cuban rebels, uniform was a marker of masculinity and an assertion of power, but they also sought to undercut its potency through their improvised approach to clothing. Enlisting women in the rebellion and softening masculinities were both gender tactics that sought to offer an alternative vision of society in order to effectively legitimise military action.

A set of images by the press photographer Burt Glinn features members of the rebel army entering Havana in January 1959, to reveal a militarism that fuses elements of past military traditions with US military influences and aspects of popular culture.[45] Glimpses of popular culture suggest that the rebels crafted their unique military image in an Americanised Cuba but also in response to the brutal reality of revolution itself. A photograph of rebels returning atop trucks, jeeps and on foot dressed in a diverse range of military outfits offer an incoherent but captivating pageant: all guerrillas wear fatigues but not of a uniform design; headgear ranges from the field cap to the beret to nothing at all; and finally some men sport long hair, some short, some bearded, some not. Such uncontrived bricolage gave the Cuban Revolution a subversive image, which arose as part of the complex reality of the military struggle, but provided compelling images that anticipated alternative social structures. Another intriguing photograph of three rebels by Glinn offers a range of military looks: on the left a man wears a heavy jacket over what appears to be a pair of overalls, along with a field cap on his head and scarf around his neck. The figure in centre of the photograph wears the familiar fatigue uniform, while the man on the right erodes any faint impression of uniformity with a gaucho wide-brimmed hat and fatigue trousers matched with a dark shirt and an improvised bandolier exposing his ammunition. All three men wear the heavy army boots. They are not military in the traditional sense, but the rebel army appeared to draw on normative ideas about military identities to then subvert their meaning, weaving in local symbols to improvise a uniform that mixed conformity with creativity.

In his autobiography Castro recalled diplomacy missions by the Cubans, where he observed a certain improvised aesthetic forming of its own accord. Castro describes Guevara playing the role of the swaggering veteran fighter, in contrast with Salvador Vilaseca whose bourgeois suit befitted his role as the prim and polished mathematics professor, while other fighters were neither, presenting instead a neat and tidy military image. Vilaseca was of the revolutionary left but not military in the sense the others were, having returned from exile after the revolution. It was the combined force of these clashing versions of revolutionary masculinities which gave these unlikely heroes a distinctive attitude, and promoted an image of diversity. The visible range of masculine tropes succeeded, according to Castro, in making their cause convincing in the eyes of the world:

> Che came out first, with that moody smile, and behind him his seven or eight companions, who were also bearded and uniformed, although they were more rigorous about wearing their jackets all pressed and proper, tucked into their pants, and finally Professor Vilaseca, with his sober dark suit, white shirt and tie. And so it was, without our having set out to do so, that we inaugurated that shabby diplomacy that has become such a deep part of the history of the Cuban Revolution.[46]

Governments that disliked the Cuban guerrillas were particularly bothered by their seeming capacity to capture the popular imagination. In 2004, the British government declassified documents written by the British embassy in Havana in 1960; it emerged that in 1967, when they had been concerned with Guevara's involvement in the revolution and his position in government, they provided a vivid description of him as a 'bearded Argentinian, with his Irish charm and his inevitable military fatigue uniform, [who] has exercised considerable fascination'.[47] What these official papers reveal is a detailed description of the threat this revolutionary masculinity represented to the British establishment at the time. Further, the reference to Guevara's Irish ancestry demonstrates a very specific fear about the transnational threat an attractive image of revolutionary masculinity might pose. Guevara's bricolage of military and masculine signifiers clearly caused irritation; his image in part built on a complex reality, partly invented as a set of fashioned poses. The revolution happened at a time when youth culture was exploding in the USA, and its distinctly oppositional and dissenting texture made revolutionaries attractive as heroic outsiders. When Guevara and Castro took the stage they somehow embodied the youthful, brave outsider, which had first been aestheticised in modern forms of military discourse, but then came to embody angry rebellious youth, as 'Castro was one piece of a larger fascination with a certain type of male rebel' akin to Elvis Presley.[48] In the 1930s, American movies, in particular gangster films, had been especially popular in Cuba, influencing forms of political violence: 'The drive-by machine-gun shooting, so much part of the film genre, became a prominent motif of political warfare in Havana.'[49] Cuban insurgency found various reference points in American popular culture that would have made images of the revolution accessible to young people in the USA. Guevara's image in particular was fashioned by the realities of the conflict, but his oppositional attitude also spoke to people who had no experience of military conflict.

Unconventional in behaviour and appearance, 'the sheer hairiness of Castro and his barbudos endeared them to North American youth, indelibly associating the Revolution with a generationally inspired insouciance and defiance of convention'.[50] If these gender styles had transnational meanings, it was not confined to military conflict. A defiant hairiness was an expression of revolutionary masculinities, but it was also emerging as a reflection of new social movements such as hippies in North America. Like Lawrence on the Middle Eastern front of World War I, Castro's outsider quality was inscribed on a body that had been racialised as white, producing a figure that Van Gosse has described as the 'White Guerrilla' who had 'thrown it all away, and chosen to live dangerously so as to truly live' – implying that his white privilege was foregone in his quest for adventure and justice. He was rewarded with popularity in the USA up until 1959 when this image began to fade.[51] While there were Afro-Cubans involved in the revolution, they do not appear much in the photographs still circulating. José Nivaldo Causse comes into view in some photographs (Figure 9.2), a prominent Cuban revolutionary who saw military action, was prominent in the propaganda arm and enjoyed a political career in the new Cuba.

What is clear is that to oppose dominant ideologies Cuban revolutionaries drew on established symbols of power, but they also embodied new kinds of identities emerging in civil society: people, usually young white men, who sought justice through rebellion. Rebels were well aware of, and regularly reflected upon, the distance between theory and reality in a revolutionary context. The rebels themselves often embodied contradictions by performing masculinity in ways that made sense in a postcolonial context, by subverting traditional military codes and fusing them with dominant symbols in popular culture. Their military bricolage gave the revolution a subversive quality that inspired youth beyond Cuba.

Cuban Revolutionary Visual Culture

The proliferation of visual imagery, political cartoons, government-sponsored advertisements and propaganda highlight just how valuable visual culture was to the Cuban revolutionary government in order for them to build a society based on collectivity, revolutionary ideals, responsibility and diligence.[52] The revolutionary process was focused on Cuban and Soviet ideology, and in particular on the value of labour, which continued to be meaningful in the new Cuba. The figure that emerged from the revolution was the New Man, a concept developed by Guevara, an idea that became central to nation-building efforts. While it drew on some characteristics of the rebel leadership there were ways in which it was clearly different. This model of the new Socialist Man, partly a Soviet-style Stakhanovite,[53] took on a more flexible form in Cuba where various roles might have to be held simultaneously by the revolutionary citizen. Most important to revolutionary Cuba, though, was the creation of citizens who could overcome future uncertainties through their physical and spiritual strength. A new citizen identity echoed the form and texture of military figures that emerged at various stages of the revolution, a key strength being flexibility and responsiveness to events.

Images of Guevara and Castro as heroic warriors were embedded in Cuba's official popular culture. Models of the 'Cuban new man were guerrilla war heroes and heroines, volunteers, work heroes' who were commemorated in various ways in communities, schools and workplaces.[54] The 1959 revolution led by Fidel Castro had brought about the transformation of Cuba's society. He was determined to support other revolutionary regimes, intervening in Angola between 1975 and 1991, to maintain opposition to a creeping US hegemony over various parts of the world. Central to Cuba's revolutionary project were the constructs of internationalism, co-operation amongst nations, and transnationalism, people-to-people relationships.[55] An important aspect of the transnational experience was cultural exchange, and for Cuba this was primarily through images, commodities, film and art. Images of heroism transcended physical borders, such as the famous image of Guevara, which spread rapidly following his assassination in Bolivia in 1967. The famous 'Che' photograph, entitled *Guerrillero Heroico*, taken by Alberto Korda at a funeral in Havana in 1960 (Figure 9.3), became one of the most reproduced in the world.

Korda took the photograph while working as a photojournalist for the Cuban government newspaper *Revolución*, but it was never published due to its poor quality. The Italian editor Giangiacomo Feltrinelli was

Figure 9.3 Popularised cropped version of *Guerrillero Heroico* ('Heroic Guerrilla Fighter'), an iconic photo of Che Guevara at the funeral for the victims of the La Coubre explosion. Photo taken on 5 March 1960, published within Cuba in 1961, internationally in 1967 (photo: Alberto Korda). Wikimedia Commons: https://commons.wikimedia.org/wiki/File:CheHigh.jpg

given the photograph by Korda, when he was in Cuba to write Castro's memoirs, and upon obtaining exclusive rights to Guevara's *Bolivian Diary* following his death in 1967 he put the image on the cover, but also used it to print posters for the Paris uprising in May 1968.[56] Another early version of the image was created by the Irish artist Jim Fitzpatrick, who found the Korda photograph in *Stern* magazine and used it to create a black and red screen-printed poster soon after Guevara's death, a version that was reproduced widely and 'universalized Guevara as a symbol of revolutionary masculinity'.[57] Artists and designers have since appropriated the 'Che' image; it continues to inspire student movements, is regularly re-purposed to sell all manner of commodities, and appears on murals in conflict zones. Most ubiquitous, however, was the Che Guevara T-shirt, which began as a countercultural statement and eventually became a fashion item. This image of Guevara was by the end of the twentieth century not only powerful but also very marketable.

Images were a powerful form of cultural exchange for revolutionary Cuba. Photographs that created the image of the revolution were circulated in newspapers, in touring exhibitions and were later appropriated and recreated by graphic artists. Images became a weapon of war not least because developments in photography synchronised with the revolution, which encouraged Cuban photographers and attracted the foreign press to the island. In 1957, René Rodriquez, from the rebel army, took a photograph of Castro in command of the Sierra Maestra, which circulated all around the world. At the time, the image clearly contradicted the Batista government's propaganda that Castro was by that time dead. Cuban photographers were integral to the construction of the new order as images acted as a conduit for positive messages about the new Cuban state and what it meant, like the Soviets did decades before. Photography, and images generally, communicated the transformation of Cuba to the world.[58] Images were also a form of propaganda feedback. The 1950s was a critical time for the growth of television and of journalism, which by this time were less inclined to be conservative and relied more on images. Guevara became an inspirational image at a critical moment in the development of the Cuban political poster.[59] Castro later said of Guevara that he was inelegant, he 'was scruffy because he thought that was the poster child for rebellion to the extreme . . . I must admit, in the end Che's worn and crumpled clothing would give things a fresh air that we hadn't conceived of beforehand.'[60] In retrospect, the scruffy appearance of the rebels and the 'shabby diplomacy' of the leadership described by Castro offered a fascinating bricolage of masculine and military signifiers that fitted a new culture of youth rebellion characterised by a vibrant visual culture that spoke to a North American audience.

The 'bearded Argentinian' who wore the military fatigue uniform, partly a response to the demands of guerrilla warfare, partly adopted as a fashioned pose, fused the myth of the unconventional military adventurer with the 'angry young man' of the 1960s emerging in the USA at the time. Cuban insurgency, which found various reference points in American popular culture, created images of soldier heroes worthy of a new age. Perhaps Guevara became the 'poster child of the rebellion' because his creative approach to performing a revolutionary masculinity involved subverting established symbols of power. Images were increasingly part of popular culture and were undoubtedly meaningful for a population who accessed information through news media, posters and television. Visual gender codes framed the story of a Marxist uprising in Latin America, by re-purposing military masculinities to create new kinds of soldier heroes that were meaningful to youth audiences beyond Cuba. The revolution reinvented the poster as a rhetorical medium with a new visual language that used iconic photographs to build up oppositional consciousness.[61] And yet this oppositional language was not sufficiently radical to include women or to incorporate the possibility of other gender positions.

Images of Guevara and Castro were reproduced to represent the revolution locally, but their innovative gender performances were very useful to communicate the complexities of both the revolution and its aftermath to the wider world. Guevara, a transnational figure who embodied the ideals of the New Cuban Man, was also an inspiration for anti-imperialist struggle in other regions. Reproducing Guevara's image in revolutionary Cuba was a significant part of nation-building efforts; he was exalted as the model citizen but also embodied a form of leadership that had surface masculine qualities but whose identity incorporated feminine attributes to articulate opposition to the military strength of US colonial power. Guevara was often pictured with children, so that his revolutionary image incorporated both a rugged masculinity and a softer nurturing side. Guevara's informal militarism aestheticised his opposition to colonial power; his 'shabby' improvised masculinity reassured with its intimacy, warmth and humanity in contrast to the distant coldness of the crisp gentlemanly colonial state. Such complexity and contradiction deflected from readings that might be made of Guevara's image that emphasise his conventional background and education. In common with Castro and Cienfuegos, Guevara represented the acceptable face of militarism on the island, which was reassuringly white and middle class. By incorporating aspects of peasant identity, femininity and a disregard for colonial gentlemanly soldiering Guevara's popular media image de-emphasised his racial and gender conformity to hegemonic power.

The Cuban Revolution gained its power from the material reality and pace of the conflict, embodied by the military appearance of rebel forces, which offered compelling visual material for image-makers to work with, whether photographers or poster artists. Castro suggests that many actions and experiences were a corrective to ideas he gleaned from books, emphasising his reliance on events to create compelling images and ideas to capture the imagination of Cubans and the international community. The visual images that form the legacy of the revolution were not carefully invented but they did exploit the distinctiveness and novelty of new and re-purposed military masculinities. Militarily, classic options were often not available, and so the rebels were forced to act with tactical flexibility. Thus, the reality of asymmetrical warfare pushed Cuban rebels to experiment with their appearance in an effort to evade the enemy and to reach out to young people, intellectuals and the media beyond Cuba.

Dress practices in the Cuban Revolution had parallels with how marginal groups used clothing under colonial rule in Latin America. Historically, in the colonial period, clothing was a visual tool to establish racial and ethnic difference and to claim the superiority of colonisers, but then became an 'avenue of self-expression . . . manipulated by marginal sectors of the society such as mestizos, blacks, mulattos and women who wanted to find a space of their own in a society governed by the categories of race, gender and birthplace'.[62] Fashioning the self was not so much an opportunity for consumption but shaped personal identity in ways that allowed people to break out of the categories created for them. The Americanisation of Cuban society from the late nineteenth century was reflected in how citizens viewed themselves as modern, sharing values with their North American counterparts: 'Cubans and North Americans not only shared similar fashions, but more significant, they invested similar psychic faith in what clothing could do for them.'[63] A belief in the power of image, and the potential for clothing to transform the self, informed a revolution that was distinctly modern in its deployment of representational aesthetics. Media developments meant that war had become entertaining spectacle and identity had also become malleable, which fused with notions of the transformation of subjectivity so critical to the building of a new Cuba.

A visual culture that drew on images of patriarchal power, but para-doxically sought its undoing, therefore explored the flexible space created by insurgency to reconcile the various social groups that made up the new Cuba. National liberation involved manipulating symbols, ideas, mate-rial objects and even bodies in order to transform society. Fashioning the self was critical to shaping personal identity and gave Cubans access to new self-identities to meet the challenges of revolutionary society. The Cuban Revolution 'meant access to the world market for culture. In the 1960s, Cuba put Latin America in fashion.'[64] While the Americanisation of Cuba appeared to put it on the map, it was the visibility and the shock of the revolution that reached the world, with its dreams of rupture and transformation. As politics and culture converged, the latter became the site of contestation, but also where citizens sought recovery: 'The growing political crisis gave new urgency to the reconfiguration of cultural forms and in the process created possibilities for radical political change.'[65] Revolutionary Cuba had to recreate itself and offer its citizens some part of the heroic event.

One of the ways revolutionary Cuba managed to offer citizens a part in heroic events, led by a few white, male rebel leaders, was through the cultural practice of re-enactment. The Pioneer movement, for instance, a Cuban youth organisation, re-enacted key battles of the revolution to offer young people on the island a material connection with those events. Castro described re-enactments in a speech to the Ismaelillo Pioneers' Camp in Las Villas Province in 1976, when he spoke of how emotional it was for comrades to 'watch the Pioneers reenacting the "Granma" landing. [applause] Eighty-two Pioneers with their back-packs, rifles and olive-drab uniforms landed on that beach to reen-act that historic event.'[66] Castro and eighty-one other revolutionaries had landed in Cuba on the yacht *Granma* in December 1956, a key moment in the revolution when Castro returned from exile in Mexico. His speech in 1976 reflected his concern that the revolution be kept within popular memory, but also revealed that for him visual culture and performance was an ideal form of commemoration. Fidelity to the minutiae of events was clearly important to him, but so too was a care-ful approach to aestheticising and embodying the *Granma*. He went on to say that 'those children did not look as if they were reenacting an event, they were so solemn and acted their roles with such emotion that it seemed as if it were a real landing. [applause]'[67] Castro clearly val-ued fidelity to historical accuracy, but re-enactments are a curious form of commemoration, which betray an interest in encouraging citizens to inhabit the costume and attitude of the revolutionaries. Military

Figure 9.4 Fidel Castro, 1950s (photographer unknown (Mondadori Publishers)). Wikimedia Commons: https://commons.wikimedia.org/wiki/File:Fidel_Castro_1950s.jpg

re-enactments, which continue to this day in Cuba, carefully recreate the clothing and general appearance of the rebels, including the signature beards.

Re-enactment reflects an interest in stabilising the revolutionary moment,[68] which was also evident in Castro's insistence on always wearing a military uniform (Figure 9.4). He wore the uniform in every photo from the late 1950s to the 1990s, which appeared to be central to how he maintained the fiction of an eternal and unchanging revolutionary masculinity. The paradox is that what eventually became a hegemonic discourse of rebellion had first relied heavily on radical images and gender performances to mobilise the movement for independence. As time went on, despite memories of the *barbudos* as a transgressive group of outsiders, 'the revolutionary movement relied on familiar imagery and discourse regarding masculine honor, sexual discipline, and even Catholicism and paternal duty'.[69] This was clear when a reporter asked Fidel Castro in 1994 why he was still wearing his guerrilla uniform

thirty-five years after the revolution. His response revealed an investment not in the flexibility of masculine performance, but an assertion
that his was immutable:

> These are my clothes. I have worn them throughout my life. They are com-
> fortable and simple. They are cheap and they are never out of fashion. I also
> have another suit, a more formal one with a tie. But forgive me if I ask you a
> question: When you interviewed the pope, did you ask him why he always
> wears that white vestment?[70]

Conclusion

Despite the fact that Castro had invented novel images to embody the
revolution, precisely by exploiting the instability and contingency of
masculinity, by the 1990s he was unprepared to admit how creative he
had been when he first constructed his military identity. By this time his
image was, as far he was concerned, immutable. Image and self-presentation techniques were critical to the Cuban Revolution, which embodied and aestheticised strategies of urban guerrilla war, to then form the
basis of nation-building programmes. This bold participatory revolution
was underpinned by a visual culture enabled by the growing currency of
images in the 1950s and 1960s. Guevara and Castro in particular were
chosen to represent the revolution; their images functioned as models of
the Cuban new man but were transnational in terms of their symbolic
and social power. The power of revolutionary images was in no small
way the result of their genesis in the events of 1953–9, whereby the anarchic form of militarism adopted by the rebels demanded flexible, informal and unauthorised military appearances. At times they came into
view as hypermasculine, complete with cowboy hats, long hair, cigars
and a cheerful contempt for uniformity. Gender was for the rebels a performance, constrained somewhat by convention, but they also managed
to manipulate established codes of military masculinity. If the range of
acceptable masculine social roles tends to limit the 'costumes' available
to men, the Cuban rebel leadership sought to push those limits and in
doing so crafted a convincing image of revolutionary masculinity in an
age of popular culture. Traditional images of uniformity might have represented conformity, gentlemanly soldiering and the interests of colonial power but none was attractive to the Cuban rebels who preferred to
exploit the space between civilian and military, masculine and feminine,
the secular and the spiritual; liminality enabled them to fashion bodies
that could embody a revolutionary Cuba, one that promised creative

rather than conformist styles of citizenship. While revolutionary images appeared to highlight creativity and subversive visual practices, performances were clearly gendered and racialised.

Aesthetics and embodiment are critical to understanding the dynamics of insurgencies, in particular how this kind of conflict creates distinctive military identities that incorporate both combatant and citizen. If insurgents invent their own myths of military strength, Cuban rebels sought to do this by fashioning their bodies in distinctive ways. Enlisting women in the rebellion and softening masculinities were gender tactics that formed part of the complex reality of military struggle. This discussion draws attention to the various forms militarisation can take and highlights the cost of ignoring specific aesthetic forms and embodiments in favour of larger motifs and narratives in research on war and conflict. The intimate politics of militarisation deserves much more attention if we are to understand how social transformations are constituted through material and aesthetic forms that are often fleeting but become critical to the formation of popular myths and memories of revolution.

Notes

1. Idean Salehyan, *Rebels Without Borders: Transnational Insurgencies in World Politics* (Ithaca, NY: Cornell University Press, 2009). See also David Lake and Donald Rothchild (eds), *The International Spread of Ethnic Conflict* (Princeton, NJ: Princeton University Press, 1998), and Mary Kaldor, *New and Old Wars: Organized Violence in a Global Era* (Stanford, CA: Stanford University Press, 1999).
2. Rafael Hernández, *Looking at Cuba: Essays on Culture and Civil Society* (Gainesville, FL: University Press of Florida, 2003), 19.
3. Julia E. Sweig, *Cuba: What Everyone Needs to Know*, 3rd ed. (Oxford: Oxford University Press, 2016), 2.
4. Sweig, *Cuba*, 2–4.
5. Sweig, *Cuba*, 23–4. The *foco* theory of warfare describes guerrilla warfare, whereby a vanguard relies on the support of workers and peasants and on fast-moving attacks to face a numerically stronger enemy.
6. Michelle Chase, *Revolution within the Revolution: Women and Gender Politics in Cuba, 1952–1962* (Chapel Hill, NC: University of North Carolina Press, 2015), 210.
7. Karen Kampwirth, *Women and Guerrilla Movements: Nicaragua, El Salvador, Chiapas, Cuba* (Philadelphia, PA: University of Pennsylvania Press, 2002), 118.
8. Chase, *Revolution*, 211.
9. See Ongiri, this volume.
10. John D. Holst, 'Ernesto Che Guevara, Dispositions and Education for Transnational Social Justice', in *Cuba in a Global Context: International Relations,*

Internationalism and Transnationalism, edited by Catherine Krull (Gainesville, FL: University Press of Florida, 2014), 302–18, 303.

11. Judith Butler, *Gender Trouble* (London: Routledge, 2007 [1990]), 45.

12. Sara Salih, 'On Judith Butler and Performativity', in *Sexualities and Communication in Everyday Life*, edited by Karen E. Lovaas and Mercilee M. Jenkins (London: Sage, 2007), 55–68, 56.

13. Rachel Woodward and Trish Winter, *Sexing the Soldier: The Politics of Gender and the Contemporary British Army* (London: Routledge, 2007), 2.

14. Marcia Kovitz, 'The Roots of Military Masculinity', in *Military Masculinities: Identity and the State*, edited by Paul Higate (Westport, CT: Praeger, 2003), 1–14.

15. See R. W. Connell, *Gender and Power* (Sydney: Allen and Unwin, 1987); Mike Donaldson, 'What is Hegemonic Masculinity?', *Theory and Society* 22:5 (1993): 643–57.

16. Joanna Bourke, *Dismembering the Male: Men's Bodies, Britain and the Great War* (London: Reaktion, 1996), 30.

17. See Evans, this volume.

18. Graham Dawson, *Soldier Heroes: British Adventure, Empire, and the Imagining of Masculinities* (London: Routledge, 1994).

19. Raymond F. Betts, *Decolonization*, 2nd ed. (London: Routledge, 1998), 55.

20. Ernesto Che Guevara, 'The Social Aims of the Rebel Army', speech given at a ceremony in Havana, 27 January 1959, reprinted in *The Militant* 63:11 (22 March 1999). http://www.hartford-hwp.com/archives/43b/103.html.

21. Jane Tynan, 'The Unmilitary Appearance of the 1916 Rebels', in *Making 1916: Material and Visual Culture of the Easter Rising*, edited by Lisa Godson and Joanna Brück (Liverpool: Liverpool University Press, 2015), 25–33.

22. Raj Desai and Harry Eckstein, 'Insurgency: The Transformation of Peasant Rebellion', *World Politics* 42:4 (1990): 441–65.

23. Guevara, 'Social Aims'.

24. Erica L. Fraser, 'Soviet Masculinities and Revolution', in *Gender in 20th Century Eastern Europe and the USSR*, edited by Catherine Baker (London: Palgrave Macmillan, 2017), 127–40, 133.

25. Norberto Fuentes, *The Autobiography of Fidel Castro* (New York: Norton, 2010), 392.

26. Dawson, *Soldier Heroes*.

27. Ruth Streicher, 'Fashioning the Gentlemanly State: The Curious Charm of the Military Uniform in Southern Thailand', *International Feminist Journal of Politics* 14:4 (2012): 470–88, 472.

28. Dawson, *Soldier Heroes*, 59.

29. See Paul Fussell, *The First World War and Modern Memory* (Oxford: Oxford University Press, 1977); Dawson, *Soldier Heroes*.

30. Arminio Savioli, 'L'Unita Reporter Interviews Fidel Castro', *L'Unità*, 1 February 1961, 1–2, as reprinted by US Joint Publications Research Service, Latin American Network Information Center (LANIC), Castro Speech Data Base. http://lanic.utexas.edu/project/castro/db/1961/19610201.html.

31. Ibid.
32. Kamilah F. Majied, 'Racism and Homophobia in Cuba: A Historical and Contemporary Overview', *Journal of Human Behavior in the Social Environment* 25:1 (2015): 26–34, 30.
33. Fuentes, *Castro*, 399.
34. Ulrich Lehmann, *Tigersprung: Fashion in Modernity* (Cambridge, MA: MIT Press, 2000), xii.
35. Van Gosse, 'Fidel Castro and the White Guerrilla', in *Cold War Constructions: The Political Culture of United States Imperialism, 1945–1966*, edited by Christian G. Appy (Amherst, MA: University of Massachusetts Press, 2000), 238–56, 241.
36. Fuentes, *Castro*, 392.
37. David Havens Photographs of the Cuban Revolution TAM. 61, Tamiment Library and Robert F. Wagner Labor Archives, New York University.
38. Ibid.
39. Fuentes, *Castro*, 398.
40. Lorraine Bayard de Volo, *Women and the Cuban Revolution: How Gender Shaped Castro's Victory* (Cambridge: Cambridge University Press, 2018).
41. Nancy Stout, *One Day in December: Celia Sánchez and the Cuban Revolution* (New York: Monthly Review Press, 2013).
42. Alberto Korda, 'Fidel and Celia Sanchez'. http://www.museumsyndicate.com/item.php?item=27818.
43. See Catherine Baker, 'Svetlana Alexievich's Soviet Women Veterans and the Aesthetics of the Disabled Military Body: Staring at the Unwomanly Face of War', this volume.
44. Bayard de Volo, *Women*, 12.
45. Burt Glinn, *Havana: The Revolutionary Moment* (New York: Dewi Lewis Publishing, 2001). This is a collection of photographs taken by Magnum photographer Burt Glinn recording Fidel Castro's entry into Havana in 1959.
46. Fuentes, *Castro*, 399.
47. Helen Yaffe, 'Ernesto "Che" Guevara: Socialist Political Economy and Economic Management in Cuba, 1959–1965', PhD thesis (London School of Economics and Political Science, 2014), 10–11.
48. Gosse, 'Castro', 249.
49. Louis A. Pérez, Jr, *On Becoming Cuban: Identity, Nationality and Culture* (Chapel Hill, NC: University of North Carolina Press, 1999), 297.
50. Gosse, 'Castro', 250.
51. Ibid., 253.
52. Yamile Regalado Someillan, 'Visual Culture and the New Cuban Man: Examining a Core Force of the Cuban Revolution, 1959–1963', *International Journal of Comic Art* 2 (2005): 164–97.
53. The Stakhanovite movement began in the Soviet Union in the 1930s and was led by the Communist Party who encouraged workers to model themselves on the success of Alexey Stakhanov.
54. Yinghong Cheng, *Creating the 'New Man': From Enlightenment Ideals to Socialist Realities* (Honolulu, HI: University of Hawai'i Press, 2009), 175.

55. Krull (ed.), *Cuba*.
56. Ariana Hernandez-Reguant, 'Copyrighting Che: Art and Authorship under Cuban Late Socialism', *Public Culture* 16:1 (2004): 1–29, 5.
57. 'Che Guevara, Jim Fitzpatrick and the Making of an Icon', *History Ireland* 16:4 (July–August 2008). https://www.historyireland.com/20th-century-contemporary-history/che-guevara-jim-fitzpatrick-and-the-making-of-an-icon/; Lisa Corrigan, 'Visual Rhetoric and Oppositional Consciousness: Poster Art in Cuba and the United States', *Intertexts* 18:1 (2014): 71–91, 77.
58. Nan Richardson, 'Image and Revolution', in Burt Glinn, *Havana: The Revolutionary Moment* (New York: Dewi Lewis Publishing, 2001), 106–10, 106.
59. David Kunzle, *Che Guevara: Icon, Myth and Message* (Los Angeles, CA: UCLA Fowler Museum of Cultural History, 1997), 29.
60. Fuentes, *Castro*, 399.
61. Corrigan, 'Rhetoric', 74.
62. Mariselle Meléndez, 'Visualizing Difference: The Rhetoric of Clothing in Colonial Spanish America', in *The Latin American Fashion Reader*, edited by Regina A. Root (New York: Berg, 2005), 17–30, 30.
63. Pérez, *Becoming*, 316.
64. Hernández, *Looking*, 40.
65. Pérez, *Becoming*, 473.
66. Fidel Castro, 'Fidel Castro Speaks at Dedication of Pioneer Camp', speech at the dedication ceremony at Ismaelillo Pioneer's Camp in Las Villas Province, 1976, Latin American Network Information Center (LANIC), Castro Speech Data Base. http://lanic.utexas.edu/project/castro/db/1976/19760718.html.
67. Ibid.
68. Katherine Johnson considers re-enactment as 'living history' that serves a variety of purposes including popular pastime, public pedagogy and commemorative performance: Katherine Johnson, 'Performing Pasts for Present Purposes: Reenactment as Embodied, Performative History', in *History, Memory, Performance: Studies in International Performance*, edited by David Dean, Yana Meerzon and Kathryn Prince (London: Palgrave Macmillan, 2015), 36–52. See also Alan Filewod, 'Warplay: Spectacle, Performance, and (Dis) Simulation of Combat', in *Bearing Witness: Perspectives on War and Peace from the Arts and Humanities*, edited by Sherrill Grace, Patrick Imbert and Tiffany Johnstone (McGill–Queen's University Press, 2012), 17–27, where re-enactment is viewed as a spectacle to stabilise historical moments but variously also to commemorate, to create fantasy or to perform a political function.
69. Chase, *Revolution*, 211.
70. Jas Gawronski, '"Exclusive" Interview with Castro', *Clarín*, 2 January 1994, 28–9, as reprinted by Latin American Network Information Center (LANIC), Castro Speech Data Base (PY0301221594). http://lanic.utexas.edu/project/castro/db/1994/19940105.html.

CHAPTER 10

Seize the Time!: Military Aesthetics, Symbolic Revolution and the Black Panther Party

Amy Abugo Ongiri

In July 1969, the founder and director of the United States Federal Bureau of Investigation (FBI) declared that the Black Panther Party (BPP) 'without question, represents the greatest threat to the internal security of the country'.[1] Hoover used the idea of the threat that the group supposedly posed as a means to stage what Black Panther Party Chairman Huey P. Newton would characterise as a 'war against the panthers'.[2] During this period, hundreds of members of the Black Panther Party were systematically harassed, incarcered and even killed by local and state police, the FBI and the Central Intelligence Agency (CIA). Surprisingly, J. Edgar Hoover would argue in an infamous memo and later during a news conference that it was not a military threat that the Black Panthers presented, but rather a public relations threat. Hoover's original 15 May 1969 memo in which he labelled the Black Panther Party 'the greatest threat to the internal security of the country' was actually addressed towards the party's Breakfast for Children Program (BCP). In this programme school-aged children were provided breakfast for free before school, prepared by party members from locally donated food. Hoover would criticise the attempt to 'provide a stable breakfast to ghetto children'. He noted: 'The program has met with considerable success and has resulted in considerable favorable publicity for the BPP.' Hoover would then write that:

> The resulting publicity tends to portray the BPP in a favorable light and clouds the violent nature of the group and its ultimate aim of insurrection. The BCP promotes at least tacit support for the BPP among naive individuals ... and, what is more distressing, provides the BPP with a ready audience

composed of highly impressionable youths . . . Consequently, the BCP represents the best and most influential activity going for the BPP and, as such,
is potentially the greatest threat to efforts by authorities.[3]

According to Hoover, the public relations success of the Breakfast for
Children Program, and by extension the BPP's other public relations
successes, proved so great that the FBI was left with only one viable alternative and that was 'to neutralize the BPP and destroy what it stands
for'.[4] Government agencies like the FBI and CIA and both local and
statewide law enforcement agencies would successfully meet the challenge of the Black Panther Party with a military intervention that would
destroy its political power, but they were relatively powerless to coun-
teract their successes in the realm of the symbolic in which the Panthers
successfully re-scripted a visual language of military might to argue for
Black liberation. While most militaries conceive of propaganda as a way
of 'selling' the violence that they are charged with conducting, the BPP
saw propaganda as one of their most primary imperatives. Just as the
Panthers used images of the Black body in military poses and formations to challenge ideas of national belonging in the USA, the Panthers'
use of a military aesthetic challenges us to think in new ways about
the uses to which a militarised body might be put beyond further state
sponsored notions of masculinity. The aesthetic that the Panthers developed was dependent on a militarisation that figured both them and
their adversaries as soldiers in a war in which they reshaped traditional
notions of the Black male body as lacking in self-discipline and in need
of the paternalised structure that the state enforced through repressive
policing and prisons. Though this form of militarisation occurred in
an organisation targeted by the state itself, rather than among a state's
public and armed forces, and might therefore seem beyond the boundaries of what much critical literature would conventionally understand
as militarisation, it too revolved around an affective logic of aesthetics
and embodiment structured by notions of gender and race.

As an organisation that had made a name for itself through the
deployment of armed actions and militarised language, the BPP was in a
unique position after the passing of the 1967 Mulford Act in California,
the state where they were founded and headquartered. This legislation
was directly aimed at disarming the Panthers by denying them the right
to openly carry firearms for any reason. The Mulford Act was signed
into law by future US president and then governor of California, Ronald
Reagan, who was horrified by the appearance of armed Panthers at a
protest at the California State Capitol in 1967. After 1967 and even as

the Panthers expanded internationally, their use of actual weaponry was so heavily curtailed at their California headquarters that their deployment of militarised rhetoric as propaganda took on a primary function.[5] While frequently celebrated and memorialised as the embodiment of armed, militarised resistance, the Black Panther Party are often under-recognised for their media-savvy representational strategies and their abilities to utilise the mainstream media for didactic purposes. Even the FBI website conflates the party's political tactics and influence with the widespread actions of social unrest carried out by a variety of organised and individual actors:

> The civil rights movement ultimately began to unleash pent-up racial frustrations across the nation. Not all protests during the '60s were peaceful, as vocal groups like the Black Panthers that advocated armed resistance and police brutality (both real and perceived) began touching off more hostile confrontations, including a decade-long string of violent riots in Los Angeles, Detroit, and many other cities. In the first nine months of 1967 alone, more than 100 people were killed in rioting in more than 60 cities.[6]

Though the Black Panther Party continues to be celebrated for the military resistance threat they purportedly posed, their greatest wins were within the realm of the symbolic rather than through armed resistance.

While militarism has traditionally been seen as the language of state entities who are able to invoke the power of armed forces, Marsha Henry has noted the ways in which Paul Higate's pioneering edited collection *Military Masculinities: Identity and the State* paved the way for work that 'challenged the idea that military values only belonged to fields where there was a formal military setting'.[7] Henry concludes that such work 'pave[d] the way for thinking about militarized masculinities in non-traditional contexts'.[8] Insurgencies and liberation movements, as Henri Myrttinen and Jane Tynan have already argued in this volume, are certainly among these. The Black Panther Party's continued embrace of a military ethos long after they were effectively disarmed by the Mulford Act in 1967 speaks to the degree in which a militarised aesthetic was evocative in a successfully contestatory manner in relationship to the BPP's primary concerns of citizenship, masculinity and liberation. They developed this ethos in relationship to Black inclusion in a recently desegregated US military, the US military presence in Vietnam, anti-war activism, and Black nationalism that argued that African Americans already constituted a separate nation within the USA and thus deserved military-like defences of their community.

The US authorities also conceived of the Panthers as a military threat. In 'Police and Panthers at War', a 1969 *Time* article, the police murder of two BPP leaders in Chicago is described as part of a 'lethal undeclared war'.[9] The article goes on to describe the ways in which 'the ranks of the Panther leadership has been decimated in the past two years' by police actions that had left most of the leadership injured, dead or incarcerated. Police became militarised in the USA largely as a result of the threat of Black activism. Evelyn A. Williams notes the escalating militarisation of the New York Police Department throughout the 1970s:

> For the first time in its history, the New York City Police Department equipped patrol cars with shotguns. More police were added to the force. Revised guidelines were issued: travel only with a backup team and use caution in the chase. Special training programs in urban guerrilla warfare became mandatory, and were distributed detailing the degree of care to be used when stopping suspicious-looking Black men in vehicles or on the street, whether alone or in a crowd.[10]

Perceptions of the dangerous possibilities of groups like the Panthers as a military threat consistently drove the militarisation of police throughout the United States. The first use of the newly created Special Weapons and Tactics (SWAT) unit in Los Angeles was to serve a warrant for illegal weapons possession at the Black Panther Party headquarters in 1969. The use of SWAT units was further popularised by *SWAT*, a 1975 television series filmed in Los Angeles, and SWAT units subsequently became standard in police departments throughout the USA after this. Similarly, the deployment of tanks and other sorts of armoured vehicles against civilian protestors by police departments in the USA primarily begun in response to moments of African American social unrest, including urban rebellions in response to the murder of Martin Luther King, Jr.[11]

The Panthers' repetition of rhetorical tropes of militarisation and the Party's embrace of a military ethos must be seen in the context of escalating violence within US anti-war groups in the 1960s, in which prominent groups like Students for a Democratic Society and the Weather Underground significantly contested the war in Vietnam with a promise 'to bring the war home'.[12] Groups such as the Weather Underground and the Black Liberation Army, a militarised and underground offshoot of Black radical groups that included the BPP, participated primarily in armed actions inspired by the writing of Che Guevara in *Guerrilla Warfare* and Carlos Marighella in *The Minimanual of the Urban Guerrilla* and the success of groups like the Tupamaros in Uruguay.[13] Eleven years after *Time*'s article, Huey P. Newton would continue to characterise the repression of the BPP as a war in his 1980 doctoral dissertation that would later become a book entitled *War against the Panthers: A Study of Repression in America*.

While the Black Panther Party continued primarily as an aboveground group, it used military language and aesthetics in its appeal to gain power through a project of reconstructing Black masculinity. The civil rights movement had made its plea for citizenship and inclusion through the invocation of dignity and respect. Martin Luther King was killed during organising in Memphis where striking garbage workers dressed up in their best Sunday church clothing and carried signs that read 'I AM A MAN'. The Panthers in contrast wore clothing that was fashionable on urban streets as their uniform and they utilised the rhetoric of armed struggle. The Black Panther Party Chief of Staff David Hilliard was famously arrested after a speech at a large Bay area rally when he said of President Richard Nixon:

> This is the man that's responsible for all the attacks on the Black Panther Party nationally. This is the man that sends his vicious murderous dogs out into the black community and invade upon our Black Panther Party Breakfast Programs. Destroy food that we have for hungry kids and expect us to accept, shit like that idly. Fuck that motherfucking man. We will kill Richard Nixon. We will kill any motherfucker that stands in the way of our freedom. We ain't here for no goddamned peace, because we know that we can't have no peace because this country was built on war. And if you want peace you got to fight for it.[14]

Though his legal team argued that Hilliard had neither the means nor the interest in actually harming Nixon, he was subsequently sentenced to serve ten years in a maximum-security prison for his words.

Though *Time* would conceive of the Black Panther Party and the police as involved in 'a lethal undeclared war', it would also concede: 'The Panthers' aim is a Marxist-style radical revolution, though so far there has been more tough talk than provable action.'[15] *Time* failed to understand that the 'tough talk', which most often took the form of militarised visual and discursive rhetoric, was a primary objective of the BPP as they contested the proprietary right of the state to invoke militarisation for an affective response. The article ends in a litany of targeted arrests, harassment and violence by the police, with a discussion of David Hilliard's recent arrest for using language that appeared to threaten Nixon. The Panther's Minister of Education, Raymond 'Masai'

Hewitt, is quoted as saying: 'We speak the language of the ghetto and we're not going to change it to suit anybody's Marquess of Queensberry rules.'[16] *Time* conflated, as the US government did, Hilliard's language of violence and Hewitt's defence of that language with the *actual* violence of the police when it ended: 'The police seem to feel just as violently about the Panthers.'

The Black Panther Party came into existence in a period in which ideas of beauty and the body were being directly challenged by artists, musicians and activists involved in the Black Arts movement. Artists like Sun Ra, Jayne Cortez, Amiri Baraka and Barkley Hendricks created work directly in response to the changing political culture created by the Panthers and the aesthetic directive that one must avoid 'art for art's sake' alone. Ideas of visual Blackness created by the Black Power movement in the 1960s and 1970s continue to be among the most influential ideas of Blackness and revolution still in circulation. Because the Black Panther Party was forced to publicly disarm so early in its existence, they made a tactical switch under the leadership of Huey P. Newton and began to develop the more instructional and didactic aspects of their organisation, including their newspaper *The Black Panther*, which would first garner a national and then international readership. Graphic designer Emory Douglas was appointed the Minister of Culture and created iconic representations of revolutionary struggle and the Black Power movement that continue to circulate globally as representations of militarised revolutionary struggle, similarly to the iconic image of Che Guevara discussed in the previous chapter.[17] According to Joshua Bloom and Waldo E. Martin, Jr, Huey P. Newton was so consumed by the question of what actions the Panthers should take after the passage of the Mulford Act that he spent the entire summer after its passage contemplating tactics to counter the contradiction of having to 'mobilize "the brothers on the block" without the legal option of publicly arming themselves'.[18] This period of intense contemplation ended in Newton's writing a series of essays, including the seminal essay 'The Correct Handling of a Revolution', in which he would insist on the Party's role as instructive rather than directly participatory in armed resistance. He would write: 'It is of prime importance that the vanguard party develop a political organ, such as a newspaper produced by the party, as well as employ strategically revolutionary art.'[19] From this intention, the Black Arts movement and Black Power emerged.

In many ways, the Black Arts movement and Black Power present the foundational moment for contemporary understandings of Blackness. However, the most commonly circulated ideas of Black

Figure 10.1 'Huey Newton, Black Panther Minister of Defense', 1968. Collection of the Smithsonian National Museum of African American History and Culture

identity out of this moment are rooted in a very limited idea of a militarised masculinity whose aesthetics are more closely related to a reductive version of Black Power politics than to all the complexities of Black masculinity as articulated and explored during the era. For this reason, I want to explore what is perhaps the most iconic image of the Black Panther Party, an image of Chairman Huey P. Newton (Figure 10.1) that continues to reappear in popular culture on objects and in everything from popular movies and memes to countless music videos.

Staging the Black Panther Party: Panther Iconography and the Making of a Revolution

In a very short time, between 1965 and 1968, the Black Panther Party grew from a small outgrowth of an Oakland, California community college Black student group with less than a dozen members to a national, and even international, Black Power organisation with thousands of members and hundreds of chapters. Though they were very much part of the zeitgeist of the moment that birthed many radical and political and cultural groups, they were also the most visible and to this day remain the most remembered of the Black Power groups to survive in popular memory beyond their historical moment. Though the Black Power movement and the Black Arts movement – the cultural movement that Larry Neal called 'the sister to the Black Power concept' – gave us many important cultural luminaries, from the writer Amiri Baraka and poets Haki Mahabuti and Mari Evans to jazz luminaries Albert Ayler and Sun Ra, the visual iconography of the Black Panther Party remains some of the most potent and broadly circulated symbols of the moment.[20]

In 1967, Eldridge Cleaver staged what would become one of the most iconic pictures of Huey P. Newton in the apartment of a Panther supporter in San Francisco. The photograph was meant to condense the cultural politics and political agenda of the Black Panther Party into a simplified visual coding. It did so through the lens of a highly symbolically potent mixture meant to simultaneously suggest, firstly, military power, and secondly a Black masculinity which was itself connected both to the cultural change being enacted by the Black Arts movement and to the movie star appeal aesthetic that the BPP so self-consciously cultivated. It is important to note that the Panthers' own writing about the moment suggests that the images that they constructed were not meant to take on the full political and ideological weight of the Black Panther Party itself. Instead, they were meant to be a rhetorical shorthand for the group's bigger ideas. In *Seize the Time: The Story of the Black Panther Party and Huey P. Newton*, Black Panther Party co-founder Bobby Seale's 1968 account of the early years of the group, he recalled the moment when he and Newton decided 'it was necessary for us to try and get a centralized symbol of the leadership of black people in the black community. We had to centralize it in some way, so we decided on a picture of Huey.'[21] The image of Newton in the Party's signature black leather jacket and black beret holding a gun and a spear while surrounded by African shields, like much of the BPP iconography, was meant to condense the more complex political agenda of the group, in keeping with Newton's command that: 'The main purpose of the vanguard group should be to raise the consciousness of the masses through educational programs.'[22] Arranged by Eldridge Cleaver, the Black Panther Party's Minister of Culture, the inclusion of Newton was meant to metaphorically 'represent a shield for black people against all the imperialism, the decadence, the aggression, and the racism in this country'.[23] In this particular image, and in many of the images created by Emory Douglas, complexity was traded for visual rhetorical power.

The demand to create a new symbolic economy encoded with the radical political impulses of the moment was one echoed by the Black Arts movement's demand for an end to 'art for art's sake' and a new language to explore Black identity that would resonate with a revolutionary praxis. Maulana Karenga's seminal 1969 essay 'On Black Art', for instance, declared that Black Art must be 'functional, collective and committing'.[24] Later in the essay, Karenga connected these demands with the possibility of revolutionary change. He wrote: 'All art must be revolutionary and in being revolutionary it must be collective, committing, and functional.'[25] In the 1965 poem 'Black Art', similarly, LeRoi Jones declared a direct relationship between art and military action. He wrote: 'We want "poems that kill". / Assassin poems, Poems that shoot / guns. Poems that wrestle cops into alleys / and take their weapons leaving them dead.'[26]

Interest in the Black Panthers' political aesthetic was derisively labelled 'radical chic' by Tom Wolfe in a 1970 book by the same name that mocked the mainstream popularity of the party and its politics, particularly among wealthy, educated whites.[27] The book was based on a 1970 essay called 'Radical Chic: That Party at Lenny's', originally appearing in *New York Magazine*, that included a cover photo of several upper-middle-class white women in party dresses raising gloved hands in the Black Power salute that the Black Panthers had helped to popularise.[28] The title of the essay made reference to a Black Panther Party fundraiser held at the home of conductor Leonard Bernstein, and the cover photo included the words 'Free Leonard Bernstein!' though Bernstein was not and had not been incarcerated. Wolfe's concept of 'radical chic' and his critique of both the Black Panther Party and their imagery seemed to be based in the strength of the Panthers' ability to operate within a widespread popular appeal. However, rather than imagining this potentially wide appeal as operating to its detriment, as Tom Wolfe created it in *Radical Chic*, returning to this imagery instead helps to imagine that appeal as part of the affective power of re-scripting the Black body into militarised poses that reflected their insurgent potential.

'Symbolic Revolution' and Social Change

In looking back at the revolutionary events in Europe of May 1968, Michel de Certeau declared that, while events in France in 1789 had freed the Bastille, the French student revolutionaries of May 1968 had created 'a revolution of words'.[29] While he saw the events of May 1968 in Paris as mostly a political failure, de Certeau proclaimed unequivocally that 'it is imprisoned speech that was freed' in what would amount to 'a symbolic revolution'.[30] Similarly, Huey P. Newton would write:

> The Black Panthers have always emphasized action over rhetoric. But language, the power of the word, in the philosophical sense, is not underestimated in our ideology. We recognize the significance of words in our struggle for liberation, not only in the media and in conversations with people on the block, but in the important area of raising consciousness. Words are another way of defining phenomena, and the definition of any phenomena is the first step to controlling it or being controlled by it.[31]

Newton discussed at length the success of reframing the notion of policing around 'a new definition of policeman' because: 'Words could be used not only to make Blacks more proud but to make whites question and reject concepts that they had always unthinkingly accepted.'[32] In popularising the use of the word 'pig' to describe policemen, Newton would draw a direct parallel between language and action for change:

> Our greatest victory, however, lay in the effect on the policemen themselves. They did not like to be called pigs, and they still do not. Ever since the term came into use, they have conducted a countercampaign by using slogans like 'Pigs Are Beautiful!' and wearing pig pins: but their effort has failed. Our message, of course is that if they do not want to be pigs, then they ought to stop their brutalization of the victims of the world. No slogan will change the people's opinion; a change in behavior is the only thing that will do that.[33]

A similar argument to de Certeau's idea of valuing a 'symbolic revolution' could be made for the enduring power of the Black Panther Party's visual rhetoric. There has been exponential growth in the prison industrial complex and other institutions that were a foundational part of the Black Panther Party's critique of the United States government since the BPP officially ceased to exist in the early 1980s. Policing and mass incarceration were a major focus of the Black Panther Party's Ten-Point Program that guided Panther organising, with three of the points specifically focused on it. Unlike the anti-war movement that spoke of 'bringing the war home' through their protest, the Black Panther Party saw policing on a continuum of racialised violence that began with policing practices and extended to US imperialist aggression abroad – a stance

Alison Howell has followed in arguing against activists' and academics' recent desire to understand the militarisation of the police as a recent phenomenon resulting from the 'War on Drugs' in the 1980s, when policing should instead be understood as already always part of a martial state structure endemic to the liberal state (that is, as part of what Howell terms the state's 'martial politics').[34] Newton and the Panthers' continuous construction of the police as 'soldiers' working in concert with other forms of militarised state power is very much in keeping with this analysis. Point six of the Black Panther Party's Ten-Point Program, accordingly, demanded that all Black men be excluded from the draft. Their demand for 'all Black men to be exempt from military service' actually collapsed policing and military intervention with the assertion: 'We will protect ourselves from the force and violence of the racist police and the racist military, by whatever means necessary.'[35]

Despite their vision and efforts, more African Americans are currently incarcerated now than at any time in US history, and police brutality has increasingly been the focus of contemporary activism.[36] While US protests successfully halted the militarised participation in Vietnam, the US imperialist project in Southeast Asia and Africa did not end. One could look at the current situation and conclude that Black Panther activism, in fact, failed. However, de Certeau's notion of 'a symbolic revolution' would call us to look beyond an overly simplistic understanding of a revolution that has otherwise failed politically to identify the ways in which transformation in the realm of the symbolic has occurred and opened new possibilities. De Certeau celebrates 'the creation of a "symbolic site" as an action' because such a site creates the possibility to imagine what has been unimaginable, since it 'demonstrates a disarticulation between what is *said* and what is *unsaid*'.[37] For the Panthers, their enduring power lay not in their ability to utilise military power to enact public policy change but rather in their ability to alter the visual rhetoric of ideas of revolutionary change. The militarised aesthetics of Black masculine embodiment in Newton's photograph were central to this symbolic revolution.

Picturing the Revolution: The Spectre of Huey P. Newton

What is perhaps most striking about the 1967 photograph of Huey P. Newton is its resilience as marked by its startling repetition throughout popular, political and fine arts culture. Images repeating the iconic structure of the original photograph began appearing during the era itself, perhaps the most famous being the album cover art for the 1979 Funkadelic album *Uncle Jam Wants You,* in which the spear in the original photograph is replaced with a giant flashlight and the rifle in the original became a futuristic ray gun. Images that restage the famous photo continue into our current moment in a wide variety of contexts from fine art and advertising to popular culture. Meme makers were quick to notice the presence of the image in the advertising for Ryan Coogler's 2017 cutting-edge superhero movie *Black Panther.* In Black popular music, everyone from Beyoncé, Missy Elliott, Chuck D, Paris and Janet Jackson to Big Boi from Outkast have restaged the photograph. The Hip Hop icon Nas has restaged the photo twice at different stages of his career, while Ab-Soul performed almost all of his 2016 song 'Huey Knew' while posed like the Newton picture as images of Donald Trump, Colin Kaepernick and Huey Newton himself flash on a screen behind him. The artist Jennifer Moon restaged the photo twice, once while posing nude for a promotional calendar in 2013 and again that year fully clothed as a commission for an art gallery show (Figure 10.2). Despite the playful and somewhat irreverent nature of both photographs, Moon is adamant that her work is 'entirely sincere' in

Figure 10.2 'You Can Kill My Body, But You Can't Kill My Soul', 2013 (Jennifer Moon)

Figure 10.3 Huey P. Newton refrigerator magnet, 2017 (Radical Dreams: Lapel Pins and Accessories with a Message and a Cause)

its homage to Newton, the Black Panther Party and their ideas of revolutionary change.[38] The image has similarly reappeared on a rich variety of objects that do not seem to suggest social change, from T-shirts to mugs to refrigerator magnets. Radical Dreams, the company that reproduces the image on a lapel pin, a patch and a refrigerator magnet (Figure 10.3), explains its corporate mission as 'Overall, we want to change the world, one pin at a time'.[39]

Another important factor of the image is its seemingly contradictory malleability. It is at once politically limited and fixed by its historical and cultural context but also imbued with a seemingly endless flexibility. The original photograph consciously played on the early postcolonial context in which it was created through its invocation of the shield and the spear that appear on the flag of the then recently decolonised nation of Kenya. It also consciously invoked the militarised armed self-defence ethos of the Black Panther Party in the early moment of the Party's creation. Given its historical specificity, the frequency and wide context of its reproduction is surprising. Chuck D, who is an originator of the genre of conscious rap, can use it to evoke Black consciousness, but so can pop music queen Beyoncé in a context that is otherwise devoid of politics. The images can be used to sell a T-shirt or to evoke a critique of capitalism itself. Its continuing reappearance seems to suggest that the visual aesthetic that it invokes, though historically specific, has as much relevance in 2018 as it did in 1967.

In 'Afro Images: Politics, Fashion, and Nostalgia', Angela Davis has written about the 'fragility and mutability of historical images', including her own, that circulate outside the moment of political struggle in which they were created.[40] Davis notes that her own image has been used in everything from fashion magazines to advertising to evoke a historical moment and feeling apart from the political movements that created that moment. Davis is suspicious of the political implications of nostalgia for its ability to re-contour the past into a 'surrogate for historical memory' that creates the realities of liberation as forever out of reach.[41] Furthermore, Davis argues:

> What is also lost in this nostalgic surrogate for historical memory – in these 'arrested moments', to use John Berger's word – is the activist involvement of vast numbers of Black women in movements that are now represented with even greater masculinist contours than they actually exhibited at the time.[42]

While Davis is suspicious of the ways in which contemporary image culture reduces 'a politics of liberation to a politics of fashion', her critique is useful as a starting point to explore the ideas central to the photograph's militarised aesthetic, including futurity, masculinity, and the centrality of visual culture for the movement.[43]

Soul on Ice: Nostalgia, Futurity and the Promise of the Panthers

Nostalgia is and has been a critical factor in the recreation of the image of Huey P. Newton, but it is a nostalgia that is seen to animate a challenge to the present moment, rather than fix the past as Davis suggests. When fashion photographer Naskademini wanted to 'change the narrative' around Black masculinity and sports while photographing the Puma Legacy Collection in 2017, he returned to the iconic photograph of Huey P. Newton (Figure 10.4). He writes:

> Rather than showcase these young black men in a gym with a basketball, I wanted to change the narrative and have them in a setting that incites reflection and shock because rarely do we see our youth holding a book in their

Figure 10.4 Legacy Collection 2017 (Naskademini)

hands. I won't analyze these shots for you, I'll leave that up to the reader but I would like to mention that one of my inspirations was the famous photo of Huey P Newton sitting in his peacock chair. I am sure you've seen it before.[44]

Naskademini's reliance on the symbolic capital of the historic photograph to 'change' the contemporary 'narrative' around young Black men emanates, according to him, on the continuing ability of that imagery to incite 'reflection and shock'. It is worth asking why an image that is over fifty years old still has this provocative possibility. The book that the young man in Naskademini's photograph is provocatively reading is Eldridge Cleaver's 1968 essay collection *Soul on Ice*.

Cleaver, who served as the Panthers' Minister of Information, gained considerable notoriety as a provocateur for exploring, among other things, the idea in *Soul on Ice* that 'rape was an insurrectionary act'.[45] Cleaver begins *Soul on Ice* writing from prison where he is incarcerated as a teenager for marijuana possession. In a chapter entitled 'On Becoming', Cleaver attempts to explore the complexities of imprisonment, emasculation and desire as he inverts the scene of one of the most infamous lynchings in US history, the lynching of Emmett Till. As a prisoner, Cleaver becomes bothered by his and other Black prisoners' extreme sexual preference for white women. This realisation and the limitations that incarceration places on his physical body precipitates for Cleaver a loss of identity. He writes:

> I am very familiar with the Eldridge who came to prison, but that Eldridge no longer exists. And the one I am now is in some ways a stranger to me. You may find this difficult to understand but it is very easy for one in prison to lose his sense of self.[46]

He suffers what he describes as 'a nervous breakdown' when he realises that when he sees the woman whose accusation of rape infamously resulted in the lynching of Emmett Till, he is sexually attracted to her. Cleaver goes through a period of destruction of the self and begins, by his own account, to reconstruct his sense of self only through performing the very acts of sexual violence for which men and boys like Emmett Till are wrongly accused and punished. In this shocking restaging of the lynching tableau, the victim could become victor by doing the very thing for which he had been accused while also making himself physically and psychically whole by ridding himself of ideologically problematic desires for white women at the expense of those women who have accused him. This provocative claim had all the caustic flair that would help catapult the Panthers to international notoriety in the years between 1967 and 1971.

By the 1970s, the idea of guerrilla violence as performing a military function had given way to the idea of acts of violence as didactic and performative rather than utilitarian. In Africa, the Caribbean and Latin America, decolonisation movements had managed to create formidable armed resistance capable of toppling governments throughout the 1960s and 1970s.[47] However, when Huey P. Newton offered Black Panther Party 'troops' to assist the National Liberation Front of the People's Republic of Vietnam, it was done at a press conference and it was largely performative.[48] No Panthers were actually ever sent. In reality, Leftist groups in the USA and Europe were ill-prepared for the reality of militarisation and armed combat. The Black Liberation Army, an armed underground splinter group formed from the Black Panthers and other nationalist groups, mostly engaged inconsistently with the police rather than the US military. Although they had some notable successes with this strategy, they were largely inoperative by the late 1970s.

Creating Terrorism: Countering the Legacy of the
Black Panther Party

If the Black Panthers were successful in creating de Certeau's 'symbolic revolution', then they were also responsible for a new area of scholarship that was being born in an attempt to counter those successes by rebranding Newton's ideas of the exemplary behaviour of the vanguard party as 'terrorism'. Brian Michael Jenkins would famously remark in 1974 that 'terrorism is theater'.[49] In 'International Terrorism: A New Kind of Warfare', written for the Rand Corporation in 1975, Jenkins concluded that terrorism 'is aimed at the people watching, not at the actual victims'.[50] Similarly, in the 1982 text *Violence as Communication: Insurgent Terrorism and the Western News Media*, Alex P. Schmid and Janny de Graaf conclude that the news media is central to the birth of terrorism:

> In the late nineteenth century two new phenomena entered social life: the mass press and modern insurgent terrorism. Both owed much of their existence to recent technical developments: dynamite, discovered in 1866, and the rotary press, introduced in 1848 and perfected in 1881. The two inventions soon started to interact. '*Truth* is two cents a copy, dynamite is forty cents a pound. Buy them both, read one, use the other,' the anarchist paper *Truth* declared.[51]

Newton would write of the central importance of the news media in creating the possibilities for revolution when he noted: 'Millions of oppressed people may not know members of the vanguard party personally but they will learn of its activities and its proper strategy for liberation through an indirect acquaintance provided by mass media.'[52]

While the concept of 'terrorism' was not new, the word itself in English was not widely used until the late 1960s and 1970s. The contemporary language of terrorism was, in other words, being constructed in this moment, not only by law enforcement agencies like the FBI but also by private corporations and academic theorists who wanted to contest the hold that groups like the Black Panther Party had on the public imagination. In fact, the notion of 'terrorism' was largely constructed in response to the public relations success of groups like the Black Panther Party, in which militarised visual images like the 1967 photo played a large role.

Scholars such as Walter Laqueur, writing in the aftermath of the Black Panther movement, took great pains to distinguish the developing concept of 'terrorism' from what radicals themselves labelled 'guerrilla warfare'.[53] In the introductory note to *Terrorism*, Laqueur stated outright: 'This essay grew out of a study of guerrilla warfare, and the conclusion that urban terrorism is not a new stage in guerrilla warfare, but differs from it in essential respects, and that it is heir to a different tradition.'[54] Later in the text, he argues:

> Terrorism is not, as is frequently believed, a subspecies of guerrilla (or revolutionary) warfare and its political function today is also altogether different. 'Urban guerrilla' is indeed urban, but it is not 'guerrilla' in any meaningful sense of the term; the difference between guerrilla and terrorism is not one of semantics but of quality.[55]

The quality that Laqueur identifies has to do with terrorism's 'unexpected, shocking and outrageous character',[56] which is not unlike Naskademini's observation about his selection of the Newton imagery for its ability to incite 'reflection and shock'. Laqueur also identifies 'the violation of established norms' as a major factor that distinguishes terrorism from other types of military engagement.[57] Recognising that the current image of those whom he wished to label as terrorists was in fact that of the 'heroic yet tragic role: the good Samaritan distributing poison, St. Francis with the bomb', Laqueur wanted to reimagine the power of the images and actions of Leftist radicals from this romanticism towards an understanding of them in relationship to the idea of terror.[58]

Despite the work of scholars such as Laqueur, Jenkins, Schmid and de Graaf to counter the attractiveness of groups like the Black Panther Party, their appeal to generations of artists and activists continued. After the National Basketball League championship win in 2018 by the Oakland-based Golden State Warriors, designer Eesuu Orundide creatively reimagined their logo and the iconic photo on a T-shirt tribute to Huey P. Newton that labelled him an 'Oakland Warrior' (Figure 10.5). In doing so, Orundide successfully reclaimed the geography, space and history denied by the recent gentrification of Oakland and its attendant erasure of Black Panther Party history. Images like this arrest time, but not in the manner that Angela Davis described as a stationary fixing of time. Rather these images engage with time as a disruption and rupture that participates in the 'unexpected, shocking' effect that Laqueur suggests was at the root of their power but also in their ability to incite reflection that Naskademini evokes.

Making the Past Present: The Black Panther Party and the Power of Historical Rupture

The images created that pay homage to the Huey P. Newton photograph speak as much to the anxiety around racial representation as they do to the work of reinscribing the symbolic political shorthand that the BPP

Figure 10.5 Oakland Warrior 2018 (Eesuu Orundide, Orundide Afro-Urban Couture)

created through its visual representation. Huey P. Newton largely considered the BPP's function to be a symbolic one and that their actions, including the aesthetic and image culture that they created, were largely there for the purposes of political education. In 'The Correct Handling of a Revolution', Huey P. Newton writes 'it is important for the party to show the people how to stage a revolution' and that 'the main function of the party is to awaken the people and teach them'.[59] Even direct political action had an instructive character, in keeping with the idea of 'armed propaganda' popularised by Regis Debray in *Revolution in the Revolution?: Armed Struggle and Political Struggle in Latin America*, a study of successful liberation struggles throughout Latin America that served as inspiration for Leftist movements around the world.[60] Newton would argue:

> Millions and millions of oppressed people might not know members of the vanguard party personally or directly, but they will gain through an indirect acquaintance the proper strategy for liberation via the mass media and the physical activities of the party.[61]

Contemporary adaptations of the Newton image typically reproduce a reductive understanding of the politics of the 1960s and 1970s. In contemporary circulation of these images, the simple didacticism of the images is retained rather than the more complex impulses that they signalled. However, nostalgia does not simply work as a denial of historical 'truths' of the past, as Angela Davis claims. Instead the historical memory as captured in photographs of Newton, Davis and others becomes the raw materiality with which people configure contemporary Blackness as a contestatory space and site of historical rupture. These images exist not so much as a dismissal of historical fact, as Angela Davis claimed, but rather an acknowledgement of the power of nostalgia as a functioning to make the past present and creatively relevant. Bobby Seale's appropriately titled memoir *Seize the Time* speaks to the complete malleability of time and of chronology as the stuff of power.

So, for example, though the Black Panther Party membership was at some points in its history as much as two-thirds female, its leadership structures and agendas reflected an investment in recuperating a masculinity that they viewed as having been disempowered by everything from slavery to lynching.[62] For this reason, despite heavy participation by women as indicated by the earlier Angela Davis quote, the Black Panther Party's primary mode of address was almost always to 'the brother on the block'.[63] Consequently, reductive views of Black Power often reduce its vision of masculinity to almost a caricature of hypermasculinity replete with misogyny and homophobia. However, it is clear from the malleability of the iconic image of Huey P. Newton that this sort of characterisation fails to give a complete accounting for the coded possibilities of masculinity as deployed by the Black Arts movement. In fact, the performative nature of the Panthers' revolution extended to their performance of masculinity. This was a performance not meant to deceive but to educate, as was all their visual material. It is for this reason that the group's early support of homosexual rights is so often read as a contradiction to the Panthers' politics when in fact it is just an expression of the depths of their exploration of the complexities of masculinity.[64]

Indeed, for many of the groups and cultural workers associated with the Black Power moment, masculinity was a much more complicated affair than it has been created in the official and popular nostalgia for the movement. This is evidenced in the importance of Sun Ra to the movement, who played not only with ideas of time and space but also with identity with his investment in African American mysticism and in his claim that he actually was a being from another world. Even the most phallocentric impulses of the moment engaged in a sort of speculative play with embodied notions of Blackness. There is no stronger example of this than the creation of Eldridge Cleaver's so-called 'penis pants' in 1975. Cleaver was on the run in Europe and Africa as the party's former Minister of Culture when he designed these pants that he labelled 'pants especially for men'. The pants were created with a separate outward-facing and differently-coloured pocket to hold and emphasise the wearer's genitalia. The pants when they were presented as a prototype were almost universally mocked.[65] When they are remembered now, they are mostly mentioned as a joke, or a testament either to the phallocentric excesses of the Party in its last days or to just how out of control Cleaver's drug habit had gotten by that point. I want to see them in relationship to the more abstract and expansive, if misguided, visionary impulses of the Black Power movement when it came to masculinity. Ultimately, they declare an allegiance not with an embodied reality of masculinity that they would seem to exaggerate but rather with a sense of exploration that, in Walter Laqueur's words, went far beyond 'the violation of established norms'.[66] They did so not for the sake of shock alone but rather in the spirit of inciting reflection. Black Power's play with militarised masculinity was not limited to a simple reversal logic of imitation in which the men of the Black Power movement were the better soldiers. Instead, people like Cleaver and Newton extended the metaphor of militarised masculinity far beyond its usual boundaries.

To Die for the People: The Enduring Legacy of Black Panther Iconography

By all accounts Huey P. Newton had a fairly ambivalent relationship to the photo that would become the most iconic image of him. Many accounts claim that he hated it, while others note that while he claimed to hate it he also hung a large copy of it in his penthouse apartment on Lake Merritt in Oakland. In 1972, Newton himself somewhat recreated the photo for *Jet* magazine. In *My People Are Rising: A Memoir of a Black Panther Captain*, Aaron Dixon writes:

> An unflattering story had run in *Jet Magazine* in May 1972, with Huey on the cover, sitting imperiously in a brown leather chair, very well dressed, labeled 'Supreme Servant of the People', a title chosen by the Central Committee. It sent a very different message than the earlier pictures of him in his leather jacket, black beret tilted to the side, shot gun in one hand and spear in the other. This new image created doubt in the mind of party members and the general public about Huey's real motives.[67]

Dixon's autobiography is just one of many accounts that reveal the ways in which by 1972 internal strife and increased pressure from law enforcement agencies meant that the disintegration of the party was on the immediate horizon. These internal and external pressures meant that recreating the symbolic power and possibility of the earlier photograph was completely impossible. The new image for *Jet* magazine, likely meant to cement the party's established prestige and signal their success, seemed to do the exact opposite. By the late 1970s, the party had all but disappeared from the political landscape of the USA. The ever-evolving, constantly changing relationship of the images of their movement to US political, social and popular culture, however, is suggestive of just how deep their symbolic impact continues to cut.

Huey P. Newton seemed to predict his own early death with the titles of an early collection of his speeches and writings, *To Die for the People*, and his 1973 autobiography, *Revolutionary Suicide*. In *Revolutionary Suicide*, Newton would argue that the crushing conditions of oppression coupled with the inevitability of an early and possibly violent death for the majority of poor African Americans meant that there was no reason *not* to participate in revolutionary practices that might led to physical harm or eventual death. This would be a 'revolutionary suicide' in contrast to the 'death of the spirit' that the majority of African Americans were forced to live with.[68] The original cover photo for *Revolutionary Suicide* was of the iconic photo of Newton that had hung in the window of the Black Panther Party headquarters in Oakland, California, only to be partly destroyed by the gunfire of a police raid. It was deliberately suggestive of the precariousness of the Panther vision of liberation.

In his memoir, *Just Another Nigger: My Life in the Black Panther Party*, Donald Cox reflected on his life in the BPP from his self-imposed exile overseas in France. Cox, who had been the Panthers' Field Marshal and a founder of the San Francisco chapter, noted the dangerous effect of hero worship: 'The actual Huey could not survive the Huey that we had created . . . We killed Huey with our love!'[69] Despite the intensity of focus on the redemptive power of the sacrificial death, the persistent argument of the larger aesthetic project of the Black Panther Party was of a desire to reconstitute the Black body in a utopian space in which it could, in the words of Newton, 'live with hope and human dignity'.[70] Panther iconography with its seemingly contradictory display of traditional militarised masculinity enshrined in an ambiguous fantasy of liberation was ultimately flexible enough that it continues to offer imaginative possibilities for thinking through revolution visually. This 'symbolic revolution' was the purpose of the Panthers' militarised aesthetics and the lasting achievement of their movement, struggling against what they regarded not as the temporary militarisation of a USA at war in Vietnam but the martial politics of an endemically white supremacist US state.

Notes

1. 'Black Panther Greatest Threat to US Security', *Desert Sun* 42:296, 16 July 1969.
2. Huey P. Newton developed this concept first as a doctoral thesis and it was later published as a book: Huey P. Newton, *War against the Panthers* (New York: Harlem Rivers Press, 1996).
3. Sanford J. Ungar, *FBI: An Uncensored Look behind the Walls* (New York: Little, Brown, 1976), 121.
4. Ibid., 121.
5. Joshua Bloom and Waldo E. Martin, Jr note that the disarming of the Panthers troubled Panther Chairman Huey P. Newton so much that it 'kept Newton up at night, posing both a political puzzle and personal dilemma': Joshua Bloom and Waldo E. Martin, Jr, *Black against Empire: The History and Politics of the Black Panther Party* (Oakland, CA: University of California Press, 2016), 65.
6. Federal Bureau of Investigations, 'And Justice for All: 1954–1971'. https://www.fbi.gov/history/brief-history/and-justice-for-all.
7. Marsha Henry, 'Problematizing Military Masculinity, Intersectionality and Male Vulnerability in Feminist Critical Military Studies', *Critical Military Studies* 3:2 (2017), 182–99, 188.
8. Ibid., 187.
9. 'Police and Panthers at War', *Time*, 29 December 1969, 22.
10. Evelyn A. Williams, *Inadmissible Evidence: The Story of the African American Trial Lawyer who Defended the Black Liberation Army* (Lincoln, NE: iUniverse, 2000), 3.
11. A strong example of the ways that federal money was used to militarise the police force existed in Cleveland, Ohio, in response to the Hough riots in July 1966 and two years later in a shootout with a Black nationalist group, now known as 'the Glenville shootout', in July of 1968. Both these incidents of urban insurrections were blamed by policymakers and the media on attempts by Black nationalists and Leftists to organise poor African American communities in Cleveland. When police were met with violence from a radical Muslim sect in 1974, 'Cleveland's 12-ton mobile armored command post, purchased with Federal funds after the 1968 riots, was used in action for the first time': '3 Captured and 8 Injured in Cleveland Police Battle', *New York Times*, 31 May 1974, 28.
12. In *Bringing the War Home: The Weather Underground, The Red Army Faction and Revolutionary Violence in the Sixties and Seventies* (Berkeley, CA: University of California Press, 2004), Jeremy Varon explores the ways that the global student movement radicalised to the point of armed struggle. In *Outlaws of America: The Weather Underground and the Politics of Solidarity* (Chico, CA: AK Press, 2006),

Dan Berger examines the specific history of Students for a Democratic Society and its move towards revolutionary violence in the formation of the Weather Underground as an underground fighting force. Daniel Burton-Rose documents the specific choice to engage in revolutionary violence on the part of anti-war activists in *Guerrilla USA: The George Jackson Brigade and the Anticapitalist Underground of the 1970s* (Berkeley, CA: University of California Press, 2010). The turn to revolutionary violence within African American organisations is much less well documented because it resulted in much more state repression, and law enforcement continues to be much more aggressive in punishing its participants than those involved in this turn outside African American organisations. Consequently, Muhammad Ahmad's *We Will Return in the Whirlwind: 1960–1975* (Chicago: Charles H. Kerr, 2007) is one of the few comprehensive attempts to document the turn towards armed struggle within Black organisations in the 1960s and 1970s. Safiya Bukhari documents her time in both the BPP and the Black Liberation Army (BLA) in *The War Before* (New York: The Feminist Press, 2010). Similarly, Assata Shakur, who remains a fugitive from the US criminal justice system, wrote an autobiography that provides important insights into the inner workings of the Black Liberation Army: *Assata: An Autobiography* (New York: Lawrence Hill, 2001). Evelyn Williams, Assata Shakur's lawyer until she escaped from prison, wrote about the experience of defending members of the BLA: Williams, *Inadmissible Evidence*.

13. Che Guevara, *Guerrilla Warfare* (New York: Monthly Review Press, 1961); Carlos Marighella, *The Minimanual of the Urban Guerrilla* (Greenville, SC: CreateSpace, 2011 [1969]).

14. 'Panther Chief Nabbed for Threatening Nixon', *The Stanford Daily*, 12 April 1969, 1.

15. 'Police and Panthers at War'.

16. Ibid.

17. Erika Doss, 'Revolutionary Art Is a Tool for Liberation', in *Liberation, Imagination, and the Black Panther Party: A New Look at the Panthers and Their Legacy*, edited by Kathleen Cleaver and George N. Katsiaficas (New York: Routledge, 2001), 175–87; Tynan, this volume. Since Cleaver and many other figures involved in the Black Arts movement and BPP changed their names for various political and personal reasons, citations and the main text of this chapter refer to them by the names used at the time of publication.

18. Bloom and Martin, *Black against Empire*, 65.

19. Huey P. Newton, 'The Correct Handling of a Revolution', in *The Black Panthers Speak*, edited by Phillip S. Foner (New York: Da Capo Press, 1995), 41–5, 44.

20. Larry Neal, 'The Black Arts Movement', in *Visions of a Liberated Future: Black Arts Movement Writing* (New York: Basic Books, 1989), 62–78, 62.

21. Bobby Seale, *Seize the Time: The Story of the Black Panther Party and Huey P. Newton* (New York: Random House, 1968), 182.

22. Newton, 'Correct Handling', 42–3.

23. Seale, *Seize the Time*, 182.

24. Maulana Karenga, 'On Black Art', *Black Theater: The Drama Review* 4 (1969), 9–10.
25. Ibid., 10.
26. This poem appeared in the highly influential Black Arts Movement collection *Black Fire*, which was edited by Amiri Baraka and Larry Neal, the major architects of the movement: LeRoi Jones, 'Black Art', in *Black Fire*, edited by Amiri Baraka and Larry Neal (New York: William Morrow, 1968), 302.
27. Tom Wolfe, *Radical Chic and Mau-Mauing the Flak Catchers* (New York: Farrar, Strauss, Giroux, 1970).
28. Tom Wolfe, 'Radical Chic: That Party at Lenny's', *New York Magazine*, 8 June 1970, 26–56.
29. Michel de Certeau, *Capture of Speech and Other Political Writings*, translated by Tim Conley (Minneapolis, MN: University of Minnesota Press, 1997), 9.
30. Ibid., 11.
31. Huey P. Newton, *Revolutionary Suicide* (New York: Penguin Classics, 1995), 173.
32. Ibid., 175.
33. Ibid., 176.
34. Alison Howell, 'Forget Militarization: Race, Disability and the Martial Politics of the Police and the University', *International Feminist Journal of Politics* 20:2 (2018), 117–36.
35. Huey P. Newton, *To Die for the People*, edited by Toni Morrison (San Francisco, CA: City Lights, 2009), 4.
36. Michelle Alexander famously notes that there are currently more Black men in prison today than there were enslaved in 1850: Michelle Alexander, *The New Jim Crow: Mass Incarceration in the Age of Colorblindness* (New York: New World Press, 2012), 175.
37. De Certeau, *Capture of Speech*, 8.
38. Jennifer Moon, personal communication, 7 July 2018.
39. 'Radical Dreams: Lapel Pins and Accessories with a Message and a Cause'. https://www.radicaldreams.net/.
40. Angela Y. Davis, 'Afro Images: Politics, Fashion, and Nostalgia', *Critical Inquiry* 21:1 (1994): 37–45, 39.
41. Ibid., 43.
42. Ibid., 43.
43. Ibid., 37.
44. Naskademini, 'Puma Legacy Collection'. https://www.naskademini.com/blog/puma-black-history-month-legacy-collection.
45. Eldridge Cleaver, *Soul on Ice* (New York: Dell Publishing, 1968), 14.
46. Ibid., 16.
47. See Tynan, this volume.
48. Newton declared his intent to send 'Black Panther troops' to Vietnam at the press conference on his release from prison after being acquitted for the killing of a police officer in 1970: Newton, *Revolutionary Suicide*, 290.
49. Brian Michael Jenkins, 'International Terrorism: A New Kind of Warfare' (Santa Monica, CA: The Rand Papers, 1974), 4.

50. Ibid., 4.
51. Alex P. Schmid and Janny de Graaf, *Violence as Communication: Insurgent Terrorism and the Western News Media* (London: Sage, 1982), 9.
52. Newton, 'Correct Handling', 44.
53. Walter Laqueur, *Terrorism* (Boston: Little, Brown and Company, 1977), 1.
54. Ibid., 1.
55. Ibid., 5.
56. Ibid., 3.
57. Ibid., 3.
58. Ibid., 4–5.
59. Newton, 'Correct Handling', 42.
60. Regis Debray, *Revolution in the Revolution?: Armed Struggle and Political Struggle in Latin America* (New York: Grove Press, 1967).
61. Newton, 'Correct Handling', 44.
62. Kathleen Neal Cleaver cites a survey that Bobby Seale did in 1969 of the party's membership in saying that the membership was two-thirds female. She contests the dominant image of the Black Panther Party as misogynist based on the heavy presence of female leadership and membership in the group: Kathleen Neal Cleaver, 'Women, Power, and Revolution', in *Liberation, Imagination and the Black Panther Party: A New Look at the Panthers and Their Legacy*, edited by Kathleen Neal Cleaver and George Katsiaficas (New York: Routledge, 2001), 123–7, 124.
63. Huey P. Newton was instrumental in developing a strategy for politicising the lumpen proletariat as the primary organising base for the Black Panther Party. He referred to this group as 'the brothers on the block', thereby revealing not only a misogynist bias but also the totality of the investment in masculinity as a focal point for the redemptive vision of the party: Huey P. Newton, 'Huey Newton Talks to the Movement About the Black Panther Party, Cultural Nationalism, SNCC, Liberals and White Revolutionaries', in *Black Panthers Speak*, edited by Phillip Foner (New York: Da Capo, 1970).
64. Huey P. Newton issued a controversial statement in defence of the Gay Liberation movement on 15 August 1970. It is reprinted in its entirety in *To Die for the People: The Writings of Huey P. Newton*, edited by Toni Morrison (New York: Writers and Readers Press, 1995).
65. In 'Eldridge Cleaver's New Pants', a journalist for the *Harvard Crimson* details at length a meeting with Cleaver in a Paris apartment to examine the prototype. While it is clear that Cleaver is very serious about the pants, the journalist treats the entire encounter humorously: Mark Stillman, 'Eldridge Cleaver's New Pants', *Harvard Crimson*, 26 September 1975, 3. *Jet* treated the product more seriously in its interview with Cleaver but addresses Cleaver's history of rape and outstanding charges, which included attempted murder, as a way of questioning his intentions: 'Eldridge Cleaver Designs Pants For Men Only', *Jet*, 21 September 1978, 22–4.
66. Laqueur, *Terrorism*, 3.

67. Aaron Dixon, *My People Are Rising: A Memoir of a Black Panther Captain* (Chicago: Haymarket Books, 2012), 244.

68. Newton, *Revolutionary Suicide*, 2.

69. Donald Cox, *Just Another Nigger: My Life in the Black Panther Party* (Berkeley, CA: Heyday Books, 2019), 208.

70. Newton, *Revolutionary Suicide*, 3.

INDEX

EU representative:
Easy Access System Europe
Mustamäe tee 50, 10621 Tallinn, Estonia
Gpsr.requests@easproject.com

www.ingramcontent.com/pod-product-compliance
Lightning Source LLC
Chambersburg PA
CBHW070842300326
41935CB00039B/1369